Stephen Beauregard Weeks

Southern Quakers And Slavery

A Study in Institutional History

Stephen Beauregard Weeks

Southern Quakers And Slavery
A Study in Institutional History

ISBN/EAN: 9783744732833

Printed in Europe, USA, Canada, Australia, Japan

Cover: Foto ©ninafisch / pixelio.de

More available books at **www.hansebooks.com**

SOUTHERN QUAKERS

AND

SLAVERY

A Study in Institutional History

By STEPHEN B. WEEKS, Ph. D.

(University of North Carolina and Johns Hopkins University)

BALTIMORE
THE JOHNS HOPKINS PRESS
1896

PREFACE.

The following study of Quakerism in the South has been entitled "Southern Quakers and Slavery," for the reason that slavery was *the* subject which differentiated Friends in the South from other religious bodies. It was opposition to slavery that made Southern Quakerism what it was; without this opposition Quakers would have been comparatively unnoticed in the presence of larger and more powerful denominations. Again, these pages deal with the Society in Virginia, North Carolina, South Carolina, Georgia and Tennessee. It was not thought well to include the Baltimore Yearly Meetings, for the reason that these lie only in part in Maryland, and extending into Pennsylvania, where the emancipation sentiment was strong, there was not the same heroism implied in opposition to slavery as in the more southern Yearly Meetings. Further, the Baltimore Yearly Meetings did not suffer so severely from the westward migration which was superinduced by slavery. The institution of slavery differentiates Quakers from other denominations; the effects of slavery differentiate the meetings in Virginia, the Carolinas and Georgia from those to the northward, hence the title of this book and its geographical limitations.

As a rule the history of the earliest Southern Friends has been either misrepresented or ignored, or both. And the importance of that great wave of Quaker migration, rising in Pennsylvania, striking Maryland about 1725, and spending its dying power on the colonization of Georgia, 1770-75, seems never to have been duly appreciated. The same is largely true of that other wave of Quaker migration which began to rise in Virginia and the Carolinas during the closing decades of the eighteenth century, and, sweeping across the mountains for the next eighty years, planted some of the first settlements in the then new Northwest, and has since made that country the greatest stronghold of Quakerism in the world. These are some of the reasons that brought the writer, now five years since, to begin the study of Southern Quakerism.

The writer is indebted to many parties for valuable assistance rendered in the preparation of this book. He desires to express his thanks to all who have assisted him in this undertaking; particularly would he mention Mr. Gilbert Cope of West Chester, Pa., Messrs. Frederick D. Stone and John W. Jordan of the Pennsylvania Historical Society Library, Dr. Colyer Meriwether and Mr. George P. Pell of Washington City, Messrs. Kirk Brown and John C. Thomas and Miss E. T. King of Baltimore, Mr. John W. H. Porter of Portsmouth, Va., and Mr. Edmund W. James of Norfolk, Va., Col. Robert A. Brock of Richmond, Mr. Philip A. Bruce of the Virginia Historical Society, Mr. Robert W. Carroll of Cincinnati, Mr. Timothy Nicholson of Richmond, Ind., Mr. Josiah Nicholson of Belvidere, N. C., Mrs. P. B. Hackney and Mr. Addison Coffin of Guilford College, N. C., Mr. Nathan H. Vestal of Yadkinville, N. C., and Mr. Albert W. Brown of Woodland, N. C. He is especially grateful to Mr. Hugh W. Dixon of Snow Camp, N. C., to Prof. F. S. Blair of Guilford College, N. C., to Rev. Rufus King of Archdale, N. C., and to Prof. Eli M. Lamb of Baltimore, who all read much of the work, and to Dr. James Carey Thomas of Baltimore, who criticised parts of the same. The writer would acknowledge also his great obligations to Mr. Francis White of Baltimore for the deep interest he has shown in the work from its very inception, to Mr. Charles Roberts, member of the Common Council of Philadelphia, who, besides assisting him in other ways, placed the MS. correspondence of John Archdale at his service, and to Mr. George J. Scattergood, of Philadelphia, who not only secured him access to the early records of Philadelphia Yearly Meeting, and showed him the MS. correspondence of Thomas Scattergood, but also took the trouble to read over the whole of this volume while still in manuscript and to make valued criticisms on the same.

Washington, D. C., Dec. 1, 1895.

CONTENTS.

CHAPTER IV.

JOHN ARCHDALE AND THE GOLDEN AGE OF SOUTHERN QUAKERISM.

CHAPTER V.

THE EXPANSION OF SOUTHERN QUAKERISM IN THE EIGHTEENTH CENTURY.

CHAPTER VII.

QUAKERS AND THE ESTABLISHED CHURCH.

CHAPTER VIII.

QUAKERS AND THEIR TESTIMONY AGAINST WAR.

SOUTHERN QUAKERS AND SLAVERY.

CHAPTER I.

INTRODUCTION.

The influence of the Quakers in the settlement and growth of the Southern States has never been sufficiently recognized. They appeared in Virginia soon after their organization; they were in the Carolinas almost with the first settlers; they were considerable in numbers and substance; they were well behaved and law-abiding; they maintained friendly relations with the Indians; they were industrious and frugal; they were zealous missionaries, and through their earnest and faithful preaching became, toward the close of the seventeenth century, the largest and only organized body of Dissenters in these colonies.

They have always been zealous supporters of religious freedom. They bore witness to their faith under bodily persecution in Virginia; under disfranchisement and tithes in the Carolinas and Georgia. By reason of their organization and numbers they were bold and aggressive in North Carolina in the struggle against the Established Church. They took the lead in this struggle for religious freedom in the first half of the eighteenth century, as the Presbyterians did in the latter half. They continued an important element in the life of these States until about 1800, when their protest against slavery took the form of migration. They left their old homes in the South by thousands, and removed to the free Northwest, particularly Ohio and Indiana. These emigrants composed the middle and lower ranks of society, who had few or no slaves and who could not come into economic competition with slavery. They

were accompanied by many who were not Quakers, but who
were driven to emigration by the same economic cause, and
so great was this emigration that in 1850 one-third of the
population of Indiana is said to have been made up of
native North Carolinians and their children.

Soon after 1800 Quakers disappeared entirely from the
political and religious life of South Carolina and Georgia.
They now number only a few hundred in Virginia. They
are now relatively less important in North Carolina than
in colonial days, but are still an important factor in the
making of that State.

The times of the English Civil War and Commonwealth
were rich in controversy. In no field was controversy more
prominent and bitter than in that of religion. Discussion
and disputes were frequent; they produced dissensions and
divisions; they were carried on by exasperating methods;
stern, harsh and vulgar language was used. The churches
were put to all sorts of uses, and men frequently inter-
rupted the minister to quarrel with him over theological
points, while the care of souls was suspended.

> Blind mouths ! that scarce themselves know how to hold
> A sheep hook, or have learned aught else the least
> That to the faithful herdman's art belongs !
> What recks it them? What need they? They are sped ;
> And when they list, their lean and flashy songs
> Grate on their scrannel pipes of wretched straw ;
> The hungry sheep look up and are not fed,
> But swoln with wind, and the rank mist they draw,
> Rot inwardly, and foul contagion spread.

In the end Puritanism triumphed over the Episcopacy,
and the Presbyterians over the Puritan; but, as Milton said,
new presbyter was but old priest writ large, and the jangling sects continued to increase. Masson enumerates more
than twenty. These sects were the logical outcome of the
revolt against the State Church; for as soon as the right
of the individual to think for himself in religious matters

is recognized, as soon as heresy ceases to be capital, so soon does the judgment of the individual assert itself; a centrifugal force begins to act, and there is no theoretical limitation to the number of divisions possible. The practical limitation is found in the gregariousness of the race. As Aristotle says, man is a social animal, πολιτικόν ζῶον, and this instinct will always have a restraining influence on the multiplication of sects.

The English sects of the seventeenth century were all advocates of religious liberty, and were filled with zeal against the Established Church. The Quakers also opposed it strongly, but they were much more decent than many others. Fox usually waited until the minister was through before replying. His followers were not always so considerate. Their zeal manifested itself particularly in bearing testimony against a hireling ministry or barbarous laws, and they frequently ascribed these actions to a divine requirement; but, notwithstanding some blemishes of this character, I think it accurate to call Quakerism the flower of Puritanism, from which it was an outgrowth.

The founder of the Society of Friends was George Fox (1624-1691). He was born at Drayton in the Clay, in Leicestershire, England, in July, 1624. His father was a Puritan weaver, and the son, originally intended for the Church, was apprenticed to a shoemaker and dealer in wool. At a very early age Fox had "a gravity and stayedness of mind and spirit not usual in children," and when he was eleven "knew pureness and righteousness." In 1643 "I left my relations, and broke off all familiarity or fellowship with young or old." For the next few years he was in spiritual darkness and groped after the light. He met with struggles and temptations, with buffets and jeers, but the work of the Lord went forward, and many were turned from darkness to light by his labors.

He dates the beginnings of his Society from Leicestershire in 1644. The course of Quakerism was at first toward the north of England. It appeared in Warwickshire in 1645; in Nottinghamshire in 1646; in Derby, 1647; in the adjacent counties in 1648, 1649 and 1650. It reached Yorkshire in 1651; Lancaster and Westmoreland, 1652; Cumberland, Durham and Northumberland, 1653; London and most other parts of England, Scotland and Ireland in 1654. In 1655 Friends went beyond sea "where truth also sprang up," and in 1656 "it broke forth in America and many other places." [1]

Fox was unremittent in his missionary labors, and traveled over England, Scotland, Wales and Ireland. He visited the West Indies and North America. He went twice into Holland. His first imprisonment was at Nottingham in 1649. It was a strange thing then to be in prison for religion, and some thought him mad because he "stood for purity, righteousness and perfection," but the simplicity, the earnestness, the devotion, and the practical nature of this system when contrasted with the dry husk of Episcopacy and the jangling creeds of the Dissenters soon won him adherents by the thousands. They came mostly from the lower ranks of society, but from all sects.

Quakerism is distinctively the creed of the seventeenth century. Seekers were in revolt against the established order. It gave these seekers what they were seeking for. In theology it was un-Puritan; but in cultus, forms and modes it was more than Puritan. The Quaker was the Puritan of the Puritans. He was an extremist, and this brought him into conflict with the established order. He believed that Quakerism was primitive Christianity revived. He recognized no distinction between the clergy and laity; he refused to swear, for Christ had said, swear not at all; he refused to fight, for the religion of Christ is a religion of love, not of war; he would pay no tithes, for Christ had said, ye have freely received, freely give; he called no man master, for he thought the terms rabbi, your holiness and right reverend connoted the same idea. He rejected the dogmas of water baptism and the Puritan Sabbath, and in

[1] Fox's *Journal*, II., 442.

addition to these claimed that inspiration is not limited to the writers of the Old and New Testaments, but is the gift of Jehovah to all men who will accept it, and to interpret the Scriptures men must be guided by the Spirit that guided its authors. Here was the cardinal doctrine of their creed and the point where they differed radically from other Dissenters. Add to this the doctrine of the *Inner Light*, the heavenly guide given directly to inform or illuminate the individual conscience, and we have the corner-stones of their system.

The Society of Friends was not organized by the establishment of meetings to inspect the affairs of the church until some years after Fox began preaching, and then a prominent part of the business of these meetings was to aid those Friends who were in prison, for persecution followed hard upon their increase in numbers. In 1661 500 were in prison in London alone; there were 4,000 in jail in all England; and the Act of Indulgence liberated 1,200 Quakers in 1673. But Quakerism flourished under persecution. They showed a firmness which has been seen nowhere else in the annals of religious history. Other Dissenters might temporize, plot against the Government or hold meetings in secret; the Quakers never. They scorned these things. They received the brutal violence of Government in meekness; they met openly and in defiance of its orders; they wearied it by their very persistence.

In July, 1656, Ann Austin and Mary Fisher, the vanguard of a Quaker army, appeared in Boston from Barbadoes. They were the first Quakers to arrive in America. They were imprisoned and shipped back. In October of the same year a law was passed which provided a fine for the shipmaster who knowingly brought in Quakers, and obliged him to carry them out again. The Quaker was to be whipped and committed to the house of correction. Any person importing books " or writings concerning their devilish opinions," or defending their " heretical opinions " was to be fined, and for the third offense banished. Nor was any person to revile the magistrates and ministry, "as is usual with the Quakers." The law of October, 1657, imposed a fine for entertaining a Quaker. If a Quaker returned after being sent away once he was to lose one ear; if he returned a second time, the other ear; and the third offense was punished by boring the tongue. The law of October, 1658, banished both resident and foreign Quakers under pain of death. In Massachusetts Quakers had their ears cut off; they were branded; they were tied to the cart-tail and whipped through the streets; women were shamefully exposed to public gaze; and in 1659-60 three men and one woman were hanged on Boston Common—such was the welcome of the first Quakers to American soil. This severity ceased to be a permanent factor in the policy of Massachusetts in 1677, and in 1728 Quakers were exempted from tithes for support of the clergy.

There is much discussion among students of New England history as to the amount of justification to be found for this treatment in the excesses of the Quakers themselves. Cotton Mather's *Magnalia* has been a storehouse of ammunition for apologists for Puritan bigotry. It was charged that Quakers worshipped the devil and said that the Bible was inspired by him; that they danced naked and denied civil authority. There were cases of Quaker excesses, but these excesses were probably not the cause, but the result of Puritan harshness. And Hallowell pertinently remarks that had "suffrage been extended [in Massachusetts] to all citizens of character and good repute, instead of being limited to church members, it is probable there would have been an infusion of true religion and humanity into the laws, and the colony would have been spared the tragic record which now mars its history."[1]

With this introduction of the Quaker into the New World we can turn to the Status of Dissent in the Southern colonies at the time of their appearance there.

---

[1] Hallowell, *Quaker Invasion of Massachusetts.* 68. See also the appendix to the second volume of Pickard's *Life of John G. Whittier.*

CHAPTER II.

In discussing the career of the Quakers in Virginia, the Carolinas and Georgia, it is necessary for us to examine, first of all, the laws of these provinces concerning Dissent. This will show us at once the legal position of Friends.

Virginia received three charters from the King in the seventeenth century. The last was issued in 1611-12. There is nothing in them of interest to us. The question of tolerating Protestant Dissenters is not considered. It had not yet been recognized in England. These times were a sort of lull between two storms. England had passed through the storm of the Catholic reaction and was now firmly Protestant. The heyday of Puritanism had not yet come. The Church of England was the church of all the King's dominions. The Jamestown colony did not prosper at first, and King James annulled the last charter in 1624. From this time the colony was governed under laws made by the Virginia Assembly, with the approbation of the King or his representative, the Governor. Many of their early enactments relate to church affairs. They were careful to establish the church, so far as law could do it, and in 1642-43, to secure "the preservation of the puritie of doctrine & unitie of the church," it was enacted that no popish recusant should hold office, and any popish priest was to be sent out of the country in five days. The Governor and Council were also to take care that all Nonconformist ministers should be silenced, and if they persisted in preaching, might be expelled the province.[1] This law was aimed at the Puritans in Nanse-

---

[1] Hening, *Statutes at Large of Virginia*, I., 268, 277. See Dr. H. R. McIlwaine's *The Struggle of Protestant Dissenters for Religious Toleration in Virginia*, p. 10, for the full text of this law, quoted from Trott's *Laws of the British Plantations*.

mond County, and thus did Virginia orthodoxy establish the
limit of religious thought beyond which none should dare
to go.

We see the same spirit in the grant of Carolina to Sir
Robert Heath in 1620. Here the King grants him "the
patronages and advowsons of all churches which shall happen to be built hereafter in the said region . . . to have, exercise, use and enjoy in like manner as any Bishop of Durham within the Bishopricke or county palatine of Durham."[1]

Nothing more is said in this charter on the question of
religion or religious toleration. There is no sort of recognition accorded to Dissenters. There was to be uniformity of
religious opinions. The grant to Heath did not bring settlers, and in 1663 Charles II. granted the Province of Carolina to eight of his favorites. It was the clear purpose of
Charles to establish the English Church, for the Proprietors
had power "to build and found churches, chapels and ora-
tories . . . and to cause them to be consecrated according
to the ecclesiastical laws of our kingdom of England."[2]

But the influence of the religious element in the Civil War
is clearly seen. That event laid the foundation for religious
liberty. The State Church was not to be absolutely supreme
in Carolina, as it was in Virginia. Section 18 provides for
religious toleration "Because it may happen that some of
the people and inhabitants of the said province cannot, in their
private opinions, conform to the public exercise of religion,
according to the liturgy, form and ceremonies of the Church
of England, or take and subscribe the oaths and articles,
made and established in that behalf, and for that the same,
by reason of the remote distances of these places, will, we
hope be no breach of the unity and uniformity established
in this nation, our will and our pleasure is and we do . . .
give and grant unto the said Edward, Earl of Clarendon,
etc., . . . full and free license, liberty and authority. . . .
to give and grant unto such person or persons . . . who

Colonial Records of N. C., I., 6, 7.   [2] *Ibid.*, I., 22.

really in their judgments, and for conscience sake, cannot or shall not conform to the said liturgy and ceremonies, and take and subscribe the oaths and articles aforesaid, or any of them, such indulgences and dispensations in that behalf, for and during such time and times, and with such limitations and restrictions as they . . . shall in their discretion think fit and reasonable; and with this express proviso, and limitation also, that such person and persons . . . shall . . . be subject and obedient to all other the laws, ordinances and constitutions of the said province, in all matters whatsoever as well ecclesiastical as civil." [1]

The ideal aimed at by the Proprietors is then clear; but for a generation the Establishment was a harmless ideal. On the other hand, the authorities took care to impress would-be settlers that there was to be what they called the fullest religious freedom in Carolina. Thus we find Sir John Colleton writing to the Duke of Albemarle, under the date of June 10, 1663, that the persons designing to settle in North Carolina "expect liberty of conscience and without that will not go." [2] Again, on August 25, 1663, the Proprietors say in their proposals concerning settlements on the Cape Fear, that they "will grant, in as ample manner as the undertakers shall desire, freedom and liberty of conscience in all religious or spiritual things, and to be kept inviolably with them, we having power in our charter so to do." [3] Furthermore, the Proprietors, writing to Sir William Berkeley, September 8, 1663, in regard to the appointment of a Governor for Albemarle, assign as their reasons for giving him power to appoint two Governors instead of one in the territory, that "some persons that are for liberty of conscience may desire a governor of their own proposing." [4]

Again, the terms offered in 1665 to Sir John Yeamans and others who had made a settlement on the Cape Fear, bore on their face the evidence of remarkable liberality. It was provided that "no person . . . shall be any ways mo-

---

[1] *Col. Rec.*, I., 32, 33.   [2] *Ibid.*, I., 34.   [3] *Ibid.*, I., 45.   [4] *Ibid.*, I., 54.

lested, punished, disquieted or called in question for any
differences in opinion or practice in matters of religious concernment."[1]   Later in the same year we find that Yeamans,
then Governor of the Clarendon colony on Cape Fear, is
instructed to do all he can to keep those in the "king's
dominions that either cannot or will not submit to the government of the Church of England."[2]   In 1667 the Proprietors direct Gov. Stephens to see to it that no persons shall
be in "any way molested, punished, disquieted or called in
question for any differences in opinion or practice in matters
of religious concernment who do not actually disturb the
civil peace of the said province or county, but that all and
every such person and persons may from time to time and at
all times freely and fully have and enjoy their judgments and
consciences in matter of religion."[3]

In the same way Locke made provisions in his Fundamental Constitutions for the toleration of Dissenters, "that
civil peace may be obtained amidst diversity of opinion."
He provided that any seven persons agreeing in any religion
should be constituted a "church or profession, to which
they shall give some name, to distinguish it from others."[4]
Three articles of belief were necessary to constitute any body
of persons a church: (1) that there is a God; (2) that God is
to be publicly worshipped; (3) that it is lawful and the duty
of every man to bear witness to the truth when called on by
the proper authority, and "that every church or profession
shall in their terms of communion set down the eternal way
whereby they witness a truth as in the presence of God."[5]
No man was permitted to be a freeman in Carolina or to
have any estate or habitation in it that did not acknowledge
a God, and that he was to be publicly worshipped.[6]   No person above seventeen years of age could have any benefit or
protection of law, nor hold any place of honor or profit who
was not a member of some church or profession.[7]   No person of one faith was to disturb or molest the religious as-

---

[1] *Col. Rec.*, I., 80, 81.   [2] *Ibid.*, I., 94.   [3] *Ibid.*, I., 166.
[4] Fundamental Constitutions, sec. 97, in *Col. Rec.*, I., pp. 187-207.
[5] *Ibid.*, sec. 100.   [6] *Ibid.*, sec. 95.   [7] *Ibid.*, sec. 101.

semblies of others,[1] nor use reproachful, reviling or abusive
language against any church or profession,[2] nor persecute
them for speculative opinions in religion or their ways of
worship.[3] But in section 96 the doctrine was enunciated
that as the country came to be " sufficiently planted and distributed into fit divisions," it should be the duty of " parliament to take care for the building of churches and the public
maintenance of divines, to be employed in the exercise of
religion according to the Church of England; which being
the only true and orthodox, and the national religion of all
the king's dominions, is so also of Carolina, and therefore it
alone shall be allowed to receive public maintenance by
grant of parliament." [4]

The settlement of Georgia was not undertaken until 1732.
Its object was primarily philanthropic, and the clauses of
the charter of 1732 in regard to religion are more liberal
than those of the Carolinas. No provision was made for
an Established Church, although this idea does not seem to
have been absent from the mind of the party drawing up the
charter. Liberty of conscience was " allowed in the worship
of God, to all persons inhabiting . . . and all such persons,
except papists," were to have the " free exercise of religion, so
they be contented with the quiet and peaceable enjoyment of
the same, not giving offence nor scandal to the government."
It was especially provided that Quakers be allowed to affirm.[5]
The Proprietary idea was a failure in Georgia also, and in
1752 the colony passed into Royal hands. This left the
Quakers without special provision save as they influenced
legislation to that end. Further, the Episcopal Church had
received official recognition in the province before any
Quaker settlements were made there.

We see, then, that the Quakers on coming into these
provinces found themselves in different positions legally.

---

[1] Fundamental Constitutions, sec. 102.
[2] *Ibid.*, sec. 106.   [3] *Ibid.*, sec. 109.
[4] It is worthy of note that this section was not in the first set of
Constitutions. dated July 21, 1669, and was inserted by Shaftesbury
against the judgment of Locke.
[5] Poore, *Charters and Constitutions*, 375.

In Virginia their status depended entirely on the will of the
Governor and Assembly; they might have liberty and they
might just as easily be deprived of all privileges. The
policy pursued toward them might be steady or vacillating.
There was no appeal from the law except to the King.
When Georgia was settled their tenets were well known and
religious freedom had made considerable progress. They
were provided for and protected under the charter, but, as
we have seen, they made no use of this privilege.

In the Carolinas, on the other hand, the right of Dissenters
to toleration was fixed in the charter and Fundamental Constitutions. But the amount of toleration, the time and way
it was to be given, were matters left in the hands of the Proprietors entirely. The establishment of the English Church
was the ultimate goal. It was not possible to introduce a
state system at once, because many of the settlers were Dissenters, and for the time it was held in abeyance. But that
the Proprietors never intended to divorce Church and State
is indicated by their frequent grants to assemblies " to constitute and appoint such and so many ministers or preachers
as they shall think fit "[1]: by their grants to " each parish " of
church sites and a hundred acres of land for the use of the
minister,[2] and by the direct and elaborate provision in the
Fundamental Constitutions of Locke.

After giving notice of their ultimate purpose, the Proprietors could only wait for a time favorable to the execution of
the ecclesiastical program. This did not come for a generation. During the seventeenth century, North Carolina, and
South Carolina up to 1698, were, in religious things, the
freest of the free; but with the organization of the Society
for the Promotion of Christian Knowledge and the Society
for the Propagation of the Gospel, and the new missionary
spirit infused into the Church by such men as Thomas
Bray, it was thought that the time for the establishment of
the Church of England had come, and a religious struggle
begins.

[1] *Col. Rec.*, I., 167.   [2] *Ibid.*, I., 81, 92.

CHAPTER III.

THE PLANTING OF QUAKERISM IN VIRGINIA AND THE CAROLINAS.

No Church since the days of the Apostles has allowed such great freedom in the Gospel to women as has been allowed by Friends. Under their system man and woman are equal, and Quaker women have repaid this greater liberty with an unsurpassed zeal and devotion.

Massachusetts was the first American colony in which Quakerism was preached. The second seems to have been Virginia, although there is little difference in the time of its appearance in this colony and in Maryland. The person to plant the standard of Quakerism in the South was Elizabeth Harris, a native of London. Of her personal history we know little. She entered Virginia in 1656, and arrived in England on her return about July, 1657, "in a pretty condition." Bowden says "her religious labors were blessed to many in that province, who were sincere seekers after heavenly riches, and she was instrumental in convincing many of the primitive and spiritual views of the Christian religion professed by Friends."[1]

We know, however, very little of the number or character of these converts. It has been claimed that Robert Clarkson, a respectable and influential planter, was one of them. He is said to have lived at Severn, probably in what is now Gloucester County, but it is more probable that it was the Severn of the Puritan colony in Maryland.[2] But Elizabeth Harris was not unmindful, after her return to England, of the needs of her proselytes in Virginia. She wrote them letters and sent them books, for one of the items in the

---

[1] *History of Friends in America,* I., 339.
[2] See McIlwaine, pp. 19. 20.

national expense account of the Quakers for 1657 is "for books to Virginia, £2 5s."

Friends soon met with opposition in Virginia. "The two messengers thou spoke of in thy letters," wrote Clarkson to Elizabeth Harris, "are not yet come to this place; we heard of two come to Virginia in the fore part of the winter, but we heard that they were soon put in prison and not suffered to pass; we heard further that they desired liberty to pass to this place, but it was denied them, whereupon one of them answered, that though they might not be suffered, yet he must come another time. We have heard that they are to be kept in prison until the ship that brought them be ready to depart the country again, and then to be sent out of the country." [1]

These Friends were, most probably, Josiah Cole and Thomas Thurston. [2] They visited Virginia toward the close of 1657 and continued to labor in the province until August, 1658, when they traveled overland to New England. [3] Thurston soon after returned to Virginia and was again imprisoned.

There is evidence that persecution of Quakers followed these visits. Our information in this matter comes from the records of the General Court of Virginia. All the originals of these records have been destroyed by fire except one volume. Extracts were made from the earlier volumes be-

---

[1] Bowden, I., 341.

[2] Cole (c. 1633-1668), whose name is also spelled Coale, was a native of Gloucester and was converted to Quakerism in Bristol in 1654. He twice visited America and the West Indies; he went to Holland and the Low Countries. In England his labors extended to almost every county, and he suffered numerous imprisonments. In Maryland, along with Richard Preston, he pushed Jacob Lumbroso, the Jew, to answer certain questions about his religious belief, which brought about his arrest for blasphemy. Cole was himself arrested under the proclamation of April 13, 1657, which required an oath of fidelity to the Lord Proprietor. Thurston was also a Gloucester man. He was imprisoned in Maryland soon after his departure from Virginia; later he sided with Perrot in his schism.

[3] Sewel, *History of the Quakers,* ed. 1834, I., 351; Bowden, I., 342, 343; Janney, *History of Friends,* I., 432, 433.

fore their destruction by Conway Robinson. These extracts consist of headings or titles, extracts of proceedings, etc., and are now preserved in the library of the Virginia Historical Society. Under date of November 27, 1657, we find (pp. 353, 354) that Thomas Thurston and Josiah Cole, Quakers, were sentenced to depart the colony on a sloop, and in the meantime were to be committed to custody; they were not to have the use of pen, ink or paper, and were not to correspond with the citizens. At the same time it was ordered that masters of sloops who brought in Quakers should be fined and compelled to take them out again (p. 354). The inference is that Cole and Thurston were kept in prison all that winter, for we hear no more of them until March, 1657(58), when they were allowed to go to Maryland (p. 382). This is probably the release referred to by one of the contemporary Quaker authorities, who says: "The governor of that place [probably S. Matthews] hath promised that he shall have his liberty in the country; where there is like to be a great gathering, and the living power of the Lord goes along with him." [1]

But this was not the end of persecution. We find that one Quaker was whipped (p. 413); that one was fined for entertaining another Quaker (pp. 413, 416); that other Quakers were punished in ways not stated; and that on June 10, 1658, a general persecution of Quakers was directed (p. 416).

The results of these severities were the opposite of what was expected. Quakerism grew by the buffets it received. About this time Virginia was visited by William Robinson, Robert Hodgson and Christopher Holder, all of whom had come over in Robert Fowler's vessel, the *Woodhouse*. Concerning this visit Robinson writes Fox from Boston jail: "There are many people convinced, and some there are brought into the sense and feeling of truth in several places." [2]

---

[1] Bowden, I., 343.
[2] Bowden, I., 346; Janney, I., 433, 434. Robinson was hanged in Boston the next year. Hodgson was probably a native of Skipton

Thus did these humble missionaries of the Cross plant their standard in Virginia in the midst of difficulty and danger. Virginia was not a land in which religious freedom thrived. Loyalty was its corner-stone, and its narrowness and devotion to the cause of the Established Church had been increased by the crowds of Cavaliers who had come over to escape from the tender mercies, political and religious, of the Puritan Establishment. Dissenters had few privileges in Virginia. A law enacted in 1643 had given the Governor and Council power to "suspend and silence" any minister who undertook to teach or preach without the ordination of the Church of England, and if he still persisted he might be expelled from the province.[1] It was under this law that Quakers were first punished. Four months' imprisonment and whippings was certainly the full extent of the law to "suspend and silence." We are to remember also that this was not the work of Sir William Berkeley. It agrees so well with his character that we are apt to credit him with it, but it was the work of the Commonwealth men, who, it might be supposed, were enough in sympathy to give the Quakers passive sufferance at least.

It was not until March, 1659(60), that there were enactments against Quakers *eo nomine*. This act was the first passed against the Society in the colonies we are studying, and one of the earliest in America. It fittingly marks the return of Berkeley to power. The prefatory remarks to this act are worthy of notice, as they give us the popular impression of the object, aims and results of Quakerism; and this misunderstanding, so far as it is sincere, is the best and the only excuse for the infamous treatment which Quakers in many places received.

The introduction to the act goes on to recite that "where-

in Yorkshire. He first appeared among Friends in Berkshire in 1655. He suffered persecution in the Old World and the New. Holder (c. 1628-1688) was of Gloucestershire, was now on his second visit to America, and had suffered imprisonment at Ilchester as early as 1655.

[1] See *ante*, p. 7.

as there is an unreasonable and turbulent sort of people, commonly called Quakers, who, contrary to the law, do daily gather together unto them unlawful assemblies and congregations of people, teaching and publishing lies, miracles, false visions, prophecies and doctrines, which have influence upon the communities of men both ecclesiastical and civil, endeavoring and attempting thereby to destroy religion, laws, communities and all bonds of civil society, leaving it arbitrary to every vain and vicious person whether men shall be safe, laws established, offenders punished, and governors rule, hereby disturbing the public peace and just interest, to prevent and restrain which mischief," etc., it was enacted: That every shipmaster bringing a Quaker into Virginia was to be fined £100; that all Quakers who have been questioned or shall hereafter arrive shall be arrested and imprisoned "without bail or mainprize till they do abjure this country or put in security with all speed to depart the colony and not to return again." If any returned after being thus deported they were to be proceeded against as "contemners of the laws and magistracy," and to be punished accordingly. If they came to Virginia the third time they were to be treated as felons. No person could entertain a Quaker, nor a person suspected of Quakerism by the Governor and his Council, nor allow a Quaker assembly in or near his house, on penalty of £100 sterling. Commissioners and officers were warned at their peril to see that the act went into effect. All persons were warned that they published books or pamphlets containing Quaker tenets and opinions at their peril.[1]

Again, in March, 1662, under the caption "Sundays not to be profaned," the Protestant legislators of Virginia could find nothing better than to rake up the statute of 23d Elizabeth, which was aimed at Romish recusants, and apply it to the Quakers. This law imposed a penalty of £20 a month for refusing to go to church, "and if they forbear a twelve-

---

[1] Hening, I., 532. This law bears striking resemblance to the Massachusetts law of 1658, and was probably a copy.

month then to give good security for their good behavior
besides their payment for their monthly absences, according
to the tenor of the said statute. And that all Quakers for
assembling in unlawful assemblies and conventicles be fined
and pay each of them there taken, 200 pounds of tobacco
for each time they shall be for such unlawful meeting taken
or presented by the church-wardens to the county court,"
and in case any members were insolvent, the more able were
to pay for them.[1]

A further act empowers the church-wardens to present to
the court twice a year all cases of offense under this law.[2]
And in December, 1662, it is enacted that, "Whereas many
schismatical persons, out of their averseness to the orthodox
established religion, or out of the new-fangled conceits of
their own heretical inventions, refuse to have their children
baptized," such persons should be fined 200 pounds of
tobacco. It is evident that this law was aimed at both
Baptists and Quakers. It is probable that the latter were
more numerous and suffered most under its provisions.[3]

It is to be noted that the law of 1659-60 was not inserted
in the revisal of the laws of the colony made in 1662. We
are probably justified in assuming that it failed to accomplish the end aimed at in its enactment. Its place was supplied by the law of September, 1663, to prohibit "the unlawful assembling of Quakers,"[4] and which is considerably
more humane than the law of 1659-60. This act recites that the
Quakers were endangering the public peace, and gave color-
ing "to the terror of the people by maintaining a secret and
strict correspondence among themselves." The law then provided that if "Quakers, or any other separatists whatsoever in
this colony," should at any time assemble to the number of five
or more of the age of sixteen, "at any time in any one place
under pretence of joining in religious worship not authorized
by the laws of England nor this country," the party offending was to be fined for first offense 200 pounds of tobacco,

---

[1] Hening. II., 48.   [2] *Ibid.,* II., 51.
[3] *Ibid.,* II., 165.   [4] *Ibid.,* II., 180-183.

for the second offense they were to be fined 500 pounds of
tobacco, to be levied by distress and sale of goods. If there
were some unable to pay this fine the sum was to be collected
" from the rest of the Quakers or other separatists then
present." For the third offense the party was to be banished. All shipmasters bringing in Quakers to reside, except in accordance with the English act of May 19, 1663,
were to be fined 5,000 pounds of tobacco, and had to take
them out again on the return voyage. Persons entertaining
Quakers to preach or teach were to be fined 5,000 pounds
of tobacco. Officers neglecting to enforce this act or con-
niving at neglect of it were to be fined 2,000 pounds of
tobacco. But if Quakers or others, after being convicted,
should give security not to violate the act again, they were to
be discharged from further penalties.[1]

The horrible character of this Virginia Conventicle Act
comes out only on close examination. By its terms all Dissenters were alike forbidden to worship; not even could a
minister or a layman offer a prayer at the bedside of the
dying if there were five grown persons present. Men were
forbidden to exercise hospitality, and as Dissent was looked
on as a social evil, the whole body of Dissenters was held
responsible for the acts of a part. What we might call the
social solidarity of Dissent was emphasized, and there was no
way of escape from responsibility save in flight to the Establishment.

Nor were these laws idle threats. Friends had experienced hardships and imprisonments in Virginia under the
Commonwealth. The Restoration in England and the return of the royalists to power in Virginia was the sign for

[1] The Parliamentary act of May 19, 1663, is clearly the original of
the Virginia statute. It provided against the assembling of Quakers to the number of five or more over sixteen years of age for
religious worship, and punished them for refusing to take an oath.
For the third offense they were to be transported " in any Ship or
Ships to any of His Majesties Plantations beyond the Seas." The
Virginia law does not contain the provision against refusing to
swear, but was in other respects considerably harsher than its
English prototype.

the beginning of more persecution. One of the first acts
of the restored royalists was to disfranchise Maj. John Bond
for "factious and schismatical demeanors."[1] We do not
know that Bond's offense was Quakerism, but it was in all
probability of a religious character, and comports with the
character of Sir William Berkeley, who was now in power.
About 1661 George Wilson, a native of Cumberland, visited
Virginia. He had been imprisoned in Cumberland for "re-
proving a priest." He had been cast into jail in Boston, and
was whipped through three towns and banished. From
Puritan New England he turned to Cavalier Virginia. Here
he was cast into a dungeon, very loathsome, without light,
without ventilation. "Here, after being cruelly scourged
and heavily ironed, for a long period, George Wilson had to
feel the heartlessness of a persecuting and dominant hier-
archy; until at last his flesh actually rotted from his bones,
and within the cold damp walls of the miserable dungeon of
James's Town he lay [*sic*] down his life a faithful martyr for
the testimony of Jesus." William Coale, of Maryland, was a
fellow-prisoner with Wilson in the jail at Jamestown, and
never fully recovered·from the effects of the imprisonment
which he then endured.[2]

But notwithstanding these persecutions, Coale was able to
report that his visit to Virginia was a successful one. "Some
were turned to the Lord through his ministry, and many
were established in the truth." Josiah Cole was also in Virginia during his second visit to America in 1660. He writes
to Fox: "I left Friends in Virginia generally very well and
fresh in the truth." He was then in Barbadoes and had
drawings to return to Virginia.[3] George Rolfe (d. 1663), a
resident of Holstead in Essex, who had suffered various im-

[1] Hening, II., 39.
[2] Bowden, I., 344-346, quoting Bishop's *New England Judged*, and
Piety Promoted, Kendall's ed., I., 97-98. Coale died c. 1678. We
are tempted to regard some of these accounts as exaggerated, because there is no provision for imprisonment in the law, but it followed naturally and necessarily on the refusal to pay fines.
[3] Bowden, I., 346.

prisonments for his faith, also visited Virginia in 1661. We
have no definite account of his work, but he writes to Stephen
Crisp, "The truth prevaileth through the most of all these
parts [Barbadoes], and many settled meetings there are in
Maryland, and Virginia and New England."[1]

In the same year Elizabeth Hooton and Joan Brocksoppe
visited Virginia from England. This seems to have been
the first voyage made direct. Elizabeth Hooton (*c.* 1600-1671)
was the wife of Samuel Hooton, of Skegby, in Nottinghamshire, and was associated with Fox as early as 1647. She
was the first woman, and the first person after Fox, to enter
the ministry of Friends. She was imprisoned as early as
1651. This was her first visit to America; she made a
second voyage soon after, and died in Jamaica while undertaking a third voyage with Fox and Edmundson in 1671.[2]
Of Joan Brocksoppe we know but little save that she was the
wife of Thomas Brocksoppe, of Little Normanton, and died
in 1680. We have no particulars of their visit to Virginia.
They then went to Boston, were banished thence, returned
to Virginia, and Elizabeth Hooton suffered because of her
testimony.[3]

The next traveling Friends in Virginia were Joseph Nicholson, John Liddal and Jane Millard. Of the last we know
nothing. Liddal, it is believed, was of Cumberland. They
all labored in New England and suffered there. Nicholson
was for one night a prisoner in New Amsterdam, and after
his return to England was imprisoned in Dover Castle.
Their visit to Virginia was about March, 1662. "They had
many hard travels and sufferings in the service of the Lord."[4]

Mary Tompkins and Alice Ambrose were the next visi-
tors (*c.* 1662). They had been associated in the work of the
ministry before coming to America. In Virginia "we have
had good service for the Lord . . . our sufferings have been

---

[1] Bowden, I., 347. This letter shows that there were settled meetings in Virginia certainly as early as 1661. They were probably
earlier still.
[2] *Ibid.*, I., 260.   [3] Sewel, I., 435 ; Bowden, I., 347.
[4] Bowden, I., 265, 268, 348, quoting Bishop, 423.

large amongst them. . . . We are now about to sail for Virginia again." [1] They returned to Virginia, and Sewel tells us what these " sufferings " were. They had been pilloried, and each had been whipped " with thirty-two stripes, with a whip of nine cords, and every cord with three knots; and they were handled so severely that the very first lash drew blood and made it run down from their breasts." They had recently experienced the same sort of treatment in Massachusetts, their goods were then seized, and they were expelled from the colony in June, 1664. [2]

It has been suggested that some of these persecutions were the work of mobs and that the people in their organic capacity are not to be held responsible for them. It is to be hoped that this is true; but even in that case the Government set the example in brutality, as we have seen. We have note of proceedings by the General Court at James City, April 4, 1662, in the Robinson Manuscripts, but the record itself has been lost.

In the case of Norfolk County our evidence is full and also unimpeachable, as it comes from the county records. In December, 1662, Col. John Sidney, high sheriff of Norfolk County, had caused a number of persons, among whom was his own daughter, to be summoned to court for holding a Quaker meeting, and they were fined 200 pounds of tobacco each. This is the first case of persecution of resident Quakers that we have met with. These fines were imposed under the law of March, 1662. John Hill became the high sheriff of Norfolk County in April, 1663. He was either tempted by the bait of one-half of the fines which the law allowed to the informer, or by religious zeal, or both, and began a systematic persecution of the Quakers. The fines against them for this year in Norfolk County alone amounted to £100 sterling and 20,750 pounds of tobacco.

---

[1] Janney, II., 97; Bowden, I., 348, 349.
[2] Sewel, quoting Bishop, I., 436; Bowden, I., 253, 349. Of the visit of George Preston and Wenlock Christison in 1663 we have no particulars.

It was a profitable year to Hill. He is the man who reported to the House of Burgesses that John Porter, the representative in that body from Lower Norfolk County, was
" loving to the Quakers and stood well affected towards
them, and had been at their meetings, and was so far an Ana-
baptist as to be against the baptizing of children." On September 12, 1663, the trial took place. Porter confessed that
he was loving to Friends, but denied that his accusers could
establish the truth of their accusations. But the Assembly
had a shibboleth of orthodoxy with which they tried him.
They administered to him the Oath of Supremacy. He refused to swear and was expelled from the House.[1]

Again, on the 12th of November, 1663, Hill found another
Quaker meeting at the residence of Richard Russell, and
summoned some 35 persons, including John Porter, Sr.,
and John Porter, Jr., to court. Ten days later Hill discovered a Quaker meeting on the ship Blissing, at anchor in the
southern branch of Elizabeth river, and summoned John
Porter, Jr., who was speaking; James Gilbert, master of the
ship; Mrs. Mary Emperor, and others, to court. December
15 they were fined 200 pounds of tobacco each, this being

[1] Hening, II., 198. There has existed much confusion in North
Carolina in regard to the career of this John Porter. Hon. George
Davis, in his paper, A Study in Colonial History, pp. 16–17, says
that Porter soon moved to Albemarle [N. C.], settled probably in
Perquimans County, and became the father of that John Porter
who was the leader of the "Cary Rebellion" in 1705. This is in-
correct. Mr. John W. H. Porter, of Portsmouth, Va., has recently
extracted his history from the records of Norfolk County. John
Porter, Sr., is first mentioned in the county records, Dec. 16, 1647,
when an order was entered allowing him 100 pounds of tobacco for
killing a wolf, and on the 16th of March, 1648, a similar order was
entered. Jan. 17, 1652, he was granted a certificate for 200 acres
of land for having brought four persons into the colony. March
29, 1655, he was appointed a justice of the county court ; August 15,
1653, was married to Miss Mary Savill. Jan. 13, 1661, was granted
300 acres of land under patent from the Governor ; Sept. 12, 1663,
was expelled from the House of Burgesses ; Nov. 17, 1663, was
fined 200 pounds of tobacco for attending a Quaker meeting, 50
pounds of tobacco for not attending public worship, and 350 pounds
of tobacco for setting out tobacco plants on Sunday, and must therefore have been a planter. Aug. 16, 1671, was appointed road sur-
veyor for the Eastern Branch section of Norfolk County. April 17,

their first trial. On the same day others were fined 50 pounds each for absenting themselves from public worship, and the grand jury presented John Porter, Jr., and Mrs. Mary Emperor and others for attending a meeting on that day at the house of Mrs. Emperor. The trial for the offense of November 12 occurred on February 14 following. John Porter, Jr., and Mrs. Mary Emperor were fined 500 pounds of tobacco each, for it was their second offense; Richard Russell was fined 5,000 pounds of tobacco for permitting the meeting to be held at his house, and the others were fined 200 pounds of tobacco each, as it was their first offense. The trial for the meeting held at the house of Mrs. Emperor on December 15 also came off then. Mrs. Emperor and John Porter, Jr., were ordered to be sent out of the colony, it being their third correction. Ann Godby was fined 500 pounds of tobacco, it being her second correction, and others were fined 200 pounds, as it was their first. The sentence of transportation passed against Porter and Mrs. Emperor was not carried out. They were persons of influence in the county, and as there was no profit to the in-

---

1672, was appointed one of the Justices of the Quorum of the county and served until his death. Aug. 17, 1675, was the last day he presided at court. Feb. 15, 1675(76), his will was recorded ; it was entirely in his own handwriting. He left nearly all his property to his widow and her heirs forever, and appointed her executrix ; he gave his best suit of clothes to "my brother, John Porter, Jr." He gave also certain cattle to be divided among the children of this John Porter, Jr., upon their arriving at the age of twenty-one years, but his will makes no mention of any children of his own. His widow married George Lawson in April, 1676 ; he died that fall ; in the spring of 1677 she married Thomas Fenwick and died in 1678. She gave her property to Fenwick for his life, and at his death it was to go to John Porter, Jr. This is another reason for thinking she had no children of her own. On the contrary, the will of Richard Russell, who died Jan. 24, 1667, appoints John Porter, Sr., his executor and leaves a lot of books to the oldest son of the said John Porter, Sr.; if he had a son at that date he must have died before his father. At the time of his death Porter was a commissioner of the Association of Nansemond River Fort, a position which would be inconsistent with the character of a Quaker (see Hening, II., 255-8). It is probable that he sympathized with but was not actually a member of the Society. See also Mr. Porter's article on "Norfolk Quakers," in Richmond *Dispatch*, Dec. 3, 1893.

former in their transportation the sentence was probably allowed to die of itself. Hill's term as sheriff expired in 1664, and there was no further persecution of Quakers in this county until 1675.[1]

It will be noticed that the penalty of fifty pounds of tobacco, inflicted for not attending church, was much lighter than the legal penalty, while the other fines were in strict conformity with the law of September, 1663. It is more than probable that the industrious Hill had something to do with securing its passage. It is evident that its enforcement was spasmodical, depending almost entirely on the personal equation of the officers.

Material comes to us to illustrate this narrow bigotry of our fathers, from records of the Friends as well as from public records. No other sect has been so careful, so anxious to preserve the record of their sufferings as have Friends. When Fox was in Virginia in 1672 he laid down rules and regulations for the guidance of the Society. Besides making inquiry concerning the payment of tithes and supporting the families of those in prison for sake of their testimony, they were to see to it " that all the Sufferings of friends of all

---

[1] See article in Richmond *Dispatch*. Dec. 3, 1893. by John W. H. Porter. I am again indebted to Mr. Porter for the history of John Porter, Jr., who was the brother of John Porter, Sr., as we have already seen from the will of the latter. John Porter, Jr., first appears in the records on the 21st of Dec., 1651, when an order was entered recording the marks on his cattle. He was appointed a justice of the county court, March 29, 1655, at the same time as John Porter, Sr. He was made high sheriff, April 21, 1656. His wife was the daughter of Col. John Sidney. He was undoubtedly a Quaker, for he was on several occasions addressing the meetings when arrested. After his third conviction and sentence to transportation he ceased to hold any public office, but remained in the colony, and quite a number of deeds are recorded from different parties giving him power of attorney to attend to their affairs, suits, bills, etc., during their absence. At the time of the formation of Princess Anne County, in April, 1691 (Hening. III , 95), John Porter, Jr., now called John Porter, owned land on the Princess Anne side of the line, became a citizen of the new county and resided in Lynn Haven Parish. His will is said to be on record in Princess Anne County. It seems strange that there should have been two brothers of the same name, but such was the case. Besides the evidence already found in the will of John Porter, Sr., we have an

kinde of sufferings in all the Countrys be gathered up & put together & Sent to the gennerall meeting, & So Sent to London to Elise Hookes, that nothing of the memoriall of the blood & cruell Sufferings of the bretheren be Lost, which shall stand as a testimony against the Murdering Spiritt of this world, & be to the praise of the everlasting power of the Lord in the ages to come, who supported & upheld them in Such hardships & cruelties, who is god over all blessed for ever Amen."

The first case of persecution which we have from this source is that of William Parratt and Edward Jones, about 1663. They were arrested for having a meeting at Parratt's house, and were kept for some time prisoners in the house of the sheriff of Isle of Wight County. Another case was that of Thomas Jordan, of Chuckatuck, in Nansemond County. He was born in 1634, received the truth in 1660, and died on the 8th of 9th month, 1699. His sufferings date from September, 1664. He was imprisoned six months for being taken in a meeting at his own house. He was released by the King's proclamation. He was taken a second time at a meeting at Robert Lawrence's, and bound over to

---

additional one in the sale on Aug. 28, 1691, by John Porter, the first Jr., and second Sr., of a tract of land taken up under patent by Col. John Sidney and sold by him to John Porter, Sr. (1st), and John Porter, Jr. (1st), Jan. 4, 1648, and also a tract of 350 acres "which was taken up by *my brother*, John Porter, Sr., on the 16th of March, 1663."

John Porter, Jr., the first, who later became the second Sr., had a son who was known as John Porter, Jr., the second. This son was not of age in 1675, as we have learned from the will of his uncle, the first John Porter, Sr. He does not appear in the court records until May 20, 1679, when his father gave him a power of attorney. We may therefore assume that he had at this time attained his majority. He was both a planter and a merchant, and on Jan. 16, 1688, bought 400 acres of land near the Currituck County line. This brought him toward North Carolina. When Norfolk County was divided in 1691 he remained in the old county, while his father's residence fell within the new. On Oct. 11, 1690, he gave a deed to one Kemp, which mentions him as "of Norfolk County, Elizabeth River Parish." Sept. 15, 1693, he obtained a judgment to a suit in the Norfolk County court, but was then a resident of Albemarle County, North Carolina, and his name does not appear again in the Norfolk County records. The proof that he

court; he refused to swear, was sent up to Jamestown, and was a prisoner ten months. The sheriff took away three servants and kept them nine weeks; he took by distress beds and other goods amounting to 3,907 pounds of tobacco; he took also a serving-man and ten head of cattle, valued at 5,507 pounds of tobacco.

Nor were the Virginia Quakers during these years free from internal discord. Tompkins and Ambrose write in 1663, "John Perrot is now amongst them; many there are leavened with his unclean spirit. He has done much hurt, which has made our travels hard and our labors sore; for which we know he will have his reward, if he repent not."

Perrot was the leader of the first schism among Friends. He was a man of great natural parts, and united with Friends at an early period. In 1660 he traveled in the ministry to Rome to convert the Pope. He manifested much spiritual pride, and the Inquisitors thinking him of unsound mind, committed him to Bedlam. His schism began in 1661. The three points in which he differed from Fox seem to have been: (1) he maintained that the practice of uncovering the head in time of prayer was a mere form and one that

---

was then a resident of Albemarle County comes from the Princess Anne records : May 3, 1693, "John Porter, Jr., of the county of Albemarle, in North Carolina," gave a power of attorney to his "brother" Thomas Solley, of Elizabeth River in the county of Norfolk in Virginia. We know that Solley had married Porter's sister. This John Porter, then, nephew of the man of that name expelled from the Virginia House of Burgesses for Quakerism. removed to North Carolina between Oct. 11, 1690, and May 3, 1693. and is, beyond doubt, the same as the man of that name who was Speaker of the North Carolina House of Burgesses in 1697 and was so prominent in the "Cary Rebellion." If we assume that he became of age in 1679, he was still in the prime of life in 1705. He remained a prominent citizen of the colony and died in 1713. His will is on file in Raleigh. As it bears date Jan. 8, 1713, and was probated Aug. 7 of the same year. it seems that Porter died in the spring or summer of 1713. In his will are mentioned Mary, his wife ; sons, John, Edmund, Joshua, Matthew : daughters. Sarah, Eliza, and son-in-law. John Lillington, husband of Sarah. He had retained some of his landed interests in Princess Anne County. It will also be seen further on. when we come to treat of the struggle between Quakerism and the Established Church in North Carolina. 1705-11, that an Edmund Porter was prominent on the side of the Dissenters. He is no doubt the son of the subject of this sketch.

ought to be testified against; (2) the second " extravagancy "
was that he let his beard grow; (3) he discouraged attendance
on meetings for worship, on the ground that this also was a
mere form.   These are the charges brought against him by
the Quaker historian Bowden (I., 349-353).   However indifferent a matter the first charge may have been, and however trifling the second, it is certain that he gained many to
his way of thinking in Virginia because of his appearance
of superior sanctity and austereness.   His influence on the
development of the Society was particularly bad in Virginia because of his third tenet, for he preached against
meetings on set days when their persecutors would know of
it and might sweep down upon them.   In this way their
peculiar testimonies were likely to be lost sight of entirely.
Thomas Jordan, who had himself gone off in the Perrot
schism, returned in 1678, and said that this effort to shirk
persecution had done the Society more harm than the persecution itself.   Many of those who had been thus led astray
returned in later years, but the immediate effect was to
cause the Society to lose vitality and languish.

When John Burnyeat (1631-1690) visited Virginia in 1665
he complained that " they had quite forsaken their meetings
and did not meet together once in a year, and many of them
had lost the very form and language of the truth," and had,
in a great measure, relinquished their testimonies in order to
shun the truth.   Burnyeat spent some months in Virginia
and Maryland, and it was with difficulty that he obtained a
meeting among them.   But " the Lord's power was with us
and amongst us, and several were revived and refreshed,
and through the Lord's goodness and his renewed visita-
tions, raised up into a service of life, and in time came to see
over the wiles of the enemy." [1]

The effects of the work of Burnyeat were very manifest
when he came on his second visit to America in 1671: " I
went down to Virginia [in November, 1671] to visit Friends

there, and found a freshness amongst them; and many of them were restored, and grown up to a degree of their former zeal and tenderness; and I found a great openness in the country, and had several blessed meetings. I advised them to have a men's meeting, and so to meet together to settle things in good order amongst them, that they might be instrumental to the gathering of such as were yet scattered, and stirring up of such as were cold and careless; and so keep things in order, sweet, and well amongst them." [1]

We have at this point some vivid and biting characterizations of the Quakers, which may be fairly taken as a sample of the way they were regarded by many of their contemporaries. There was a settlement of Quakers on the border line between Accomac County, Virginia, and Somerset County, Maryland. Edmund Scarborough, who was surveyor-general of Virginia, was sent to collect taxes on the Eastern Shore, and sought to bring these settlers under the rule of Virginia. They refused to recognize her authority and claimed to be under Maryland. This angered the Virginia officer and gave him an opportunity to characterize them after his own fashion. One was "repugnant to all government, of all sects, yet professed by none, constant in nothing, but opposing church government, his children at great ages yet unchristened." Another was the "proteus of heresy . . . notorious for shifting scismatical pranks." A third was a "creeping Quaker." A fourth "was often in question for his quaking profession, . . . a receiver of many Quakers, his house the place of their resort." [2]

For the next five years we have no account of Virginia Quakers, save from Burnyeat, who has been quoted already. There are no other journalists, no manuscripts, no records. The blank comes to an end in 1672, when Virginia was

[1] *Journal,* in *Friends' Library.* XI., 144.
[2] Neill's *Virginia Carolorum,* 301-303. See also *Wenlock Christison and the Early Friends in Talbot County, Maryland,* by Samuel A. Harrison. M. D., Baltimore, 1878. Christison visited Virginia in 1663.

visited by William Edmundson and George Fox. From
their visit the Society clearly began to revive. They may
be said to have replanted Quakerism in Virginia, for under
their ministrations the membership was more than doubled.
Further, the American visit of Fox and Edmundson was
pre-eminently a visit for organization. The Society had
received a definite organization in England for the first
time in 1669. In 1672 meetings for discipline were established in Virginia, and their earliest records, in which they
recount the efforts of Fox in this direction, have been preserved. The same was the case in Maryland. It was on
this occasion that Edmundson and Fox laid the foundations
of their Society in North Carolina.

The history of Quakerism in Virginia and North Carolina is one. It is one in its origin, it is one in its development; it is one in its struggles; it is one in its protest against
slavery; it is one in its decline. The two States will be
treated as one.

William Edmundson, the founder of Quakerism in North
Carolina, was a man of rude eloquence, of earnest piety and
shrewd common-sense. He showed unusual self-denial, and
was charitable to a fault. Born in 1627, he was apprenticed
to a carpenter in York. As soon as his apprenticeship was
over he joined the Parliamentary army and accompanied
Cromwell to Scotland in 1650. He took part the next
year in the battle of Worcester and the siege of the Isle of
Man. In 1652 he was engaged in recruiting for the Scotch
army. A little later he married and settled in Antrim, Ireland, and opened a shop there. During a visit to England
in 1653 he again met with the Quakers and embraced their
creed. He began to preach, and suffered numerous persecutions and imprisonments. From 1661 he was recognized
as the leader of the Quakers in Ireland, and his house became practically the headquarters of the Society. In 1665
he was excommunicated for not paying tithes, and suffered
more persecutions. He first visited America with Fox in
1672, and about April, 1672, sailed from Maryland with

three companions for Virginia.[1] He traveled through Virginia, where he found "things were much out of order" as regards church discipline. He had several powerful meetings among them, got their minds a little settled, and passed on to Albemarle, in the northeast corner of the present State of North Carolina.

The fact that none of the traveling Friends had visited Albemarle before Edmundson is conclusive proof that no Friends were there. The visit of Edmundson was full of importance to that little colony. This was about the first of May, 1672. He had two companions, whose names have been lost. They do not deserve remembrance, however, for they were "weak-spirited" men and deserted their leader in his hour of need. They were probably little more than guides picked up in Virginia for the journey. He encountered many natural obstacles, and tells most graphically of a night spent in the primitive forest. "It being dark, and the woods thick, I walked all night between two trees; and though very weary, I durst not lie down on the ground, for my clothes were wet to my skin. I had eaten little or nothing that day, neither had I anything to refresh me but the Lord."[2] In the morning he and his two companions reached the house of Henry Phillips, situate on "Albemarle" (Perquimans) river, where the town of Hertford now stands.[3] Phillips "and his wife had been convinced of the truth in New England, and came here to live; and not having seen a Friend for seven years before, they wept for joy to see us." Edmundson reached the house of Phillips on Sunday morning and desired him to appoint a meeting for about noon of the same day. Many people attended the services, "but they had little or no religion, for they came and sat down in the meeting smoking their pipes." But the power of God was there; some of their hearts were softened and they "received the testimony." One Tems (Toms), a justice of the peace, and his wife were among the converts. They desired

[1] Fox's *Journal*, II., 146. [2] *Journal*, ed. 1774, 66-68.
[3] Moore, *History of North Carolina*, I., 20, quoting Martin, I., 155.

the preacher to hold a meeting at their house, which was about three miles off and "on the other side of the water." A meeting was held there the next day, and with success, "for several were tendered with a sense of the power of God, received the truth and abode in it." Edmundson left Albemarle on Tuesday of the same week and returned to Virginia.

Thus ended the first missionary journey to North Carolina. It lasted but three days; only two sermons were preached, but here is the beginning of the religious life of a great State and here were laid the foundations of the Society of Friends.

Before tracing further the history of Friends in North Carolina it is necessary for us to go backwards a little. The beginnings of this State are shrouded in mystery. We do not know the time settlements were begun. A permanent government was first organized in 1664.[1] We know nothing of the religious feeling of these settlers. They probably leaned to the Established Church.

Until recent years it has been the fashion to parade these settlers as religious refugees. Historians have delighted to represent the province as a home for the weary and oppressed of every sect and nation, as a common refuge for the lovers of soul-liberty the world over. The belief seems to have started with Williamson,—on what authority we cannot say, unless it was a misreading of Hening's *Statutes at Large of Virginia.* He has been followed by Martin, Wheeler, Hawks and Moore.[2]

---

[1] For an account of the organization of the government see my paper on William Drummond, first Governor of North Carolina, 1664-1667, in *The National Magazine*, April, 1892.

[2] It has always been believed that F. X. Martin would, under no circumstances, warp the facts of history to prove a theory. But we know that he has deliberately done this in the case of the Quaker settlers of North Carolina. About 1808 Martin wrote to the North Carolina Yearly Meeting requesting an account, for his history, of their first settlement and growth in the State. This information was furnished him, and a copy of the reply, dated 15th of 10th month, 1808, and signed by Francis White, was preserved. This copy came to light and was published by Charles F. Coffin, in *Friends' Review*,

The belief has become incarnated in the person of George Durant, who gave his name to a neck of land in lower Perquimans County. He was the first white man of whose settlement within the bounds of North Carolina we have distinct record. He purchased the tract of land between Perquimans and Little rivers from the Indians in 1662. He spent the remainder of his days in Perquimans, and died there probably not long before February, 1694,[1] as his will was presented for probate at that time.

Mr. Bancroft has suggested that Durant might be the same as the Mr. Durand who was an elder in the Puritan "very orthodox Church" in Nansemond County, Va., and who was banished from Virginia by Sir William Berkeley in 1648.[2] Building on this suggestion as a basis, some have made Durant a Presbyterian,[3] but the favorite belief has been that he was a Quaker. This view has been strengthened, no doubt, by the fact that he purchased his lands from the Indians instead of *taking* them after the usual English fashion.

Durant was a leader in the colony, and was its attorney-general in 1679.[4] This does not indicate, however, that he was not a Quaker, as others claim, for we know that Archdale and Akehurst and Toms were all Quakers, yet held high offices under the colonial government; but the part taken by Durant in the Culpeper uprising does indicate that he was not a member of the Society of Friends. This movement was severely denounced by the Society, who declared themselves a "separated people," and that they "stood

---

1858-59. vol. xii, pp. 532-534, 548-550. This narrative begins with Edmundson and Fox, and the writer had evidently seen their journals. He "states that this [Edmundson's] appears to have been the first meeting of Friends held in North Carolina." He gives the names and dates correctly. A reference to Martin (I., 119, 155) will convince the reader that these variations could not have been accidental.

[1] *Col. Rec.*, I., 893.   [2] *Hist. U. S.*, II. 134 note. ed. 1837.
[3] So has Dr. Vass in his *History of the Presbyterian Church in New Bern, N C.*, p. 11, following Bancroft's *United States* and Charles Campbell's *Virginia*.
[4] *Col. Rec.*, I., 317.

single from all the seditious actions" which occurred in
1677, 1678 and 1679.[1] If Durant was a Quaker, how could
his Society denounce the movement so severely and yet
consistently refrain from expelling from its communion one
of its own members who was a leader in it?

Further, Rt. Rev. Joseph Blount Cheshire, Jr., D. D.,
Bishop of the Diocese of North Carolina, who has seen the
family Bible of George Durant, son of the settler, tells me
that there are no Quaker phrases in the genealogical entries
there. We might have expected some of these, like *first
day*, *first month*, etc., to have remained, even after the faith
of the family had changed.

It is to be remembered also that when George Fox visited
Perquimans and Pasquotank counties in 1672 it was necessary for him to pass on his journey within sight of Durant's
house, and although Durant was one of the most prominent
men in the colony, and we may suppose he would have been
the same in the Society, Fox made no mention whatever of
him in his journal. Still stronger testimony of his non-
membership with the Society is shown by the fact that his
name nowhere appears in the original journals of the
Friends.

The writer has found no contemporary evidence to prove
that George Durant was either a Quaker when he came to
the colony, that he ever became a convert to that faith, or
that he professed any form of religion whatever.

As the claims of Durant to Quakerism have gone glim-
mering, so has gone the broader claim of settlement by religious refugees. The first person to attack the theory was
Doctor, now Bishop, Cheshire; then came Col. William L.
Saunders in the Prefatory Notes to the first volume of the
North Carolina Colonial Records. The arguments against
this claim are derived from three separate sources: (1) From
the Dissenters themselves, (2) from the Church party, (3)
from other contemporary authorities. Briefly stated, they

---

[1] *Col. Rec.*, I., 250-253.

may be summarized as follows: There is no evidence in the journal of William Edmundson to indicate that he found any sort of religious belief at all emphasized when he came on a missionary tour to the Province in 1672. He mentions one Quaker family only. There is no indication that Fox found many Quakers when he arrived in November of the same year, and those whom he found were most probably converts of Edmundson. But when the latter visited them in 1676-77 he found Friends "finely settled," and "there was no room for the priests." This change inside of four years indicates that much work had been done by those who had been convinced in 1672. It indicates also that there were no religious refugees of other denominations in North Carolina, for had there been such the success of the Quakers could not have been so marked; nor have the Quakers themselves set up the claim that they were the first settlers.

Further, Governor Walker, writing in 1703, says the Quakers began with Fox's visit, and in 1709 William Gordon, missionary of the Society for the Propagation of the Gospel, denies that the Quakers were the first settlers.

Again, Governor Johnston said in 1749 that North Carolina was first settled by people seeking "a larger and better range for their stocks." Lawson, in his history, first published in 1709, attributes the first planting of the colony to economic motives, and in 1666 Thomas Woodward, the surveyor-general of Albemarle, says it is "land only that they come for."[1]

We may safely conclude that in 1672, when Edmundson arrived in Albemarle, there was only one Quaker family in the colony. This was the family of Henry Phillips, and Edmundson went directly to his house. Phillips came to Albemarle in 1665, and his is the only case of immigration in the earliest days of the colony that bears on its face any indica-

---

[1] For an extensive examination of the former views and the arguments against them, see my *Religious Development in the Province of North Carolina,* Johns Hopkins University *Studies* in Historical and Political Science, IX., 239-306, 1892. In this I follow substantially the lines of argument laid down by Bishop Cheshire.

tions of religious persecution.[1] The religious meeting at
his house was in all probability the first ever held in Albemarle, and Edmundson, the Quaker, was the first to proclaim there the gospel of peace.

After preaching at two places in North Carolina, which
was then called Albemarle, Edmundson returned to Virginia
and held meetings in what is now, no doubt, Nansemond
County. He visited " several places in that country," and
traveled thirty miles above Jamestown to Green Spring,
where there were Friends. A meeting had been settled here,
" but was lost, the people being stumbled in their minds, and
scattered by the evil example of one Thomas Newhouse,
who had been a preacher among them, and went from truth
into filth and uncleanness of the world." These Friends
were restored. On his return he held meetings at William
Wright's house, which was probably in Nansemond, "and
a blessed, heavenly meeting it was; many were tendered by
the Lord's power." His meetings grew in size and so did
the Society. Some of the converts were men of prominence,
among them being Major-General Richard Bennett, the first
governor sent out to Virginia by Cromwell. "He was a
brave, solid, wise man, received the truth and died in the
same." Edmundson also visited Governor Berkeley, seeking some relief for Friends who "were great sufferers in the
spoiling of their goods." He found the Governor "very
peevish and brittle, and I could fasten nothing upon him
with all the soft arguments I could use." It was in connection with this visit that General Bennett drew a picture of
Berkeley, summing up his career in a nutshell. "He asked
me if the governor called me dog, rogue, &c.? I said, no,
he did not call me so. Then said he, you took him in his
best humor, they being his usual terms when he is angry,
for he is an enemy to every appearance of good." From

<hr />

[1] *Col. Rec.*, I., 215. A petition signed by Quakers in 1679 says
that most of them had lived in Albemarle since 1663 or 1664, but it
does not follow that they came as Quakers.—*Ibid.*, I., 250-253.

Virginia Edmundson traveled into Maryland,[1] having labored seven weeks in the two colonies.[2]

We left George Fox going over to the Eastern Shore.[3] In
a day or two he set out for New England. He labored there,
then returned to Maryland, held meetings on both sides of
the Bay, and on the fifth of November set sail for Virginia
from Patuxent River. In three days they came to Nance-
mund (Nansemond).[4] Fox reached it by going down Patuxent River, down Chesapeake Bay and up Nansemond
River. Here a great meeting was held. To this meeting
came one Col. Dewes, "with several officers and magistrates,
who were much taken with the declaration of truth." Then
Fox "hastened towards Carolina; yet had several meetings
by the way, wherein we had good service for the Lord: one
about four miles from Nancemum water, which was very
precious; and there was a men's and a women's meeting
settled, for the affairs of the church. Another very good
meeting we had at William Yarrow's, at Pagan Creek, which
was so large that we were fain to be abroad, the house not
being big enough to contain the people. A great openness
there was, the sound of truth spread abroad, and had a good
favor in the hearts of people: the Lord have the glory forever!"[5]

"After this," Fox continues, "our way to Carolina grew
worse, being much of it plashy, and pretty full of great bogs
and swamps; so that we were commonly wet to the knees,
and lay abroad a-nights in the woods by a fire: saving one
of the nights we got to a poor house at Summertown [Som-
erton], and lay by the fire." The whole of this itinerary can be traced pretty clearly; coming down the Chesapeake and sailing up Nansemond River, as we have seen,
Fox and his companions, Robert Widders, James Lancaster

---

[1] *Journal*, 68-72. [2] *Fox's Journal*, II., 153. [3] *Ibid.*, II., 146.
[4] It is to be noticed that all of these early Friends refer to the
southeastern corner of the present State as "Virginia."
[5] *Journal*. II., 161, 162. This establishment of a regular meeting
for discipline indicates that the Society was now organized and
moving forward.

and George Pattison,¹ probably took horse before they
reached the Widow Wright's. They entered North Carolina
by way of Somerton, Va., and went by canoe down Bennett's
Creek, called by Fox Bonner's Creek, into "Macocomocock
river," which is doubtless the modern Chowan, to the house of
Hugh Smith, "where people of other professions came to see
us (no Friends inhabiting that part of the country)." This
house was probably situate in the western part of the present
county of Chowan. "Then passing down the river Mara-
tick² in a canoe, we went down the bay Connie-oak [Eden-
ton] to a captains who was loving to us and lent us his boat
(for we were much wetted in the canoe, the water plashing in
upon us). With this boat we went to the governor's; but
the water in some places was so shallow, that the boat being
loaden, could not swim; so that we put off our shoes and
stockings, and waded through the water a pretty way." The
Governor's residence was probably near Edenton. Fox says
he and his wife received them "lovingly," but they found a
sceptic in the person of a certain doctor, who "would needs
dispute with us," declaring that the light and the spirit of
God were not in the Indians, and who "ran out so far that
at length he would not own the Scriptures."

"We tarried at the Governor's that night; and next morning he very courteously walked with us about two miles
through the woods, to a place whither he had sent our boat
about to meet us. Taking leave of him, we entered our
boat and went about thirty miles to Joseph Scot's, one of
the representatives of the country [probably in Perquimans,
near Pasquotank County]. There we had a sound, precious

---

¹ Lancaster was a resident of Lancashire and became a convert
of Fox in 1652. He was perhaps more closely identified with Fox
in his labors than any one else. He accompanied him on his travels
in America, was with him on a visit to Scotland in 1657, to Ireland
in 1669, and acted as his private secretary. Widders (c. 1618–1686)
was also a Lancashire man and was also associated with Fox in his
work. He was with him in Scotland, and traveled much in western
England, suffered much and was "a thundering man."—Bowden,
I., 420, 421, and *Piety Promoted*, I., 141.

² In the last edition of Fox's *Journal* this is given as Roanoke
River.

meeting; the people were tender, and much desired after meetings. Wherefore at an house about four miles further, we had another meeting; to which the Governor's secretary came, who was chief secretary of the province, and had been formerly convinced."

Fox also went among the Indians and spoke to them by an interpreter, and "having visited the north part of Carolina, and made a little entrance for the truth among the people there, we began to return again towards Virginia, having several meetings in our way, wherein we had good service for the Lord, the people being generally tender and open. . . . In our return we had a very precious meeting at Hugh Smith's . . . the people were very tender, and very good service we had amongst them. . . . The ninth of the tenth month we got back to Bonner's creek . . . having spent about eighteen days in the north of Carolina.[1]

"Our horses having rested, we set forward for Virginia again, traveling through the woods and bogs as far as we could well reach that day, and at night lay by a fire in the woods. Next day we had a tedious journey through bogs and swamps, and were exceedingly wet and dirty all the day, but dried ourselves at night by a fire. We got that night to Sommertown. . . . Here we lay in our clothes by the fire as we had done many a night before. Next day we had a meeting; for the people . . . had a great desire to hear us;

[1] Fox's *Journal*, II., 159-162. This journey has many perplexing problems. Fox evidently went down Bennett's Creek, which he calls Bonner's Creek, and got into Macocomocock River. This could only be the Chowan, for Bennett's Creek empties into the Chowan. But immediately on leaving Hugh Smith's they are in Maratick River, which is the name then applied to Roanoke River and Albemarle Sound. Colonel Saunders thought Connie-Oak Bay the modern Edenton Bay, and he is doubtless correct. Did Joseph Scott live in Perquimans? Who was the Governor and his chief secretary? Was Peter Carteret Governor at this time? The colony of Albemarle is often called Roanoke by the early writers, and is "Nathaniel Batts who had been governor of Roanoke" one of the lost governors of Albemarle? Is he kin to the "Nathaniel Battson" mentioned in Hening, I., 383, 385? He was known as Capt. Batts, and Fox again speaks of him in a letter to Virginia Friends in 1673 as "Captain Batts, the Governor."—Bowden, I., 412.

and a very good meeting we had among them, where we
never had one before." After traveling about a hundred
miles from Carolina into Virginia they were again among
Friends. They spent about three weeks in Virginia, mostly
among Friends. They had large and precious meetings.
At the Widow Wright's "many of the magistrates, officers
and other high people came. A most heavenly meeting we
had; wherein the power of the Lord was so great, that it
struck a dread upon the assembly, chained all down, and
brought reverence upon the people's minds." The parish
priest threatened to interfere, "but the Lord's power . . .
stopped him. . . . The people were wonderfully affected with
the testimony of truth. . . . Another very good meeting we
had at Crickatrough, at which many considerable people
were, who had never heard a Friend before; and they were
greatly satisfied, praised be the Lord! We had also a very
good and serviceable meeting at John Porter's which consisted mostly of other people, in which the power of the
Lord was gloriously seen and felt, and it brought the truth
over all the bad walkers and talkers; blessed be the Lord!"

During the last week of his stay Fox spent time and pains
correcting evils that had come into the Society and in "working down a bad spirit that was got up in some," and then,
"having finished what service lay upon us at Virginia, the
thirtieth of the tenth month [30 December, 1672] we set sail
in an open sloop for Maryland."[1]

Thus ended the only visit of George Fox to Virginia and
Carolina. It was his good fortune to see his Society organized and prospering in each. In Virginia the number of
Friends was more than doubled by his preaching, while "a
large convincement" was upon many others who had not
yet professed. The connection between these bodies and
the English societies was close. An exchange of letters
began. Fox sent copies of Edward Burrough's *Works* to
Col. Thomas Dewes at Nansemond; to Major-General Ben-

[1] *Fox's Journal*, II., 162, 163.

nett; to Lieutenant-Colonel Waters, in Accomack; to Justice Jordan, near Accomack, in Potomac; to the Governor of Carolina, and others.[1] There was soon, no doubt, some sort of union between the meetings in Virginia and Carolina, but this has not been at any time an organic one, for the Quakers of North Carolina steadily fought against the idea of being absorbed by their Virginia neighbors. There has always been unity of thought and feeling between the Society in the two States and their history is one.

No visiting Friends came to Virginia or Carolina from 1672 until the return of Edmundson in 1676. We know that they were engaged during these years in missionary labors among the Indians from a letter of Fox to Virginia Friends in 1673, in which he says: "I have received letters giving me an account of the service some of you had with and amongst the Indian king and his council; and if you go over again to Carolina, you may inquire of Captain Batts, the governor, with whom I left a paper to be read to the emperor, and his thirty kings under him of the Tuscaroras." Later he exhorts Friends of Carolina as follows: "You should sometimes have meetings with the Indian kings and their people, to preach the gospel of peace, of life, and of salvation to them "[2] : and again in 1681 he urges this on Friends in Carolina.

The next account we have of Southern Friends is from Edmundson, who again visited them in 1676-77.[3] He came down the Chesapeake from Maryland, entered a branch of Elizabeth River, and reached the house of one Yeats, where he had been before. He "had many precious meetings with Friends, both for the worship of God, and the affairs of

---

[1] Bowden, I., 356-358.   [2] *Ibid.* I., 412.
[3] Edmundson does not trouble himself to give dates. This journey is usually put down as occurring in 1676, but I think it must have been made during the closing months of 1676 or the beginning of 1677, for he says that it was cold, with sleet and snow. He notes also the death of Nathaniel Bacon, which occurred October 1, 1676, and that "several of his party were executed." I do not know that any of these executions took place earlier than January 11, 1677.—Hening, II., 545.

truth relating to gospel order. There was indeed need enough of help for things were much out of order, and many unruly spirits to deal with. I had good service and success, for the Lord blessed his work in my hand." Then comes a passage in the narrative that rings with Hebraic simplicity and shows the influence of his Puritan training. " Now I was moved of the Lord to go to Carolina, and it was perilous travelling, for the Indians were not yet subdued, but did mischief and murdered several: the place they haunted much was in that wilderness betwixt Virginia and Carolina, scarce any durst travel that way unarmed: So Friends endeavored to dissuade me from going, . . . so I delayed some time. . . . In the mean time I appointed a meeting on the north side of James river, where none had been, and there came several Friends a great way to it in boats, there came also the widow Hout-land's eldest son, with whom I walked near two miles the night before the meeting, advising him of some disorders in the family, and so we parted; . . . but before morning a messenger came to tell me the young man was dead. . . .

"Then the word of the Lord came to me, saying, All lives are in my hand and if thou goest not to Carolina, thy life is as this young man's: but if thou goest, I will give thee thy life for a prey. . . The next day I made ready for my journey."[1]

He seems to have gone over nearly the same route as in 1672, but the difference in the forms of expression in his journal is significant. It is no longer the preacher who appoints the meetings, but we find that " they," the members, say when and where these should be held, indicating that the Society of Friends was now on a sure footing in North Carolina, and not unorganized and non-existent as it had been in 1672. Edmundson held a meeting at the home of his old friend Toms, and says in concluding: " I had several precious meetings in that colony, and several turned to the

---

[1] He had as companion, "one ancient man, a **Friend**," name unknown.

Lord; people were tender and loving, and there was no
room for the priests (i. e., hirelings), for Friends were finely
settled and I left things well among them." He then returned to Virginia, had meetings in several places, settled
things among Friends, sailed for England and saw America
no more.[1]

About 1678 John Boweter (*c.* 1629-1704), another Cumberland man, visited Virginia. He appears to have traveled
through most of the settled parts of the province, but no
particulars of his journey have been preserved. He did not
visit Carolina; we do not know the reason why. He has
preserved the names of the places visited in Virginia: James
River in Virginia, James River at Chuckatuck, Pagan Creek,
Southward, Nansemun, Accomack, Pongaleg by Accomack
shore, Pocomock Bay, Annamesiah, Moody Creek in Accomack, Savidge Neck, Nesswatakes, Ocahanack.[2]

The Society had more trouble in Virginia. In December,
1680, the minutes of Friends on the Eastern Shore of Maryland record: " The sad estate and condition of the church in
Virginia being seriously considered by this meeting, it is the
sense of the meeting that they should be visited for their
good by such Friends as find a concern on their minds."
William Berry and Stephen Keddy signified their willingness to go, and their object was doubtless to advise, encourage and help.[3]

It is probable that this trouble was due to persecution by
the Government. We have some instances of this from the
records. As early as 1674 we find an order in the General
Court records to proceed against conventicles in Nansemond
County. And again (p. 218), under date of June 15, 1675,
" The Hon'ble Governor being informed that there are Several conventicles in Nansemond County, it is ordered by
this Court that if there be any meeting in this Country that
they be proceeded against according to the laws of England

[1] *Journal*, 110-114 : parts relating to North Carolina reprinted in
Col. Rec., I., 215, 226.
[2] Bowden, I., 359.   [3] Janney, II., 359.

and this Country. Col. Bridger[1] is desired Strictly to Command the Justices of Nansemond, Lower Norfolk, and the Isle of Wight counties to make Strict inquiry of the same. And if any person shall be found to meet, as aforesaid then they be proceeded as aforesaid."[2]

On the same day we find a presentment against John Bigg for not baptizing his child (p. 218). It is more probable that he was a Quaker than a Baptist. "John Edwards informing against John Bigg, upon the act for not baptizing his children which appearing to this court it is ordered that the said John Bigg pay 1000 lbs tobacco and cask to the Said John Edwards and 1000 lbs tobacco & casks to the p'sh according to act and pay 1225 lbs. of tobacco & casks in full of his costs."

In 1678 we learn that parties were fined for entertaining Quakers, and the next year, " At a Court held 21st day 9ber 1679 Present His Majesties Dept Governor & Council Order that if John Pleasants does not pay 1500 pounds of Tobacco—to Mr. Tho Cocke Jr his Costs & Charges in prosecuting a suit agst him & if he do not at next Heno County Court give security that he will not suffer any meeting of Quakers at his house for the future then execution is to issue upon a former judgment obtained agst ye sd Pleasants upon ye act of Assembly about Quakers."[3]

Pleasants seems to have been particularly obnoxious to the powers of the day. In February, 1682, we find, " Information by Lt Col Thos Grendon & Wm Randolph that John Pleasants & Jane Tucker lias Larcome alias Pleasants (Quakers) that they unlawfully accompany themselves together in living as man & wife without legal marriage. That they have absented themselves from church for twelve months & upwards That they have refused to have their

---

[1] It appears later that he was a Quaker sympathizer, and there seems to have been a number of prominent men who felt the same way.

[2] Order made at a court held at James City, June 15, 1675, in the afternoon. Sir William Berkeley, Governor.

[3] Minute Book, Henrico County Court, p. 116.

children baptised. That said John Pleasants did Suffer a
Convention at or near his house That they were present
at said Convention.

"Defts in open Court confsed the first & owned the breach
of the peace laws

"Judgment is granted said Lt Col Thos Grendon & W^m
Randolph for 24ol sterling that they give Security 2000 p^ds
Tobacco for refusing to have their children baptised, 500
pounds Tob for being members of Convention & John
Pleasants for suffering same 5000 p^ds of Tobacco

"Appeal taken by pleasants." [1]

Pleasants came from Norwich, England, in 1668, and was
the founder of the Virginia family of that name.[2] We do
not know whether he was a Quaker when he came over, or
whether he became a convert of Edmundson and Fox. As
we have already seen, he was an important and prominent
member among Virginia Quakers. On December 3, 1683,
we have the instructions of the King to Lord Effingham,
Governor of Virginia, "to represent the case of John Plais-
ance, a Quaker, indicted in Henrico Co. for not coming to
church and to continue to stop execution against him." [3]

These records indicate that life in Virginia for the Quaker
during the seventeenth century was by no means an ideal
one, free from religious vexations, trials, persecutions and
fines. These entries will help to explain the troubles to
which we find reference in the records of Maryland Friends.
Much of this persecution came, no doubt, from a misunderstanding of Friends' principles; thus we find from the
records of Accomac that Friends brought up for trial there
were charged with "villifying the ministers, disobeying the
laws, and blaspheming God." As their principles became
better known and their numbers increased this persecution
was less. Lord Culpeper, who became Governor in 1680,

[1] Minutes. Henrico County Court, Feb., 1682, to April, 1701.
[2] Brock, *A Colonial Virginian.*
[3] Sainsbury, *Extracts from English Public Records.*

is said to have particularly manifested a desire to save them from persecution.[1]

There was likewise some trouble in North Carolina. The Half-Yearly Meeting of Maryland writes to Fox in 1683: " Here are many Friends of this province who find a concern laid upon them to visit the seed of God in Carolina, for we understand that the spoiler makes havoc of the flock there; so here are many weighty Friends, intending [to go] down there on that service, and may visit Virginia and Accomack and then we may inform thee how things are on truth's account in those places."[2] This probably refers to the militia fines that we shall examine later.

The organization of the Society went on in the midst of persecution. It is doubtful if there was any organization in Virginia beyond the particular meetings or individual congregations prior to the coming of Edmundson and Fox in 1672. We know that monthly and quarterly meetings were established in England in 1669 and that the Yearly Meeting followed soon after. It is not at all probable that any definite plan of organization could have been evolved among the feeble meetings in America. We may safely conclude that monthly and quarterly meetings were organized in Virginia by Fox in 1672. He tells us that he settled a men's and women's meeting, presumably a monthly meeting, in eastern Virginia. Burnyeat had advised them the year before to have a men's meeting,[3] and we know that organization in Maryland dates from Fox's visit. We know also that the Henrico Monthly Meeting was organized as early as 1698, perhaps a little earlier. In Virginia in 1700 there was one quarterly, with two, possibly three, monthly meetings. The Virginia Yearly Meeting seems to have been organized not later than 1698.

Bowden states (I., 425) that there were half-yearly meetings in Virginia and Carolina in 1682. We have the records

<hr>

[1] McIlwaine, pp. 26-28.   [2] Bowden, I., 385, 386.
[3] *Journal*, in *Friends' Library*, XI., 134.

of a monthly meeting in Perquimans County, N. C., as early as 1680. In that year Christopher Nicholson and Ann Atwood announce their intention of marriage before a "general meeting." It was deferred for the space of "one month." The parties were married 11th of 2d month, 1680 (April). These records are said by the committee of copyists appointed in 1728 to be the earliest records that were kept in Carolina. This was a men's and women's meeting, and was kept at the house of Francis Toms. A men's and women's meeting was also held at Henry Prows's, and on 10th of 7th month, 1681, a six weeks' meeting was established at Christopher Nicholson's, and a six weeks' meeting was established at said Prows's "at Little River." "At a quarterly meeting" held at Christopher Nicholson's, 2d of 10th month (1681, year shown by context), it was concluded that a monthly meeting be established at the house of Jonathan Phelps, the first fourth day in every month. I take it that these were monthly meetings for business and that this was the organic beginning of the Society in the colony. We find also in 11th month, 1684(85), mention of a monthly meeting held at the house of William Wyat, at Yopim." It seems to have been a meeting for worship only. As the Pasquotank Monthly Meeting goes back to this early period also, I conclude that in 1700 there were three monthly meetings, one in Pasquotank, one held at the house of Francis Toms, and the third at the house of Jonathan Phelps. The last two were located in Perquimans County, as was the quarterly meeting.

The date of the organization of North Carolina Yearly Meeting has been preserved: "at a quarterly meeting at the house of henry whites this 4 day of the 4 month 1698: it is unaninus agreed by fr'nds that all the quarterly meetings be altered from: the first seventh day of month to the last seventh day and that all the quarterly meeting be held the last seventh day of the same month they were formerly held on and the last seventh day of the 7 month in Euery yere to be the yerely meeting for this Cuntree at the house of francis

tooms the Elder and the second day of the weke following
to be seat aparte for busines and that a meeting be held at
the house of Thomas Catreke in pastotanke the first day
Euery month."

By what body were these meetings set up? New England Yearly Meeting, the first in America, covered all the
colonies, of course. In 1683 it was set off from London
Yearly Meeting as a regular Yearly Meeting for discipline.
Philadelphia Yearly Meeting was first held in Burlington,
N. J., in 1681. It was held there again in 1683, and then
embraced the meetings as far northward as New England
and as far southward as Carolina. The Yearly Meeting of
1684, held in Philadelphia, had delegates from Herring
Creek and Choptank in Maryland, but none from the meetings farther south; but in a letter to Friends in England they
say: " We are to send an epistle to Carolina, Virginia, Maryland and all thereaway."[1] This was doubtless the first organic relation Virginia and Carolina had had with others,
and it leads us to the conclusion that the quarterly and
yearly meetings in these Southern colonies were established
by Philadelphia Yearly Meeting instead of London Yearly
Meeting, as some have held.

These meetings were of enough importance for Philadelphia Yearly Meeting to note the fact in its records in 1686
that no delegates appeared from them. But about this time
George Hutchinson, of Burlington, N. J., and James Martin,
a member of Philadelphia meeting, traveled in Maryland,
Virginia and Carolina. They gave an account of their service to the meeting of ministers (and elders) in February,
1686(87). "They found their travel among Friends there
very acceptable and a door was opened on Truth's account."
We have no other information concerning Friends in Virginia and Carolina until the visits of Dickinson and Wilson
in 1691-92.

---

[1] Ezra Michner, *Retrospect of Early Quakerism*, pp. 22, 29. See
also the records of Philadelphia Yearly Meeting.

The first settlement in South Carolina, unlike that in North Carolina, has a definite beginning. It dates from the landing of a colony, under command of Governor William Sayle, on the shores of Kiawah River, now called Ashley, in April, 1670. Here they laid out a town. Ten years later the site was changed from Albemarle Point to Oyster Point, and there Charleston was built. The government of this colony, civil and religious, was the same as that of Albemarle. There was no Establishment until 1698.

Quakers were in South Carolina as early as 1681. We do not know their origin further than that they came by sea, and doubtless direct from England. In 1682 their Society was small, but a monthly meeting had been established, probably by London Yearly Meeting, and they enjoyed liberty. Their "yea" was taken instead of an oath, and they served alike in the Assembly, on juries and in other offices. In 1681 Fox suggested an organic union with the Society in North Carolina: "If you of Ashley River and that way, and you of Albemarle River and that way, had once a year or once in half a year, a meeting together somewhere in the middle of the country, it might be well." [1] It does not seem that this program was immediately carried into effect, for communication between the colonies was difficult and tedious. There was a stretch of territory several hundred miles wide between the two which was unexplored and inhabited by savages. Edmundson and Fox got no further south than Albemarle, and it was not until well in the eighteenth century that we find Friends undertaking this hazardous journey overland.

---

[1] Janney, II., 359, 361 ; Bowden, I., 413.

CHAPTER IV.

JOHN ARCHDALE AND THE GOLDEN AGE OF SOUTHERN QUAKERISM.

The heyday of Quakerism in the South is indissolubly connected with the name of John Archdale, Governor-General of Carolina. To Carolina Friends the seventeenth century was a Golden Age, a time of ease and of release from the restraints of Church and State. The Society grew in numbers and importance, and its cosmopolitan character made Friends the connecting link with the outside world.

We have already seen that a quarterly and three monthly meetings, the executive bodies of the Society, had been established in North Carolina before 1700. Friends seem to have fixed also on definite places of worship, for in 1698 we find an entry which directs "that meeting houses be kept decent and in good repair." This would indicate that the meeting house had now become a part of their regular expense, but of their location, or whether they were the dwellings of Friends that had attained a semi-public character, we do not know. In 1702 a request for help in formulating and establishing church discipline went up from Virginia and North Carolina to Philadelphia Yearly Meeting. This would indicate that they were then undertaking to put into practice some system or arrangement which had not been tried before. A committee was appointed to attend to the matter, and seem to have sent an answer to both provinces. The one to North Carolina is addressed to " The Yearly, Quarterly and Monthly Meetings of Friends in North Carolina." It is signed by Samuel Jennings, Griffith Owen, Nicholas Waln, John Blunstone, Antho. Morris, and is dated 18th of 7th mo., 1703.[1] The records of North Carolina Yearly Meeting begin with 1708.

The records show that Friends were coming into Albemarle (North Carolina) from Pennsylvania and Ireland prior to 1690, but we know little of their history from the visit of Edmundson to North Carolina in 1676-77, and of Boweter to Virginia in 1678, until the coming of Wilson and Dickinson in 1692. Under date of 1685 Bowden (II., 52) quotes a passage from a London epistle which expresses joy that some Friends in Pennsylvania and New Jersey "were stirred up in the spirit and power of the Lord to visit the churches of Christ in New England, Virginia, Maryland and Carolina." But we have no account of any visits coming from this determination.

Thomas Wilson and James Dickinson landed in New York in November, 1691; they traveled south, first visited the Eastern Shore, and about January, 1692, passed over the bay to James River, Virginia. They had "many good and comfortable meetings," and "went from Virginia towards North Carolina, where the floods were so great, that we could not travel on horseback, but waded bare foot through swamps and waters; Friends and people were exceedingly glad to see us, they not having had any visit by a travelling Friend of the ministry for several years before. We had good service amongst them, for the Lord's heavenly power wonderfully supported us under our difficulties and hard travel, the country being so full of wild creatures, that wolves would come and roar about the houses in the night time. So after having had many good and heavenly meetings with Friends there, we took leave of them and returned through the wilderness to Virginia." At Chuckatuck, in Nansemond County, they warned Friends "to keep out of the superfluous fashions of the world," and traveled toward the falls of James River; they had some meetings here and "found a

---

[1] A copy of the letter is in the archives of Philadelphia Yearly Meeting. In 1702 we find James Bates, of Virginia, in Philadelphia. Some North Carolina Friends were there about the same time. They may have brought up the request for assistance.

great openness among the people." At Black Creek the
sheriff undertook to prevent them from speaking, but was
induced to desist, and a successful meeting was held. From
here they returned overland to Maryland.[1]

Dickinson landed in Virginia again in July, 1696; held
meetings at Queen's Creek; visited New Kent, where Friends
"were glad to see us"; had a meeting at Curles, where he
had been in 1692 with Wilson; had a dispute at Merchant-
hope with a priest, and visited Chuckatuck. In Accomac
County he met an Indian king, "who was a very solid man,"
and was pleased with the visit; to another Indian he also
unfolded the doctrine of the Inner Light and advised him
of the evil nature of swearing. "He said he never swore
before he learned to speak English, for they had no swearing
in their language; but so soon as they could speak English
they learned to swear; but if he had more of my company I
would teach him better, and wished he was a Quaker, then
he would not swear."[2]

Dickinson then visited the North, and in the spring of
1697 was again in Virginia. His destination was North
Carolina, and Story tells us that Jacob Fallowfield was his
companion.[3] They held meetings on the way; visited Friends
at Pagan Creek and Chuckatuck; "so through the wilderness to Carolina, and there met with Governor Archdale,
who traveled through Carolina with us. We had good service in that wilderness country, and found a tender people
who were glad to be visited. Being clear, we returned in
peace, and attended the shipping for England."[4]

John Archdale was made Governor-General of Carolina,
August 31, 1694.[5] His patent as a Landgrave of Carolina is
dated November 24, 1694, and his salary was £200 a year.

[1] Dickinson's *Journal*, in *Friends' Library*, XII., 381; Wilson's
Journal, ed. 1784, 29-31. In 1693 Maryland, Virginia and North
Carolina were visited by Richard Hoskins, who had just settled in
Pennsylvania, but we have no particulars of his visit.—Bowden,
II., 52.
[2] *Friends' Library*, XII., 388-390.   [3] Story's *Journal*, ed. 1747, 156.
[4] *Friends' Library*, XII., 396.   [5] *Col. Rec.* I., 389.

Less has been preserved concerning his career than we could desire. This is due, no doubt, in a large measure, to the overshadowing of William Penn. Were pictures of Penn's government in Pennsylvania less vivid, the administration of Archdale in Carolina might be better known.

The details of the life of John Archdale are few. The genealogy of the family has been traced to about 1520.[1] In the reign of Elizabeth they were settled at Norton Hall, Norfolk, and were in good circumstances. In 1604 Richard Archdale purchased of John Rounce the Loakes estate in Bucks County, which is now known as Wycombe Abbey and is the seat of Lord Carington. In 1628 he purchased from the same person the manors of "Temple Wycombe" and "Chapel Fee." It is probable that he thus became the principal landholder in the parish. About the time that Richard Archdale came to Bucks, his brother John received a grant of land from Elizabeth at Castle Archdale, County Fermanagh, Ireland, where that branch of the family has been established ever since, the present representative being Captain Edward Mervyn Archdale, of Castle Archdale and Trillick Castle, County Tyrone. The motto of both branches of the family is *Data fata secutus.*[2]

It seems probable that John Archdale, Governor of Carolina, was the son of Thomas Archdale, who was the son of that Richard Archdale who settled in Bucks in 1604. Richard Archdale probably died before 1633, and John was born in 1642. His first connection with American affairs seems to have been in 1664, when he came out as agent of Governor Ferdinando Gorges, of Maine. In that year Sir Robert Carr and Samuel Maverick, as royal commissioners, carried to Gov. Gorges two letters from the King, both bearing date June 11, 1664.[3] The first of these letters was to

---

[1] By Rev. Geo. P. Jarvis, High Wycombe, Bucks, England.
[2] Private information from Rev. W. H. Summers, Reading, England.
[3] Article on Archdale in *Quakeriana*, May, 1894. Mr. Jarvis says Archdale was not the brother-in-law of Gorges, and not a commissioner with Carr and Maverick, as there stated.

the people of Maine, commanding them to submit to the
government of Gorges. The second letter was to the Governor and Council of Massachusetts Bay, and was an order
from the King to surrender Maine to Gov. Gorges. Archdale arrived in Maine in November, 1664, and on November 30 was in Boston along with Henry Joslin and Edward
Rushworth as commissioners for Gov. Gorges. The commissioners sent a letter to the Massachusetts Council about
the proposed surrender. The Governor and Council made
reply that Maine was claimed by the colony of Massachusetts and that they could not give it up without consent of
the General Court. Archdale appealed to the King's commissioners, and the General Court seems to have given its
consent, for Archdale reported to the Council in England
on February 6, 1671(72), that the commissioners appointed
by Gorges to govern the province met and summoned the
inhabitants, who submitted to their rule: that about April,
1665, the commissioners, being at York, summoned every
town to send two deputies to a general council to be held at
Wells in May, and that they met and enacted several laws.
Gorges was confirmed in his possession by the King, April
10, 1666; but after three years of quiet possession, the Government of Massachusetts again took possession of Maine
by force, turned out the officers and seized the records. The
Board of Trade and Plantations heard the testimony of
Archdale in the matter and recommended that Gorges be
restored.[1]

We learn from these records that Archdale was then a
man of some maturity, and that he was not a Quaker, for he
says that the Maine authorities elected him a colonel of
militia in 1665, and that he held several private trainings.
He probably returned to England in 1666, and we know
little of his history for the next fifteen years. He probably
lived at his country-seat during the period, for Isaac Milles,

<hr />

[1] *Calendar of State Papers*, Colonial Series, II., 258, 272, 492 ; III.,
54, 329.

the vicar of the parish, 1673-81, says that he was the "chief gentleman of the village."[1]

The first time we find Archdale mentioned in connection with Carolina is on March 26, 1681, when he commissioned Daniel Akehurst as his deputy.[2] He was no doubt acting here as the representative of his minor son, for all papers are signed by "John Archdale for Thomas Archdale." This was not the share of Sir William Berkeley, as Dr. Hawks states,[3] but from the materials before me I conclude that the share which came into the possession of Thomas Archdale in 1681 was that of Sir John Berkeley, who died in 1678, for the shares of Craven, Shaftesbury, Colleton, Albemarle, and Carteret were still in the original families; Sothel had purchased the share of Earl Clarendon,[4] Amy purchased that of Sir William Berkeley, and only that of Sir John Berkeley could have then been on the market.[5]

Archdale is said to have lived a loose and careless life, but the preaching of Fox, he says, "convinced . . . and separated me from my father's house."[6] Since Isaac Milles, the vicar of the parish, bewails his apostasy, we may conclude that this occurred between 1673 and 1681. But this conversion does not seem to have been of any consequence as far

---

[1] Milles was presented to this vicarate by Matthew Archdale, probably the uncle of John. Matthew Archdale made presentations in 1660, 1664, 1669, 1673, and probably in 1681. In 1661 he took part in the persecution of Quakers and arrested Isaac Pennington and Thomas Ellwood at Chalfont St. Peter.

[2] S. C. Hist. Soc. *Colls.*, I., 104.

[3] *History of North Carolina*, II., 499.

[4] *Col. Rec.*, I., 339.

[5] *Ibid.*, I., 345. May 25, 1681, a letter was sent to the Governor and Council of Ashley River, in which it is said Mr. Archdale had bought "Lady Berkeley's share."—S. C. Hist. Soc. *Colls.*, I., 106. The Wheeler MSS. say that Archdale purchased Sir William Berkeley's share in 1679, also that Archdale held the rank of Chief Justice of Carolina in 1681.

[6] Letter to Fox, reprinted in Hawks's *North Carolina*, II., 378, from Bowden, I., 415. It is said also that Archdale was turned Quaker by the writings of Henry More, the Platonist. Isaac Milles took counsel with Rev. Timothy Borage, vicar of Marlow, and Henry Dodwell, Camden Professor of History at Oxford, about winning Archdale back to the Church. They asked More to write a letter to Archdale, giving a true idea of the light within and refuting the

as the management of their share of Carolina is concerned. We know, from instructions sent to Governor Sothel, that he was in Albemarle on December 14, 1683, or earlier, " and that he [Sothel] do forthwith with the advice of Mr. Archdale choose four of the discreetest honest men of the county," etc.[1] Again, in February, 1685, the Proprietors write Sothel about the same matter and insist that he, "with the advice of Mr. Archdale," fill certain blanks with names of men who were to serve as Lords Proprietors' deputies.[2] From the letter quoted above we know that he was also in North Carolina in March, 1686. It is probable, then, that he came out to Carolina in a year or two after he became a virtual Proprietor, to look after the common interests, and while there his co-religionists, the Quakers, were not allowed to feel the need of any help he was able to give them. His presence did much, no doubt, to give them prestige in the colony, to protect them from persecution, should such be attempted, and to increase their numbers. During the temporary absence of Sothel from Albemarle in 1685 and 1686, Archdale acted as Governor of that colony, whether by the special appointment of that infamous dignitary, or because of his position as a virtual Proprietor, we do not know. It is probable that he was in Carolina during this visit for three years or more, for in a letter written in 1705 he says that he had lived five years in Carolina in all, and his visit in 1695-97 was hardly more than two years in duration.

When made Governor-General of Carolina he was not

Quaker belief. In reply More sent an unsealed letter to the trio. They were to read, seal, and forward to Archdale, but after reading the letter over two or three times they judged it best to suppress it, as more likely to confirm than to convince him of error. The effort to redeem John seems to have resulted in keeping some of his family from leaving the Established Church.—See *Memories of Jordans and the Chalfonts*, by Rev. W. H. Summers (London, 1895), pp. 213-215

[1] *Col. Rec.*, I., 346. July 29, 1682, a blank commission was given Archdale to receive the quit rents due the Proprietors in Albemarle (*S. C. Hist. Soc. Colls.*, I., 105). This would indicate that he was then preparing to come out.

[2] *Col. Rec.*, I., 350, 351.

yet a Proprietor, for his name is not on the list of " the true
and absolute Lords and Proprietors," and we learn from a
communication to the commissioners of customs, dated
November 10, 1696, that he was administering the share of
the proprietorship for his own son, who was a minor.[1] He
came into this dignity a few years later, probably by the
death of the son.

Archdale was appointed Governor of Carolina with the
express hope that he would be able to heal the disturbances
in South Carolina. This trouble had arisen through the
popular ferment about the tenure of lands, the payment of
quit-rents, the naturalization of Huguenots, and the recent
annulment by the Proprietors of the laws of Ludwell's Parliament relating to juries and the election of representatives.[2]
At last Governor Smith wrote in despair to the Proprietors
that " it was impossible to settle the country, except a Proprietor himself was sent over with full power to heal their
grievances."[3] Lord Ashley, grandson of Shaftesbury, was
first chosen for this duty, but he declined, and the Proprietors chose Archdale in his place with almost unlimited
powers. He could sell, let, or escheat lands, appoint deputy
governors in both provinces, make and alter laws. His
powers were so great, in fact, that the Proprietors were careful to say his case should not be taken as a precedent for
future governors.

Archdale left England on his difficult mission in December, 1694. In April, 1695, he landed at "Pasca in New
England." From here he traveled overland to Boston, and
seems to have come all the way south overland. He arrived in North Carolina, June 25, 1695. Here he found
Thomas Harvey acting as Deputy Governor. He had been
filling this office since September 24, 1694,[4] at least, and

---

[1] *Col. Rec.,* I . 467, 545.
[2] Rivers, *History of South Carolina.* 171.
[3] Archdale's *Description of Carolina*, and his MSS.
[4] Archdale succeeded Thomas Smith as Governor-General. Ludwell had been made Governor-General, November 2, 1691. Smith
was appointed Nov. 29, 1693 (S. C. Hist. Soc. *Colls.,* I., 134). He

was now established in his office by Archdale, who, along
with his son, then passed on to South Carolina by water.
He took up his residence in Charleston, assumed the government, August 17, 1695, and on August 23, in addition to
his other duties, was commissioned as deputy to Earl
Craven. His administration of South Carolina was, as it
had been formerly in North Carolina, wise, prudent and
moderate. He found a keen spirit of hostility to the French
refugees. They were subjected to many discriminations
and suffered much hardship. Mr. Ash and some of the Dissenters desired the French to have no more privileges than
negroes; so sharp was the opposition that he thought
best to summon his first Assembly from the English inhabitants only. On petition of the Commons, three years' rent
was remitted to those who held land by grant, and four years'
to those who held by survey without grant. Arrears of
quit-rents were to be paid in money or commodities, as was
most convenient. The price of land was reduced from £50
to £25 per 1,000 acres, and he was authorized to sell lands
and grant titles to immigrants after they got to Carolina,
which had not been the case previously.

Archdale established a special board for deciding contests
between white men and Indians, and in this way won the
friendship of the latter. He was careful to keep those Indians who were friendly to his Government from causing
diplomatic trouble with the Spaniards in Florida, and by
several little acts of kindness won the good-will of the latter.
Under his quieting administration the many bickerings of
the colonists became less harsh, and under his successor,
March 10, 1696(97), an act for the naturalization of aliens

was thus put over the whole province and had authority to appoint
a Deputy Governor for North Carolina. But Ludwell seems to
have been acting as Governor of North Carolina as late as May 1,
1694 (*Col. Rec.*, I., 391). Ludwell was Governor-General, 1691–93,
and Edmund Randolph says that "one Jarvis" was appointed
Deputy Governor of North Carolina by Col. Ludwell, "then Governor of all Carolina" (S. C. Hist. Soc. *Colls.*, I., 206 ; II., 196). Was
Alexander Lillington governor of North Carolina during any part
of this period, as is commonly said ?

and for granting liberty of conscience was passed. This act covered the case of the Huguenot refugees, and further provided "that all Christians which now are or hereafter may be in this province (Papists only excepted) shall enjoy the full liberty of their consciences." Archdale stood between the extremes in these quarrels, and no doubt had a care for his co-religionists at the same time, and while administering a general military law, secured a special act, passed March 16, 1695(96), exempting Quakers from its provisions. In 1704 and 1705, when the line was sharply drawn between Churchmen and Dissenters, Archdale steadily and strongly opposed the church acts. He refused to give his sanction to these acts, and received thanks from the Dissenters for the same. Writing to Sir Nathaniel Johnson in 1705, and remembering the instructions from Lord Granville, perhaps, he reminds Johnson that he is also a Proprietor, and therefore has an equal voice in affairs, and counsels him: "I earnestly desire thee to be a reconciling instrument of peace; else," he adds, with a prophetic ring to be heard later from one end of America to the other, "Saxons will goe for Pensilvania if you continue obstinate towards y^m being a free people they expect in a wilderness an enlargement not a lessening of their priviledges" (MSS.). Again, in his *Description of Carolina*, he makes an unanswerable plea for liberality and religious freedom: "It is stupendous to consider how passionate and preposterous zeal not only vails but stupefies, oftentimes, the rational powers; for cannot Dissenters kill wolves and bears, &c., as well as Churchmen; as also fell trees and clear ground for plantations, and be as capable of defending the same, generally, as well as the other? Surely Pennsylvania can bear witness to what I write."

The administration of Archdale had a soothing effect on the people of South Carolina. Through his skill the province began to increase in wealth; the disputes and quarrels of the day were quieted for the time, and remained so until the efforts of the Churchmen to set up an Establishment again threw the province into an uproar.

Toward the close of 1696 Archdale left South Carolina
on his return to England. He was succeeded in the chief
command by Joseph Blake as Deputy Governor (commission dated December 20, 1695). He carried with him the
thanks of the House of Representatives to the Proprietors
for sending them such a successful governor. He again
visited North Carolina on his way; was present at a Palatine's court held December 9, 1696; again confirmed the
government of Thomas Harvey, and in the winter, or spring,
of 1697 traveled through the province with James Dickinson, as we have seen. Here he was also highly esteemed,
for in the address to the Proprietors by the North Carolina
House of Burgesses, which is signed by John Porter, a man
to become famous in the colony ten years later, it is said
that he was a man "whose greatest care it is to make peace
and plenty flow amongst us" (February 4, 1696(97).

Archdale left Carolina in the spring of this year and saw
America no more. One of his daughters had married in
North Carolina in 1688. Her husband was Emmanuel
Lowe, who became prominent in the Cary troubles, 1705-11.
Her family has become extinct in the State within a generation. In 1705 Archdale was speaking of coming to Carolina again. He says that he had then, besides his daughter
in North Carolina, a sister's son in South Carolina (Blake?),
"a sober discreet and hopeful young man about 27: yea:
old: . . . my wife hath also a son there who principally on
my acc⁰ is gouʳ of yᵉ North." This was Thomas Cary,[1]
Governor of North Carolina, 1705-07, 1708-10. He had been
secretary of the Council of South Carolina in 1695; was register of the admiralty court in February, 1697(98)[2]; was
receiver-general or treasurer of the province from about
August, 1697, to August 16, 1698. He was appointed to
this office by Archdale, but a commission was afterwards

[1] It seems that Cary married the daughter of John Archdale's
wife by her first husband, the daughter probably being Cary's
cousin.
[2] S. C. Hist. Soc. *Colls.*, I., 207.

created to inspect and audit his accounts. He died prior to November 21, 1718, "greatly indebted to their Lordships."[1]

Archdale was succeeded in the proprietorship on April 9, 1709, by John Dawson, his son-in-law.[2] His work was perhaps more permanent in the northern colony. Here the good work inaugurated by him was continued under Harvey; the colonists enjoyed peace within and without, and their general progress was steadily upward. He had been sagacious, prudent and moderate. His arrival was like balm to this colony, long torn and bleeding from political dissensions and from the misrule of ignorant Proprietors and villainous governors. These troubles were ended by his coming. The colonists set themselves at once to recover lost vantage-ground, and seem to have entered on a period of prosperity and quiet which had hitherto never been known in their troublesome history. Archdale's faith tended also to encourage religion and morality. The Quakers thus received an impetus in North Carolina which gave them the prestige and power needed to carry them through the struggle of the next twenty years. They now began to appear more frequently than formerly as holders of office in both the Carolinas. The Council, the courts and the Assembly soon showed a preponderance of Quaker influence. There was a material reward for being a Quaker, and Churchmen and others who thus found it to their interests deserted their own creeds to enroll themselves among Friends. They were thus prepared for the coming struggle with the Establishment.[3]

Although the effect of the administration of Archdale was long felt in the Carolinas, the personal element seems to have disappeared with the close of the century. But his return to England did not mean retirement to private life. In 1698 he was elected to Parliament from the borough of Chipping Wycombe, and was the first Quaker elected to a   ＊

---

[1] S. C. Hist. Soc. *Colls.,* I., 192.   [2] *Ibid.,* I., 156.
[3] *Col. Rec.,* I., 708 ; Hawks, II., 364, Fox's letter, *ante.*

seat in that body. But his seat was never occupied. He
preferred to bear testimony to the honesty of his convictions rather than enjoy the honor of personal distinction
and advancement. The story of this public testimony can
best be told in the language of the journals of the House of
Commons for January 3, 1698(99):

"The House was, according to order, called over, and the
names of such members as made default taken down, and
their names being called over a second time, several were
excused upon account of their being sick; and others upon
the road coming up, and others upon account of extraordinary occasions in the country; and the name of John Archdale, Esq., a Burgess for the Borough of Chiping Wicomb,
in the County of Bucks, being called over a second time,
Mr. Speaker acquainted the House that Mr. Archdale had
been with him this morning, and delivered him a letter
sealed, which Mr. Speaker presented to the House. And
the same was opened and read, and is as followeth, viz:

"'London, 3rd of the 11th /mo called January, 1698-9.

Sir,—Upon the call of the House it will appear that I am
duly chosen and returned to serve in Parliament for the
Borough of Chipping Wycombe, in the county of Bucks,
and therefore I request thee to acquaint the Honourable
House of Commons the reason that I have not yet appeared;
which is, that the Burgesses being voluntarily inclined to
elect me, I did not oppose their inclinations, believing that
my declarations of fidelity, etc., might in this case, as in
others where the law requires an oath, be accepted; I am
therefore ready to execute my trust if the House think fit to
admit of me thereupon, which I do humbly submit to their
wisdom and justice; and shall acquiesce with what they may
be pleased to determine therein. This being all at present,

I remain, Thy real and obliged friend,

JOHN ARCHDALE.'"

The case came up for settlement on the 6th of January,
when Archdale was ordered to be present. "The House

being informed that Mr. Archdale attended according to order, his letter to Mr. Speaker was again read, and the several statutes qualifying persons to come into, and sit, and vote in this House were read . . . and then the said Mr. Archdale was called in, and he came to the middle of the House almost to the table; and Mr. Speaker, by direction of the House, asked him if he had taken the oaths, or would take the oaths, appointed to qualify himself to be a member of this House? To which he answered back, in regard to a principle of religion, he had not taken the oaths nor could take them, and then he withdrew."

With this great public testimony to the then startling principle that a man's yea and nay are sufficient and that a super-added oath is unchristian, John Archdale withdrew from the Parliament of England, and his vacated seat was soon occupied by his brother Thomas.[1]

In March, 1696(97), James and Ann Dilworth, of Philadelphia, expressed their purpose to visit the South. They were probably accompanied by Richard Gove. In June, 1698, they reported that in Maryland and Virginia they found an openness to come to meetings; people were anxious to come to the Truth and to be visited. Jonathan Taylor, an English Friend, was in Carolina in 1697 or 1698. In 1698 William Ellis (1658-1709), of Airton, in Yorkshire, and Aaron Atkinson (1665-1740), of Cumberland, visited the South. They started about March and intended to stay three or four months. At Chuckatuck, " we find many poor dejected people that profess Truth, who for want of true care

---

[1] *Quakeriana*, May, 1894. Archdale printed in London in 1707: A New Description of that Fertile and Pleasant Province of Carolina, etc. This little book deals almost exclusively with South Carolina affairs and does not expressly state that he had ever visited North Carolina. It is hardly a description ; it is rather a memoir. rambling, discursive, defensive, recounting his personal experience and work as governor. etc. About 1700 Thomas Archdale conveyed all the estate of Loakes to Henry Petty. Lord Shelbourne, son of Sir William Petty. There are buried at the parish church of Wycombe : Thomas Archdale. probably the father of John, obiit Sept. 5, 1676 ; Matthew Archdale, obiit Dec. 10, 1685 : Ann Archdale, obiit Oct. 25, 1719.

in themselves, and of visiting by Friends in love and zeal,
are grown too cold." In May he wrote that they had been
once through Virginia and Carolina, "things being much
out of order amongst Friends, and wrong minded people
bearing sway." He spoke of being present at a yearly
meeting. This was no doubt in Virginia. He left Atkinson there.[1]

Thomas Chalkley was also in Virginia toward the close of
1698, accompanied by Richard Hoskins and Richard Gove.[2]
He did not go to Carolina; in Accomac and Northampton
counties, Va., they had "large meetings. . . . In those parts
we had several meetings, where we were informed Friends
had not had any before." He visited the Middle and New
England colonies, then traveled south. "And after we had
had several good and open meetings in Virginia, we found
ourselves clear of America," March, 1699.[3]

The next traveling Friends in the South were Roger Gill
and Thomas Story. They sailed from England in November, 1698, and cast anchor in Mobjack Bay, Virginia, in
February, 1699. Of Roger Gill we know little. He had
professed with the Baptists in his youth, but joined Friends
at nineteen. After traveling in the South, they went to New
England. The yellow fever was then raging in Philadelphia. Gill felt himself called to go there and administer to
the sick. During the Yearly Meeting he prayed God to
stay His hand, and offered his own life if God "would be
pleased to accept" it for a sacrifice. He was impressed
with the belief that his prayer had been heard, took the
fever and died in a few days (1699).[4]

Thomas Story was one of the most important of the An-
glo-American Quakers. He was born about 1662, near Carlisle, in Cumberland. His parents were members of the
Church of England. He was well educated and was de-
signed for the law. He became a Quaker in 1691, and
traveled in Scotland the next year. He visited America in

[1] *Life and Correspondence of William and Alice Ellis*, by James
Backhouse, Philadelphia, 1850.   [2] Bowden, II., 53.
[3] *Journal*, ed. 1790, 15-17, 23. 24.   [4] Bowden, II., 45.

1699, as we have seen, and was preparing to return to England when William Penn invited him to remain in Pennsylvania and take office under that government. He consented, and was appointed a member of the Council of State, keeper of the Great Seal, master of the rolls for recording patents of land, one of the commissioners of property, and later became the first Recorder of Philadelphia. He did not discontinue his ministry, but visited most parts of America. He returned to England in 1714, settled there, and visited Holland, Germany and Ireland, being imprisoned in the latter country in 1716. He died at Carlisle, June 21, 1742.[1]

The American labors of Story and Gill began in Virginia. "On the 11th of 12th month [1698(99)] we set sail in the long boat for Queen's creek in York river, where we got with some difficulty, and were made welcome at the house of our friend Edward Thomas; had a meeting with the family, and a few of the neighborhood, who, though not of the society, were several of them much tendered; which was the first fruits of our ministry in that country, and good encouragement. We went from hence to Warwick River, Martin's Hundred, and Bangor House, and had meetings to satisfaction. At Scimmino in York county, at the house of John Bates, we had a meeting appointed, where no meeting had been before. The people were generally tendered and humbled, and we comforted in a sense of the love and visitation of God towards them. . . . Next day we had a meeting at the house of Daniel Akehurst,[2] in which many were humbled and tendered by the word and power of truth, and de-

---

[1] Bowden. II., 47.
[2] Akehurst was a minister of the Society. Archdale appointed him his deputy, March 26, 1681. He was witness to a marriage in Isle of Wight County, November 9, 1692. February 8, 1692(93), the Proprietors appointed him secretary of that part of their province north and east of Cape Fear. His original commission is now in possession of the writer and is signed by John Archdale for Thomas Archdale, Shaftesbury, Colleton, and Craven. I do not know how long he held this office. He seems to have returned to Virginia after his term of

parted in a solid frame of mind. . . . The next morning we went down to Thomas Cary's towards the foot of the creek. He had been lately convinced . . . and his brother Miles Cary." Then they crossed over James River and went to Chuckatuck, where they lodged at the house of John Copeland, "and upon some discourse with our friend, I found he was one of the first of those who had their ears cut off by the Independents in New England for the testimony of truth, in the first publishing thereof to that rebellious generation: and at my request he showed us his right ear, yet bearing the badge of their antichristianity."[1]

" From hence we went to Derasconeck, Western Branch and Southern Branch, having meetings to our comfort and satisfaction." Then they had a meeting at Barbican, "being the last meeting in Virginia towards Carolina. That night we lodged at our friend's, Nathan Newby's, and had some discourses with him concerning the Indians."[2]

Their first meeting in North Carolina was on Perquimans River, at the house of Francis Toms, now a member of the Provincial Council. This meeting was largely attended, including persons of note, although " the noises and elevations of some professing truth, occasioned their admiration and was hurtful to them." Toms conducted Story from this meeting to the court, where they met Governor Harvey, to whom Story presented letters of introduction from England. He was kindly received and hospitably entertained, and this, together with his appointment by Archdale, will lead us to think that Harvey was himself a Quaker. March 9, 1699, Story held another meeting at the house of

---

office in Carolina expired, as the quotation from Story indicates. He died 8th of eleventh month, 1699, probably in Virginia, and we find an Ann Akehurst mentioned in 1703, who was probably his widow. Yet the records of North Carolina meetings spoke of him and entered a memorial of him on their pages as if he was still a member of their meeting. In *The National Magazine*, August, 1892, I published his commission as secretary of North Carolina and such biographical facts as I could gather.

[1] Story's *Journal*, ed. 1747. 153 155.   [2] *Ibid.*, 155-156.

Henry White, on Little River, also one at Stephen Scott's. This meeting "was small, but well and tender." Later they crossed the Sound and preached to the settlers on the southern side, at the widow Anne Wilson's; but the scene of Story's labors lay principally in the precinct of Perquimans, for the largest part of the Quakers lived in that precinct and in Pasquotank adjoining.[1]

After preaching in Carolina, Story and Gill "set forward for Virginia and were at Chuckatuck, Southern Branch, Elizabeth's River, and had meetings. . . . After this we had a meeting at Pagan Creek, Lyon's Creek, and from hence went to Burleigh, to the house of James Johns." They cheered themselves on the way with "drams, sugar and nutmeg, we made punch in a little horn cup; and so had good entertainment." At the house of Johns, Story was exercised over the welfare of some Indian servants, and unfolded to them spiritual things. "After this, we had several meetings, and came to our friend Jane Pleasants" at Curles. Here he heard that her son was likely to marry outside of the Society. They had a meeting, and "my concern in it was, for the most part, about marriage, and the displeasure of God against his own people in the old world, and in all ages of this, against mixed marriages between them and the world."

---

[1] A meeting-house, to be built "at Pasquotank with as much speed as can be," was provided for by the monthly meeting of May 1, 1703 (*Col. Rec.*, I., 596) ; not March 1, as Dr. Hawks states (II., 367). This is the oldest Quaker meeting-house of which we have distinct record, and it places their church edifices among the very oldest in the colony. In 1705 it was determined to erect a meeting-house on the plantation of Joseph Jordan, "at the charge of Friends belonging to Pasquotank" (original record in Hawks, II., 321), and in the next year Caleb Bundy asked the approval of the Society in regard to the erection of a place of worship near his residence. (*Ibid.*, II., 368.) We cannot fix accurately the position of these early churches. Traditions still point to the sites of two Quaker meeting-houses in Pasquotank, the one near Weeksville, and the other about a mile from Symons's Creek, on the road from Nixonton to Weeksville, and about two miles from the former place. These houses were doubtless erected during this early period.

[2] Story's *Journal*, ed. 1747, 156-158.

From Curles, Story and Gill visited the Chickahominy
Indians toward the upper part of the Mattapony River. "The
town consisted of about eleven wigwams, or houses, made
of the bark of trees, and contained so many families: we
were directed to the sagamor, or chief; and when we went to
his door, he came out with a piece of cloth about his middle
but otherwise naked, and invited us in, and being set down,
several of his people came to look upon us. After a time of
silence and the company increased, we asked him if they
were all there for we desired to see as many of them together
as we could." This caused the chief some uneasiness, for he
"was a grave, serious and wary old man." But they won
his confidence and spoke to them of the things of God.
When ready to leave "we took them by the hand, one by
one, and they seemed well pleased with our visit."

The missionaries then went to Queen's Creek, Hickory
Neck and York City, in York County, where the people
"were very rude, and senseless of all good." They had
"meetings in a good degree to satisfaction" at Pocosin in
Warwick County, and also at Kickatan and thence into
Maryland.¹ Daniel Akehurst traveled with Story over a
part of this route.

Unfortunately, most of the Quakers have little to say
directly as to the growth of the Society or of the religious
and moral condition of the people among whom they traveled; but we may conclude from the number of places visited
that Friends were increasing in numbers and influence.
They seem to have suffered little at this time from the presence of the Establishment. We find John Copeland residing
in peace in Virginia, and probably preaching his doctrines
without let or hindrance. The people seem to have received
them well for the most part, and were eager for meetings.
But Story gives one notable exception. At Elizabeth's
Town he found some of them "a very rude, senseless people,
devoid of all relish of truth, and the fear of God in general:

¹ Kendall's *Story*, ed. 1786, 111-122; *Life of Story*, ed. 1747, 158-167.

yet to the meetings many of them came; some were civil, others tender; but the bulk of them, airy, wanton, and scoffers; sometimes rushing into the meeting and leering under their hats, and then again running out of the house, mocking at what they had heard; both to the great disturbance of the few who were sober, and us who went to visit them in the goodness of God." [1]

With Story's visit the history of the seventeenth century closes.

---

[1] *Life of Story*, 159.   See also Hawks's *North Carolina*, II., 365.

CHAPTER V.

THE EXPANSION OF SOUTHERN QUAKERISM IN THE EIGHTEENTH CENTURY.

During the seventeenth century there was no large or sudden immigration of Quakers into any of the provinces under consideration. The Society enjoyed during that period a quiet and steady growth. It received some' accessions from the incoming of persons who were already Friends, but these were comparatively few. Its greatest increase came from the numerous converts to Quakerism that were made at home. In 1700 Quakers were the most numerous and the only organized body of Dissenters in any of these provinces.

During the first generation of the eighteenth century there was no marked change in either of the provinces. But a wave of Quaker migration, southward bound, was rising during these years in Pennsylvania and New Jersey. This wave reached the Monocacy region in Maryland about 1725. It crossed the Potomac and struck Hopewell, in Frederick County, Virginia, in 1732. A monthly meeting was organized here in 1735. About the same time another branch of the same wave passed from Maryland into Loudoun and Fairfax counties, Va. From these northern counties it moved southward, touched slightly Fauquier, Culpeper, Stafford and Orange counties; stopped in full force in Campbell and Bedford, and to a less extent in Pittsylvania and Halifax; thence it moved into Surry, Stokes, Guilford, Alamance, Chatham and Randolph counties, N. C.; thence it passed into South Carolina and Georgia.

It is therefore possible for us to divide the history of Southern Quakerism in the eighteenth century into two pretty well defined parts: 1. The counties lying on and near the sea-coast represented the old Quaker stock, the native

element; 2. The inland counties represented the incoming
of the later immigrants, many of them Germans or Welsh-
men by birth or descent, who were destined to replant Quakerism in the South, and without whose representatives the
Society would be almost extinct in these States to-day.

This southward-moving wave of Quaker migration is almost identical in character, as it is in time, with the movement of the Scotch-Irish. It started from the same province, Pennsylvania; it moved over the same territory, and it
has left its indelible impress on much of this territory. It
did not have a Southern wing coming in at Charleston, as
did the Scotch-Irish; it did not spread itself over the whole
country; but it also stood for education, morality and religion; it did not bring the sword and it did not seek political
advancement. It, too, was instrumental in the settlement of
the West and is still a great and growing power.

In this chapter I shall undertake to develop the history of
the older settlements first, and shall then treat as a separate
element what I have ventured to call "the replanting of
Southern Quakerism."

1.—*The Expansion of the Native Element.*

One of the most distinguishing features of Friends is their
cordial recognition of the power of the press. The *Diction-
ary of National Biography* has remarked that Friends,
admitting the use of no weapon but the pen, have made
unstinted use of that, and a look into Joseph Smith's *Catalogue of Friends' Books* will convince of the truth of the
saying. So far as my own observations and experience go,
Friends have been more careful than other denominations in
preserving materials for their history. But their manuscript
records are, of necessity, filled with routine matters, and the
Society in its larger aspects is seldom considered. Further,
the records of nearly all these meetings are imperfect; some
have lost all their records, and none are full for the period
prior to 1750. In this dearth of material we turn with joy

to the journals of the "Public" Friends, but these have
much that is of little value to the historian. These preachers,
intent on the higher life, failed, for the most part, to notice
the moral, intellectual, political and economic condition of
the people among whom they moved. As a rule they failed
utterly to avail themselves of their magnificent opportunities
to gather materials for social history. The itinerary, the
bare mention of the different meeting-houses visited, is the
main feature of the narrative, and in some cases the only feature; but still there is generally much in their journals of
value. Occasionally we have a journalist like Story who
gives a larger setting to his labors, thus affording us
glimpses of the colonies as a whole, and whose work for
this reason is doubly valuable. It is from these journals
and from what we have of manuscript records that we must
reconstruct, as carefully as we can, the history of the expansion of this native element of Quakerism in the South.

The first traveling ministers in Virginia and Carolina,
after the beginning of the new century, were John Richardson and John Estaugh,[1] English Friends. They arrived in
March, 1701, and found "great openness in these two provinces amongst the people, and a tender-hearted remnant of
Friends scattered abroad in these wilderness countries." In
Virginia Richardson had some experiences with a priest
who was seeking to collect from Friends the tithe allowed
him by law. "I was also in company with the governor of
Virginia [Francis Nicholson] at our friend Richard John's
house, upon the West Cliffs, in Maryland, for we both
lodged there one night, and I heard that he had been studious in a book against Friends, called the Snake, and Friends
greatly desired he might have the answer called the Switch,
but knew not how to be so free with him as to offer it to
him; I told Friends, I would endeavor to make way for it.

---

[1] Estaugh (c. 1675–1742) was of Dunmow, in Essex, and later
settled at Haddonfield in New Jersey. He joined Friends at seventeen and traveled extensively both in Great Britain and America.
He died in Tortola.

Altho' he had seemed to be a man of few words, yet at a suitable interval I said to him, I had heard that he had seen a book called the Snake in the Grass; he confessed he had. I desired he would accept of the answer, and be as studious in it as he had been in the Snake; which he promised he would and took the book."[1]

During the same year John Salkeld[2] visited Virginia and North Carolina. We have few facts in regard to the journey, but he could give a good account of the people: "There is a loving people in each of these places, and especially in Carolina, amongst many that are not yet fully in the profession of truth." He had "divers large and good meetings," and "the Lord's blessed power did much appear to his glory and his people's comfort." But he warns traveling Friends to be on their guard, "the meetings being much mixed, some watching for evil, and others too ready to take offense and be stumbled."[3]

But these were among the lesser lights of Quakerism. In March, 1703, came Thomas Chalkley, who was to become one of the most prominent of the American Quakers. He was born at Southwark, England, in 1675, and had been piously trained. His first visit to America was in 1698. He saw it again in 1701: "We were about eight weeks from Land's End to the Capes of Virginia, had meetings twice a week on board, and they helped to stay our minds on our Maker, though our bodies were tossed to and again on the mighty waters." He and his family went on shore at Patuxent River and prepared to settle in America.

---

[1] Richardson's *Journal*, ed. 1783. 63–67, 144. Richardson (c. 1666–1753) seems to have visited Virginia and North Carolina again in 1731, with Henry Frankland, p. 224.

[2] Salkeld (1672–1739) was of Westmoreland. Some years later he migrated to Pennsylvania and settled at Chester. He traveled several times through most parts of America, and about 1712 revisited England, and also traveled in Scotland and Ireland. Salkeld was accompanied by Robert Roberts, of Philadelphia. John Rodman and Vincent Caldwell, both of Philadelphia, visited Maryland, Virginia and Carolina in September, 1702.

[3] Janney, III., 127–128.

"After some time, I was drawn forth to visit Friends in Maryland, Virginia, and North Carolina, and went with the unity of Friends, having their certificate (according to the good order established among us); so about the 26th of the first month, 1703, I went thro' Maryland, and visited Friends in Virginia and North Carolina, to the river Pamphlico, where no traveling public Friends (that I ever heard of) were before, and we had several meetings there on each side of the river. . . . And on our return through North Carolina, we had several large meetings, and an open time it was; as also at Nansemond and Chockatuck, and several other places in Virginia; and when my service was over in these two provinces, I went back to Maryland and visited meetings there, and then went home. As near as I can compute it, I rode about a thousand miles in this journey." [1]

This is the first indication we have of the expansion of the Friends of Albemarle. Up to this time they had been only in Pasquotank and Perquimans counties. They had now crossed Albemarle Sound, and with the tide of population had drifted into the section watered by the Pamlico and its tributaries. This is beyond doubt the beginning of the Core Sound and Contentnea settlements of Friends which were quite prominent a generation later. The Quakers were still practically the only religious organization in this province.

Chalkley seems to have visited only the meetings in Nansemond County and the adjoining southeastern section of Virginia. It was different with Thomas Story, who visited the colony in 1705. He had much discussion with priests and others; was treated with much kindness by Governor Nicholson; visited meetings at Black Creek, Curles in Henrico, Levy Neck or Pagan Creek in Isle of Wight, Chuckatuck, Western Branch of Nansemond, Southern Branch, and then passed down into North Carolina. He held a "large and comfortable" meeting in Perquimans County, besides others. At the house of Emmannel Lowe he had

---

[1] *Journal*, 38-39.

an interview, perhaps by appointment, with Thomas Cary, then Governor. He had much discourse with Cary "about matters of government, and informed him of the methods taken by some other governors in other governments, concerning our Friends and in favor of us against the severity of some laws, and found him likewise very inclinable to favor us so far as in any construction he could consistent with his office." Dr. Hawks argues from this that Cary, the "artful demagogue," was "even then cajoling them into partizanship, which was afterwards fully developed in his rebellion."[1]

Story visited Pasquotank and held a meeting there. "Many of the country people came to it, who were generally sober; and the Lord opened the truths of the gospel very clear and with authority." The next day he held a meeting in upper Perquimans, "which was the best and most powerful meeting I had in that country."[2]

"The next day I went back into Virginia fifty miles, being exceeding hot weather, and no wind, nor house in the way to entertain us. On the 14th I was at a monthly meeting at Chuckatuck; which was very large, and the whole public service fell upon me." He attended other meetings in Surry, Isle of Wight, Nansemond and York counties, and at Hicquotan, now Hampton, in Elizabeth City County. His record shows that the Virginia meetings were still clinging closely to the tidewater section.

There were at this time three monthly meetings in Virginia: at Chuckatuck, York, and Curles. The Chuckatuck monthly meeting was soon divided into two, and one was then held at the meeting-house called Buffkins, on the east side of Nansemond River.[3] The meetings in this section

---

[1] *History of North Carolina*, II., 366.   [2] *Life of Story*. 375–378.

[3] These are not the earliest houses erected in Virginia, but as they are the earliest of which the record has survived, it may be of interest to give a few items. The Buffkins meeting house, on the South Branch of Nansemond River, was 20 x 20 feet; the inside was ceiled and the floor laid with planks, and was fitted with forms and seats. It was on Leavin Buffkin's plantation, hence

formed a quarterly meeting that came to be known later as the Lower Quarter. At first it is referred to under the name of the meeting-house where it was held for the time.

The records of the monthly meeting at Curles, in Henrico County, begin with 1699. It is probable that the meeting was settled not later than 1692 (see *post*, p. 147). The Quakers of Henrico had obtained recognition under the Toleration Act as early as 1692. We have contemporary authority to show that they were in this county as early as 1678, and that they had suffered persecution there. Their meetings were held at first in the house of William Porter. This was continued for a number of years. In 1699 we find the following parties subscribed tobacco to build a meeting-house at Curles: James Pleasants, 500 pounds; James Howard, 500 and three days' work; Henry Watkins, Sr., 500; Edward Hughes, 500; Wm. Porter, Jr., 300; John Crew, 400; John Robinson, 250; Ephm. Gartrite, 150; Wm. Lead, 150; Robert Boyes, 20 pounds and three days' work; Samuel Gartrite, 10; John Pleasants, 55; Joseph Pleasants, 50; Nich. Hutchins, 40; Edward Mosby, 25; Joseph Parsons, 15; Henry Watkins, Jr., 15; Benj. Woodson, 5; John Woodson, 50.

This monthly meeting seems to have been migratory like the others. Within the next few years we find various particular meetings attached to it: Merchant's Hope in Henrico; Black Creek in New Kent; one at James Howard's, which

---

the name. It cost 3,868 pounds of tobacco. The principal contributors were: Robert Jordan, 580 pounds of tobacco; John Mardah, 550 pounds; Ben Small, 520; John Porter, 500; Nathan Newby, 500; John Hollowell, 350; Reid Hopkins, 350; Nath. Small, 250; Elizabeth Mald, 100; Moses Hall, 350. Other members gave "nales of all sorts," besides tobacco.

Another house was built on the Western Branch of Nansemond in 1702. It was 20x25 feet, was fitted with benches and cost 3,000 pounds of tobacco. Francis Bridle gave nails. This was an important item and was deemed worthy of special mention. The contributors of tobacco were: Isaac Rickes, Sr., 400 pounds; Wm. Scott, Sr., 400; James Denson, 400; Jno. Denson, 300; Abraham Rickes, 100; Jno. Rickes, 100; Robert Rickes, 100; Jno. Sikes, 150; Thomas Hamton, 200; Francis Denson, 500.

was also called Old Man's Neck; and one held in the woods near Herring Creek. In 1722 these uncertain names give place to Curles, Wainoak, Black Creek, and White Oak Swamp, or Swamp. The last was then a new meeting. We also find a meeting at this time at Cedar Creek in Hanover, and a new one at "Appomattox at the widow Buller's," which seems to have been in Prince George County. In 1722 Burleigh also belonged to this monthly meeting. The names of Friends in this monthly meeting indicate that they came from the more eastern meetings and that they received little increase from the immigrants who came into the Hopewell section. We find here such names as Pleasants, Howard, Woodson, Watkins, Porter, Ellyson, Jordan, Binford, Cate, Hunicut, West, Johnson, Clark, Maddox, Crew, Goode, Stith, Janet, Fleming, Lankford, Thomas, Atkinson, Randolph, Lead (Lad, Ladd), Bates, Magehe, Elmore, Scott, Wilmore, Stanley, Mayo, Holmes, Harris, Massie, Lane, Munford, Saunders, Peebles, Cheadle, Wooddy, Simmons, Sebrell. Add to this list a few other names that are found more frequently in the eastern counties: Rickes, Small, Newby, Denson, Nixon, Hubbard, and we have representatives of a majority of Quaker families in eastern Virginia.

During the first quarter of the eighteenth century there had been no material expansion of the North Carolina Yearly Meeting. There was then one quarterly meeting, with three monthly and perhaps five or six meetings for worship. Of the number of members we have no means for determining. The North Carolina meetings, however, exerted relatively a much wider influence, and the evidence is that the Carolinians were less tractable. The Carolinians had from time to time received considerable additions of strength from the Virginia meetings. To a certain extent these Carolina meetings were a continuation of, we may say an overflow from, the meetings in Virginia. This view is confirmed in part by the family names of these early Carolina Friends: Elliott, Nicholson, White, Newby, Morris, Nixon, Scott, Saint, Parker, Toms, Bundy, Jordan, Symons, Pritchett.

John Fothergill visited both provinces in 1707, and says
of the trip: "We got over the great bay of Chesapeak, so
through the lower part of Virginia and into North Carolina,
and had many strengthening and comfortable meetings in
those parts, through extendings of the love and power of
God towards a well disposed people, both professors of
Truth, and some others; among whom we had some good
service."

After the departure of Fothergill there is a break of seven
years in the history of Southern Quakerism.[1] It will be
noticed also that little has been said about the meetings in
Charleston. This is because we have little to say. They
were seldom visited by the journalists; their local records
are scanty, and the State historians know next to nothing of
the Quakers and their work. In 1713 Chalkley went to
Charleston from Philadelphia by sea. So far as we know
he was the first Friend to take this trip, and his account is
the first we have of South Carolina Friends since the days of
Governor Archdale. It is very noteworthy. "We were
about a month at sea; and when it pleased God that we
arrived at Charlestown, in South Carolina, we had a meeting there, and divers others afterwards. There are but few
Friends in this province, yet I had several meetings in the
country. The people were generally loving, and received
me kindly . . . and there was openness in the people
in several places. I was several times to visit the governor [Charles Craven] who was courteous and civil to me.
He said I 'deserved encouragement,' and spoke to several
to be generous, and contribute to my assistance. He meant
an outward maintenance; for he would have me encouraged
to stay among them . . . The longer I staid there, the larger
our meetings were."[2]

This entry furnishes a striking contrast to the reception

_____

[1] Esther Champion (*d.* 1714) came about 1710 ; Daniel Gould (*c.*
1625-1716), and Jonathan Tyler (*c.* 1669-1717), also visited Virginia
and Carolina, but we have no particulars.—*Piety Promoted*, II.
[2] *Journal,* 81, 82.

which Friends had been accustomed to meet in other parts. We can perhaps explain the difference as due in part to the fact that Friends were few there and were regarded with a certain degree of curiosity. There had been sharp ecclesiastical disputes in South Carolina, as we shall see when we come to treat of the relations of Quakerism and the Established Church. It was due in part, no doubt, to the personal equation of Governor Craven, who was a man of personal courage, upright character, and devotion to the best interests of the province; to the natural kindness and hospitality of the people; perhaps in part to the Huguenots, who knew the evils of religious intolerance; and to a certain extent, doubtless, to the desire to hear a purer gospel than was furnished by many of the professional guides in affairs spiritual. Under these conditions we can but wonder that so few Friends ever visited this promising field. It could not have been because of the difficulties of the way, for natural obstacles have never impeded Quakers when the spirit led. Or did they act on the principle that those who welcomed all Christians were more nearly Christ's?

Traveling Friends were probably kept out of North Carolina by the civil troubles there, 1707-11. In February, 1714, Thomas Wilson and James Dickinson landed on Rappahannock River, Virginia. Wilson had visited America once before and Dickinson twice. They went on shore at Queen Anne's Town. They passed over York River and then "took our saddles, bags and great coats upon our shoulders and traveled several miles." They went on towards Carolina and "had many good meetings, both among Friends and others." Truth was manifested, and the gospel of life and salvation freely declared. In Carolina "we found a hopeful stock of young people whom the Lord was qualifying for his service; and they received the testimony of Truth with gladness; we also met with several who had been convinced when we labored in these parts before, and it was a great comfort to us to find them walking in the Truth."

On their return they held meetings in Nansemond;

passed up James River; visited Friends in York County, and
traveled in Kent, "where we had labored in the work of the
ministry twenty three years before: several were then convinced, and a meeting settled from that time." They traveled next into Westmoreland, where several were convinced
and "the testimony of Truth exhalted over all."[1]

Benjamin Holme (1682-1749) was in both provinces in
1717. He visited both yearly meetings; reports disputes
with priests, and an effort on the part of some to revive the
anti-Quaker laws of 1663. But the general conditions were
good, for persons out of Society desired meetings; a new
meeting-house had been built in New Kent, and there were
many meetings there.[2]

John Fothergill arrived in York River in July, 1721, with
Lawrence King of Yorkshire, on a second visit to the meetings in Virginia and Carolina. They spent the next three
months in traveling through these provinces, and seem to
have visited most of the meetings. Fothergill gives us a
very minute account of their journey in the form of notes.
These notes may be taken as a fair sample of the average
journal, and indicate the sort of materials, the dry skeletons
of itineraries, clothed with little flesh, with which the historian of Quakerism has to contend so often.

In North Carolina he first held meetings in Perquimans
County, "to which many sober people came," and in Pasquotank, "whither came many Friends; and we had an edifying season together, through the abounding of gospel life
and wisdom"; at a meeting on the other side of Pasquotank
"some hundreds of people were gathered; the meeting was
held under the shade of a large tree, it being extremely hot.
. . . We came to Little river meeting again, which was very
large of Friends and others." And at the lower meeting-
house on Perquimans River "the meeting was very large,
and very solid and edifying. We took leave of most of

---

[1] Dickinson's *Journal,* in *Friends' Library.* XII., 403-405; Wilson's
Journal, 48, 49, 56, London, 1784.
[2] *Epistles and Works,* 23-27.

the Friends of Carolina here, in a sense of the love and tendering power of truth, and in much nearness to one another." They had been less than a month in Carolina, but
it seems visited most of the Friends' meetings in Perquimans and Pasquotank. It does not appear that they went
outside of these two counties. In Virginia they visited
most of the meetings in Nansemond, Southampton, Surry
and Henrico. In August "we came down to a French
settlement called Manikin town, and on the first of the
seventh month [September], we had a meeting there; to
which divers of the French people, with others, came; and
the Lord was graciously mindful of us." They passed over
Pamunkey River, "where few or no Friends had ever been,
or had a meeting before." Then they seemed to have turned
west; crossed the James and Appomattox, and, after spending most of September visiting the meetings in the eastern
and southeastern part of the colony and attending the
Yearly Meeting at Chuckatuck, passed north by land into
Maryland. In November they visited the meetings on the
Eastern Shore of Virginia, where they "were much afflicted
in the sense of the prevailing of an earthly spirit."

To the Yearly Meeting of London Fothergill could say of
his work in the South that they had "many large and open
meetings, both among Friends and others. . . . In both
these provinces we found great willingness in many people
to hear the truth declared, divers of whom appeared very
loving and tenderly affected. There seemed to be a comfortable opening among the youth . . . and rather a growth
among some of the elder, in a religious care. . . . Divine
mercy still reaches freely to them, and in some places there
is an increase in righteousness, and truth is in good esteem;
but in others the love and friendship of the world occasion
a decay."[1] All the regular meetings mentioned here are in
southeastern Virginia.

About 1722 North Carolina was visited by Susanna Mor-

---

[1] *Journal,* in *Friends' Library.* XIII., 365, 378-382, 400.

ris (1682-1755) and Ann Roberts (1677-1750). There is
little of interest in the visit, save that in attempting to cross
Chesapeake Bay they encountered a storm and were driven
to sea. They finally got into Currituck Inlet, and from
thence reached the Quaker settlements in eastern North
Carolina.[1]

Rarely do these missionaries think to give us anything in
their journals that concerns directly the expansion of the
Society. But we have some accounts of this character from
Samuel Bownas (1676-1753), a Friend of Westmoreland,
who had come out on his second visit to America in 1727.
He was an unusually close observer. He had visited Virginia and North Carolina in 1706, "and had good satisfaction" in his meetings. In 1727 he landed at Hampton,
Va. He visited most of the meetings in Virginia, was at
various places in York, Charles City, Henrico and Hanover
counties, which had not been mentioned so prominently
before, "and had fine meetings, people being ready to attend them." His journal indicates that the Society was becoming stronger in the upper section. He was twice in
Carolina and reports successful meetings, particularly in Pasquotank, "for the inhabitants mostly came to meetings there
when they expected a preacher, and at other times pretty
much." He was twice among the lower Virginia meetings.
The progress of American Friends, as seen in his travels,
was very encouraging. He reports that the Society was
steadily increasing in numbers and importance. Many of
the old meeting-houses had been enlarged to two, three or
even four times their original capacity, new ones had been
built, and private houses were no longer adequate for their
needs. Within the last twenty-two or twenty-three years
fifty-six new meeting-houses had been erected in America, of
which nine were in Virginia and three in North Carolina.

Bownas is also the one to give us the next account we
have of South Carolina Friends. While in Virginia he

---

[1] Morris, *Journal*, in *Friends' Miscellany*, I., 141-151.

" met a friend of London, his name was Joshua Fielding, who had visited the island, and South Carolina, and had traveled by land to North Carolina, about five hundred miles, in about three weeks, mostly alone, which was a difficult and hazardous attempt: Some thought it too great an undertaking and seemed to blame him for it, but he got safe through, tho' he had no provision but what he carried with him, and met with but four or five houses or plantations in all that five hundred miles travel, which obliged him to lodge in the woods frequently; but having a small pocket compass, that was his guide, when the sun and stars were hid from him. But I have since heard, that some others have since traveled over this same ground, (plantations and settlements being now placed at proper distances) with less hardship, viz. they have a road marked out by government, and now they may accomplish this journey without so frequently lying in the woods, as when this friend came from thence."

This seems to have been the first time that province had been visited since Chalkley left it. Overland communication with North Carolina was more frequent from this time, for the intervening country began to be settled; but it was not until about 1770 that organic connection with the North Carolina Yearly Meeting began.

John Fothergill visited most of the Virginia and North Carolina meetings again in 1736. He was the first to pass from the older meetings in lower Virginia to the new ones in Frederick and Loudoun counties. Between his departure and the middle of the century there were a number of traveling Friends in these colonies, but their journals are little more than bare itineraries. Thomas Chalkley was there in 1738 and had some good meetings. Jane Hoskins, an English Friend, had traveled in Virginia in 1726 with Abagail Bowles, of Ireland. In 1744 she " had a certificate to go a second time to Maryland, Virginia, and Carolina, in company with Margaret Churchman; concerning which visit I could say much, but it may suffice to remark that it

appeared to me to be a time of gathering, and great openness among people of various ranks. They followed us
from meeting to meeting, treating us with respect, and the
marks of real love and affection."[1]

John Woolman made his first visit south in 1746. We
shall hear more of his work in connection with slavery. He
visited most of the meetings in the colony, but "our exercise in general was more painful in these old settlements,
than it had been among the back inhabitants." In Perquimans County, N. C., they "had several meetings, which were
large; and found some openness in those parts, and a hopeful appearance amongst the young people.... In our journeying to and fro, we found some honest hearted Friends
who appeared to be concerned for the cause of Truth among
a backsliding people."[2]

It appears that the native element in Virginia had reached
its greatest expansion by the middle of the eighteenth century, or even a few years earlier. From that time it began
to decay. The scepter passed from the descendants of the
converts of Edmundson and Fox to those of the companions
of Penn. The same course of development, the same evolution westward, with the allowance of a generation more in
time, was to go on in North Carolina. By the Revolution
the balance of power had passed in that State also from the
eastern meetings to the western, from the native to the immigrant element. That struggle for superiority between the
eastern and western halves of these States, a struggle in
economic, social and political life, which was founded on
race differences and has been and is still a source of considerable bitterness, particularly in North Carolina, has also
made itself felt in the Society of Friends.

In Virginia the native element attained the most of its
growth at an early period. We have seen that it was first
planted in the region bordering on the lower James. Be-

[1] *Journal*, in *Friends' Library*, I., 470, 471.
[2] *Journal*, London, 1824, 33-35.

fore the death of Fox in 1691 there were Quakers in Norfolk, Nansemond, Southampton, Isle of Wight, Prince George, Surry, Charles City, York, Warwick and Henrico counties; perhaps in others. It became well rooted, and powerful. It is a generation before we hear of a further expansion. In 1721 there was a meeting at Cedar Creek in Hanover County. This became a monthly meeting later and included the particular meetings at Cedar Creek, Genito and Caroline, and perhaps others. The native element does not seem to have established any other meetings in Virginia, for while the monthly meetings of South River and Goose Creek belonged to Virginia Yearly Meeting and had some members from the older meetings in eastern Virginia, they lay directly in the line of southward migration and drew most of their strength from meetings to the northward.

As the meetings in eastern Virginia are the oldest under consideration, so they are the first to decline. Quakers seem to have disappeared from Norfolk County before 1700. They had no doubt "gone West." That migration, which was to assume such gigantic proportions a century and a half later, had already begun. In September and October, 1736, John Fothergill was on the Eastern Shore of Virginia. He was in company with Edward Mifflin, and came down from the Eastern Shore of Maryland to Paul Crippin's, "a Friend near Muddy creek, where formerly a meeting had been settled; but by gradually mixing with the spirit of the world, and so into marriages with others out of the way of truth, the elders being dead, the youth turned their backs on truth, and the meeting was quite dropped. I had no freedom to appoint a meeting there, and so set out the next day towards Neswaddacks [Nassawadox] where notice had been given of our intention to have a meeting the next day, which was the first of the week. The meeting was held in the meeting house where formerly there had been a pretty number of Friends, but now they are nearly gone, through the love of the world, with its enjoyments and liberties; so that a meeting is hardly kept there; but a pretty

many of the neighbors gathered, and we had a meeting
which was comfortable to me, in my faithfulness to the
Lord; though they seemed to have little sense of God, or
the operation of truth; for indeed a cloud of carnal indiffer-
ency appeared to me to have overspread almost all that part
of the country in an uncommon manner."

This is the first instance we have of the decadence of
Southern Friends. From this time the Eastern Shore of
Virginia disappears from their records. Daniel Stanton
visited the meetings in eastern Virginia about 1761 and
gives us further information of the same character. Of the
meeting at Chuckatuck he remarks: " I was informed [this]
had been one of the largest in Virginia, but is now reduced
to two or three families; things were at a low ebb among
them." Another meeting was somewhat open " and attended by several who did not profess with Friends." The
meetings at Surry and Burleigh were also attended mostly
by people who were not Friends. There was a " large
meeting at the burial of an ancient Friend near Wainoak; it
was held in an orchard, was an awful solid time, and of
brokenness of heart among the people." At Curles there
was a large meeting, " though not many Friends." [1] From
these reports it is clear that there was a decided decrease in
the strength of the older Virginia meetings. It will be
noticed also that most of the meetings held are made up of
persons other than Friends. This is also evident from the
journal of Griffith (1713-1776), whose visit occurred in 1765.

When Quakerism was thus expanding toward the west in
Virginia, a similar but independent movement was going on
in North Carolina toward the south. The first Quaker
counties of North Carolina were Perquimans and Pasquotank.[2] Here it was planted by Edmundson and Fox in

---

[1] *Journal,* in *Friends' Library.* XII., 168-172.
[2] But there were no Quakers in Camden, which formed the eastern
half of Pasquotank until 1777 ; nor in Currituck, which lies east of
Camden ; nor have they ever been numerous in Chowan, the county
just west of Perquimans.

1672. Migrations from these original seats of the faith began as early as 1703. The movement crossed Albemarle Sound and went south. By the middle of the century there were Quakers in Hyde, Beaufort, Craven, Carteret, Jones, Bladen and Lenoir counties. They probably had meetings for worship in all of these counties.

In Carteret County, Core Sound Monthly Meeting was set up in 1733. It was probably the oldest in the section and its records have been preserved. In 1747 Quakers in Carteret were strong enough to send one of their number to the Assembly. But in 1771 Core Sound Monthly Meeting was small, for it seems that most of its members had moved farther into the interior of the State. At the end of the last century the principal families of Quakers in the meeting bore the names of Stanton, Williams, Harris, Brown, Howard, Mace, Thomas, Davis, Arnold, Hollowell, Horn, Overman, Dew, Bogue, Bishop, Bundy, Borden, Parker, Chadwick, Hellen, Scott, Physioc, and Cartright.[1]

In 1748 we find mention of a monthly meeting on Falling Creek, then in Dobbs, now in Lenoir County.[2] This monthly meeting was probably not far from the present town of Kinston, and continued here until January 6, 1772, when it was the judgment of Friends that, since most of the Friends about the meeting-house on Lower Falling Creek had died or had moved away, the monthly meeting should be held at Richard Coxe's, near Upper Falling Creek. In July, 1772, it was said that Friends had settled on several branches of Contentnea Creek, and as they were distant from meeting, it was agreed to put a first day's meeting at Arthur Bryant's, and "at a monthly meeting held at Great Contentney, the 12th of the 9th mo., 1772," it was also agreed that the

---

[1] Stephen F. Miller, in his *Recollections of Newbern Fifty Years Ago,* notes the presence of one Quaker family there in 1820.

[2] In 1746 there are indications that there was then a monthly meeting at Bath, but there are no records. It is probable that this was the same as the Core Sound Monthly Meeting and that it got this variant name from the place where it was held for the time, after the Virginia fashion.

monthly meeting should be transferred to Arthur Bryant's. From this time the Falling Creek Monthly Meeting disappears and Great Contentnea takes its place. It was at the time of its organization farther from the sea-coast than any other monthly meeting in North Carolina. It was known later as Contentnea Monthly Meeting. We find among its members in the eighteenth century the following names: Beeman, Overman, Bogue, Hollowell, Cox, Pike, Pearson, Hall, Mayo, Wooten, Edgerton, Arnold, Copeland, Bundy, Morris, Doudna, and Outland. From these names we are led to infer that connection with the meetings in Carteret County to the east and Northampton County on the north was close.

There are still to be considered in this connection the two monthly meetings in Northampton County, Rich Square and Jack Swamp, which are, strictly speaking, to be classed somewhat between the two divisions we have made and represent a division of their own. This settlement began about 1750. It seems that the meeting for worship was set up in 1753, and the monthly meeting was settled in 1760 by Eastern Quarterly Meeting for Friends in Northampton, Hertford and Edgecombe counties. The meeting-house was finished in 1760, and, in accordance with the law of the province, was registered. The main strength of the monthly meeting lay in the community about Rich Square, but there were Friends in Hertford County, and it seems that regular meetings were held, but it does not appear that a meeting-house was ever built there. In Edgecombe County regular meetings were held as early as 1768, but these also were in private houses. We are certain that a considerable number of Friends' families lived there. In 1775 a meeting-house was built at Jack Swamp, which was then becoming a considerable settlement and which was evolved into a monthly meeting in 1794. Rich Square Monthly Meeting had grown strong enough in 1773 to ask for a quarterly meeting, but the request has never been granted. This meeting was large in extent: Tar River Friends were transferred to

Contentnea Monthly Meeting in 1782, and Fishing Creek was made the dividing line. A list of those thus transferred, and who lived therefore on the south side of Fishing Creek and in Edgecombe County, has been preserved. It contains families by the name of White, Thomas, Vick, Wilson, Watkins, Horn, Denson, Rush, and Westra. Many of the names remain in the section, but their form of belief has changed. In Hertford County were found Josiah Brown and John Copeland; in Bertie lived Joseph Sanders and Thomas Howel; and Joshua Fletcher lived in Halifax. These were all members of Rich Square Monthly Meeting. In Northampton County were found other members of the same meeting, the families of Page, Dougherty, Hall, Copeland, Peelle, Gray, Ross, Horn, Pitman, Knox, Hollowell, Brown, Griffin, Elliott, Baughm, Chapel, Brittain, Richardson, Farmer, White, Parker, Davis, Bryant, Lancaster, Newsom, Beeman, Ratcliff, Jordan, Outland, Lawrence, Collier, Purvis, Judkins, Blanchard, Denson, Pike, Crew, and Binford. To Jack Swamp Monthly Meeting belonged the Pattisons, Merrimons (or Merimoon), Binfords, Halls, Taylors.

Whence came these Friends in Northampton, Edgecombe, Hertford, Bertie and Halifax counties? They came mostly from Virginia, and present a parallel to that larger mass of Quaker migration whose rise in Pennsylvania and southward movement to Georgia we are soon to trace. As we have seen, there was a large settlement of Friends in southeastern Virginia in the eighteenth century, and the Quakers in northeastern North Carolina were at first but a continuation of the Virginia Quakers. The natural increase drove them southward to seek new homes. This is the beginning of the settlement. They came mostly from Isle of Wight, Surry, Prince George and Henrico counties, Va. A few reinforcements came from Perquimans and Pasquotank counties in North Carolina. Many of these settlers, like those who were coming into central North Carolina at the same time, made the Rich Square Meeting a basis for farther progress, and from this pushed out across Roanoke

River to the meetings in Dobbs County and even to South
Carolina.

Perhaps we can illustrate the expansion of Quakerism in eastern Virginia and eastern North Carolina in no
better way than by quoting the journal of William Reckitt,
who visited these meetings in 1756-57. He says of the
meetings in Virginia: " I visited all the little handfuls scattered up and down in these parts, and often had service in
families. I met with Samuel Spavold, who likewise was
much engaged in the service of truth. His labor of love in
the work of the gospel was indeed great in this part of the
world; those of other societies being much reached by his
ministry."

Reckitt then set forward to North Carolina; held meetings at Piney Woods, Wells, Old Neck, and Little River,
all in Perquimans County; lodged with Thomas Nicholson,
the author; probably did not go into Pasquotank County,
but turned to the west, accompanied by Joshua Fletcher and
Francis Nixon. " I then set forward towards a wilderness
country, where the inhabitants were very thin. . . . Our
first meeting after we left Perquimans was at John Coupe-
land's. . . . There were but few friends, but people of other
societies came in, who had notice; amongst whom was an
officer of the army . . ." The first established meeting
they reached was at Fort River (Roanoke?), " where a meeting had been recently settled, of such as had been convinced." They then came to Henry Horn's in Edgecombe
County, who had been convinced from among the Baptists,
for the inhabitants of this section belonged principally to
that faith; then they came to a small meeting at Neuse in
Wayne County, and then ninety miles to the meeting at Core
Sound. The destination of Reckitt was to the Friends in
South Carolina. " The first meeting we had after we left
Core sound, was at Permeanus Hanton's who gave us an in-
vitation to his house, and sent to give notice to his neighbors, though some lived several miles distant. We got to
his house about the time the meeting was appointed, where

we found seats placed, and every thing in such convenient order for a meeting, as I thought I had seldom seen. His rooms being little, he had placed seats in his court yard, and under the windows, that I believe all could sit and hear without the least troubling one another; and indeed I thought his labor and good inclination were blessed, for a solid time it was, and I found openness to declare the truth amongst them. . . . We staid one night at Wilmington, the capital town in North Carolina; but it being their general court time and the privateers having brought in prizes, the people's minds were in great commotions, so that I could find no room nor freedom to have a meeting, though several called Quakers lived there, but held no meeting, except when strangers came." They crossed a branch of Cape Fear River and then went to Carver's Creek. "Here was a small gathering of Friends. We staid their first day meeting over, and then went to Dan's [Dunn's] Creek, where we found another gathering of such as call themselves Friends, but had been much hurt, and scattered in their minds from the true shepherd, by an enemy that had sown tares."[1]

As a part of these coast settlements, coming from the seeds of Quakerism planted in South Carolina in the seventeenth century, we must count two of the older meetings in that province. These were the meetings in Charleston and Edisto. We have seen that Chalkley visited Charleston in 1713. We find no further visits from traveling Friends for forty years. In 1753 Mary Peisley and Catherine Peyton, afterwards Phillips, landed at Charleston. They visited most of the meetings in the South, and both kept journals of their travels. They visited all the Quakers in the place, and found that few kept to plainness of language; discipline was lax and they had to revive it. The city had become a place of refuge for the disjointed members of Society, "where they may walk in the sight of their own eyes, and the imagination of their own hearts, without being accountable to

---

[1] *Journal,* Phila., 1783, 63–83.

any for their conduct and yet be called by the name of
Quaker." [1]

Samuel Fothergill was the next Friend to visit South
Carolina, and his account agrees with the former report. He
writes from Charleston, February 13, 1755: "Since I wrote
you from Waynoak [Va.] I have visited all the residue of
Virginia and North Carolina, and last night arrived here,
and have had a meeting here this day, amongst a poor miserable handful of professors, and believe I must visit all their
families before I can easily leave this place. I expect to be
in Georgia, 150 miles south of this place, sometime next
week, and then return northwards, 800 miles, upon a line,
without much stop, except seven meetings which I left as I
came southwards.

"On the 2d instant, after a ride of fifty miles, we were
obliged to lie in the woods all night.

"I have this day had a large, good meeting, to my satisfaction; but the meeting house being small was incon-
venient. Most of the principal inhabitants attended, and I
expect the use of the Baptist meeting house on first day
evening, to take leave of the inhabitants of this place, who
have given general instances of their regard.

"George Whitfield passed through this town a few days
ago, to Georgia, having travelled very hard from Philadelphia, to get to his flock before we came amongst them.

"The state of the church is generally low, and exceedingly so in this place; there is very little of the form, and
much less of the power, of truth amongst them. My heart
has been bowed into strong concern, and close labor for and
with them, and hope for some little reviving of secret care
in particular; but alas, many seem awakened for a time, and
sink afresh into lukewarmness." In the same letter he
says: "I have now been to the extent of my visit southward, being 120 miles further than any Friend hath travelled on religious account, and am setting my face north-

---

[1] *Life* of Mary Neale, formerly Mary Peisley. 1860 ; *Memoirs* of
Catherine Phillips, 1797, 63–101.

ward. I propose another public meeting in this place to-morrow, and then to leave." He was also invited to visit the Sea Islands, and expected to do it, but "found a prohibition." These people seemed "desirous the testimony should be exalted by others, but won't lend a hand. . . . When we left Charleston we had near 450 miles to ride to the next settlement of Friends, through a country little inhabited, and in which accommodations were scarce enough, though we made shift to get into some cabin or other at nights, but had not my clothes off for several nights successively, or any things at times to lie down upon but a bear skin or boards." [1]

Reckitt was also in Charleston in 1757. "We found but few steady Friends, yet we had some good opportunities together." The Charleston meeting dates, as we have already learned, from 1680. It was established by London Yearly Meeting and Charleston Friends considered themselves under the jurisdiction of no Yearly Meeting save London; they retained their connection with that and were bound by its principles and testimonies. They corresponded with London and Philadelphia, and many of the Friends there kept their membership in the old meetings. They were few in numbers, and for some twenty years prior to 1718 no settled meeting for business was held. In that year what was practically a monthly meeting was set up in Charleston. Its records continue, but with many breaks, until 1786. This may be taken as the probable limit of their ability to hold business meetings. Their first meetings were held in a private house, but they had a meeting-house as early as 1715. They did not come into the title to their property until 1731, when it was secured for them through English Friends. It was then conveyed to trustees, but the last survivor claimed the property as his own, locked up the meeting-house and would allow no meetings there. At this juncture Philadelphia Friends appeared on the scene, purchased all the claims

---

[1] *Memoirs and Letters*, New York, 1844, 164-178, 264.

of the heirs of this original trustee and then vested the property in others. Philadelphia Friends incurred much trouble
and expense and got little return, for there did not "appear
to be more than fifteen members in the place" in 1791;[1] the
property was going to decay and some of their agents were
dishonest. In 1796 the property was transferred to Bush
River Monthly Meeting, but there was little improvement,
and as this meeting had become very weak in the meantime, trustees of North Carolina Yearly Meeting, appointed
for the purpose, reconveyed the property to Philadelphia
Yearly Meeting in 1812. Several unsuccessful efforts have
been made by North Carolina Yearly Meeting since that
date to again get possession of the property. The meeting
for worship was finally laid down in 1837, when only three
persons attended, two of whom were not Friends. The
meeting-house was burned in 1837; a new one was built in
1856, but burned in 1861. In 1875 the income from the lot,
on which there was a dwelling, amounted to some $12,000.
The sum of $4,000 was reserved to build a meeting-house in
Charleston whenever there should be a sufficient number of
Friends to hold a meeting, and an act of the South Carolina
Legislature of 1876 authorized Friends to spend a part or
the whole of the remainder in building, or in repairing,
meeting-houses elsewhere. A number of meetings in North
Carolina have been helped from this fund. The property
remains *in statu quo.*

  The meeting on the Edisto seems to have been at first entirely independent in government. It was possibly due to
the work of a few zealous Charleston Friends. Job Scott
says he found in 1789 "a little meeting of Friends though
not members," about fifty-eight miles from Charleston, while
on his way to Wrightsborough, Georgia. This is evidently
the same as the meeting on the Edisto mentioned by William Savery in 1791. "Left the city and got to T. Lewis's the
5th, about 54 miles. Here are about seven families who
have built a small meeting house, being convinced mostly

[1] Savery's *Journal,* in *Friends' Library,* I., 329.

without instrumental means; they meet in the manner of Friends twice a week, and appear to be an innocent people." [1] They seem to have been at that time an entirely independent organization, for Thomas Scattergood tells us that they met, but did not have the consent of Bush River Monthly Meeting. But a committee was appointed "to take some care of matters here," [2] and in 1798 they were under the control of that body.

These two meetings seem to have had little in common, as far as the origin goes, with the other four centers of Quaker influence in the central part of South Carolina. These centers were Pee Dee and Gum Swamp in Marlborough County, Wateree in Kershaw County, Bush River in Newberry County, and Cane Creek in Union County. These last were the product, mostly, of the southward migration and will be treated in the second part of this chapter. It will be noticed also that these coast settlements were nearly all planted during the infancy of Quakerism and that they never extended to Georgia.

We may say, in a general way, that the meetings mentioned above, except Carver's Creek and Dunn's Creek, represent the expansion of the native element in the three States. It represented men of English descent almost exclusively. It was less progressive than the foreign element, which we are now to study, because it came less in contact with others, was more provincial, had less new blood, and so got fewer new ideas. Further, these meetings were called on to furnish many recruits to the newer meetings in the western parts of these States, and many others migrated to the Western States. The result has been that these older meetings have either disappeared entirely from the history of the States or have sunk to a subordinate position. The largest and most progressive meetings found in North Carolina today are not among the representatives of the native stock, but among those who came in from the North during the

---

[1] *Friends' Library.* I., 330.   [2] *Ibid.,* VIII., 42–43.

eighteenth century. It is the planting and the development
of these meetings that we are now to trace.

2.—*The Replanting of Southern Quakerism.*

In the half-century included between 1732 and the close
of the Revolution a new and vigorous element was in-
jected into the life of Southern Quakerism. Most of these
new settlers were from Pennsylvania, but some had delayed a few years in Maryland; some were from New Jersey,
and some from Nantucket. Some were of English an-
tecedents, but many were Pennsylvania Germans, and some
were Welsh. The influence of these new settlers was so
distinct and overwhelming that I have ventured to call this
movement the replanting of Southern Quakerism, for had
this movement not taken place, Quakerism would hardly
be an appreciable factor in these States to-day.

These immigrants seem to have had but one motive in
coming South. This motive was distinctly economic. Their
movement is parallel to that of the Scotch-Irish. These
two waves passed over the same ground at the same time,
but the two did not intermingle, for the gentle and peace-
loving Friend, who decried all war, avoided the holding
of office, sought not his own, and put his abiding faith in
the personal presence of God, free grace and the powers
that be, had little in common with the restless, aggressive,
fighting, ruling Scotch-Irish, or with the democratic but
stern tenets of Calvinism.

About 1725 the vanguard of the Quaker movement appeared at Monocacy, Maryland. Here, like a true wave
of Teutonic migration, it rested for a time. It reached
Hopewell, Va., in 1732, and the next twelve or fifteen
years were spent in subduing northern Virginia. In 1743
an advance-guard had gotten as far as Carver's Creek, in
Bladen County, N. C. The next twenty years are marked
by the swarms of Quakers that came pouring into the
central sections of North Carolina, many of them falling

by the wayside, however, in Campbell and Bedford counties, Va., where South River Monthly Meeting was organized, in 1757. From about 1760 to the Revolution the horde passed through North Carolina and pressed into South Carolina and Georgia.

· Like a true migration again, this movement did not take the form of an overflow, but of successive waves. Many parts of the line of march were comparatively or even absolutely free from Quakers. It is idle for us to speculate on the reasons why they settled in the particular sections they did. It is possibly due to that "invincible attraction" which Walter Bagehot points out as playing such an important part in the formation of national character. Some accidental advantage, perhaps the excellence of the soil, located the first immigrant, and the gregarious instinct did the rest.

It now becomes us to narrate the planting of these meetings more in detail.

The beginning of this new movement southward, the counterpart of the movement of the next century westward, is to be found in the Hopewell settlement in Frederick County, Va. About 1725, Friends from Salem, N. J., and Nottingham, then in Pennsylvania, but thrown by Mason and Dixon into Maryland, settled in the upper part of Prince George County, Md., near the Monocacy, a tributary of the Potomac. They were erected into a meeting by New Garden Monthly Meeting, Pa. In 1732 Alexander Ross and a company crossed the Potomac, and thus initiated the migration of which we are now to write. In that year they obtained a charter for 100,000 acres of land situated on Opequan Creek, a tributary of the Potomac in what is now Frederick County, Virginia.[1] A settlement was begun here by Alexander Ross, Josiah Ballenger, James Wright, Evan Thomas and other Friends from Pennsylvania and Elk

---

[1] The surveys for Ross's warrant were made along Opequan Creek, north of Winchester, and up to Apple-pie Ridge. See Kercheval, *History of Valley of Virginia.*

River, Md.[1] A meeting called Hopewell, or Opeckon, was
established the same year, and one called Providence in
1733. They were organized in 1735 into Hopewell Monthly
Meeting, under the auspices and care of Chester Quarterly
Meeting in Pennsylvania.[2]

In 1733 other Friends removed from Bucks County, Penn.,
and settled in Fairfax, now Loudoun County, about ten
miles south of the Potomac, east of the Hopewell settlement, and near where the town of Waterford now is. When
these parties settled in northern Virginia there were no
Quakers in this section, and few inhabitants. The meeting
for worship of the Fairfax settlement was at first held in
the house of Amos Janney, the first Quaker settler here.
The Janneys became a large and influential family, produced among others the historian, Samuel McPherson
Janney,[3] and some of the name still reside in the county.
The meeting was called Fairfax, and dates from 1733. A
meeting-house was erected in 1741 and called by the same
name. In 1744 Fairfax Monthly Meeting was established.

---

[1] Janney, III., 248.   [2] Bowden, II., 249 ; *Records.*
[3] Samuel M. Janney was born in Loudoun County, Virginia, January 11, 1801.   His ancestors were from Cheshire and had been
among the earliest converts to Quakerism.   They removed from
Bucks County, Pennsylvania, about 1745.   On the division he became a Hicksite and labored long in the work of the ministry.   He
visited nearly or quite all of Friends' meetings in America :
was liberal in his feelings toward the other branch ; was earnest in
promoting a better educational system in Virginia, and constant in
his efforts to advance the cause of emancipation, being once presented by the Grand Jury for a paper on emancipation.   During
the Civil War he was useful in ameliorating the horrors of war for
the Virginia counties lying on the border, by reason of his interces-
sions with the Federal Government and the respect entertained for
him by the Confederates.   In 1869 he was appointed by President
Grant superintendent of Indian affairs and served until 1871.   He
died in Loudoun County, Va., April 30, 1880.   In literature he was
the most prolific of all the Southern Quakers.   Besides a number of
books and pamphlets on doctrinal matters, he published a volume of
poems in 1839 ; a Life of William Penn (Philadelphia, 1852), a Life
of George Fox, and A History of the Religious Society of Friends,
from its Rise to the Year 1828, in four volumes (Philadelphia, 1861–
1870).   A memoir of his own life, properly an autobiography, appeared in Philadelphia in 1881.

This also became a branch of Chester Quarterly Meeting and Philadelphia Yearly Meeting.[1]

These meetings soon attracted the watchful care of traveling Friends. John Fothergill visited them in 1736. The state of the Society in Virginia, he said, was "low and painful"; those advanced in years were, in general, "very insensible of true feeling, or suitable zeal for truth's advancement in themselves, their families or the church." John Churchman (1705-1775) went down in 1741 to see if the Friends at Fairfax "were in number and weight sufficient to have a meeting settled amongst them." He also visited the families on the Shenandoah and says, "I believe that the delight in hunting, and a roving idle life, drew most of them under our name to settle there."[2]

The meetings in Loudoun, Fairfax and Frederick counties were never as distinctively Virginian as those farther south. They looked first to Philadelphia Yearly Meeting, and after 1789 to Baltimore Yearly Meeting. Their distance and the inconvenience in traveling were doubtless important factors in this division. Then, too, the origin of the settlers had its effect. They were an offspring of the Pennsylvania meetings and looked naturally to them.[3]

These meetings in turn began to extend their boundaries. Various meetings were established in Frederick, Loudoun,

---

[1] Janney, III.. 248-249.   [2] *Journal.* 66, 67. 278, 279, 319.

[3] Friends at Hopewell had not purchased their lands from the Indians. This gave great uneasiness to Chalkley, who in 1738 had urged the Society to "endeavor to agree with and purchase your lands from the native Indians or inhabitants." The matter was not settled at once, and it gave Hopewell meeting so much trouble that in 1765 they declined to give certificates of removal until they learned whether the site of the proposed settlement had been purchased from the Indians. In 1778 the Monthly Meeting said that "Notwithstanding it may by this distance of time be difficult to find out the particular tribe that occupied these lands, yet it becomes us, as a religious Society, to demonstrate that testimony of justice and uprightness which we have ever held forth." They made an effort to find the Indian owners, and in 1794 the Tuscaroras laid claim to the reward, evidently with the purpose of exploiting the scrupulous Friends. It was shown that they had no right to it. But a valuable present was given them, as they "entertained strong expectations of receiving a donation." (Janney, III., 266. 440-441.)

Culpeper and the adjoining counties. In 1756 a meeting-house was built and a meeting settled at Goose Creek. In 1760 Crooked Run meeting was settled. A monthly meeting was established at Crooked Run in 1782, and one at Goose Creek in 1785; at Southland in 1789, or earlier; and at Alexandria in 1802. Migration from Pennsylvania to northern Virginia continued brisk until the Revolution. Day, Barrett, Beeson, Piggott, Sidwell, Kirk, White, Brown, Wilson, Ross, Johnson, Bailey, Carter, Ballinger, Pugh, Rees, Branson, Webb and Wright were the names of some of the families that came south from Pennsylvania and settled in this section. There were in this immediate section one quarterly and five monthly meetings, with twenty or more meetings for worship. There was much interchange between these meetings; as the settlers increased in numbers they took their certificates from the older meetings like Hopewell and Fairfax to the newer ones like Goose Creek. The meetings in this locality are now reduced to about eight. In the schism in 1828 a majority accepted the views of Hicks. The census of 1890 gives 96 as the number of Orthodox and 506 as the number of Hicksite Friends in Fairfax, Frederick and Loudoun counties. Friends have entirely disappeared from the adjoining counties of Culpeper, Stafford and Orange, Va., as well as from Hampshire, Berkeley and Jefferson counties, W. Va., in all of which they had members during the last century.

We may safely conclude that the meetings in Campbell and Bedford, Pittsylvania and Halifax counties, Va., were built up almost entirely by this southward movement. There were two monthly meetings in this section, South River and Goose Creek. The former dates from 1757; the latter, which is not the same as the Goose Creek Monthly Meeting in the Hopewell Quarter, from 1794. These monthly meetings applied for a quarterly meeting. It was granted in 1797, and was known as Western Quarterly Meeting; but the number of Friends in the section decreased so much that Goose Creek Monthly Meeting was laid down in 1814

and the Western Quarterly Meeting in 1817. South River
Monthly Meeting survived the Virginia Yearly Meeting,
and was laid down in 1858. These meetings lay in the
direct path of southern immigration. I conclude that they
received most of their increase from persons who got
stranded, as it were, on the way South. But they were
also a mixture of the native and foreign elements. The
Clarks of Louisa and Albemarle counties, and the Terrells
of Caroline, seem to have been in the Society before 1730,
and had been turned toward Quakerism by the preaching of
Joseph Newby of North Carolina. The Lynch family, from
whom the city of Lynchburg is named, and who have
also given us the term " lynch law," became members about
1752. It was the widow of Charles Lynch, died about 1753,
Irishman and founder of the family, who organized the
meetings in this locality. The Lynches, Davises, Johnsons,
Cadwalladers, Douglasses, Anthonys, Holloways, Strattons,
Fishers, Stantons, Moormans, Burgesses, Butlers, Pid-
geons, Perdues, were some of the prominent Quaker families in Campbell and the adjoining counties.[1] At a later
period the migration from northern Virginia became more
frequent. Between 1775 and 1800 we find thirty parties,
some with families, taking certificates from Fairfax and
the northern Goose Creek Monthly Meetings to South
River Monthly Meeting.

But before the meetings were strong enough to stand
alone in south-central Virginia, many emigrants had gone
beyond them and passed down into North Carolina. The
large settlement of Friends in Alamance, Chatham, Guilford, Randolph and Surry counties was formed by Quaker
immigrants, not by the expansion of the native element.
This stream of immigration was strong and healthy. It
added a stable element, fortified still further by the presence

---

[1] Cabell, *Sketches and Recollections of Lynchburg*, 24 et seq., and
Records. Lynchburg was founded in 1786 by John and Charles
Lynch, sons of the immigrant. John Clark, Achilles Douglass,
Micajah Moorman and others. The site of the city was the property
of the Lynch family. See Howe, *Historical Collections of Virginia.*

of thrift, frugality and energy, to the making of the State. These immigrants have been ignored by the historians of the State; but this has not been because of the lack of materials.

The earliest of these meetings in North Carolina seems to have been that at Carver's Creek, in Bladen County. It was so named from the founder of the settlement, who removed from Pennsylvania. It was begun about 1740, and asked for a monthly meeting as early as 1743; in 1746 one had been settled. It belonged to the Eastern Quarter. We find among its representative families (mostly 1749-52) Carver, Clayton, Benbow,[1] Beals, Ballinger, Channess, Cox, Kemp, Mayer, Mathews, Sommers, Wright, Clark. Most of these settlers were from Fairfax Monthly Meeting, Va., but others were from Pennsylvania. We find that at least fourteen parties, some with families, had removed to it. Unfortunately we know little of its history, for the records are lost. It continued till toward the close of the century; about 1797 it broke up, some of its members going west, and others joining their Quaker brethren in Guilford and Randolph. About the same time a monthly meeting was established at Dunn's Creek, probably either in Cumberland or Bladen County. Richard Dunn was probably the founder and leader in the settlement. Its connection was at first with the Eastern Quarter, for in 1746 Thomas Nicholson and others visited it as a committee of the Eastern Quarterly Meeting to quiet some troubles there. Some of these settlers had come from Pennsylvania, and they had a meeting-house as early as 1746. It was joined to the new Western Quarter by North Carolina Yearly Meeting in 1760. It was at this time, perhaps, half as strong financially as Cane Creek or New Garden. It did not prosper from this time, and was laid down in 1772, the first monthly meeting to be laid down within the limits of North Carolina Yearly Meeting. In 1781 the meeting for worship disappears also.

---

[1] Ancestors of the family in Guilford County.

The oldest of these meetings which has come down to the present is Cane Creek Monthly Meeting, in Alamance County. This was established in December, 1751, by Eastern Quarterly Meeting, then the only one in the Yearly Meeting. There were then some thirty families in the section, and some of the certificates presented were dated in 1748 and 1749, indicating that the settlement was of some standing. Fortunately the records of the monthly meeting have been preserved. During the four years, 1751-54, sixty-eight certificates were presented to this monthly meeting; of this number twenty-eight came from various meetings in Pennsylvania; two came from Hopewell and six from Fairfax; seven from Camp Creek, Va.; two from New Jersey; one from Falling Creek, N. C.; one from Gunpowder, Md.; and one from Ireland. The records indicate that they were mostly young men without families. Who were some of these founders of the present strongholds of Quakerism in North Carolina? John Powell, Joseph and John Doan came from Bucks County, Pa.; Simon Dixon, John Stanfield, John Lambert, Solomon, William and Thomas Cox came from Newark in Kennet, Pa.; William Reynolds, Richard Sidwell, Jeremiah Piggott, from East Nottingham; Isaac Jackson and Thomas Lindley, from New Garden, in Chester County; Joseph and Benjamin Ruddick, Matthew and William Ozburn, from Warrington; James and Robert Taylor, from Exeter; Bowater Beales, from Fairfax, Montgomery County, Pa.; Thomas Carr, from Gunpowder; John, Martha and William Hiatt, Aaron Jones, Eli Vestal, Benjamin and William Beeson, Mordecai Mendenhall, Thomas and William Thornburg, William Hunt, the Edwardses, Baldwins, Knights, Dillons, Millses, Joneses and Browns, from Hopewell. The Summers, Ballingers, Hunts, Matthews and Coxes came from Fairfax; the Hendersons, Clarks, Hoggatts and Moormans, from Camp Creek.

Nor were these men by any means idle after their arrival. William Reckitt, who was there in 1757, gives the sum of their history in a nutshell: " There is a large body of Friends

gathered thither in a few years from the several provinces.
They told me they had not been settled there above ten years,
but had found occasion to build five meeting-houses, and
then wanted one or two more. I had good and seasonable
opportunities among them."[1]

Their zeal and activity appear clearly in their minutes
also. This monthly meeting was set up in 1751; the same
year a meeting for worship was set up at New Garden, and
the monthly meeting was held by turns at Cane Creek and
New Garden. Deep River midweek meeting was set up
in 1753; Eno week-day and New Garden Monthly Meeting
in 1754. This was the expansion of the first four years.

During the next twenty years, 1755-75, a pretty steady
stream of immigrants came to the Cane Creek Meeting,
but owing to the imperfection of the records—a thing that
is very rare among Quakers—we are ignorant of their origin.
With the Revolution the tide of migration changed; many
went to other meetings, and some passed on to South Carolina and Georgia. This movement was hastened no doubt
by the War of the Regulation. Eight certificates of removal
were granted in 1772, and between 1771 and 1775 twenty-
two removals occurred, but the interchange of residence
among Friends was so frequent that the general average of
its population was probably maintained.

When we come to the New Garden settlement we have
an open field from 1754. The monthly meeting was established this year, and their records, kept with the scrupulous fidelity of Friends, begin then and extend in an unbroken
line to the present. Of the settlers who formed the New
Garden meetings the first to arrive were doubtless the immigrants from Pennsylvania by way of Maryland. They
brought the name with them from Pennsylvania. It has
always been a characteristic of Quakers to reproduce the
names of the sections with which they have been associated
in former years. Many English Quaker names are repro-

---

[1] *Journal*, pp. 60-81.

duced in America. There is a New Garden and a Springfield in Pennsylvania. They were carried thence to North Carolina, and from there, in turn, to Indiana.

The first settlement at New Garden was about 1750. In 1751 a meeting for worship was granted by Cane Creek Monthly Meeting, as we have seen.[1] For the next three years the monthly meeting circulated between Cane Creek and New Garden, and the latter was of enough importance in 1753 for Catherine Peyton and Mary Peisley to visit it and work for two months in the neighborhood. The settlement must have grown rapidly, for the monthly meeting was set up in 1754. This was the second monthly meeting set up by the Yearly Meeting out of the distinctively foreign element. New Garden was destined to become the most important meeting in the State, and was the mother of many others. In the first year, 1754, we have settlers coming in from Pennsylvania, from Hopewell and Fairfax meetings, Virginia. In this we see a revival of the idea of migrations. During 1755 nine certificates were received, representing Pennsylvania and Virginia only. According to the official minutes of New Garden Monthly Meeting, which note all certificates received, there were brought in during the sixteen years, 1754-70, inclusive, eighty-six certificates in all. Of these we have record that twenty-four represented families. It is probable that there were more families than this. Of these eighty-six immigrants—the actual number of persons received into Society from outside sources—the records show that forty-five, including fourteen of the families, came from Pennsylvania; thirty-five came from Virginia, one from Maryland, and four from northeastern North Carolina.

---

[1] About 1752, Richard Williams, with his wife, Prudence Beals, and two children, removed from Monocacy River, then in Prince George, now in Frederick County, Md., to Guilford County, N. C., and settled upon the lands where the New Garden meeting-house now stands. The county was then thinly settled. Williams gave the site for the meeting-house.

It will be of interest to us to see the names of some of
the persons who were the leaders in this extensive migration, for their children became prominent in the Society
in North Carolina, and their grandchildren went to the
West and became equally prominent there. From Warrington Monthly Meeting, Pa., there were twenty-three arrivals;
among them were Isaac and Peter Cox, Peter, Nathan and
Zacharias Dicks, Isaac Pidgen, John Beeson, Joseph Ozburn, Isaac Jones, Jacob and Abram Elliott, Thomas Kendall, William Reynolds, James and Aaron Frazer. Eight
came from Bradford Monthly Meeting; among them were
Ebenezer Worth, Phineas, John and Richard Mendenhall;
while another Richard Mendenhall, William Reynolds and
Thomas Dennis, Jr., came from New Garden, Pa.; eleven
came from Cedar Creek Monthly Meeting, Va., including
Phillip Hoggatt, William and Zachariah Stanley, Robert,
John and William Johnson; eight from Caroline Monthly
Meeting, Joseph Hoggatt, Stringman and Nathan Stanley,
Talton and James Johnson; eight from Hopewell and six
from Fairfax; from Hopewell came Richard, Isaac, Na-
thaniel and John Beeson, Benjamin Brittain, John Beals,
James Langley, Joseph Hiatt; from the neighboring Fairfax
came George Hiatt, William Kersey, Micajah Stanley, Wil-
liam Ballinger; Joseph Unthank and family came from
Richland, Bucks County, Pa.; James Brown, James Johnson
came from East Nottingham, then in Pennsylvania, now in
Maryland. While the westward movement from the eastern
North Carolina meetings was begun from Perquimans
Monthly Meeting by Henry, Jacob and Joseph Lamb, who
came up in 1760, and thus set in motion a movement that
was to attain large proportions fifty years later.

The names given in the above lists do not represent all
the Quaker settlers who came to central North Carolina
between 1751 and 1770, it gives only representatives of certain families that have since attained considerable distinction in the section and who first made this and the surround-

ing Quaker settlements a success.[1] They represented some of the oldest and best Quaker families in Pennsylvania. The New Garden settlers were soon reinforced by other immigrants who also came from old Quaker stock. These were the settlers from Nantucket Island, Mass. This movement began in 1771, and Libni Coffin was the first Nantucket man to arrive at New Garden.

We get some particulars from the life of Elijah Coffin: "The island of Nantucket being small, and its soil not very productive, a large number of people could not be supported thereupon. . . . The population of the island still increasing, many of the citizens turned their attention to other parts, and were induced to remove and settle elsewhere, with a view to better their condition as to provide for their children, etc. A while before the Revolutionary war, a considerable colony of Friends removed and settled at New Garden, in Guilford County, North Carolina, which was then a newly settled country. My grandfather [William] Coffin [1720-1803] was one of the number that thus removed. His removal took place, I believe, in the year 1773."[2] Again, Obed Macy,[3] writing of the period about 1760, says that because of the failure of the whale fishery some went to New Garden, N. C., others to Nova Scotia and Kennebec: "Very few of whom benefited themselves, and some, after a few years' stay, returned." Again, about the outbreak of the Revolution, because of the derangement of their business by the war, others went to New York and North Carolina.

---

[1] In 1764, Friends had begun investigations to find out who were the original Indian owners of their new homes, in order that they might pay them for the land, as they were trying to do at Hopewell, Va. It was reported that the New Garden section belonged to the Cheraws, who had been since much reduced and then lived with the " Catoppyes "—Catawbas. The matter was referred to a future meeting and seems to have been dropped.

[2] Page 10. This volume was published privately in 1863. See the same account substantially in the *Reminiscences* of Levi Coffin, Cincinnati, 1876.

[3] *History of Nantucket*, Boston, 1835.

In 1780 two-thirds of the inhabitants of Nantucket were
Quakers. We find among their leaders the Coffins, Star-
bucks, Folgers, Barnards and Husseys. Some of these became leaders in the Carolina migration, which was particularly large, 1771-75. During this period of five years
there were no less than forty-one certificates recorded at
New Garden Monthly Meeting from Nantucket out of a
total of fifty certificates received. In this number there
were eleven families, and it included many families that
have since been prominent in that section of the State. We
find among these immigrants Libni Coffin, William (Jr.),
William, Barnabas, Seth (and wife), Samuel (and family),
Peter and Joseph Coffin; Jethro Macy, David, Enoch, Na-
thaniel, Paul (and family), Matthew (and five children) and
Joseph Macy; William, Gayer, Paul (and family) and Wil-
liam Starbuck; Richard, William, Stephen, and Stephen
Gardner; Tristrim, Francis and Timothy Barnard; Daniel
Francis and Jonah Worth; John Wickersham; William
Reece; Jonathan Gifford; Reuben Bunker; Nathaniel Swain;
Thomas Dixon.

This southward migration stopped almost as suddenly
as it began. This was caused by the War of the Revolution.
In 1775 there were eight certificates from Nantucket. In
1776 there was but one. In that year the migration from
Virginia begins again with an occasional belated settler from
Delaware or Maryland. But it never attained important
proportions. During the seventeen years, 1783-1800, there
were thirteen certificates received, less than one a year;
some came from Nantucket, the most from Pennsylvania,
but these were partly counterbalanced by the five certificates
granted to parties who returned to their old homes.

It seems accurate to say that all of these new meetings
had practically attained their full growth by the outbreak
of the Revolution. Migration from the northward was
steady until then. It then ceased largely, and from that time
the meetings were kept up by the natural increase, not by
the new arrivals.

From New Garden as a center most of the meetings in this section of the State take their rise. It was this monthly meeting which settled a first-day meeting at Centre in 1757 and made it a monthly meeting in 1773. Thomas Scattergood, while visiting this meeting in 1792, was told by Peter Dicks "that there were but four or five families settled near him, when he moved to this place, about forty years ago [1755, from Warrington M. M.]. They held their meeting first in a private house, then built a small meeting-house, which is yet standing and used for a school; and near it is a large meeting-house, built within these few years, and a large settlement of Friends." [1]

New Garden Monthly Meeting also established a preparative meeting at Deep River, in Guilford County, in 1758. This was made a monthly meeting in 1778 and a quarterly meeting in 1818. In 1787 it established Westfield in Surry County. This became in due time the center of a large and important Quaker community; as a result, Westfield Quarter was set off in 1803. It consisted of the monthly meetings of Westfield and Mount Pleasant. The latter is of particular interest from the fact that it lay partly in Grayson County, Virginia, and was a sort of stopping-place in the migration westward. Toward the close of the eighteenth century there were three or four flourishing meetings within its limits in Virginia—Mount Pleasant, Chestnut Creek and Fruit Hill, all established in 1792. It received quite a number of members by certificate from the Virginia Yearly Meeting, particularly from the South River Monthly Meeting.

There was also a migration of Nicholites to this section, but the time of their arrival is unknown. The Nicholites were a religious sect who were organized in Caroline County, Maryland, about the time of the Revolution, by Joseph Nichols. It may be called the independent evolution of a

---

[1] *Friends' Library*, VIII., 35. He also says that at Back Creek there was a settlement of Germans who held meetings by themselves for a time like Friends. Later five or six of these families joined Friends.

Quaker Society, as we have seen was the case at Edisto, S. C., for the two societies were one in the vital, fundamental principle of their professions. They established a regular order of discipline about 1780, and organized three churches in Caroline County. It is probable that they migrated to North Carolina after the Revolution. Job Scott found some of them at Deep River in 1789, where they had a meeting-house. Scott says: "I had a lively evidence that some among them were humbly endeavoring to serve the Lord; but at the same time I saw clearly that many of them rested too much in their outside plainness; and valuing themselves upon that, and stopped short of more living acquaintance with the well-spring of eternal life." [1]

John Wigham visited them in 1795. [2] In 1797 Joshua Evans was among them. "I had two favored meetings among a people called Nicholites. The first was largely attended by others; but at the close I requested a meeting with them and their children by themselves. In about half an hour they came together, and a solid instructive season it was. They appear to be plain, sober people, are reputed honest in their dealings and otherwise maintain a good character. . . . I observed they had nine queries, which in substance were much like ours; these they read at times in their meetings. The last one was this: ' Are Friends careful to bear a steady testimony against slavery and oppression in all its different branches, endeavoring in every thing to do to others as we in like case would have others do unto us?' " [3]

Stephen Grellet met some of them in 1800, but from this time we hear no more of the Nicholites in North Carolina. About 1800 the Maryland branch joined themselves with Friends, and we may assume that the North Carolina branch followed their example. They disappear from the history of the State, and there is now but the faintest recollection of them in the section they inhabited.

---

[1] *Journal*, 203.   [2] *Memoirs*, 52.
[3] *Journal*, in *Friends' Miscellany*, X., 173-174.

The new settlements had an immediate effect on the course of the travels of Friends in the South. In 1761 Virginia and North Carolina were visited by Daniel Stanton (1708-1770), a Friend of Philadelphia, who had already paid religious visits to England and the West Indies. He was accompanied by Isaac Zane. The route of their journey indicates that the center of Quaker population was drifting away from the Atlantic seaboard. This was particularly the case with North Carolina. There the Quaker immigrants of a few years before were now predominant.

Stanton and Zane crossed the Potomac, and after preaching in Fairfax and Frederick counties, passed almost directly south. Their meetings were well attended and successful. Then to the meetings at Camp Creek, Fork Creek and Genito; then across James River to Amelia meeting, and across South River to Goose Creek. "That night we lodged at Peter Holland's, lying down in one room like a flock of sheep in a fold, being sixteen in number with the Friend's family." This entry will give some idea of the relative position of Friends in Virginia financially and socially. They were not among the wealthier Virginians. They had an experience of the same kind in North Carolina: "We stopped at a house to enquire for entertainment, where was a woman and several children. She gave us liberty for house room, and there being no bed for us we laid on the floor, and it being cold and snow falling, we were sometimes obliged to get to the fireside to warm us."[1]

John Griffith covered much of the same ground in 1765, and gives us his opinions in plain language. His reports of the state of Society are gloomy and discouraging. He says he had "two poor small meetings" at Camp Creek and Fork Creek, "where the life of religion seemed to be almost if not wholly lost." On their way to the back settlements of North Carolina: "We had four small poor meetings, viz., Genito, Amelia and Banister, and a meeting

---

[1] *Journal,* in *Friends' Library,* XII., 168-172.

at Kirby's, on the banks of Dan river; to some of them, many of other societies came, and gospel doctrine was opened largely for their help and information; in which labor there was good satisfaction; but alas! few under our name in those parts, let the true light shine before men, but were most of them stumbling blocks in the way of serious inquirers." Some of the North Carolina meetings were better than those in Virginia, and some were not. "We had a meeting at Centre; it was extremely cold, and, as some observed, the like had not been known there in the memory of man; and being quite an open meeting-house, and very little of anything to be felt amongst them of religious warmth, it was really a distressing time inwardly and outwardly."

He was at the monthly meeting at Cane Creek. "This was large, but most of the members seemed void of a solid sense and solemnity; a spirit of self-righteousness and contention was painfully felt. . . . I am persuaded many of those under our name have removed out of Pennsylvania and other places to those parts, in their own wills, having taken counsel of their own depraved hearts, and when they have got thither, have set up for something in the church; but it seemed to me most of them were very unfit for the spiritual building, not having been hewn in the mount. We went to their meeting on first day, but there was much darkness and death over them."[1]

The superiority of Carolina Friends over Virginia Friends, both in temporal and spiritual affairs, is also shown clearly by Hugh Judge, who visited Southern Quakers in 1784. In speaking of his travels in the Hopewell section of Virginia he says: "We arrived there safely; but though it was a poor place, it was much better than the former, for we got a tolerably good bed, and corn blades for our horses; but they had no bread, milk, cheese nor butter for us. I asked whether we could have some water boiled, which

[1] *Journal*, 370-380.

they did in a large kettle, for they were entire strangers to tea and tea-tackling, having nothing of the kind. However, getting some hot water, I made some tea in a quart mug; and, having tea and sugar as well as bread and meat with us, we fared pretty well on our own.

"Set out before sunrise, and called at several places before we could get any breakfast, or anything for our horses to eat. At length we obtained some corn blades for them, and a broken kettle to boil water for ourselves a breakfast. So sorrowfully poor is the situation and condition of many of the inhabitants of old Virginia that travelers are hardly beset to get a little refreshment; yet they abound with negroes."

From Virginia Judge passed on to North Carolina and held meetings at Springfield and Muddy Creek: "Things carry a different appearance here to what they did in Virginia. Here is a large body of Friends, many of whom appear livingly concerned for the right ordering of things amongst them."[1]

When South Carolina is reached there is found to be no essential difference in the evolution and development of the meetings in the northern and central part of the State, save that immigrants coming into this province, 1760-75, unlike those in Virginia and North Carolina, found some Quaker meetings already established in their line of march. Two of these, Pee Dee and Gum Swamp, were in Marlborough County, S. C. "The Friends there," says Reckitt, "though their circumstances in the world were but low, treated us very kindly. Their love to truth and diligence in attending meetings are worthy of notice; for they had nigh-one hundred miles to go to the monthly meeting they belonged to, and I was informed very seldom missed at-

---

[1] *Journal,* 32-48.

tending it." These Friends "were truly glad to see us, they being seldom visited."[1]

Another Quaker meeting on their line was that at Wateree. It was in, or near, Camden, in Kershaw County. It was also known as the Fredericksburg or Camden meeting. Mary Peisley and Catherine Peyton visited it in 1753. They found the Society very low as to religious experience, but "some of the youth were under a divine visitation, which afforded comfort and encouragement."[2] Reckitt visited them in 1757, and says "several of the Friends from Ireland had been settled about six or seven years."[3]

They seem to have grown rapidly, for in 1755 we find Wateree mentioned as a monthly meeting, but whether it was established by North Carolina Yearly Meeting we do not know. In 1757 we find that certificates were taken from New Garden to Wateree, and in 1761 parties returned to New Garden. In 1762 they were visited by William Hunt of North Carolina. So far as any evidence to the contrary is to be found, this monthly meeting, as well as other meetings in South Carolina, at first led a purely independent existence. They were congregational as far as government goes, and it seems some did not elect at first to come under North Carolina Yearly Meeting. Up to this time all South Carolina Quakers seem to have come by the sea route. Charleston, Edisto, Wateree, were all of the same character in this respect. But when the south-

---

[1] This meeting belonged to the Cane Creek Monthly Meeting, North Carolina, and all that Reckitt says of their faithfulness in attending their business meetings is borne out by the records. Prior to the organization of the Bush River Quarter in 1791 it was seldom that the monthly meetings of South Carolina and Georgia did not have representatives at the Western Quarterly Meeting.

[2] Janney. III., 318, 319.

[3] In the *Life* of James Gough, London, 1783, p. 101, we find an account of some families of Friends who "came to Dublin to embark for North Carolina, to settle on my cousin Arthur Dobbs's lands there, who was their landlord at Timahoe." By mistake the captain carried them to South Carolina and they settled in that province. They are probably either the Friends at Wateree or at Pee Dee and Gum Swamp, although there is a slight discrepancy in dates, as Dobbs did not come to North Carolina until 1754.

ward migration swept over North Carolina and reached South Carolina these older meetings became less important relatively, and their connection with North Carolina Yearly Meeting becomes more distinct as the immigrants become more powerful. In 1768 Fredericksburg Monthly Meeting was joined to the Western Quarter of North Carolina Yearly Meeting, and was held at Bush River, which was a settlement mostly of parties who had come overland from the north. In 1770 a committee was appointed to investigate the state of these Friends. They recommended the settlement of a monthly meeting at Bush River, in Newberry County, which was done, and that Fredericksburg Monthly Meeting "should return to the Wateree until further orders." This was also done, and from this time Bush River increases while Fredericksburg decreases. It dragged its slow length along through the Revolution and was laid down about 1782. Job Scott was there in 1789. "I had a very small, yet precious meeting at Camden, S. C., where no member of our Society liveth, except one very ancient woman; though once there was a settled meeting of Friends there." [1] To this meeting there had come the families of Lamb, Parkins, Cox, Smith, Thomas, Pierson, Gant.

The group of meetings clustering around Bush River was the most important in South Carolina. The origin of this meeting and the time it began cannot be discovered. William Coate was living near Bush River before 1762, and Samuel Kelly, a native of King's County, Ireland, removed to Newberry County, from Camden, in 1762. Other early Quaker settlers were John Furnas, David Jenkins, Benjamin and William Pearson. Robert Evans came from Camden, probably between 1762 and 1769. Judge John Belton O'Neall, author of *The Bench and Bar of South Carolina*, and of the *Annals of Newberry*, had a birthright membership in this meeting. His parents were both

---

[1] *Journal*, 193.

from Antrim, Ireland, and this would indicate a mixture
of races in the settlement. We may conclude that it had
the Irish as a base, with a superstratum of immigrants from
the States to the north.[1] Samuel Neale reports that they
were strong in 1771.[2] This was about the beginning of the
overland migration from the northward. These immigrants
caused them to enlarge their borders. A meeting was established at Padgett's Creek in 1774, and in the same year
we find mention of " Cane Creek meeting on the waters of
Tiger River." This became a monthly meeting before long,
and the same year another meeting was wanted by Friends
of Little River. It is only from 1772 that we have the
record of certificates. Between 1772 and 1777, six years,
there were twenty-nine certificates taken to Bush River
Monthly Meeting. Of these, fourteen came from Pennsylvania, ten from North Carolina, two from Maryland, two
from Virginia. Migration came, therefore, we can easily
see, in part from the country that had supplied the meetings of middle North Carolina and partly from these meetings themselves. The tide had set toward the South, and
in its onward movement swept with it many who had stopped in Virginia or Carolina for a season or for a number
of years. The list of settlers within the limits of Bush
River included persons by the name of Pearson, Coppock,
Merrick, Clark, Edmundson, Galbreath, Harmar, Heaton,
Battin, and others, from Pennsylvania; from North Carolina came some of the Mendenhalls, Joneses and Hendersons. From Pine Creek, Md., came Benjamin VanHorn;
Hannah Hooker came with four children from Gunpowder,
Md.; from Hopewell, Va., there came the families of Ruble,
Haworth, Babb, Taylor, Pearson, Jay, Jacob, Bull, Hol-
lingsworth, Buffington, Pugh,[3] Barrett, Roberts, Thompson;
from Fairfax, Mathews, Brown, Whitson; from Cane Creek,
N. C., Bray, Cox, Thornton, Henderson; from New Garden,

---

[1] *Annals of Newberry*, 30, 31.   [2] *Journal*, 179–185.
[3] Azariah Pugh, one of these immigrants, was the ancestor of
Senator Pugh, of Ohio.

Brown, Jones, Mendenhall, Wickersham, Stewart. There were still others named Ballinger, Wright, Brooks, Gaunt, Hasket, Stedman, Edmundson, McCool, Miles, Reagan, Cook, Thomas and Duncan, most of whom came with the southward migration.[1]

To Bush River Monthly Meeting reported the meetings for worship at Bush River, Mudlick, Henderson's or Allwoods, Rocky Springs, Raybourn's Creek, Charleston and Edisto; to Cane Creek Monthly Meeting reported Cane Creek and Padgett's Creek. They were visited by most of the traveling missionaries after the Revolution. We have already quoted from Reckitt and Scott and Savery. Thomas Scattergood was there in 1792. He attended Padgett's Creek meeting, "which was large, but long in gathering; and when mostly settled, a rude company came past and disturbed it. Yet through favor we had a pretty good meeting afterwards." At Mudlick "a poor little company collected, but we fared much better than I expected." He then went to "Raban's Creek [Raybourn's Creek] meeting, held in a poor house with an earthen floor, which was damp with the beating in of the rain and snow. I thought on sitting down that it seemed a very poor beginning, but I was enabled to preach the gospel amongst them, and came away easy." "Went to a meeting at Allwoods; very poor, and continued so for a season." On his return from Georgia, Scattergood went "to Rocky Springs meeting, which was large and mixed. A number of Anabaptists came to it."[2]

There seems to have never been more than one Quaker center in Georgia. Quakers were particularly favored un-

---

[1] *Records.* See also Judge O'Nealle's *Annals of Newberry.* Judge O'Neall states that the screw augur was invented by Benjamin Evans, a Newberry Quaker. In 1779, a body of Friends from a "distant land," probably Ireland, settled within the limits of Bush River Monthly Meeting, but as they had no regular certificates, Western Quarterly Meeting advised that they be not received as full members.

[2] *Journal,* in *Friends' Library,* VIII., 37–42.

der the Georgia charter, but it is not probable that any
Friends appeared in the colony early enough to avail themselves of the advantages offered. Samuel Fothergill was
the first Quaker preacher to visit Georgia. This was in
1755. " I went thence [Charleston] to Georgia, and had a
large meeting in the court-house, and some opportunities in
the inn where I lodged, to some service, though there were
not any there who bore our name." The vagueness of this
letter leaves us in doubt as to the sections visited.[1]

The first effort at Quaker settlement was in 1758. In
that year " Certain Quaker families entered the province
and formed a settlement about seven miles above Augusta
upon a tract of land known to this day as the Quaker
Spring. The territory within which they fixed their abodes
had been formerly owned by a tribe of Indians called the
Savannahs. Thence were they expelled by the Uchees, who
occupied adjacent lands. Peacefully inclined as they were,
these Quakers hoped to dwell in amity with the neighboring Indians. While engaged in clearing lands and in building comfortable homes they were alarmed by the intelligence that the Cherokees were on the eve of invading the
white settlements. Without pausing to ascertain the truth
of the report, they hastily abandoned the country, leaving
behind them no trace of their short occupancy save a spring
and a slender memory." [2]

The next effort was more successful. On the third of
July, 1770, the General Assembly of Georgia granted to
Joseph Maddock (or Mattock) and Jonathan Still a tract
of 40,000 acres of land in St. Paul's Parish, Columbia (now
McDuffie) County, Ga., to be held in trust for the Quakers.
Here they began the town of Wrightsborough, on Town
Creek, sixteen miles from Appling, the county seat, and
named it for Sir James Wright, Governor of the colony.[3]

<hr/>

[1] *Memoirs and Letters*, 283.   [2] Jones's *Georgia*, I., 440.
[3] White's *Statistics of Georgia*, 1849, p. 193 ; Crawford and Marbury's *Digest of the Laws of Georgia*, 1802, p. 392. It is to be noticed
that these grantees have the same names as two of the men who

The records date from 1773. In that year a preparative and a monthly meeting were organized in Wrightsborough township by representatives sent from New Garden. The certificates recorded show that the Quaker population was made up of settlers from South Carolina, North Carolina, Virginia, Pennsylvania, and Burlington in West New Jersey. The outlook for a speedy development of their settlement was very promising when Indian troubles in 1774 prevented further expansion.[1] We have an account of this Indian incursion from one who was so close to the sufferers that it may be interesting to reproduce. It is written by Rachel Price (*née* Kirk) in her *Account of the Kirk Family* (MS.). It tells how her sister, Tamar Kirk, married Phineas Mendenhall and removed with him to Guilford County, N. C. This was about 1763. The account continues: "I have retained the recollection of a young man of the name of John Wickersham, who was acquainted with my sister Mary. He went to Carolina some time after her, where they renewed their attachment and were married and settled there for a time, but the State of Georgia opened for settlement, inducing many to move there. My sisters and their families were both of them amongst those who went about 300 miles from their then settlement into the State of Georgia to a place settled by Joseph Mattock and Mattock's Settlement. There they lived in peaceable possession of their homes undisturbed by the natives for a considerable time until there was a new purchase made by Government, with which the Indians seemed dissatisfied. My brothers-in-law, with others, bought land in it; as it was considered very good, many were induced to make settlements on it, to clear and sow it with grain, but the frequent incursions of Indians was cause of great discouragement to them, so that it was deemed

were concerned in the trouble in Cane Creek Monthly Meeting in 1764. It is possible and probable that they were induced to migrate by the troubles that culminated in the War of the Regulation.

[1] Jones's *Georgia*, II., 132.

best by many not to reside on it. They therefore left it, but when the grain that they had sown was ripe, they thought that they would go there and gather it, the distance not being far from their first settlement where they resided. Sister Tamer, her husband and three sons went for that purpose, leaving their two daughters behind at home. Early one morning sister went to milk a cow they had with them; while her hands were thus engaged a party of Indians were lying in wait, fired on them, put an end to her useful life, also killed her eldest son; the youngest they took captive, and kept him in captivity about two years. They adopted him and were kind to him, and when redemption was offered for him, he had become so much attached to them and to their manner of life, that it required some persuading to get him from them. The father and other son made their escape.

"This awfully trying circumstance made such an impression on the minds of sister Mary and husband that they came as soon as they could get away to North Carolina to their former settlement. In that neighborhood they lived for many years. . . . They of later years moved with their children and their families to Indiana, where they are settled."

There were then about twenty families in the Wrightsborough connection. They report at that time: "Meetings are middling well kept up and love and unity subsist in a middling good degree amongst us." But the Indian incursion caused the population to become unsteady, and many returned to the older colonies. We find, however, a few who ventured that far South during the War of the Revolution. Daniel Williams went down from Pennsylvania in 1777 to Wrightsborough, and in 1778 writes back to the people of Pennsylvania: "I got liberty to move into an empty cabin near my uncle, where we staid about six or seven weeks. During our abode there I dealt with a man for 100 acres of land in the old purchase. There were about seven acres cleared, and a nice house just built thereon, and about 40 bearing peach trees planted out. We moved there near the beginning of the second month, and I fell to grubbing and clearing a piece of ground, and got five acres ready to plant in corn in pretty good season, and have ten acres now growing of likely corn. . . . Our country is exceedingly fertile, and takes but little to render it complete. One discouragement there is to the settlement of it, and that is the frequent incursions of the savages, who almost every year cause some part of the settlement to break, though it is hard to penetrate above two or three miles within the English boundaries. Though we have often heard it was their decision to cut us off, yet the interposition of the Divine Hand has hitherto frustrated their intentions when no human power seemed sufficient. Notwithstanding discouragements of this kind appear, yet it is truly astonishing to see with what rapidity the country is settled and improved; this country which 11 years ago was a wild uninhabited wilderness. There are several people here this fall that are much indisposed with a fever that is not common in this country, for we have generally good water and clear, wholesome air in the middle of summer. . . . I shall advise if any of our friends should incline to come out here soon, that they bring no more money with them than what will bring them out, for we have no scarcity of paper currency. I would be very desirous if brother Isaiah would send 10 or 12 lbs of iron out by William Benson, for it is a very scarce article here and rates I believe at $2.00 the pound."[1]

Georgia Friends were drawn from all the meetings to the northward almost without exception. We find among them the families of Farmer, Pugh, Stubb, Jones, James, Vernon, Moorman, Upton, Williams, Webb, Dixon, Seypold, Coppock, Brown, Hodge, Mendenhall.

---

[1] Williams was born July 17, 1748, and died about 6 mo., 9th, 1800. His widow and her seven daughters moved after a few years to Stillwater, Ohio. Friends in South Carolina and Georgia suffered much from the effects of the war, and received donations from English Friends in 1783, but it was misused by the managers.

In 1789 Job Scott attended Friends' meeting at Wrightsborough, and the next day went to their "new meeting-house, four or five miles from the first."[1] I conclude from the journal of William Savery, who visited Georgia in 1791, that this new meeting was called Mendenhall's, for some of that name went from North Carolina: "The 19th, had a meeting at Mendenhall's; a large number of Methodists and Baptists attended. Two women fell on their knees and trembled, and shook, and prayed and exhorted. I could scarcely account for such an extraordinary appearance." But we can account, for we see here the influence of primitive Methodism. He continues: "The 22nd being first day, had a meeting at Wrightsborough: the people of different professions and ranks came in great numbers; it was thought to be a solid, tendering time; but not feeling quite easy, I appointed another at four o'clock in the afternoon, the people continuing in the woods. This was truly a relieving time, and we thought we had never witnessed so much brokenness throughout: they were loath to part with us, and many tears were shed on both sides. I endeavored as soon as possible to retreat, but they stopped the sulkey frequently, and seemed reluctant to let us go. Accompanied by several Friends, we passed on to Augusta."[2]

Joshua Evans visited the Georgia meetings in 1797. He went up from Charleston and took the little meeting at Edisto on his way: "I had a meeting with them, in their meeting-place, which is a few logs put up like a house, with holes cut out for doors and windows, but all open without shutters. I told them I thought the condition of their house, if it continued, would be a dishonor to them and their good cause.

"After a solid meeting in a Methodist house, at their request, we travelled towards Augusta in Georgia; . . . . but being strangers, and without a guide, we met with some difficulty in finding the place where our Friends reside.

---

[1] *Journal,* 198, 199.   [2] *Journal,* in *Friends' Library,* I., 330-331.

At length obtained information, and found them about thirty miles from Augusta, up the Savannah River in Columbia County. We had a solid and satisfactory meeting with them, and also visited most of them in their families. Here are divers valuable members of our Society; one of whom is William Farmer, at whose house we had an evening meeting.

"We had the third meeting among them, which was a comfortable season; a number of Friends of Wrightsborough Monthly Meeting attended, on a request for permission to hold a meeting twice a week at William Farmer's. With these friends, I went to Wrightsborough, and was at their fourth day meeting, which was closely exercising to me. Next day I was at a week-day meeting at Williams' Creek, about ten miles distant. It was a time of favor, a considerable number attending. I believe the Lord hath a little remnant in these parts, who testify against slavery and are favored to keep themselves clear. . . . Having visited near fifty families within the limits of the Monthly Meeting, I again attended their first day meeting, which was uncommonly large, many not being able to get into the house. . . . Thus we parted, and I came again to William Farmer's in Columbia County."[1]

The Georgia meetings reported to the Bush River Quarterly Meeting, and this in turn to the North Carolina Yearly Meeting. In 1775 we find Georgia mentioned in the North Carolina Yearly Meeting records. South Carolina had been mentioned for the first time in 1770. The change in the center was soon felt; in 1777 came the proposition to remove the Yearly Meeting from the east; in 1786 request was that it be held at Centre, in Guilford County. It was held here the next year, and then alternated between the east and the west until 1812, when the last Yearly Meeting in northeastern North Carolina was held at Little River.

---

[1] *Journal,* in *Friends' Miscellany,* X., 155-157.

In 1791 the monthly meetings at Bush River and Cane Creek, S. C., and Wrightsborough, Ga., request a quarterly meeting among themselves. It was granted, and was known as Bush River Quarter. According to the *Almanac* of Isaac Briggs for 1799, there were then ten meetings in South Carolina and three in Georgia, all but one in the Bush River Quarter. Of the Georgia meetings, one was held at Wrightsborough, " and two meetings held by permission at William Farmer's on third day; at Williams' Creek, fifth day." These meetings were probably among the first to decline. In 1799 the Assembly of Georgia incorporated a body of five trustees, authorized the Quakers to elect their successors, and authorized them to sell the land held there.[1] In 1800 Joseph Cloud, a minister of North Carolina who had been among the meeting on " the western waters," visited South Carolina and Georgia, no doubt in the interest of removal. Borden Stanton wrote them urging them to go west in 1802. A certificate from Wrightsborough Monthly Meeting to Cane Creek Monthly Meeting, N. C., dated June 4, 1803, is the last evidence we have of Georgia Friends. They had departed to the great West.

It is now possible for us to take a summary review of the results obtained thus far. The promise of an aggressive and rapid growth made in the youth of Quakerism was not fulfilled in its maturer years. This promise was particularly clear in North Carolina. During the seventeenth century the records show that the Society in that colony was quietly but steadily extending its outposts and was being strengthened by immigration and conversions. To such an extent was this true, that in 1716 Rev. Giles Rainsford writes to the S. P. G. that the " poor colony of North Carolina will be soon overrun with Quakerism and infidelity if not timely prevented by your sending over able and sober missionaries as well as schoolmasters to reside among them."[2]   But this almost phenomenal growth of the

---

[1] Crawford and Marbury's *Digest*, 392.   [2] *Col. Rec.*, II., 245.

native element ceased soon after the Established Church became well organized. Quakers never played in North Carolina under royal government the part they had played under the government of the Proprietors. They were still less important, relatively, in Virginia. During the last third of the eighteenth century they obtained their fullest growth in each of the several States under consideration. Soon after the beginning of the nineteenth century their decline becomes visible. The period of highest and fullest growth has itself a period of depression. The Revolution, like the Civil War, was a time of suffering to the Quakers. Many left their ranks and were disowned to take part in the struggle for liberty, and the Society was much depleted. On the other hand, the convincements were much more numerous than they had been in former years. Despite all the care which Friends might use to keep unworthy and timid persons out of the Society, the number of "war Quakers" was considerable, and the Society did not prosper for some years after the end of the war.

CHAPTER VI.

Quaker Social Life.

A study of Friends would be incomplete without some reference to their social life. I shall consider this subject in its broader aspects.

One of the most important of the early questions demanding the attention of Friends was marriage. It seems that from the first marriage was kept strictly within the Society. As early as 1661 Friends had forced the English law to recognize the legality of their forms of marriage. The initial step was by the parties who declared in meeting their intentions. The women's meeting then appointed a committee to see if the woman was " clear " from other " marriage entanglements " ; the men's meeting did the same, and when this was settled the parties were " left to their liberty to take each other," which was done by calling on the congregation as witnesses: " Friends, you are my witnesses that in the presence of you I take this my friend Elizabeth Nixon to be my wife, promising to be a loving and true husband to her, and to live in the good order of truth so long as it shall please the Lord that we live together or until death."

It was necessary for them to guard against excesses on these festive occasions. Friends were warned to " keep out of superfluity at maredges and bueriels." At the latter no provisions for food and drink were to be made except for such as came from a distance. Again, it was directed " that Friends in general do take care to keep out of unnecessary providing of strong drink, . . . but to keep in christian moderation at births, burials and marriages." In 1714 Chalkley speaks of these entertainments as a " growing thing amongst us," [1] and the use of liquors among Friends is taken as a matter of course by Chalkley and Richardson, but Friends were always opposed to excesses.

Friends were appointed to attend marriages "as governors [2] of the marriage feast, and see that things are managed in decency and good order, and bring report to the next monthly meeting," and those who had attended a marriage as overseers reported that "things were managed in good order and according to truth." Friends were watchful for the orphan in the event of a second marriage. On one occasion Henry Keaton and Elizabeth Scott, widow, appeared and declared their intention of marriage. Friends were appointed "to see that the fatherless children have their due of their father's estate, also that Henry Keaton give security for the same." They were always advised against marrying outside of their own communion. We find many reports against Friends for "accomplishing disorderly marriages" and for "outgoings in marriage." They were frequently disowned for such marriages, and it was even an offense to be married at home instead of in meeting.

The second marriage was a cause of considerable trouble. The Virginia meeting put the shortest limit at twelve months. This satisfied the Virginians, but the Carolinians believed more firmly in marrying early and often. They began with twelve months, but cut it down to eight. The conservatives again raised it to twelve, but this was too long a period of waiting, and in 1776 it was ordered that no widower should propose, or widow receive a proposal, under nine months. There could be no marriage between persons nearer akin than second cousins. An amusing instance of domestic infelicity comes to us from the Rich Square records. In 1801 John Knox was up before the meeting for whipping his wife. He was not "in a disposition to give Friends satisfaction but intimates that he through necessity

---

[1] *Journal*, 82.
[2] "Overseer" is the usual term in this connection, and it involves oversight of the whole event.

was in duty bound to do so in order for a better regulation in his family." He was disowned.

Friends were warned against costly attire, " new fashions," " superfluity of aparil "; against " striped and flowered stuffs in making or selling or wearing of them." They were to have no " faulds in their coats or any other unnecessary fashions or customs in their dresses." In 1752 one of the North Carolina meetings advised that Friends keep out of superfluity of meats and drinks and apparel, viz.: "Coats and other Garments made after the new & superfluous fashions of the times and that no friend wear a WIG but such as apply themselves to the Monthly Meeting giving their reason for so Doing which Shall be Adjuged of by the said Meeting." But there were Friends who insisted on their right to " wair wigs," and the meeting desired instruction " in relation to the Manner of Dealing with Those that had Gotten Wiggs Contrary to the order of the Yearly Meeting: And friends think proper to refer the Case to the next yearly meeting." The matter came up duly: " After several disputes and conferences " the majority agree " that no person wearing a wig shall be dealt with so as to amount to a denial for that offence only."

We find a testimony against excess in smoking in Virginia as early as 1701, and those who used tobacco in North Carolina were warned to use it with " great moderation as a medison and not as a delightsom companion." Complaints were frequently based on the trio of evils, chewing tobacco, taking snuff, and sleeping in meeting.

We find testimonies against such " vain and viceeious Prosceedings as Frollicking Fiddling and Dancing." Some Friends delighted in plays of diversion; some were concerned in gaming and lotteries, and in 1777 a North Carolina Quaker was acting as clerk to a lottery. We do not see many indications that they drank liquors to excess, and at a later period they were forbidden to keep taverns and retail liquors. In these matters Virginia Quakers were at least a generation ahead of those in North Carolina. In the former State distillers were to be disowned as early as 1782.

During the earlier years of the Society Friends held many offices of trust and honor in the Carolinas. Daniel Akehurst, who was a judge, a councillor and secretary of the northern province; Francis Toms, a councillor; Governor John Archdale; Emmanuel Lowe, the son-in-law of Archdale; Thomas Symons, a judge of the general court, and others were members of the Society. In later years their sentiments in regard to the holding of office changed. They discouraged Friends from becoming members of the Legislature, and in 1787 actually tried one in North Carolina who became a justice of the peace. In 1809 it was proposed to North Carolina Yearly Meeting that any Friend who held office as a member of the Federal or State Legislature, as justice of the peace, clerk of the court, coroner, sheriff or constable, should be disowned. It was the same in Virginia. The explanation is that in filling these offices they must take and would frequently have to administer the oath; would have to assist in enforcing laws against slaves, and in executing the death penalty. In more recent times the views of Friends in regard to office-holding have changed materially.

Public paupers are never Quakers, for Quakers have always been thrifty and industrious. It was so in the earliest years of the Society. One of these early Quakers was Richard Russell, of Norfolk County, Va. We know that he was fined to the amount of £100 sterling and 5,250 pounds of tobacco, but he had something at his death. His will was recorded January 24, 1667. He had a considerable library, which was distributed among his friends. He gave Richard Yates " a booke called Lyons play," " John porter junr. Six books," " John porter (1), my exer'r ten books," " Katherin Greene three bookes," " One book to Sarah Dyer," " unto Wm. Greene, his wife two books & her mother a booke," " Anna Godby two books," " Jno. Abell One booke in Quarto," " Richard Lawrance One booke."

He gave half of his property to his wife. He gave an eighth to his executor: " the other pte of my Estate I give & bequeath One pte of itt unto Six of the poorest mens Children in Eliz: Riv'r. to pay for their Teaching to read & after these six are entred then if Six more comes I give a pte allsoe to Enter them in like manner."

Would it be straining this gift too much to call it one of the corner-stones of the educational system of Virginia of to-day?[1]

We have the inventory of William Bresse in 1701. He had made considerable gifts to the meeting at Levy Neck, Virginia. In his inventory we find two and a half dozen pewter dishes, pewter "Pye" plates, candlesticks, sockets, porrengers, basons, flagons, and pots, brass kettles and pans, bell metal skillets, iron pots, also sheets, tablecloths, napkins, one damask tablecloth, fine towels, books, negroes, one English man-servant, sheep, horses, hogs, cows, " canvis," toweling, " doalis," " lynnen," Kersey broadcloth, " 7 yards of painted calico," printed and colored linen; also the following silver articles: two large tankards, one large plate, one beaker, two dozen spoons, two forks, two salt-cellars, one saucer, one sack cup, four dram cups.

In 1717 John Hawkins bequeathed " 3 score pounds " to the use of the Society in North Carolina. Friends were careful to warn their members against launching too heavily in business or getting more obligations than they could meet. In 1803 Friends decided that the bankrupt law could not excuse them from paying their debts. In Virginia in 1810, in the case of business failure, it was recommended that the party withdraw from the meeting until it was discovered that nothing discreditable had been done.

Friends occasionally misbehaved in meetings. Story remarks in 1699 that the " noises and elevations " of some in North Carolina was hurtful. In 1702 many men were anx-

---

[1] See John W. H. Porter's article on Norfolk Quakers, in *Richmond Dispatch*, Dec. 3, 1893, and *Virginia Historical Magazine*, I., 326.

ious to speak at the same time in the meeting in Virginia. Minutes were sometimes passed to make them pull off their hats in meeting, to keep them from calling the days of the week "after the heathenish customs," and to keep out of drowsiness in meetings.

In 1748 we find a committee appointed to sit in the gallery at the yearly and quarterly meetings to see that Friends behave themselves orderly. They were not to run in and out during service, and young people were not "suffered to sit too much in companies in the back part of the meeting house, without having some solid Friend or two to sit with them."

There seems to have been an epidemic of worldliness about the beginning of the present century. They complain bitterly of "the great deviation from plainness so apparent amongst us." In 1824 they record their condemnation of "such articles of dress as lapell coats, bell crowned hats, ruffles, and ornamental ribbands, and the use of the word 'you' to a single person [which] are such prominent traits of worldly fashions." And in 1826 we find a very curious minute in the journal of North Carolina Yearly Meeting: "On the subject of our deviations from plainness in dress and address, through the medium of an epistle from the yearly meeting of Indiana, we have received a very solemn message from the Indian Shawnee nation informing [us] that during a council which had lately been held amongst them, while they were under deep concern on account of the many deviations from their ancient simplicity, and were laboring to reform their people, they likewise felt a concern for our society generally on the same account; stating that in former days, they knew us from the people of the world, by the simplicity of our appearance, which in times of war, had been a preservation to us; but they have to lament that now there are many amongst us, whom they know not, by reason of their departure from our ancient plainness."

The struggle for plainness reached its climax in 1829, when the monthly meetings were instructed to continue "their labors in love with those that have artificial grave-stones in our grave yards, to have the same removed."[1] The Quakers condemned the fashions and frivolities of society in others, but there were manners and customs among themselves which they nursed as carefully and as persistently as the veriest devotee of the gay world, and in seeking after plainness of speech and simplicity of dress it sometimes happened that the Society strained at a gnat while its members were swallowing a camel.[2]

But notwithstanding some weaknesses, there was in the Society, along with a vigilant care for political interests, for which their thorough organization made them better prepared, a deep and genuine piety, a tender love for souls, a deep sympathy with the erring, a watchful regard for the morals of the Society, and a strict determination to bring all misdemeanors to account. Friends were regularly appointed to examine into and to report on the state of the Society. Did a member neglect to attend on the means of grace, or was he guilty of "disorderly walking," he was

[1] This is no doubt explained in part by the fact that Friends do not believe in the resurrection of the body. But they have not been slow in cherishing the memory of their dead in other ways, as their extensive memorial literature bears witness.

[2] This becomes evident when we take into consideration the large number of men who voluntarily confessed to the monthly meeting that they had had improper relations with their wives before marriage. It sometimes happened that the women first came forward to make confession. We find from time to time in the records of Southern Friends an entry of this kind : " —— —— offered a paper condemning his conduct in having carnal knowledge of her that is now his wife before marriage which was read and received." This epidemic of looseness reminds us of a similar state of affairs in colonial Massachusetts, 1761–1775. Here the abbreviations "C. F." —confessed to fornication—were well known in the records, and Mr. Charles Francis Adams, in discussing the subject (*Proceedings* Mass. Hist. Society, 1891), finds the compelling cause of confession to be " the parents' desire to secure baptism for their offspring during a period when baptism was believed to be essential to salvation, with the Calvinistic hell as an alternative." In the case of Friends we have found no compelling cause except a literal interpretation of the scriptural passage.

exhorted in a brotherly way, lest the "enemy might draw and vail his understanding and bring darkness over his understanding." And had two Friends quarreled, they expressed the idea in Anglo-Saxon terseness: "the Devil who is our Great Enemie has crept in between said" Friends.

The disposition of Quakers to segregate themselves from the people among whom they lived tended to make them distinctively an *imperium in imperio*. This distinction and separation was brought out by their dress, speech, religious services, marriage ceremony, opposition to oaths, and particularly by their position with reference to courts of law. Friends might go to law with one who had been disowned, but to take a Friend into court required first the agreement of the meeting, and, in case of disobedience, the Society did more than rebuke; it sometimes required a disorderly member to "bring a paper of his condemnation to the next monthly meeting, and also publish it at the court-house door in full of all he hath done." The Society did not hesitate to enforce its dictum, "swear not at all," even if it was necessary to disown the refractory member.

Some of the members were men of distinction in the Society at large; they wrote and received letters from Friends abroad. Perhaps the first North Carolinian to go on a religious visit to other parts was Gabriel Newby, who went to Pennsylvania and the Jerseys in 1701. He went again in 1715. Matthew Pritchett, also of North Carolina, was with him.[1] James Bates, a public Friend of Virginia, visited England and Ireland about 1717.[2]

Henry White, of North Carolina, "was a minister of the gospel and a faithful Friend, whose christian conduct and loving behavior towards the Indians, who were numerous in these parts at that time, was such, as we have been credibly informed, not only procured him great esteem and respect from them, but for his sake they showed great love and tenderness towards others in the infant settlement of these

---

[1] Bowden, II., 232.   [2] Chalkley's *Journal*, 192.

parts. He dwelt in Pasquotank County, and died 3d of 8th month, 1712, aged about seventy seven years."[1]

Daniel Akehurst, a public Friend who came over to North Carolina in 1681 as the deputy of John Archdale, has been mentioned already. Joseph Glaister was another Carolina Friend who was well known. He was a native of Cumberland, England, and was born there in 1673. He was converted in 1692, and at twenty-one began to preach. He traveled in England and Scotland, and in 1695 was in Ireland. He visited America, but returned to England; he was in Ireland in 1704,[2] and in the same year traveled with Chalkley on Long Island and in New England. He removed his family to America and settled in Pasquotank County, N. C., about 1709. He died there 31st of 11th month, 1718(19). His wife, Mary, died 5th of 6th month, 1740. He was a gifted man in the ministry and excellent in discipline and church affairs.[3]

William Matthews was a Virginia Friend of prominence. He was born in Stafford County, Va., in 1732, and much of his time was spent in religious labors. He visited most of the meetings in America, and spent several years in the work of the ministry in England, Ireland, Scotland and Wales.[4]

The Jordan, Ladd, Pleasants and Stabler families were prominent in the Society in Virginia and furnished several valuable ministers. Joseph Jordan (1695-1735) was born in Nansemond County, Va. He became a minister, labored in Virginia and the adjacent provinces, and visited most parts of England, Ireland and divers parts of Holland.[5]

Robert Jordan (1693-1742), the elder brother of Joseph, was also a man of much prominence in the Society. His first religious visit was to Maryland. He often traveled in Virginia and Carolina in the service of truth when young.

[1] *Collection of Memorials*, Phila., 1787, pp. 41, 42, from North Carolina Yearly Meeting.
[2] Wight's *Quakers in Ireland*, 353, 355.
[3] *MS. Records, and Memorials*, Philadelphia, 1787, 56-58.
[4] Janney, III., 398.
[5] *Memorials*, Phila., 1787, 99-102, from Virginia Yearly Meeting.

In 1722 he went to New England. He suffered for his testimony on account of militia laws and church rates. His experience with the latter will be given in a later chapter. In 1728 he embarked for Great Britain with Samuel Bownas; visited the meetings of Friends in England, Scotland, Wales and Ireland, then proceeded to Barbadoes, and returned to Virginia in 1730. In the same year he visited as far as eastward as Rhode Island. He removed to Philadelphia in 1732; was in Great Britain again in 1734, and within the next four years visited the Southern colonies, going as far as South Carolina and Georgia.[1]

Another valuable member of this family was Richard Jordan, born at Elizabeth, Norfolk County, Va., Dec. 19, 1756; died at Newton, N. J., Oct. 13, 1826. He was the son of Joseph and Patience Jordan, who were both Quakers and trained their children in this profession. They removed about 1768 to Northampton County, N. C., and settled in the Quaker community of Rich Square. Here young Richard was thrown more into the society of Friends than he had been in Virginia. He married and settled in North Carolina. He began to preach when about twenty-five years of age, and being interested in the manumission of slaves attended the sessions of the North Carolina Assembly several times between 1790 and 1797 in their behalf. His first travels were in North Carolina and Virginia on the same account. In 1797-98 he visited the meetings in Virginia, Maryland, and northwards as far as Massachusetts; he was absent on this journey eleven months; traveled 3,000 miles and reported good services. In 1799 he felt himself under a concern to pay a religious visit to Friends in Europe, and after again visiting most of the meetings in North Carolina, Virginia, Maryland and Pennsylvania on his way, sailed from New York in March, 1800. He traveled in England, Scotland, Wales and Ireland; crossed to the Continent, traveled in Germany, and went by land to

---

[1] *Memorials*, pp. 109-118.

Holland, to what is now Belgium, and through France, returning to England via Bordeaux. He reports that they
were everywhere treated with a courteous consideration.
" Thus it often appears to me that we make our way better
in the minds of people, when we keep strictly to our religious
profession, in all countries and amongst all sorts of persons." He landed in Philadelphia on his return, October 28,
1802, and writes: " I was from home on this journey three
years, one month and ten days, in which time I traveled by
land and water, about 15,000 miles." He continued the
work of a traveling minister, and writes in 1807: " I have
now attended all the yearly meetings for discipline in the
world, and some of them several times over." In 1804 he
removed with his family from North Carolina to Hartford,
Conn., and in 1809 removed to Newton, N. J., where he
died. His journal is largely in the form of a diary, and
shows all the marks of the Quaker character, naïve, simple,
but highly figurative, with a certain flavor of self-conceit.[1]

A prominent Friend in the early history of Tennessee was
Isaac Hammer. He was born near Philadelphia, April 8,
1769. His parents removed with him to Tennessee about
1783. He was at first a Methodist preacher, then a Dunk-
ard preacher, but became a Quaker about 1808. He visited
Ohio in 1811; traveled within the limits of North Carolina
and Virginia Yearly Meetings in 1816, including the weaker
meetings in South Carolina and the older meetings in Virginia. He was in Virginia, Maryland and Pennsylvania in
1818; visited Ohio and Indiana in 1821, New York and New
England, 1822. In 1826-27 he visited England, Holland,
Westphalia, Würtemberg, Austria, Baden, Switzerland and
France. After returning to America he renewed his travels

---

[1] It is printed in *Friends' Library*, XIII., Philadelphia, 1849, pp.
292-349. A separate edition is as follows: A Journal of the Life
and Religious Labours of Richard Jordan, a Minister of the Gospel
in the Society of Friends, late of Newton, in Gloucester County,
New Jersey [three lines quotation] Philadelphia, Thomas Kite,
1829, 12mo, pp. 172. See also a biographical memoir published in
Philadelphia, 1827.

and died in Tennessee, Oct. 14, 1835. He has left a manuscript journal, which is preserved among the archives of the
Society at Guilford College.

William Hunt was born in Pennsylvania about 1733. His
parents removed to Guilford County, N. C. His maturer
years were spent in North Carolina. His travels in the service of the gospel began at twenty; he visited all the American provinces and nearly all the meetings they contained.
His first travels were probably, and his second were certainly, in Virginia and North Carolina. In 1755 he visited
the settlements of Friends in South Carolina. These were
scattered and required him from time to time to spend a
night in the woods. In 1761 he left home in company with
Bowater Beales to visit Friends in Virginia, Maryland, Pennsylvania and New Jersey, and six years later we find him
again visiting these provinces and extending his work still
farther into New York and New England, his companion
on the former part of the journey being Zachariah Dicks,
from the same section of North Carolina. They went as far
east as the present State of Maine. He was again in New
England in 1768. In 1770, in company with Thomas Thornburgh, his nephew, he visited Europe. They set out from
New Garden in November, 1770; visited the meetings in
eastern North Carolina, again visited meetings as far north
as Massachusetts, and set sail from Philadelphia in May,
1771. He visited meetings in England and Scotland, went
to Dublin and passed into Holland. On his return from the
Continent he was taken with smallpox and died at Newcastle-upon-Tyne, September 9, 1772. He was a cousin of
John Woolman. Like him, he was deeply interested in the
negro and much opposed to slavery.[1]

Nathan Hunt was the son of William Hunt, and was born
within the verge of New Garden Monthly Meeting, Guilford

---

[1] *Memoirs* of William Hunt by Enoch Lewis, based on his journals
and letters. In the sketch of Hunt given in Janney, III., 326-327,
it is stated that he was born on Monocacy, Frederick County, Maryland. This is not at all improbable.

County, N. C., October 26, 1758. He married at twenty, but did not become a minister until 1792. The next four years were spent in ministrations among the local meetings. His first extended visit was to the meetings in South Carolina and Georgia in 1797. The next year he visited meetings in Tennessee, and in 1798 the Northern and Eastern States. The next few years were spent in work at home; in 1804 and 1805 he was again in the Northern, Eastern and Middle States, and again in 1810 and 1811, when he visited some Indian tribes in Canada. He visited England, Scotland and Ireland in 1820-21. He extended his visits to the newer meetings in Ohio and Indiana in 1832, and from this time was able to travel little. He died at Centre, Guilford County, N. C., August 8, 1853. He was an ardent admirer of proper and useful education and was liberal in the support of schools. He took a deep interest from the first in the establishment and maintenance of the New Garden Boarding School, which has since become Guilford College. Like the most of his contemporaries in pre-revolutionary North Carolina, the principal part of the learning he had was obtained by the light of a pine-knot on the hearth after the day's work was done.[1]

Unfortunately we know very little of Jeremiah Hubbard. He was a contemporary of Nathan Hunt, and was born, I believe, in Caswell County, N. C. He was a minister of the Society and the most learned and eloquent of his generation. He was one-fourth Indian, and with two Cherokee chiefs visited President Jackson with the request that no spirituous liquors be sold in the Indian Territory. Jackson granted the request, and it afterwards proved the salvation of the Territory. As an educator Hubbard was second only to Dr. David Caldwell.[2] He had a school at New Garden, and was instrumental in founding the Boarding School there.

---

[1] *Brief Memoir* of Nathan Hunt: chiefly extracted from his journals and letters.
[2] See C. F. Tomlinson's article on N. C. Manumission Society, in *N. C. University Magazine*, XIV. (1894-95), 221-227.

A younger contemporary of Nathan Hunt and Jeremiah Hubbard, and one whose life connects the past with the present generation, was Nereus Mendenhall. He was born Aug. 14, 1819, and was descended from one of the oldest Quaker families in the New Garden section of North Carolina. He learned the printer's trade with Lyndon Swaim; was graduated at Haverford, and became principal of New Garden Boarding School. After taking the degree of M. D. at Jefferson College, Philadelphia, in 1845, he again taught in the Boarding School. He then became a civil engineer and was engaged on the survey of the North Carolina Railroad. He was an abolitionist, and was summoned before a justice for distributing Helper's *Impending Crisis.* He was connected with the Boarding School during the war and was a strong Union man. After its close he acted with the Conservatives; was twice in the State Legislature, and was Democratic candidate for superintendent of public instruction in 1872. He afterwards taught in the Penn Charter School of Philadelphia and at Haverford, where he also acted as superintendent. His last years were spent at New Garden, N. C., where he died, Oct. 29, 1893. He was a deep thinker and a man of weight and influence in that section of the State.[1]

The names given above are mostly those of ministers who traveled and preached. Some of them kept valuable journals. There are others who deserve notice for the literary work which they did. This work is very crude, and most of it is valueless to us, but it is doubtless as good as the similar productions of Friends and Puritans, and it shows (and this is the point of main interest to us) that Southern Friends, although far from the intellectual center of the Society, and laboring under many educational disadvantages, were not idle. And it probably represents a greater literary output during the eighteenth century than any other denomination in these States, with the possible exception of the Presbyterians. Nor were they indifferent to books in general.

---

[1] See sketch by Mrs. Mary Mendenhall Hobbs, in *Guilford Collegian.* VI., 57-68, 93-105 (1893), with portrait.

The Yearly Meetings of London and Philadelphia sent down
books and tracts from time to time to be distributed. In
1760 we have the complaint that Friends have been too
"careless and negligent" in dispensing these books. But
that this was not always the case is shown by the proposition to send to Europe for a quantity of Barclay's Apology.
In 1764 thirty-eight subscriptions for a new edition of Fox's
Journal, with Penn's Introduction, were given in North
Carolina.

The first committee to oversee the press—a Quaker *Index
Expurgatorius*—in North Carolina was appointed in 1755,
when it was advised "that no Friend or Friends, write, print
or publish any Book or writeing whatsoever tending to
raise Contention or Breech of Unity amongst Friends or that
have not first had the perusal & approbation of Such friends
as shall be appointed by this Meeting for that affair."
Samuel and James Newby, Thomas Nicholson, John and
Phineas Nixon, Josiah Bundy and Joseph Robinson were
appointed "to peruse all such Books & writeings as shall be
offered them." This committee was changed from time to
time, but was a regular part of Quaker economy. The tendency of this committee was to narrow the limits of thought,
to take away that wide freedom which the early Quaker
enjoyed, and to make a sect out of the Society.

South Carolina leads the list of writers on controversial
and religious subjects, and so far as I have learned there were
no other South Carolina Quaker authors. This one was
Sophia Hume (*c.* 1701-1774). She was a native of South
Carolina and a granddaughter of William Baily and Mary
Fisher. The latter was one of the first to preach Quakerism
in New England. Sophia was not reared a Friend, but was
convinced of Friends' principles and removed from South
Carolina to London. About 1747 she revisited South Carolina and traveled north to Philadelphia.[1] She was again in
South Carolina in 1767-68. She published: An Exhorta-

---

[1] *Piety Promoted*, Kendal's ed., IX., 15.

tion to the Inhabitants of the Province of South Carolina (Philadelphia, 1748; London, 1752, etc., 8°, pp. 152); An Epistle to the Inhabitants of South Carolina; containing Sundry Observations proper to be considered by every Porfessor of *Christianity* in general (London, 1754, 8°, pp. 114); A Short Appeal to Men and Women of Reason (Bristol, 1765, 8°, pp. 35, 1); A Caution to such as Observe Days and Times (London, 1766, 8°, pp. 39).

Another of these early authors was Thomas Nicholson, who was born in Perquimans County, N. C., about 1715. Fortunately his journal has come down to us in the original manuscript. It is not a continuous record of his life, but is a narrative of the three principal journeys he made in the service of truth, and contains also some of his minor writings. His first trip was in 1746, and was made along with other Friends from Perquimans County to the Cape Fear section to settle things among Friends there. His words suggest that his committee might have been sent down to settle a monthly meeting at Carver's Creek. He also visited the meeting at Dunn's Creek and those about Newbern and in Carteret County. He says that Gov. Gabriel Johnston was " loving " to Friends and returned thanks for their visit to him.

But Thomas Nicholson's most important service was the trip which he made to England, 1749-51. He left home in May, 1749, and got back in January, 1751. Between July, 1749, and September, 1750, he was engaged in visiting the meetings in England. He rode on horseback during these journeys between 2,500 and 3,000 miles; he preached almost every day; visited most, if not all, of the meetings; was in all parts of the country, and his ministry was attended with many manifestations of the Spirit. He did not go into Wales, Scotland or Ireland. While in London he visited Lord Granville, who still retained large landed interests in North Carolina. At their parting Lord Granville expressed his good wishes for him and for Friends in America, saying he was pleased so many Friends were tenants under him.

Nicholson landed in Boston on his return home in December, 1750, and visited the meetings on his overland journey to the South.

In 1771 he was one of a committee to present a petition to the Assembly, and again visited the meetings in the vicinity of Newbern. He died, probably in Perquimans County, N. C., March 4, 1780. In 1782 we find that subscriptions were taken in the North Carolina meetings for the proposed publication of his journal. This was never done. The manuscript is in possession of Philadelphia Yearly Meeting.

His principal writings, so far as known, are: An Answer to the Layman's Treatise on Baptism (Williamsburg, Va., 1757, 8°); An Epistle to Friends in Great Britain (1762). In 1774 he presented to the Yearly Meeting a "small piece of MS." entitled "The Light upon the Candlestick." It was examined, approved and a committee appointed to assist in making it public.[1] He also presented a paper on "Liberty and Property." This was an argument in favor of altering the law in regard to the freeing of slaves. He was an ardent champion of emancipation. A committee was appointed to bring this paper to the attention of the members of Assembly. I do not know that it was ever printed.[2]

Another Quaker author was Barnaby Nixon, of Perquimans County, N. C. He was born about the first month, 1752. He led a life of self-denial, zeal and persevering integrity. He wholly declined the use of flesh as food. He advocated the manumission of slaves, and was engaged in the important struggle in their behalf in Perquimans and Pasquotank counties in 1777-78. He married Sarah Hunnicutt about 1778, and settled near Burleigh meeting, in Prince George County, Va. His interest in the negro continued, and about 1805 he made a serious address to the people of Virginia on slavery. He died, February 13, 1807.

---

[1] In the appendix to the second volume of Sewel's *History* there is a piece of this name. Were they the same?

[2] See some notes on his career, which had been prepared by John Pemberton (d. e. 1794), in *The Friend*, XVII., 1843-44, 404, 413; XVIII., 1844-45, 4, 13, 21. See also his MS. *Journal*.

A part of his manuscripts are still in possession of Baltimore Yearly Meeting. His published papers appeared post-humously: Extracts from the Manuscript Writings of Barnaby Nixon (Richmond, Va., 1814, sm. 8°); reprinted under the title Biographical and other Extracts from the Manuscript Writings of Barnaby Nixon (York, 1822, sm. 8°).

In 1807 Thomas Hollowell, of North Carolina, presented a "piece of MS." to the North Carolina Yearly Meeting, which was examined and passed upon; it was ordered that from 500 to 1,000 copies be printed. We do not know its character.[1]

Some efforts toward education were made by Friends in colonial North Carolina. It does not seem that they were extensive or long continued. The first difficulty to be overcome was the need of books. In 1743 North Carolina Friends in Perquimans and Pasquotank counties, "for the benefit of teaching young children and others," wished to send to Boston to have Fox's Primmers [*sic*] reprinted. Robert Wilson, Thomas Nicholson and Joseph Robinson were appointed a committee to edit the primers, *i. e.* "to Collect out of those primmers Such a part of them as shall be Suitable for young persons that are just entering upon Learning," and that each monthly meeting "raize a Sum of money According to each mans Liberallity for y[t] purpose." But these efforts met with small success.

Robert Pleasants, in a letter to Samuel Fothergill, mentions a scheme which was on foot to promote education in Virginia in 1759, but nothing came of it. The South River Monthly Meeting seems to have led in this work later. It reported progress in 1783, and in 1788 said that schools were set up as far as circumstances would allow. In 1784 it was the sense and judgment of the Yearly Meeting of Virginia "that Friends endeavor to have suitable schools, kept by

---

[1] I have purposely omitted from this list all men like Warner Mifflin, William Williams, Charles Osborn, Elijah Coffin, Levi Coffin, Elisha Bates, who, though born in these States, left them at an early age and did most of their work in other States. Samuel M. Janney has been mentioned elsewhere.

Friends under the inspection of fit persons chosen for the purpose." The first school opened under the Yearly Meeting plan, so far as I have been able to learn, was that of the Cedar Creek meeting in 1791. The proceedings of the Cedar Creek School Company have been preserved. The school seems to have prospered during 1791 and 1792. Then there was trouble in securing a proper teacher and in collecting subscriptions. In 1799 it was discontinued because of the small number of Friends' children in attendance and because the original intention of the school had not been fulfilled. In 1805 there was a school at Gravelly Hill under care of White Oak Swamp Monthly Meeting. It existed longer and seems to have been comparatively successful.

There was always considerable discussion concerning the education of the negro, and constant complaints appear in the records that it was "too much neglected," but this talk does not seem to have taken any practical form, and could hardly do so under the severe laws of the States against negro education.

CHAPTER VII.

QUAKERS AND THE ESTABLISHED CHURCH.

No religious denomination has stood out more unbend-ingly for the right of freedom of worship than the Society of Friends. Organized during the decline of Puritanism, they were made to feel the full weight of the royalist and ecclesi-astical reaction; persecuted all the time, they had never ceased to demand freedom of worship for themselves, and have seldom failed to recognize it as an inalienable right in others.

The American colonies partook of the civil and ecclesias-tical reaction that marks the close of the seventeenth and beginning of the eighteenth century. There had been an Establishment in Virginia for many years and the Church party was strong. From the records of Henrico County we find that the Virginians after the Revolution of 1688 took certain steps that look much like an effort to restrain the greater religious freedom of the Quakers, but which were in reality a military move and were intended to protect Vir-ginia from the spying of Frenchmen, with whom England was then at war. An order of the authorities of Henrico County in April, 1692,[1] after noting the danger of an incur-sion of the French into Pennsylvania, recites: "it being con-sidered that at ye frequent Meeting of ye Quakers in Several places in this Colony of their own appointing without ever acquainting the Governmt with ye same or doing what is required by" the Toleration Act, and noting also that "not only ye Inhabitants of this Colony, but those of Maryland, Pensilvania and other places are usually present By means whereof the French or Indians if possessed of Pensilvania have fitt opportunity of knowing the affairs of this their

---

[1] *Record Book* of Henrico County, p. 92.

Maties Governm^t or ordering them selves to do mischief accordingly for preventing whereof for ye future and to the end that the aforesaid Act of Parliament may be putt into Effective Execution, It is ordered that after publication thereof (wch all their Maties Justices of ye peace in their respective Counties in this Colony are required to Cause to be done at ye next Court to be held for their said Counties).

" That none of ye persons usually Called Quakers do presume to meet at any place whatso ever w^{th}out first doing & performing what by ye before recited Act of Parliament is required & commanded upon Penalty of being presented & suffering such pains & penalties as by ye said Act are to be inflicted on those who do not comply. And to the End the s^d Act may be duly performed all their ma^{ties} Justices of the Peace Sherr^{fs} & others their ma^{ties} officers whatsoever, are hereby required & Commanded to take *Care* that noe person or perssons whatever presume to doe an Act anything Contrary to ye true intent & meaning thereof. And it is further ordered, That if ye s^d prssons Called Quakers have performed what is required by ye aforesaid Act of Parliament any Stranger from any other Governm^t shall come among them they shall give an acct of every such prsson to ye next Justis of ye peace who is hereby ordered to cause ye s^d prsson to appear before them and to take his or their Examination under his or their hands to what place he or they belong whether going & when & of all things else, which may be for their ma^{ties} Service & forthwith return the same (if he see Case to ye R^t hon^{ble} Francis Nicholson Esq their ma^{ties} Lt Govern^r that such further orders may be had therein as shall be agreeable to the Law; and it is also ordered that if any prsson whatever shall receive by letter, or hear any strange news which may tend to ye disturbance of ye peace of this Governm^t that they doe presume to publish ye same but wth ye first Convenience repair to ye next Justice of ye peace & acquaint him therew^{th} who is to act therein according to law."

In accord with this new legal requirement we find that on October 12, 1692, "John Pleasants, in behalf of himself and other Quakers, did this day, in open court p'sent ye following Acc't of ye Quaker places of public meeting in this county, viz: At our Public Meeting House, p [per] Thomas Holmes [presumed to be the minister]; Att Mary Maddox's, a monthly meeting; Att John Pleasants'."[1] These as places of worship are directed to be committed to record as the act of Parliament enjoined.[2]

It does not appear that Friends in North Carolina registered their meeting-houses before 1758, and it never became a common practice there.

On April 1, 1700, the county court of Henrico, in answer to an order for information from Gov. Nicholson concerning the various bodies of religious Dissenters in the county, "how long they have been kept, how lycensed, how many and what persons resort thereto," etc., mention no Dissenters besides Quakers, and say there was one meeting-house in the county near Thomas Holmes', "to which place several persons deemed Quakers doe Resort upon Sunday & Thursday in Every week under pretence of Religious worship, but have no constant preacher. Except Mrs. Jane Pleasants (widow) whose qualification & Lycence we know not we are also informed that of late there have been monthly meetings,

---

[1] Pleasants was the ancestor of the Virginia family of that name. Some of its members are still Quakers. His will is dated Oct. 1, 1690: "I give, grant, and bequeath unto friends in these parts, called Quaquers—(which now are or hereafter may be) that small parcell of land by me purchased of Benjamin Hatcher, joyning upon Thos. Holmes' land, for a meeting house and burying place—with the meeting house now upon it, and ye land purchased aforesaid I doe give, devise, and bequeathe unto friends abovesaid called Quakers, for the worship and service of God forever."—Henrico County *Records*, 1688-1699, p. 154.

[2] Henrico County *Records*, 1688-1697, p. 353 ; see also R. A. Brock, in *Southern Historical Society Papers*, XIX., 129. Foote, *Sketches*, I., 51-52, says that Francis Makamie was the first Dissenter licensed in Virginia, 1699 ; but Dr. H. R. McIlwaine has recently shown that Josias Mackie was licensed to preach by Norfolk County Court, June 22, 1692. The Presbyterians thus antedate the Quakers by three months.

kept (by these persons deemed Quakers) at ye house of William Porter Junr in the County, and that several Wandering Strangers Come here as Preachers, and upon pretense of Religion, Resort to the two meeting places."

Their strength in Henrico can be better appreciated when we learn that as early as the 3d of March, 1700, it was agreed that John Pleasants build a new meeting-house, 30 x 70 feet, instead of repairing the old one.

There are no such prominent episodes in the history of the struggle of Quakerism against the Establishment in Virginia as we shall see further on enlivened the monotonous annals of the Carolinas. There are various reasons for this. The Establishment there was older, richer, stronger than in either of the Carolinas, and Quakers were always weak in Virginia in comparison with the numbers of the Established Church. In Virginia Quakers did not undertake to overthrow the Established Church as they did in North Carolina, but devoted their energies instead to securing such exemptions from the payment of tithes and military fines as were possible, in bearing testimony against these and in exhorting their members to be faithful.

As far as concerns Virginia, we have only to trace the church acts as they influenced the Friends to show what their position in regard to these acts was, what their sufferings were, and how their legal status was altered by the Bill of Rights and later legislation.

The law of 1663, although severe against Friends, had not always been enforced, as we have seen. It seems to have been left largely to the caprice of the high sheriff of the separate counties, whose duty it was to enforce it, and this was mild or severe according to the individual greed for the informer's share of the fines. In 1680 the Virginia Assembly passed an act prohibiting unlawful disturbances of divine worship " by words, or any other manner or means whatsoever," and any person who " shall there appear in any unseemly or indecent gesture" was to be put " under restraint during divine service." Such offenders were to be fined 200 pounds of tobacco and cask for the first offense, and for every subsequent offense the fine was fixed at 500 pounds of tobacco and cask.[1]

This law was aimed against what we have seen to have been a characteristic development of the seventeenth century. In Virginia it probably affected the Quakers more than any others, but as it was aimed at unjustifiable interference with regular worship, no exception can be taken to it.

In 1696 a new law for the support of the clergy of the Established Church was passed. It fixed their salary at 16,000 pounds of tobacco, besides their lawful perquisites; collectors were appointed in each district, who could levy by distress. The vestries were empowered to purchase glebes at the expense of the parish and to erect a convenient dwelling-house for the minister.[2]

It does not seem that the Toleration Act of William and Mary, passed May 24, 1689, received any formal statutory recognition in Virginia earlier than 1699, although Mr. Brock has shown that the Quakers had obtained practical recognition of their rights under it as early as 1692. In 1699 it was provided in a law "for the more effectual suppressing of blasphemy, swearing, cursing, drunkenness and Sabbath breaking,"[3] that all Protestant Dissenters, who were qualified according to the terms of the Toleration Act, were to be exempted from the penalty of 5s. or 50 pounds of tobacco inflicted by the Virginia law on all persons twenty-one years of age who "neglect or refuse to resort to their parish church or chapel once in two months to hear divine service upon the Sabbath day." But that this was toleration in name rather than in reality is pointed out clearly by Hening, who calls attention to the fact that "nothing could be more intolerant than to impose the penalties, by this act prescribed, for not repairing to church, and then to hold out the idea of exemption by compliance with the provisions of such

---

[1] Hening. II., 483.
[2] *Ibid.*, III., 151. This law, with various modifications, is the basis of all the Church legislation up to the Revolution.
[3] *Ibid.*, III., 168; see also 360, V., 226.

a law as the statute of 1 William and Mary, adopted by a
mere general reference, when not one person in a thousand
could possibly know its contents."

Friends were careful in both colonies to make their protest
against payment to the Establishment in any form. The
Virginia Yearly Meeting of 1707 issued exhortations to
members to be faithful in the testimony against tithes
" either for themselves or servants and that the monthly
meeting do deal with such offending persons in the power
of truth." They were equally careful that the record of their
sufferings be preserved. In the first month, 1701, George
Norsworthy, high sheriff of Nansemond County, had taken
by distress from Margaret Jordan 125 pounds of tobacco for
" priests dews," and the year before 530 pounds. Robert
Jordan had lost 200 pounds in 1700 for the same cause, and
300 more in 1702. There is a record of but 35 pounds
taken in 1703 and 179 in 1704. There is then a break until
1717.

The next law relating to the Establishment was passed in
1727.[1] It provided for the payment of the clergy, etc., but
there was no exemption for Dissenters. There was, however, a case in 1705 when the " French refugees, inhabiting
at the Manakin Town, and the parts adjacent," were exempted from the payment of " publick and county levys."
This exemption was to extend over a period of three years.[2]
But it is clear that it was not made on religious grounds, but
was for their " encouragement," and was more comprehensive than exemption from priest's dues.

In 1730 certain German Protestants living in Stafford
County were exempted from the payment of " parish levies."[3]
It is probable that this exemption was of the same sort as
that of the French refugees and was not especially religious
in character, because parish dues were used for other things
than church affairs. They went for the general expenses of
the parish, for the poor, etc.

---

[1] Hening, IV., 204.   [2] *Ibid.*, III., 478.   [3] *Ibid.*, IV., 306.

As early as 1701 the Yearly Meeting of Virginia ordered
" that every monthly meeting doe appoynt on friend or more
as nead may bee to goe to ye vestry at a sett time and thear
to endeavor to bee Informed what Tobb is levied on euery
Tithable in the parish for the Priests demands & Church
Rates so Called & soe to make Report of to the meeting
before the officers goe About to gather their demands that
such friends as Can not for Concience sake pay the Priests
dews & other Church demands may know what to keep back
on that acc^t."

There were cases of suffering because of this refusal. One
of the most noteworthy is that of Robert Jordan. He was
sued in the beginning of 1723 for priest's wages. He refused to comply with the demand, and offered to the magistrates in writing sundry considerations in his own defense.
This action was taken amiss; he was indicted by the grand
jury and summoned before the Governor and Council. He
pleaded in his own behalf that the case could not come up
for trial unless it was brought within three months of the
commission of the offense, and it had been seven months;
but the trial was continued nevertheless, and he was sentenced to a year's imprisonment, or bonds with security, etc.

" Being committed to prison, I was first placed in the
debtors' apartment, but in a few days was removed into the
common side, where condemned persons are kept, and for
some time had not the privilege of seeing anybody, except a
negro who once a day brought water to the prisoners; this
place was so dark that I could not see to read even at noon,
without creeping to small holes in the door; being also very
noisome, the infectious air brought on me the flux, that, had
not the Lord been pleased to sustain me by his invisible
hand, I had there lost my life; the governor was made acquainted with my condition, and I believe used his endeavors for my liberty: the commissary visited me more than
once under a show of friendship, but with a view to ensnare
me, and I was very weary of him. I wrote again to the governor, to acquaint him of my situation; for so after a con-

finement of three weeks. I was discharged, without any acknowledgment of compliance, and this brought me into an
acquaintance, and ready admittance to the governor, who
said I was a meek man," etc.

In 1725 "a malicious person getting into his possession
the judgment obtained against him for the demand of tithes
before mentioned, had seven of his cattle seized and ap-
praised, but deferred taking them away until about two years
after, when he procured a new action against him, alleging,
but not proving, that Robert had converted at least a part of
them to his own use, and so managed the matter in his absence as to make the debt amount to twenty pounds, tho'
the demand was but eight pounds, and serving the execution
on his body, he was again committed to prison in the twelfth
month, 1727, where being confined fifteen weeks, he was at
length discharged, without any person paying anything for
him, which he would not suffer."[1]

In 1739 Friends protest to the Governor and Assembly
against these forced payments. They claim for the members of their Society that they are mostly descendants of
early inhabitants, who have been subject to great losses in
"substance and employments by annual seizures and dis-
tresses made on our goods and persons, on the account of
parish levies." They asked to be relieved of this hardship,
and thought it was within the power of the authorities to do
this, as they had been "pleased to bestow the like favor on
sundry German protestants, by exempting them from parish
levies." They reminded them that in most British colonies
they are easy on this either by charter of privileges or
special laws, and pertinently add: for "we pay all taxes for
support of government. We transgress no laws of trade,
we keep back no part of the revenue due to the crown, the
publick are not charged in the least with our poor, and we
nevertheless willingly contribute to the public poor and en-
deavour to follow peace with all men."

[1] *Memorials*, Philadelphia, 1787. Bownas visited Jordan while
he was in prison and says, "We had a meeting in that prison to good
satisfaction, many people came to it and were very orderly."

This petition met with no favorable response, but Friends thought in 1742 that distress for tithes would cease, "for the men whose business it is to make distress on our goods seem to do it with great reluctance." They were to meet with disappointment. In 1748 a new Clergy bill was passed. It was based on and is essentially the same as that of 1727. Some sections are clearer and more direct. The collectors were now given power to distrain on "slaves, goods, and chattels" of the "person or persons chargeable therewith."[1] There is no provision for any class of Dissenters. We are to note also that Dissenters were strongest in those counties that did not produce good tobacco, for the clergy of the Established Church were paid in this, went to the counties where the best was grown, and left the poorer counties to Dissenters and others.

The act of 1748 was the last of the three Virginia acts having as their distinctive purpose the support of the clergy of the Established Church. The first had been passed in 1696, the second in 1727; the third lasted until the Revolution and the Declaration of Rights.

Quakers continued to suffer under its provisions. They have preserved a record of these. Unfortunately during some of these years the sufferings for "priest's wages" and "church rates" are not differentiated from militia fines, and for the years just prior to the Revolution the records are lost. We have the sufferings for the years 1737-55; these may be taken as an average of the sufferings. They were collected by distress; other parish levies were paid without hesitation.[2]

It does not appear that Friends were often imprisoned in Virginia because of their religion. Such had been the case in the early days of the colony, and occasionally this was re-

---

[1] Hening, VI., 88.

[2] Sufferings for "church rates," 1737-1755:—1737, £99 11s. 11d.; 1738, £47; 1739, £53 7s. 1d.; 1740, £78 10s. 6d.; 1741, £83 16s. 11d.; 1742, £54 10s. 10d.; 1743, £101 7s. 5d.; 1744, £50 4s.; 1745, £54 6s. 7d.; 1746, £34 4s. 7d.; 1747, £77 1s. 4½d., includes also militia fines; 1748, £76 18s.; 1750, £16 11s. 5d.; 1755, £43 19s., mostly church rates.

sorted to. Robert Pleasants mentioned a case in his *Letter Book* where Friends were imprisoned as late as 1773 for preaching. Unfortunately we have no particulars of this case. They were probably soon released, as we find no further mention.

The next step in the relations between the Society of Friends and the State in Virginia is the Bill of Rights adopted by the Virginia Convention on the 12th of June, 1776. Although the Quakers before this time had made repeated efforts to secure recognition from the Establishment and to escape from its requirements of church tithes, all their efforts had been unsuccessful. It was reserved for the trying days of the Revolution to snap asunder the bonds of Church and State, which in almost every age and country have been an evil and a retarding force in the development of each. It seems to be true, as Mr. William Wirt Henry has asserted in the *Papers of the American Historical Association* (II., 23), that at this time the absolute separation of Church and State, although claimed by different sects, had been allowed by no government in the world. To Virginia, then, belongs the great glory of the first recognition of the principle that all men have the right to worship God according to the dictates of their own conscience.

It does not appear that Virginia Quakers were very prominent in the struggle which led up to the adoption of the Bill of Rights. In fact, so far as the present writer knows, they exercised no influence further than a moral one. They were far too small to have much weight in a political way; their protests took only the form of patient suffering, and we may doubt the efficacy of this method. But Quakers began the fight; others then built upon the foundations which they had laid. Pre-eminently is this true of their career in North Carolina, and to a less extent in Virginia. It was through the efforts of Baptists and Presbyterians that the demand for freedom of religion took definite shape in Virginia. This demand was embodied in the sixteenth section of the Virginia Bill of Rights, of which Patrick Henry was the author.

" That religion, or the duty which we owe to our Creator, and the manner of discharging it, can be directed only by reason and conviction, not by force or violence, and therefore all men are equally entitled to the free exercise of religion, according to the dictates of conscience; and that it is the mutual duty of all to practice Christian forbearance, love, and charity towards each other." [1]

It appears that at first this was not judged sufficient, for it was a question whether the older acts were in force or not. In October, 1776, " that equal liberty, as well religious as civil, may be universally extended," it was enacted that all laws prescribing punishments for " maintaining any opinions in matters of religion, forbearing to repair to church or the exercising any mode of worship whatsoever," should be repealed. They were also exempted from " all levies, taxes, and impositions " toward supporting " the said church, as it now is or hereafter may be established, and its ministers." [2]

The language of this act indicates that the Legislature had not arrived at the conception of a complete divorce of Church and State. Jefferson says that at this time two-thirds of the Virginians were Dissenters, but the Church was not disestablished by it. The salaries of its clergymen, however, were suspended and cut off entirely in 1779. The question whether there should not be a general assessment laid on all for the support of pastors of their choice was reserved for future consideration. In 1785 we find the Yearly Meeting discussing a bill framed by the Assembly of October, 1784, entitled: A bill for establishing a provision for the

---

[1] Hening, IX., 112. The right of Virginia to priority in the matter of religious liberty has been disputed by Dr. Charles J. Stillé in the next volume of the *Papers of the American Historical Association* (III., 205–211). He argues that a Bill of Rights is not a law, or there would have been no necessity for the activity of Jefferson in this regard. But Mr. Henry replies to this (*Ibid.*, III., 457 *et seq.*) that the Bill of Rights was a law and was so interpreted by the Virginia Court of Appeals. The trouble was that the Virginia Legislature failed to recognize it as such. In theory religious liberty was complete, although the law-making body had not yet learned to adjust itself to new conditions.

[2] *Ibid.*, IX., 164, 312, 387, 469.

teaching of the Christian religion. It provided that Quakers
and all others might dispose of money collected from them
for religious purposes to any denomination they thought
proper. It was published to secure expressions of opinion.
Friends " signify their intire disapprobation of it; not only
as it would if passed into a law subject them into sufferings,
but (as they conceive) be an infringement of religious and
civil liberty established by the Bill of Rights, and tend to the
real disadvantage of the community at large." It failed to
pass.[1]

In the same year, 1784, Jefferson's famous bill for establishing religious freedom was introduced and championed
by Madison. It met with much opposition and was not
passed until the next year. In 1799 all laws for the benefit
of religious societies were repealed, and thus, after a struggle
of twenty-three years, the Church was disestablished.

The last phase of the quarrel of the Quakers with the Establishment in Virginia was in 1792, when they complained
about the employment of a paid chaplain for the Assembly
while in session. They sent one of their members up to the
Assembly with a formal protest. The Assembly replied that
they had too much work to attend to this and suggested that
the protest be renewed at the beginning of the next Assembly. Quakers got no relief, and for a number of years the
answer to one of their queries appears in the regular form
that no tithes had been paid except such as were paid out of
the public taxes to support a chaplain. They did not refuse
to pay the taxes on this account, satisfied themselves with
this protest, and after a few years the question disappears.[2]

The struggle for religious freedom was not waged by

---

[1] Presbyterians and Baptists also opposed it ; see Foote's *Sketches*,
I., 335-345.

[2] In contrast to the hostility which so frequently marks the relations between Quakers and the Episcopal Church, it is pleasing to
make note of two exceptions to the general rule at least. Stephen
Grellet records that in 1809 he preached in the Episcopal Church
in Petersburg after the rector had *insisted* that he do so. Henry
Hull held a meeting in the Episcopal Church in Winchester, Va., in
1799.

Friends in Virginia, but in North Carolina. It began in South Carolina in 1704. We cannot speak accurately as to the part played by Quakers there. It was probably small, for they do not seem to have ever been very numerous in South Carolina. But it is necessary for us to note the movement there, for it has its counterpart the next year in North Carolina, where Quakers were not only prominent, but the leading spirits, and throws much light upon those confused and harassing events.

Many of the inhabitants of South Carolina were Dissenters. The Act of Uniformity had driven many thither,[1] and promises of religious freedom had also served as an inducement to migration. The act of 1698, which settled a maintenance on a minister resident in Charleston, created neither suspicion nor alarm, for it referred to one man only and he was a worthy minister.[2] Blake and other prominent men were Dissenters and they at this time gave aid to the Establishment.[3] But there was a different view taken of the tendency of affairs in 1704. In that year the Dissenters had four churches in the colony. The Establishment had but one. In the revolution which followed we cannot claim that the Quakers played an important part, for they were not numerous. There were no considerable groups of new immigrants to South Carolina between 1696 and 1730. Ramsay estimates the population in 1704 at five or six thousand. In 1724 it was estimated at 14,000 whites. There were, perhaps, 10,000 in 1710; of these, 42.5 per cent were Episcopalians. The Presbyterians appeared in the province at an early date, and, including the French, represented 45 per cent. The Anabaptists had appeared about 1685 and had 10 per cent. The Quakers had only 2.5 per cent.[4]

The Quakers can claim, then, little part in the South Carolina uprising. This was mainly the work of the

---

[1] Rivers, in Winsor, *Nar. and Crit. Hist. of Amer.*, Vol. V.
[2] Ramsay, II., 3.
[3] Rivers. *Sketch of the History of South Carolina*, 216.
[4] Gov. Glen's *Account*, in Carroll, II., 248, 260.

Presbyterians and Baptists; but it is necessary to give a summary of the affair to understand the movement in North Carolina. Sir Nathaniel Johnson had been appointed Governor-General of Carolina in 1702, and, as usual, took up his residence in Charleston.

Lord John Granville was the Palatine. He was a bigoted Churchman, and instructed Sir Nathaniel to see that the Church of England was made the Church of Carolina. Johnson labored assiduously to accomplish the desires of the Palatine.[1] By dint of political trickery, some of it suggested by Lord Granville himself,[2] Johnson secured the passage of a law by the South Carolina Assembly, on May 6, 1704, which reproduced the essential principles of the Test Act of 1673. It required all members of the Assembly to subscribe to the act of 1678, which disabled the Papists; to take the oath of allegiance to Queen Anne; to receive the sacrament according to the rites and usages of the Church of England, or to swear and subscribe to an oath of conformity to the Church of England. A penalty of fifty pounds for the first time the representative sat and ten pounds for every day thereafter was inflicted on all who refused to conform to this act, because it "hath been found by experience that the admitting of persons of different persuasions and interests in matters of religion to sit and vote in the commons house of Assembly, hath often caused great contentions and animosities in this province, and hath very much obstructed the public business."[3] On November 4 of the same year the act was supplemented by a further act for "the Establishment of Religious Worship in this Province according to the Church of England, and for the Erecting of Churches for the Public Worship of God, and also for the Maintenance of Ministers

---

[1] Hawks, II., 504 ; Caruthers, *Life of David Caldwell*, 60.
[2] Hawks, II., 505. See also *Col. Rec.*, I., 639, 640. The General Assembly was chosen with "very great partiality and injustice." "This act was passed in an illegal manner by the Governor's calling the Assembly to meet the 26th of April, when it then stood prorogued to the 10th of May following."
[3] Act in *Col. Rec. of North Carolina*, II., 863-867.

and the Building Convenient Houses for them." [1] It established a commission of twenty laymen, which was given the
power, on the request of nine parishioners and a majority of
the vestry, to cite the minister or rector before them, hear
complaints against him, and if in their opinion the charges
were sustained, to remove him either by delivering such an
announcement into his hands, by leaving it at his home, or
by fixing it to the church doors.[2] Under the first of these
laws it is evident that Friends were disfranchised. "Some
of the Proprietors absolutely refused to join in the ratifica-
tion of these acts," [3] and in the meantime the Dissenters, including the Quakers we may reasonably suppose, drew up
a petition in which their grievances were recited, and forwarded it to the Proprietors by the hands of Joseph Boone.[4]
About the same time Edmund Porter, a Quaker, appeared
in England as the representative of the complaints and
grievances of the northern colony.[5]

Lord Granville, the Palatine, received the petition of his
subjects from the wilds of Carolina with haughty coldness.

---

[1] In *Col. Rec.*, II., 867–882.
[2] Secs. xv. and xvi., *Col. Rec.*, II., 873. 874. The acts were signed
by Granville, Carteret, Craven and Colleton.
[3] *Col. Rec.*, I., 635 *et seq.*
[4] Petition in *Col. Rec.*, I., 637 *et seq.*
[5] Martin, I., 219 ; Caruthers's *Caldwell*, 60 ; Hawks, II., 508. Dr.
Hawks says that Porter accompanied John Ash, who was sent to
England from South Carolina in 1703 to complain of the undue
election of an Assembly, of heavy taxes and impositions on trade
(*Col. Rec.*, II., 901 *et seq.*); but this could not have been the case.
The complaints which Ash carried are dated June 26, 1703, and his
published account of his mission was issued in the same year. This
was before the death of Walker, and consequently there had been
at that time no fresh disturbances in North Carolina. I have been
able to find no contemporary authority for the statement that
Edmund Porter was the man who went to England on this occasion,
but that such a messenger was sent there can be no doubt. Missionary Gordon, writing in 1709, says that about 1704 "the Quakers
sent complaints against Colonel Daniel." "In the year 1706 they
sent one Mr. John Porter to England, *with fresh grievances and new
complaints.*" (*Col. Rec.*, I., 709.) This view is sustained by De
Foe's Party-Tyranny; or, An Occasional Bill in Miniature : As now
Practiced in Carolina. London, 1705 ; reprinted in *Col. Rec.*, II.,
891 *et seq.* It is not improbable that Edmund Porter went over with
Boone.

It was pushed into the House of Lords. After hearing the complaint of the colonists, and the Proprietors through their counsel, the Lords spiritual and temporal declared that the law passed by the Legislature of South Carolina for the establishment of religious worship was "not warranted by the charter granted to the Proprietors of that colony, as being not consonant to reason, repugnant to reason, repugnant to the laws of this realm, and destructive to the constitution of the Church of England." They declared further that the act requiring all members of the Assembly to take the oath, subscribe to the declaration and conform in religious worship, "is founded upon falsity in matter of fact, is repugnant to the laws of England, contrary to the charter granted to the Proprietors of that colony, is an encouragement to atheism and irreligion, is destructive to trade, and tends to the depopulating and ruining the said province."[1] This was not all. On the tenth of June, 1706, the obnoxious laws were repealed by proclamation of the Queen, and the attorney-general was ordered to proceed against the Proprietors *in quo warranto* for a forfeiture of their charter.[2]

The first effort to put into active operation in North Carolina the theory of the Proprietors in regard to an Establishment was in 1701, when the Churchmen, by "a great deal of care and management," secured the passage of an act under which the province was divided into parishes, the erection of churches and the salary of the minister provided for. The Quakers were at this time the largest body of Dissenters in the province and the only organized one. They did not represent the wealth nor the intelligence of the colony, but had much influence. The Church party on this occasion seems to have caught them napping, but they collected their forces, elected a majority of the members of the next Assembly from their ranks, and were ready to repeal the vestry act of 1701 at the next session, but were spared this trouble by the Proprietors, who disallowed it. This ends the first struggle.

---

[1] *Col. Rec.*, I., 636, 637.   [2] *Ibid.*, I., 642, 643.

The second effort occurred while Daniel was Deputy Governor of North Carolina. Late in 1704, or early in 1705, a law, known as the " Vestry Act," was passed by the North Carolina Assembly by " one or two votes." No copy of the act has been preserved, and its loss has caused two views to be taken of the events of the next six years. Some think that no conformity was required. I examined the matter very carefully in my *Religious Development in the Province of North Carolina*, and while admitting fully the difficulty and complexity of the subject, I still hold to the view advanced in that paper, that the North Carolina act was substantially identical with the South Carolina acts of 1704, and by means of a test oath virtually disfranchised all Dissenters. Now it seems that at about the time the troubles caused by the Church Act were at their height, an act passed in the first year of Queen Anne, requiring an oath of allegiance to her and her heirs in the Protestant line, reached North Carolina. Daniel presented this oath to the Quakers, who refused, it is said, to take it because they swore not at all. They were thereupon dismissed from the Council, the Assembly and courts of justice; moreover, a law was made that no one should hold any office or place of trust without taking these oaths.[1] To complain against this new regulation seems to have been one of the duties of Edmund Porter, who was sent to England from North Carolina about this time, but it is self-evident that this did not represent the whole of his mission. It is probable also that the declaration of the House of Lords in regard to the religious acts in South Carolina was not without its good effect, for we find that the Proprietors, through the influence of Archdale,[1] who was opposed to this system of legislating religion into the colony, were prevailed on to remove Daniel from his overlordship in North Carolina and to appoint another deputy governor in his place. This was done in 1705,[2] and Thomas Cary was nominated as

---

[1] *Col. Rec.*, I., 709. *Cf.* also Hawks, II., 509.
[2] *Col. Rec.*, I., 709 ; Hawks, II., 440, 508.

the successor of Daniel. His appointment seems to have given satisfaction at first to the Dissenters generally. When he came into power the Quakers made fresh efforts to obtain offices and a majority of the seats in the Assembly;[1] but Cary, like Daniel, tendered them the oath of allegiance, which they again refused to take, and were again dismissed from the Council, the Assembly and the courts of justice. Cary procured, moreover, the enactment of a law by which any party who procured his own election or who sat and acted officially under any election without first taking the required oaths should forfeit five pounds for each offense.[2]

This law exasperated the Quakers and their allies, whom we may call the popular party. It seemed now that all their struggles for liberty were to become of no account, and that they were to be disfranchised by the man whose nomination they had sanctioned. They had wasted time and incurred expense in the struggle, and victory was too near in sight to be given up without another effort. In 1706 they sent John Porter as an agent to England, "with fresh grievances and new complaints."[3] Porter sympathized with but probably was not a member of the Society of Friends. He was successful in his efforts with the Proprietors. The authority of Governor Johnson was suspended; Cary was removed; several of the old deputies of the Proprietors were turned out of office; new appointments were made, and the power was given these deputies, who formed the Council of the chief magistrate, to choose a new President of the Council from among themselves and he was to act as Governor. Porter returned to North Carolina in October, 1707, and from his return the "Cary Rebellion" may be said to date.

The historians of North Carolina, taking the aristocratic Pollock as their guide, have been constant in their denunciations of the principles of Cary and his followers; with them they are rebels and indefensible. A more charitable view, that

---

[1] *Col. Rec.*, I., 709.   [2] *Ibid.*, I., 709; Hawks, II., 509.
[3] *Col. Rec.*, I., 709 *et seq.*

these men were struggling for political rights against the representatives of despotic power, has been recently advanced by Hon. William L. Saunders and Captain Samuel A. Ashe, and has been adopted by Hon. Kemp P. Battle; but the writer believes that the "rebellion" stands for more than a political struggle. It was the uprising of a free people against the attempt of foreign and domestic foes to saddle on them a church establishment with which they had no sympathy, and he has treated it as such. He does not believe it possible to explain the extent of the commotion on any other basis.

After Porter announced the instructions he had received from the Proprietors, a day was appointed on which the old officers were to be suspended and the new ones to be qualified; but before that day arrived Porter called the new deputies together, a majority of whom were Quakers, and had them choose William Glover as President of the Council. He thus became Governor of the province *ex officio*, and Cary was suspended as Daniel had been.[1] Glover was a Churchman, but the popular party seem to have thought him favorable to their interests, and his election was sanctioned by Col. Cary, Porter and other leaders.[2] It was believed that the hateful laws against which they had been struggling, *whatever the nature of these laws may have been*, would now be regarded as a dead letter, since the action of the Proprietors in removing Daniel and Cary, who had both undertaken to enforce them, was the plainest and most direct evidence that these laws were not intended for the province. It was not to be supposed that the Governors of the province would undertake to do more than was required of them by the Proprietors, or what was directly against the will of the Proprietors, as the enforcement of the hateful acts and oaths was. Whatever may have been the legal relations of the popular party to the Proprietors hitherto, they now appear not as rebels hindering the course of

---

[1] *Col. Rec.,* I., 709 *et seq.*   [2] *Ibid.,* I., 727.

law, but as patriots defending the rights granted them
by the Proprietors and the English government; while their
opponents could no longer pose as the representatives of
law and order, but had clearly become usurpers, tyrants and
autocrats, as far as they were able. It is no wonder, then,
that when Glover, like Daniel and Cary, tendered the popular party the ever present and ever hateful oaths, they, with
their leader Porter, turned against him. Porter gets the
old and the new deputies together, reverses the election of
Glover, strikes up a friendship with Cary, who had perhaps
promised to accede to their demands, and gets him chosen
President of the Council and therefore *ex-officio* Governor,
and all this by virtue of the very commission that had removed him from office.[1]

Just as was to be expected, Glover and his party refused
to recognize Cary as Governor; but the popular party did
not cease their efforts, and the result was that the colony
enjoyed for a while the tender mercies of rival governments.
In this struggle the popular party is not so clearly in the
wrong as some historians of the State, most notably Dr.
Hawks,[2] would have us believe. He says that Cary's second
election was accomplished by men who were unqualified for
the duty, the old deputies having been suspended and the
new ones unsworn; but Dr. Hawks forgets that Glover had
been elected by the new deputies before they had been
sworn; his election was therefore illegal and void and Cary
was still Governor *de jure*. The truth is that John Porter
was the cleverest politician in all colonial North Carolina.
He outwitted the Church party so completely on this occasion that its defenders are still unable to comprehend his
policy. The pretended election of Glover was simply intended by the astute politician as a feeler to indicate the true
position of the two aspirants for gubernatorial honors toward the great question of the day, the test oaths. No one
knew better than Porter that under the circumstances the

[1] *Col. Rec.*, I., 709 *et seq.*   [2] *History of North Carolina*, II., 510.

election of Glover was null and void. He soon discovered that Glover was not the friend of the popular party. Cary probably promised to respect their wishes if allowed to retain his office; this promise was accepted and the last instructions of the Proprietors were ignored.

The double government continued during 1708. The matter was finally referred to an Assembly, the Cary or popular party won, were recognized by the Proprietors and continued to hold sway until the arrival of Hyde as Governor in the summer of 1710. It is no doubt true that Cary and the Quakers fell into errors and committed blunders that are not to be defended. There was a reaction in 1710 in favor of the Establishment, and the Assembly of 1711 passed various offensive laws, among them one, evidently aimed at the Quakers, which fined every officer 100 pounds who refused to qualify himself "according to the strictness of the laws of Great Britain now in force."

The hostility to Cary was so great that he was driven into active rebellion. He collected a company of men and made an effort to capture Governor Hyde. The uprising was put down in July, 1711.

This period of civil discord has been frequently called a " Quaker rebellion," and writers on the history of the colony, notably Dr. Hawks, have accused the Quakers of all sorts of crimes, from furnishing Cary and his followers with arms and ammunition from England, to inciting the Tuscaroras to murder the whites. It has been said, and has been generally believed, that the Quakers were prominent in the appeal to arms.

It is clear that Quakers took an important part in the first half of the struggle. They were fighting the Establishment and most probably a test oath at the same time. There was certainly more at stake than the simple oath of allegiance, for this would suffice to draw neither other Protestant Dissenters nor Churchmen to their side. Their actions in this part of the struggle seem to have been perfectly legitimate, but they were sometimes unnecessarily harsh. When we

come to the second outbreak under Cary in 1710-11 we find
some actions that are blameworthy and not in accord with
their well-established principles. There are two parts to the
quarrel: the first was waged in the arena of politics: the
second was tried with the sword. In the first, Quakers had
a large share, but I am coming more and more to the
opinion that they had little to do with the second part. Of
the few names coming down to us of individuals who took a
hand in 1710-11, few Quaker names are found except that
of Emmanuel Lowe, the son-in-law of Archdale. Cary was
also a son-in-law of Archdale, but we do not know that he
was a Quaker. I have recently discovered from the records
of the Quakers that they brought Lowe to trial for his part
in the uprising. The Yearly Meeting of 1711 appointed a
committee to examine into the action of Lowe " in stirring
up a parcell of men in Arms and going to Pamlico, And
from There to Chowan In a Barkentine with men And Force
of Arms Contrary to our holy Principles." Lowe was not
only tried, but was deposed from his position as a member
of the executive committee of the Yearly Meeting and
another was chosen to fill his place, " the said Low having
acted divers things contrary to our ways and principles."[1]

Now, if Lowe, one of their most prominent men, was
tried, it follows that the lesser offenders would have been
tried likewise; but there is no provision for such trial. The
conclusion is that the Quakers, as an organization, had nothing to do with this part of the movement, but that they
continued steadfast in their testimony against war. They
refused during the next four years to take part in the Indian
war, and this discovery relieves them of the inconsistency of
bearing arms at one time and refusing at another, and agrees
with the statement of Pollock that they became good citizens
when left to themselves.

___

[1] See *Minutes of Meeting for Sufferings.* January 26, 1713, the
Proprietors ordered the President of North Carolina to restore to
Lowe a barkentine which had been seized and condemned. I pre-
sume that this was the vessel in which Cary sailed to capture Hyde.

There were no more religious rebellions in these provinces. The Quakers maintained steadily their testimony against tithes and a hireling ministry until the Revolution, when the Establishment was overthrown; but as that time drew nearer their influence became relatively weaker, and the work of resistance to the State Church passed from Friends to the Presbyterian and other stronger denominations.

Quakers, like other Dissenters, suffered in all of these provinces under the law which made the Church of England the Established Church and gave it a tithe for its support. But in no other body, perhaps, do we see as much of that thirst for the martyr's crown which characterized to such a large extent the lives and actions of the early Christians. In 1696 we find one of the regulations for the guidance of North Carolina Friends advising: " That all Friends suffering for truth's sake be kept upon record, and the names of those who takes away their goods, and the names of him for whom they are taken, with the day of the month and year be set down." This was renewed in 1723 and again in 1756.

That the Quakers kept up their testimony steadily is evident from the small amounts the Churchmen were able to collect out of them in North Carolina. In 1726 Friends in Perquimans complain of unlawful distraint, and report the case to the Meeting for Sufferings in London. In 1755 a remissness was found in some who did not keep up the " ancient and christian testimony against tithes and priests' wages," and a committee was appointed whose duty it was " to take the opportunity with some of the vestry so as to inform themselves on what account the levies are laid, before the time of the same, in order to prevent the like hereafter." Sufferings in 1756, chiefly for the maintenance " of an hireling priest," £10 14s. 5d.; two years later it was £14 17s. 6d. for same cause. The next year there was " a shortness in some Friends in respect to a compliance with the payment of the demand to support a hireling ministry. Friends are recommended to be more careful, diligent,

watchful." Sufferings for tithes and "malissia" fines, 1759,
£85 and over; 1760, £23; 1761, "Friends have had no sufferings this year; part we believe is owing in a great measure
to the moderation of the officers." No sufferings in 1762,
nor in 1765; 1768, fines reported amounted to £5 4s., "being
for priests' wages and repairing of their houses called
churches." In 1772, no suffering, except 30s., "church
rates so-called"; none in 1773 or 1774.

In South Carolina the first Church act, passed in 1698,
the acts of 1704, which had caused such an uproar, and all
others then in force, were repealed in 1706 and a new one
enacted which remained in force until the Revolution. It
established the Church of England, making such minor provisions as are usual in such cases, and forbade all marriages
contrary to the established fashion. The Quakers were too
few to influence legislation; they report no sufferings to the
North Carolina Yearly Meeting, but it is more than probable that they suffered for tithes and muster fines as in other
colonies.[1]

The religious history of Georgia is very much like that of
the other colonies. The trustees of Georgia were very much
in accord with the Society for the Propagation of the Gospel,
and on March 17, 1758, an act was passed which established
the Church of England in the province. It remained until
the Revolution. There had been special favors shown the
Quakers in the charter as an inducement to settle, and, although under an Establishment, no complaints of hard
usage have come down to us.

Besides tithes, Virginia Quakers suffered under the laws
relating to marriage. So far as I have been able to find,
there were no provisions for them to celebrate the rites of
matrimony after their peculiar fashion before the law of 1780.
In this matter North Carolina was ahead of Virginia. But
we have the clearest evidence that they had married in their
own fashion from very early times. The Virginia law of

---

[1] Cooper's *Statutes at Large of South Carolina.* II., 281 *et seq.*

March, 1662, provided that all marriages should be by license or publication of banns and be performed by a minister, all others being declared illegal.[1] The laws of 1696 and 1705 provided that marriage should be celebrated only in accordance with forms in the Book of Common Prayer.[2] It was the same under the law of 1748.[3] The laws of 1780 and 1784 legalized marriages which had been celebrated previous to this date by Dissenters, and gave the Quakers authority to celebrate the rite after their own fashion.[4] This is substantially the history of the matter in North Carolina. They married after their own fashion, but without consent of the Government and therefore illegally, until the passage of the law of 1778. It was presumably the same in South Carolina and Georgia.

The first provision in any of these States in the matter of the oath was made in Virginia. Such provisions had been made in England in 7 and 8 William III., 1696-97, and in the Virginia act of October, 1705, for the establishment of a general court, provision was made that they be allowed to affirm and declare, as was provided for by the English act.[5] How they had fared in Virginia in previous years we can judge in part from the experience of Porter in 1663, when the oath was made the test of orthodoxy. Whether there were many cases under this law, or whether Virginia Friends refused to take it, as is probable, we are not informed. This antedated the North Carolina law of the same character by ten years. Under the North Carolina act of 1715 every Quaker who was "required upon any lawful occasion to take an oath in any case" was permitted to make his affirmation instead,[6] as follows: "I, A. B., do declare in the presence of God, the

---

[1] Hening. II., 49.　　[2] *Ibid.*, III., 149, 441.　　[3] *Ibid.*, VI., 81.
[4] *Ibid.*, X., 361 ; XI., 504.　　[5] *Ibid.*, III., 298 ; IV., 354.
[6] *Col. Rec.*, II., 884. This is in substance the same as the act of 7 and 8 William III., which was continued by 13 and 14 William III., chap 4, and was made perpetual by an act of 1 George I. But it is evident that the form of the affirmation was not satisfactory, for by 8 George I., chap. 6, 1721, the affirmation required was modified to : "I, A. B., do solemnly, sincerely and truly declare and affirm."

witness of the truth of what I say." It seems this was intended to meet all conditions, for the preamble recites that the oath was to be taken in "courts of justice *and other places.*" But it is added, "that no Quaker or reputed Quaker shall by virtue of this act be qualified or permitted to give evidence in any criminal causes, or to serve on any Jury, or bear any office or place of profit or trust in the government."[1] It was probably under this act that William Borden was not allowed to take his seat in the Assembly. In 1747 Borden appeared as a member of the Assembly duly elected from the county of Carteret. He informed the authorities that he was a Quaker and "therefore desired his solemn affirmation might be taken," which he evidently expected to be done. This affirmation a committee of the Council appointed to qualify the members of the Lower House refused to receive, and a new election for a successor to Borden was ordered.[2]

No reports were sent up to the Yearly Meeting on these matters from South Carolina and Georgia. In Georgia the matter was settled by the charter. In South Carolina Quakers enjoyed the right of affirmation in 1682. It is probable that some later law took the right from them. There is nothing in Cooper's *Statutes at Large of South Carolina* to indicate that they were enjoying the right in 1776.

---

[1] In 1741 a proposed new liberty of conscience act was defeated.
[2] *Col. Rec.*, IV., 855-857. We are constrained to ask what sort of an oath the Quaker had to take to attain these things and of what particular service this high-sounding act "for liberty of conscience" could be to him? Was this act a sort of plaything for exhibition only? Did the Quakers avail themselves of it? In Pennsylvania they refused to make the affirmation, which was simply the regular oath prescribed by the English government with a simple substitution of "affirm" for "swear."

CHAPTER VIII.

QUAKERS AND THEIR TESTIMONY AGAINST WAR.

I.—*Before the Revolution.*

Southern Quakers have been pretty uniform in their testimony against war. Their position met with small respect in any of these colonies. They refused to train and were fined. They refused to pay the fine and it was collected by distress or they were imprisoned. They were alike unmoved by distress or imprisonment. The officers were forced to abandon persecution by the firm meekness of the persecuted.

Friends were always careful to put their sufferings on record. Whatever else the Quaker might suffer, he could not bear for the shade of oblivion to come over the record of his testimonies. They seem to have suffered from militia laws at an earlier period in Virginia than in North Carolina. The first law that comes under our notice is the one of 1666, which recites that "divers refractory persons" have "refused to appeare upon the dayes of exercise and other times when required to attend upon the publique service," and then imposes on them for each neglect a fine of 100 pounds of tobacco.[1] The new militia act of 1705 [2] makes no exemption of Quakers. The fine was the same as before. It was collected by distress, or imprisonment was inflicted, and the records indicate that Friends suffered from the law.

The first trial of this kind in North Carolina dates from 1680. In the Culpeper rebellion in this colony in 1677, Friends first gave their allegiance to the government of Miller and Eastchurch. When the party of the people

---

[1] Hening, II., 246.　　　　[2] *Ibid.*, III., 335.

came into power, in accord with their well-known principles of non-resistance, they submitted to it; but declared
themselves a "separated people," and that they "stood
single from all the seditious actions" which had taken
place in Albemarle in 1677, 1678 and 1679.[1]

"Then some suffering fell upon friends which we not
finding in ye old Book, we thought good to insert here;
so that it may be seen generations to come," says the
chronicler, writing of the year 1680. "It was thus, the
government made a Law that all that would not bear arms
in ye Musterfield, should be at ye Pleasure of ye Court
fined, accordingly friends not bearing arms in ye field;
they had several friends before ye Court, and they fined
them he that had a good Estate a great sum & ye rest
according to their estates; and Cast them into prison, &
when they were in prison, they went & levied their fines
upon their estates; There were nine friends put in prison,
viz. William Bundy John Price, Jonⁿ Phelps James Hogg
John Thusstone Henry Prows Rich. Byer Sam¹ Hill
Steven Handcock. They were put in prison about ye
fourth or fifth month, 1680 and continued in about six
months."

This record of persecution comes to us from the manuscript records of the Society. It is a new one, and one
which the author is inclined to attribute entirely to the dis-
ordered state of the colony. The "rebellion" of Culpeper
was at an end, but its leaders were still the controllers of
the policy of the government, and the persecution may have
been due to vindictiveness against the publishers of the protest which we have noticed. This is borne out by the
fact that of the nine Friends imprisoned, the names of three,
perhaps of five, were signed to the protest. There seems
to have been no further persecution.

The North Carolina Quakers were prominent in the first
part of the "Cary Rebellion," 1705-07. This was a war

[1] *Col. Rec.*, I., 250-253.

of words only, and has been discussed in another chapter. They refused to fight in the Indian war of 1711-13. They steadily exhorted each other not to go to this war, and even punished such of their members as paid the five pound penalty attached to the refusal. As soon as the Government ceased to persecute them, they settled down to quiet and made good citizens.

North Carolina Quakers seem to have had a comparatively easy time. In theory they were under disadvantages from muster laws, but in reality they suffered little. · In 1740 they protest against the tax levied to provide a magazine for each county, for that would be "to wound" their tender conscience. In the same year they consult London Friends as to paying the tax levied in provisions to support troops. We do not know the answer. Committees were appointed from time to time to confer with the authorities on this and similar matters. They seem to have come to little conclusion. Muster fines, sometimes collected by distress, are reported at nearly every meeting, but they were small in amount, and the muster law, like the tithe law, seems to have been spasmodically enforced.

In Virginia, on the other hand, Friends had a harder road to travel. Fines were heavier and were more rigidly collected. As early as 1702 the Yearly Meeting recorded that "Friends are generally fined for not bearing arms and that grand oppression of priests wages, though the magistrates are pretty moderate at present and truth gains ground." In 1711 Governor Spotswood came in conflict with Friends over this testimony. He undertook to force assistance from them on the ground that otherwise the lazy and cowardly would plead conscience;[1] some Friends yielded so far as to assist in building forts. The sense of the Yearly Meeting was "that those Friends who have given away their Testimony, by hiring, paying, or working, to make any fort, or defence against enemies, do give

---

[1] Spotswood's *Letters*, I., 120.

from under their hands to the monthly meeting for the clearing the truth."

It is to be understood, of course, that there was no recognition or exemption of dissenting ministers in the military acts. The military law of 1705 exempted "ministers,"[1] while that of 1723 confined it to ministers of the Church of England.[2] This indicates that dissenting ministers had claimed exemption under the broader law, and that the Assembly was not willing to recognize them.

The act of November, 1738, exempted all Quakers from personal service, but required them to furnish a substitute,[3] or to be fined for neglect. This law, while seeming to be one looking toward recognition of the peculiar views of Friends, was not in reality such. To a society which condemns war and all its paraphernalia *in toto*, personal exemption can be no favor. It was no favor to a Quaker to allow him to send a substitute or pay a fine. In 1739 they record that their sufferings had been "very considerable." both on account of "militia and priests' wages," and are of the opinion that they "are likely to increase greatly on that account." In 1742 they say "the men in military power act toward us in several counties with as much lenity and forbearance as we can reasonably expect, as they are ministers of the law; tho in some places they are not so favourable," and Friends had been in prison for neglect of military duties during the visit of Bownas.

The year of the French and Indian war and the period just preceding it were times of great trial to Friends in this matter. The English settlers believed that French agents were trying to stir up the Indians, and that in the onslaught against English civilization the Indians would be led by Frenchmen, little more civilized or humane in their conduct of war than the savages themselves. To guard against this the Assembly of Virginia passed various acts in 1748, 1754, 1755, 1756, 1757, 1758, 1759, for raising

[1] Hening. III., 336.   [2] *Ibid.*, IV., 118.   [3] *Ibid.*, V., 16.

levies and recruits, for the better training of militia, and keeping them in readiness. The Assembly also undertook to increase the number of available troops, and, to fill the quotas of the militia, passed laws in May and August, 1755, requiring the members of the county militia who had no wives or children to stand a draft; but any person drafted might secure a substitute, or be released on the payment of ten pounds. If they refused they were imprisoned until they agreed to serve, to procure a substitute, or paid the fine. From time to time it voted various sums to be expended on these matters and on the better defense of the province.[1]

The tax, since it was laid for war purposes, was a source of trouble. But Friends generally complied in paying this tax without inquiring too closely into the way it was spent. English Friends wrote that this was their custom, and it was also the custom of the Pennsylvania Friends.[2] This caused some of the Friends who were not anxious to pose as martyrs to treat the fine for refusing to stand the draft or procure a substitute as a part of the general levy. This fine when paid also went for war purposes, but the Society as a whole denounced the practice and warned their members against it.

The act of August, 1755, did not exempt the Quakers.[3] An act of March, 1756,[4] provided that every twentieth man of the county militia should be drafted and sent to the frontier at Winchester under Col. Washington. This is followed by another for "better regulating and discipling the militia,"[5] which exempted ministers of the Church of

---

[1] Hening, IX., 112, 435 *et seq.*

[2] Applegarth's *Quakers in Pennsylvania*, J. H. U. *Studies* in Hist. and Pol. Science, X.

[3] Hening, VI., 521. The next act, for "the better regulating and training the militia," in prescribing accoutrements says "that every person so as aforesaid inlisted (except the people commonly called Quakers, free mulattoes, negroes and Indians)," etc., which indicates that they were not on the same footing as others, but that this did not mean exemption is shown clearly from their records. Nor are they included in the list of exempted persons mentioned in section three of the same act.

[4] Hening, VII., 9 *et seq.*   [5] *Ibid.*, VII., 93.

England, but no dissenting ministers. Nor were Quakers
mentioned in the section directing the accoutrements, as
was done in the similar act of August, 1755. They were
shown no favors, and the Yearly Meeting records of 1757
state that seven young men had already been carried to
the frontier. They asked advice of London Yearly Meeting
in the case. They exhorted the men thus tried to remain
faithful to their testimony, took up a collection for their
relief, and recorded that Friends were "pretty generally
faithful." In their epistle to London Yearly Meeting in
1757 they stated that those Friends were now released who
had been imprisoned the year before, that application had
been made to the Assembly about this requirement, and
that the officers now had a more favorable opinion of
Friends. This was probably the severest trial through
which Virginia Friends were called to go because of this
testimony.

The North Carolina Quakers also thought it necessary
for them to attend the courts-martial in 1758 and give the
reasons of Friends for not attending musters, and likewise
to send a petition to the Governor against the militia law,
but it does not appear that they were brought to trial on
these points during the French and Indian war.

In 1766 Virginia Quakers appointed a committee to petition the Assembly for relief from military fines, etc. This
petition may have had influence on the law passed in November, 1766.[1] By this law Quakers were exempted from
appearing at private or general musters, and were not required to provide a set of arms as all other exempts were.
So far the law is good; it is further provided that the chief
militia officer in each county should list all Quakers of
military age, and if needed, these would have to go into
actual service just as other persons, except that they might
furnish a substitute or pay a fine of ten pounds. But the
number of Quakers who were thus required to serve or
find substitutes was not to exceed the proportion the whole

[1] Hening, VIII., 241.

number of Quakers bore to the whole number of other militia. The law required also that no Quaker should be exempted from musters unless he produced a testimonial that he was a *bona fide* Quaker.

This law was a decided gain for the Quaker, although it was not a complete recognition of his position on war. It recognized this position absolutely in times of peace by exempting him from musters, and even gave him a privilege over other exempts by relieving him from the requirement to furnish a set of arms. But it failed him entirely in time of war. As early as 1755 an attempt had been made in North Carolina to get a law exempting Quakers, but it was opposed by the Council, who offered to substitute in place of the regular equipment of the soldier that of the pioneer—axe, spade, shovel or hoe.[1] This failed to become law; but by the terms of a special act, which is substantially a copy of the Virginia law of 1766, passed in 1770 for five years, Quakers were released from attendance on general or private musters, provided that they were regularly listed and served in the regular militia in case of insurrection or invasion.[2] From a petition which the Quakers presented to the Governor and the Assembly of North Carolina in October, 1771, we may conclude that Tryon had in some cases exempted them from the penalty of the laws. We find also certificates of unity given to some of their members, who were liable to military duty, in 1771. These certificates seem to have relieved them practically from all militia requirements.

At the beginning of the Revolution, Friends had been exempted from attending musters in Virginia and North Carolina, but not from being enrolled in the militia or from serving in case of insurrection. I have found no indications that Quakers had been exempted at this time from military laws in South Carolina and Georgia. They were too weak in both of these provinces to affect their legisla-

---

[1] *Col. Rec.*, V., 269, 291, 506, 538.
[2] Davis's *Revisal*, ed. 1773, 455 ; see also the acknowledgment of the Quakers in *Col. Rec.*, IX., 176.

tion. There had been some suffering in South Carolina on account of this testimony about the time of the Yemassee war in 1715.

Quakers kept a careful record of all the fines they suffered by distress or otherwise. These sufferings varied from year to year according to the personal feeling of the officers. They were heavier in Virginia than in North Carolina; only in 1759 do we find an entry in that State of sufferings amounting to £85 and over for tithes and "malissia" fines. The chief cause of suffering there was for tithes. In Virginia, on the other hand, the fines seem to have been about equally divided.[1]

There has been an extensive belief that Friends were active in the War of the Regulation in North Carolina in 1771. This belief is founded partly on the charge of Governor Tryon, that the Regulators were a faction of Baptists and Quakers who were trying to overthrow the Church of England. This charge, like the similar charge made by the aristocracy in North Carolina in 1705-11, is more easily made than proved. The Quakers are easily shown from their records not to have been Regulators. There were, of course, individual Quakers who took part in the Regulation; many more no doubt sympathized with the principles advocated; but no complicity with the events of 1766-71 was tolerated by the meetings in their organic capacity.

The foundation for this charge lies, no doubt, largely in the fact that Hermon Husband,[2] the leader of the Regu-

---

[1] They have recorded fines for neglect of military duty in Virginia as follows: 1740, £12 5s.; 1741, £34 11s. 5d.; 1742, £61 1s.; 1743, £131 8s. 1d.; 1744, £59 14s. 8d.; 1745, £10 9s. 2d.; 1746, £16 14s.; 1750, £4 11s. 6d.; 1757, £86 19s. 4½d., mostly military. From this time there is no distinction between "priests' wages" and militia fines. The sums are as follows: 1758, £98 13s. 5d.; 1759, £108 6s. 10d.; 1760, £90 14s.; 1761, £80 13s.; 1762, £103; 1763, £74 12s. 6d.; 1764, £113 11s. 10d.; 1765, £109; 1766, £133; 1767, £67; 1768, £3 5s.

[2] His Christian name was evidently pronounced "Harmon."

This autograph was kindly furnished by Mr. Jacob L. Husband, of Baltimore.

lators, had been a Quaker. He had been disowned by the Society, however, but not for immorality, as Governor Tryon states. Since no North Carolina Quaker is more widely known than Husband, it is desirable that we know as many facts as possible of his life. Hermon Husband was born October 3, 1724, in all probability in Cecil County, Md. His grandfather, William Husband, made a will, March 25, 1717. He writes himself as of "Sissil" County, Maryland; he had cattle, "Hoggs and sheape," and negroes, and speaks of "the Iron works that belongs to me." He had a good deal of land. William, the father of Hermon, was also of Cecil County. His will was probated March 10, 1768. He also had negroes, and was not a Quaker. His son Joseph,[1] born February 15, 1736(37), was the first of the family to turn Quaker. His convincement influenced Hermon among others. Hermon became a prominent man among the Quakers of East Nottingham, Md. He once got a certificate to visit Barbadoes. He was first in North Carolina about 1751, when he removed to Carver's Creek Monthly Meeting in Bladen County. How long he remained here we do not know, but on December 6, 1755, he presented a certificate of removal to Cane Creek Monthly Meeting. He returned from Cane Creek to Nottingham in 1759, and, on February 27, 1761, presented a certificate of removal from Cane Creek to West River Monthly Meeting, Md. He got a certificate to go back to Cane Creek, July 24, 1761, and on July 3, 1762, Friends report to Cane Creek that the marriage of Hermon Husband and Mary Pugh had been orderly.[2]

---

[1] See *Memorials of Deceased Friends*, Philadelphia, 1787.

[2] At this period Husband also set up some claims to authorship, as the following title will show: Some | Remarks | on | Religion, | With the Author's Experience in Pursuit thereof. | For the Consideration of all People; | Being the real Truth of what happened. | Simply delivered, without the Help of School-Words, or Dress | of Learning. | *Philadelphia:* | *Printed by William Bradford for the Author.* | M,DCC,LXI. Octavo, pp. 38. (Hildeburn's Issues of the Press in Pa.) The copy in Library Company of Philadelphia has the author's name noted on the title-page in the handwriting of Du Simitiere. At the end of the tract it is said to have been "written about the year 1750."

This year a commotion began in Cane Creek Monthly
Meeting which led to the disownment of Husband, the
suspension of others, and involved the monthly meeting,
the quarterly meeting, and even the Yearly Meeting, in a
religious wrangle. The origin of this trouble was as follows: In 1762, Rachel Wright, a member of Cane Creek
Monthly Meeting, committed some disorder. She offered
a paper condemning the same. This seems to have been
accepted, and in 1763 she asked for a certificate of removal to Fredericksburg, S. C. But some members of the
monthly meeting thought she was not sincere in the paper
offered and did not wish to give her the certificate. A
wrangle resulted, and the case was appealed to the quarterly meeting, which recommended that the certificate be
given. Husband, evidently a man who was accustomed
to speak fearlessly, was thereupon "guilty of making remarks on the actions and transactions" of the meeting; he
spoke "his mind," and was guilty of "publicly advertis-
ing the same"; for this he was disowned by Cane Creek
Monthly Meeting, January 7, 1764. But in the meantime
his party had grown, and a number of Friends signed a
paper in which they expressed dissatisfaction with the disowning of Husband. The quarterly meeting then appointed a committee to advise with the malcontents, of
whom the leaders were said to be Hermon Husband,
Joseph Maddock, Isaac Vernon, Thomas Branson, John
and William Marshill, and Jonathan Cell, "with divers
others." In February, 1764, the committee report "that
it would be of dangerous consequences to allow them the
privilege of active members, or to be made use of as such
in any of our meetings of business until suitable satisfaction
is made for their outgoings." Maddock, Cell and the Mar-
shills felt "uneasy and aggrieved with the proceedings and
judgement of this meeting," and filed notice of an appeal
to the Yearly Meeting. The Yearly Meeting decided that
Western Quarterly Meeting did wrong in granting a certificate to Rachel Wright, "if it was to be made a prece-

dent," and that the minute of the quarterly meeting which suspended from active membership those who had signed the other paper expressing dissatisfaction with the disowning of Hermon Husband should be reversed. The quarterly meeting thereupon acknowledged itself wrong in the matter of Rachel Wright; Fredericksburg Monthly Meeting was informed of the conditions surrounding the certificate, and the parties under ban were restored to active membership, for we find Joseph Maddock and William Marshill serving as representatives from Cane Creek Monthly Meeting to Western Quarterly Meeting in February, 1765. But this did not restore Husband. He had been formally disowned, and disappears from this time from the records of North Carolina Quakerism. It is probable that some of these discontented Friends were led by this trouble to join the Regulators. It does not appear that the trouble was healed, for we find that two men, Joseph Maddock and Jonathan Sell, laid the foundation of the Georgia settlement of Friends in 1770. They were no doubt the same as the persons who have just been mentioned. It is probable that they carried a considerable contingent of settlers with them from Cane Creek.

It is now time for us to return to Hermon Husband and the part taken by Friends in the War of the Regulation. Caruthers, who gives the traditions among the people who knew him, characterizes Husband as a man of superior mind, grave in deportment, somewhat taciturn, wary in conversation, but when excited, forcible and fluent in argument. He was a man of strict integrity and firm in his advocacy of the right. He had considerable property, and took the part of the people in their complaints against the extortions of the officers. He was a member of the Assembly in 1769 and 1770. . His participation in the Regulation movement brought the Government down on him, and he was imprisoned for more than fifty days, awaiting trial on charges on which the grand jury could not agree to return an indictment. He was also presented for riot under an *ex post facto* law, and was six times acquitted by juries in Craven and Orange counties of all offenses alleged against him. He was expelled from the Assembly, and after the battle of the Alamance, at which he was not present, was outlawed, and a reward of £100, or 1,000 acres of land, was offered for his arrest, dead or alive. He soon left North Carolina, returned to Pennsylvania, and became prominent in the Whiskey Rebellion in 1794.[1]

Husband's career was clearly inconsistent with the unwarlike creed of the Quakers. His intentions were probably good, but because he had been a Quaker, the Society has had the credit of being a leader in the movement that culminated in the battle of the Alamance on May 16, 1771. Without entering at all into the merits of that struggle, it is sufficient to say that Friends, as a body, had nothing to do with it, and in their official capacity condemned it to the fullest extent. A few extracts from their records will show this clearly. Cane Creek Meeting was in the center of the disturbance. The first mention we find of the troubles is in 1766, when seven members were disowned for attending a "disorderly meeting," probably one of the mass-meetings with which the country was then alive. In 1768 two Quakers were complained of for joining a body of persons to withdraw from the paying of the taxes. They were disowned. In 1769 Hermon Cox was disowned for joining the Regulators. In 1771 ·denials were published against Benjamin and James Underwood, Joshua Dixon, Isaac Cox, Samuel Cox and his two sons, Hermon and Samuel, James Matthews, John and Benjamin Hinshaw, William Graves, Nathan Farmer, Jesse Pugh, William Tanzy, John and William Williams, who all seem to have been Regulators. Thomas Pugh was also disowned for joining, and Humphrey Williams for aiding them. Three men were

---

[1] I find in the minutes of Western Quarterly Meeting in 1766 a notice of the disorderly marriage of "Amey Allin now Husbands." Was this a second wife of Hermon Husband? In May, 1788, William Husband was disowned by Cane Creek for fighting. Was he a son of Hermon?

disowned by New Garden Monthly Meeting for joining, and a fourth condemned himself in meeting for aiding " with a gun."

These are all the cases I have found that indicate the participation of the Quakers in the political and civil troubles of the day. They remained faithful to the Government. Governor Tryon made a requisition on them for twenty beeves and ten barrels of flour for his army. They agreed to furnish the things demanded, but pleaded that they could not do it within the limits of time set. In 1772 Friends asserted their loyalty and attachment to George III., and at the beginning of the Revolution the Yearly Meeting, in its letter to the Society in North Carolina, South Carolina, and Georgia, gave forth their " testimony against all Plotting, Conspiracies, and insurrections against the king and government whatsoever as works of darkness."

The Regulation, no doubt, had a bad effect on the Society in this section. The minutes of Cane Creek Monthly Meeting from January, 1770, to June, 1771, fill but two pages, as if outside matters were attracting their attention. There were, moreover, many removals and few arrivals at Cane Creek. These troubles caused, no doubt, a considerable exodus of Quakers to Bush River, S. C., and to Wrightsborough, Ga., just as they sent many members of the Sandy Creek Baptist Association from the same section to the banks of the Watauga in Eastern Tennessee.

2.—*Quakers in the Revolution.*

The Revolution begins the differentiation of the conduct and fortunes of the Society of Friends in Virginia and North Carolina. Their experience was different in each, and this experience seems to have had a marked influence on future action.

Their peace policy caused American Friends to be regarded by many as hostile to the cause of American independence. Some went to the Society to escape the war,

and some left it. Some of the younger generation broke
over the peace limit, organized themselves as "Free Quakers," entered the American Army, and were still maintaining their separate organization as late as 1798. In the
gloomy aspect of affairs which greeted them at the beginning of the struggle, Friends were induced to appoint representatives from New England, Virginia and North Carolina to attend the Philadelphia Yearly Meeting in 1776 to
consult on the condition of their affairs, and this course
was followed during the most of the war.[1] The war
brought much distress and suffering to Friends. In this
extremity the noble character of the creed of Friends stands
out in bold relief. Many thousand pounds were raised in
England to be applied to their aid. During the time of
actual hostilities this was applied mostly to Friends in New
England and the Carolinas.[2]

It does not appear that Friends during the Revolution
often acted inconsistently with their well known peace policy;
but this policy was a source of weakness to the American
cause and one of strength to Great Britain. Some Friends
refused to pay the State levies for war purposes, and, as the
Continental currency was issued to carry on war, many
refused to receive it. A minute to this effect was passed
by the Virginia Yearly Meeting. We are tempted to ask
how much of the religious and how much of the economic
element was present here? This action was unfortunate.
The result was to hasten the decline of the money and
to throw the influence of the Society on the side of the
British Government. In 1776 North Carolina Quakers declined to vote for delegates to attend the convention, but
left Friends to take the paper bills or not. In 1778 they
were in doubt whether they were able "to pay the taxes
demanded under the present unsettled state of affairs." In
1780 they refused to pay the tax in provisions. There was

[1] Bowden. II., 307.
[2] Bowden, II., 356. quoting epistles of Phila. Meeting for Sufferings and Gough MSS.

no general minute on part of American Friends forbidding
their members to receive the Continental currency, but the
Virginia Yearly Meeting made such an order. That they
were much more bitter and determined in the matter of
the tax in Virginia is shown by a letter of Robert Pleasants
to Thomas Nicholson in 1779, in which he argues against
the payment of the tax, blames the Eastern Quarter of
North Carolina for paying, and praises the Western Quarter for refusing to pay. This quarterly meeting also wrote
to Bush River Monthly Meeting to warn its members not
to meddle in politics, for it was learned that some had voted
for delegates to the convention.

But Friends were not spared when these States were
invaded. Between the requisitions of the Americans and
the thefts and robberies of the British and Tories, there
was small chance for them to escape serious damage.

As soon as the war was over Friends accepted the results. But they had never been blindly obedient to des-
potism. They had steadily resisted it in England; they
did the same in America. Believing, as they do, in
the common brotherhood of man, they have been of necessity democratic, and have been found in every question
on the side which sought to elevate the lower classes.
They were, then, logically and historically, on the side of
the colonists in the question at issue. They differed from
them in regard to the method that should be employed to
attain the end.

Their property was sometimes seized for the commis-
sariat, and Friends were sometimes arrested on the charge
of being unfriendly to the American cause. In August,
1777, certain papers containing a set of questions relating
to the American Army, and some other notes that might
assist the English, were found on Staten Island, N. J., by
General Sullivan and sent to Congress. This body re-
solved at once to arrest persons who were notoriously
inimical to American freedom, and directed that the records
and papers of the Meetings for Sufferings in the several

States be secured and transmitted to Congress. In September, 1777, twenty Quakers of Philadelphia were arrested by the Council of Pennsylvania on the charge of having given information to the British, and seventeen of them were hurried down to Winchester, Va., as prisoners of war. The original charges seem to have been utterly baseless, and the proceedings against them were arbitrary and unjust, for they were given no opportunity to defend themselves; they were refused a hearing, and the writ of *habeas corpus*, issued in their behalf by the Chief Justice of Pennsylvania, was disregarded. Further, they were forced to support themselves while thus involuntarily removed from their regular occupations, and the feelings of the community were poisoned against them. This injustice was all done on the basis of certain papers pretending to come from "Spanktown Yearly Meeting," which bear unmistakable evidence of being the work of one who was wholly ignorant of the phraseology peculiar to Quakers.

The history of the arrest had preceded the prisoners. "The inhabitants in this part of the country are," writes the county lieutenant of Frederick, "in general, much exasperated against the whole society of Quakers. The people were taught to suppose these people were Tories, and the leaders of the Quakers, and two more offensive stigmas, in their estimation, could not be fixed upon men; in short, they determined not to permit them to remain in Winchester, for fear of their holding a correspondence with the Friends of the adjoining counties." He says, further, that this sentiment was manufactured to keep them from holding such communication, and so strong was the feeling that on the day after their arrival, about thirty armed men collected at their lodgings and demanded their immediate removal. The question was settled for the time by the Quakers agreeing not to leave their house. But this feeling of fear and hostility soon subsided, the people became more friendly, and not only allowed them to remain, but administered to their comforts, granted them the freedom of the

surrounding section of country, and attended their meetings. They were released in April, 1778.[1]

But in the midst of war and war's alarms, Friends did not
forget their work of love. In February, 1778, Joshua
Brown of Pennsylvania and Achilles Douglass of Virginia
visited the meetings in Virginia, passed through North
Carolina, proceeded south, and were arrested at Ninety Six
in South Carolina. They were tendered the oath of allegiance to South Carolina, which they refused to take, and,
refusing also to give security in £10,000 to leave the State,
were imprisoned. But this was not grievous, for Friends
from a settlement twenty or thirty miles distant visited
them. They held meetings regularly, first in the prison
and then in the court-house; many persons attended, and
"ability was given to preach the gospel with acceptance."
From Ninety Six they were taken to Charleston; they were
not released, but were given liberty to visit the meeting at
Bush River, which had about one hundred and thirty
families connected with it. In October, 1778, they were
released by act of Assembly.[2]

Again, in 1781, Abel Thomas and Thomas Winston traveled through North Carolina and South Carolina into Georgia
on a religious visit. They passed through both armies. They
met with rough treatment at times, but were allowed to
go on. General Greene himself had been bred a Quaker
and wrote them: "I shall be happy if your ministry shall
contribute to the establishment of morality and brotherly
kindness among the people, than which no country wanted
it more."[3]

After the beginning of the Revolution the first matter
in Virginia that related in any way to the Quakers was
the first ordinance of Convention of July, 1775, which exempted "all clergymen and dissenting ministers" from serving in the militia. But no dissenting minister could avail

---

[1] Gilpin's *Exiles in Virginia.*
[2] Janney, III., 466-467; Cooper, IV., 452.
[3] *Journal* of Abel Thomas, in *Friends' Library*, XIII., 474-478.

himself of this privilege unless he had been "duly licensed by the general court, or the society to which he belongs."[1] This law met a part of the complaint of the Quakers; it recognized their religious standing and gave their ministers, and other dissenting ministers, the same legal exemption as had always been granted to the clergymen of the Church of England. This is the first step in the movement which led up to the sixteenth section of the Virginia Bill of Rights.

The act of May, 1776, seems to have been a sort of continuation of the act of 1766. It required Quakers and Menonists to be enlisted in the militia, but exempted them from attending musters.[2] The act of May, 1777, went backward. It makes no exception in their favor in regard to enrollment, mustering or drafting.[3] This was probably an oversight, for the new law of October, 1777, recruiting the Virginia regiments, discharges all Quakers and Menonists taken by draft from personal service, but provides that a number of substitutes, equal to the number thus discharged, be secured and paid for by a general levy on the Society as a whole, and this levy was to be collected by distress.[4] There was the same provision in the laws passed in 1780 and 1781.[5] We see in these laws an evident effort to recognize the peculiar views of Friends, but the need of their services is stronger and still keeps them under disabilities.

The law of May, 1782, relieved Quakers from personal service when drafted, imposing instead a penalty of fourteen pounds, which might be collected by distress.[6] The law of October, 1782, relieved them from personal service, but the county lieutenant was required to appoint a suitable person "to procure a substitute upon the best terms possible." This amount was to be collected from the property of the drafted Quaker; if he could not pay, from the Society.[7]

---

[1] Hening, IX., 28, 89.
[2] *Ibid.*, IX., 139.
[3] *Ibid.*, IX., 267 *et seq.*
[4] *Ibid.*, IX., 345.
[5] *Ibid.*, X., 261, 314, 334, 417.
[6] *Ibid.*, XI., 18.
[7] *Ibid.*, XI., 175.

Unfortunately we have very imperfect data for determining what the conduct of Virginia Friends was during this period. But we know that Friends were exhorted to be faithful and firm in their testimony; that a committee was appointed to consult with those who were under trial for their faith, to comfort and encourage them; that, following the lead of Pennsylvania, they refused in 1779 to pay the taxes for the support of the war.

North Carolina Quakers seem to have remained pretty faithful to their peace policy during the whole war, and carried it to the extreme of asking if it was lawful for them "to pay taxes demanded under the present unsettled state of affairs." But it does not appear that they ever went to the extreme of refusing to pay these taxes or to take the State issues of script; although Western Quarterly Meeting—the foreign element—declared in 1778 that Friends could not pay the war tax. The refusal of the Virginia Quakers, when in former wars they had paid their taxes without inquiring into their destination, at once caused them to play into the hands of England.

As we have seen in an earlier chapter, John Archdale, the Quaker Governor of the Carolinas, enforced the military law in South Carolina, but exempted Friends from its provisions. Under his administration they were exempted from all military requirements. After the arrival of Sir Nathaniel Johnson in 1702 their fortunes were changed. In 1703 a military law was passed which required that "all inhabitants" between sixteen and sixty should be armed and drilled. If persons refused they were subject to a fine of 10s. for the first offense and 20s. for each subsequent one. This could be collected by distress. Among the exempts were "ministers of the gospel,"[1] which term was changed to "the clergy" in 1747, and to "all licensed clergymen, belonging to any established church in this state," in 1778.[2] This law underwent various changes and modifications

---

[1] Cooper. IX., 617–621.   [2] *Ibid.*, IX.. 673.

from time to time, but these were matters of detail, not of principle. There is no recognition of Quakers in the laws passed during the Revolution. The penalty for neglect of military duty under the law of 1778 was £500; and Quakers, like others, must stand the draft.[1] So far as I have been able to learn, there was no deference at all paid to the peculiar views of the Quakers. I have not found any mention of the Society whatever in the South Carolina laws.

In the case of Georgia, Quakers report to the North Carolina Yearly Meeting that under the laws of the State, passed in 1777 and 1778, they were exempted from military service if properly reported. In 1775 they complain that they "have been misrepresented in their conduct respecting the said contest," and in 1780 complain of being "opprest by the violent behavior of the militia of these parts and been illegally deprived of both Liberty and Property." An account of the amount thus lost was to be secured and sent to the monthly meeting, and in the same year Quakers write to Georgia from New Garden, N. C., and exhort them to stand fast in their refusals to comply with requisitions and demands for war needs. But notwithstanding all exhortations, quite a number of Quakers in all of these three States enlisted in the American Army, while others carried arms for personal defense; some were disowned for these actions.

The North Carolina Quakers seem to have been more uniformly non-combatants. They had suffered somewhat from military fines in the colonial period. In the Revolution this became heavier. In 1778 they paid £1,213:9:2 in military fines, in 1779 it amounted to £2,152:5:10, and in 1780 to £841:15:7, "good money, silver dollars at eight shillings"; 1781, to £4,134 and upwards; 1782, £741; 1783, £718. In 1781 Western Quarterly Meeting reports £2,148 8s. and £675 18s. as the amounts taken from them by the American and British armies respectively. But that these forced drafts on the resources of the Quakers did not im-

[1] Cooper, IX., 674.

poverish them is evident from the fact that when Rich Square Monthly Meeting decided in 1781 to raise £40 in gold and silver, one man, Robert Peelle, agreed to advance the whole amount.

Another source of trouble to the Quakers in the Revolution was the oath of allegiance. This was provided for by the Virginia Assembly of May, 1777. The affirmation was allowed, in accord with the terms of the act of 1705, in lieu of the oath. Those who now refused to take the test were disarmed and compelled to attend musters without arms. They were further deprived of electoral privileges, could not hold office, sue for debts, serve as jurors, or buy lands, tenements or hereditaments.[1] But in none of the Southern States were they forbidden to teach school because of this refusal, as was done in Pennsylvania.[2]

The question came up before the Virginia Yearly Meeting of 1778. It was decided that " it would be proper for the Yearly Meeting to direct the quarterly and monthly meetings, to watch over, and caution their members not to join with or engage in any measures which may be carried on by war and bloodshed, or take any test that may bind them to join with either party whilst the contest subsists "; and if any have taken the tests, they are to be labored with to convince them of the inconsistency of their actions; if they persist and refuse to condemn their action, they are to be excluded from being active in the discipline, and are not to be appointed to any service in the Society.

North Carolina provided for an oath of allegiance in 1777 also.[3] This State also granted Quakers the affirmation. The penalty for refusing the oath was expulsion from the province. Like Virginia Friends, they declined, substantially, to take this test, but they expressed[4] their position in a much happier and more forcible style: " As we have always

---

[1] Hening, IX., 221. This law was repealed. May, 1783, Hening, XI., 252.
[2] Bowden, II., 332.   [3] Iredell's *Revisal*, 285.
[4] Letter to the Assembly in 1777.

declared that we believed it to be unlawful for us, to be
active in war, and fighting with carnal weapons, and as
we conceive that the proposed affirmation approves of the
present measures, which are carried on and supported by
military force, we cannot engage or join with either party
therein; being bound by our principles to believe that the
setting up and pulling down kings and governments, is
God's peculiar prerogative, for causes best known to himself; and that it is not our work or business to have any
hand or contrivance therein, nor to be busybodies in matters above our station; so that as we cannot be active either
for or against any power that is permitted, or set over us
in the above respects: We hope that you will consider our
principles a much stronger security to any state than any
test that can be required of us; as we now are and shall be
innocent and peaceable in our several stations and conditions under this present state;.and for conscience sake are
submissive to the laws, in whatever they may justly require,
or by peaceably suffering what is or may be inflicted upon
us, in matters for which we cannot be active for conscience
sake."

In 1778 it was decided to labor with those who took the
"affirmation of allegiance or fidelity," in love and tenderness; if they remained stubborn they were not to be considered active members.

We do not know that the letter of the law was ever used
against them. The Assembly seems to have granted them
some favors in the matter of the test, for in 1779 we find
them expressing their thanks to the Assembly, "and do
humbly request that you will be pleased to grant us the
privileges that we have hitherto enjoyed until proof be made
that our behavior manifests us to be unworthy thereof and
we hope our conduct will always demonstrate our gratitude."
They remained faithful to their testimony, however, and
concluded that they could not "consistently take any test
while things remain unsettled and still to be determined
by militia force."

In 1780 we find an act securing them their lands against various persons who sought to possess themselves of these on the plea that the Quakers under the law, if not sent out of the State, were deprived of the benefit and protection of the laws and disabled from prosecuting or defending any suit either in law or equity.[1] We may conclude then that in North Carolina they were released from the required test.

In 1783, "Friends taking under consideration a former minute of this meeting, which was a prohibition of taking any test to either of the powers while contending, do apprehend that the said order is not now in force, but that Friends are now at liberty either to take or refuse the said test according to the clear freedom of their own minds. And as the present form of affirmation prescribed by law is not easy and satisfactory to some friends, therefore the following form is agreed to in this meeting (to wit) I, A. B., do solemnly and sincerely declare and affirm that I will truly and faithfully demean myself as a peaceable subject of the independent state of North Carolina, and will be subject to the powers and authorities that are or may be established for the good government thereof not inconsistent with the constitution, either by yielding an active or a passive obedience thereto and that I will not abet or join the enemies of this state by any means, in any conspiracy whatsoever against the said state or the United States of America," and the same was established "with some small additions" by the Assembly of 1784.[2]

In South Carolina the test of allegiance, established by the Assembly in February, 1777, provided for affirmation instead of an oath.[3] Those who refused to take the oath were to be transported, and if they returned, were to suffer death as traitors. The severity of this law insured its defeat. In March, 1778, a new law for the enforcement of the test

---

[1] Iredell, 400.
[2] See Iredell, 505, 541, for the law as finally adopted for Quakers and others.
[3] Cooper, I., 135.

was passed, which imposed on those who refused to take
it the same disabilities as were imposed by the Virginia
statutes.[1] We have seen what the sentiment of the North
Carolina Yearly Meeting, to which the South Carolina meetings belonged, was on the question of allegiance. It is more
probable that the South Carolina Quakers, few as they were,
preferred to suffer under the law rather than sacrifice their
testimony.

In Georgia also Friends refused to take the oath of allegiance. I have found no references to them in this connection in the laws of this State. They had been permitted to
affirm as early as 1756.

3.—*After the Revolution.*

The question of the testimony against war becomes un-
important in North Carolina after the Revolution. It does
not appear that Quakers ever served in the American armies
in that State, that they took the oath of allegiance, or that
they suffered serious inconvenience from their refusal. On
the 29th of December, 1785, a new militia act was passed,
which exempted all Quakers from attendance on private or
general musters.[2] This clause was re-enacted in the new
militia law passed in 1786,[3] and with the enactment of this
law Quakers obtained all their demands in the matter of
military affairs. But it is probable that Friends suffered
more or less in North Carolina in the war of 1812. They
had renewed their testimony against military training in
1799. In 1813 they repeated their warning and prepared
a protest against the war tax, but it does not appear that
they refused to pay it.

The North Carolina law of 1786 remained substantially
unchanged until 1830. Chapter twenty-eight of the laws of
that year repealed the clause exempting Quakers and others
from bearing arms because of religious scruples. It pro-

---

[1] Cooper, I., 147, 148.   [2] Laws 1785, ch. I.   [3] Iredell, 591.

vided that such persons should be exempt on the annual payment of a fine of $2.50, which was to go to the literary fund. The Quakers expostulated against this law. They did not object to a tax for schools, but in this form it " is a groundless and an oppressive demand. It is a muster fine in disguise and violates the very principle which it seemed to respect." Public opinion forced the repeal of this law in 1832, and with this exception I have not found that Friends suffered in North Carolina from military laws from the Revolution to the Civil War.[1]

As already stated, I have been able to find the name Quaker nowhere in the exhaustive index to Cooper's *Statutes at Large of South Carolina.*

The Georgia military law of 1792 provided that Quakers should be exempted from service on producing a certificate from a Quaker meeting of their being *bona fide* Quakers and paying an extra tax of 25 per cent in addition to their general tax. This was re-enacted in the supplementary act of 1793.[2]

In these States Quakers seem to have remained, theoretically, under disabilities; but from the fact that they nowhere speak of sufferings to the North Carolina Yearly Meeting, we may conclude that these disabilities were in reality very small—that they were really suffered to go without performance of military duty.

Their experience in Virginia was by no means so pleasant. In that State they continued under disabilities longer. The law of May, 1784, exempted Quakers from attending private or general musters provided they produced testimonials showing their affiliation with the Society.[3] The law of October, 1785, renewed these privileges.[4] The new law of October, 1792, exempted all Quakers,[5] but the law of De-

---

[1] See Laws of 1803, ch. 18; Laws of 1830, ch. 28, and Laws of 1832, ch. 4. In 1829 Friends of Core Sound found that some of their members had been furnishing materials for " warlike fortifications now in building "—probably Fort Macon, N. C.
[2] R. and G. Watkins' *Revisal*, 467, 524.
[3] Hening, XI., 389. [4] *Ibid.*, XII., 24. [5] *Ibid.*, XIII., 343.

cember 2, 1793, exempted Quakers and Menonists only
on condition that they held certificates indicating that they
were regular members, and furnished "a substitute for
such service, to be approved of by the commanding officer
of the company."[1] The law of January 23, 1799, repealed
all earlier laws exempting Quakers and Menonists from
militia service.[2] But the law of February 4, 1806, provided that they were not to be fined for refusing to receive
public arms.[3]

In Virginia there were instances in 1814, and probably
in 1815, when Friends were fined and imprisoned for not
bearing arms, but the officers were said to be very friendly
to them, so far as the case would admit. About 1816 they
presented to the Legislature of Virginia a protest against
the then existing militia law, in which, and in an accom-
panying letter, Benjamin Bates presents a remarkably strong
plea for release from this species of discrimination. The edi-
tor of Niles's *Register*, which reprints on November 30,
1816, the petition and letter, says that it perhaps "forms
a body of the ablest arguments that have ever appeared in
defense of certain principles held by this people."[4] This
petition had, unfortunately, no effect. But there is no mention of Quakers in any way in the later codes of Virginia,
and we might conclude that the law was allowed to die by
non-enforcement. But such was not the case. In 1801 a
complaint was made in the Yearly Meeting that some
Friends were acting in a military capacity; in 1804 the
meeting directed that Friends make a report of their sufferings under the militia law. In 1821 the meeting discussed
the propriety of addressing the Legislature on the subject.
This was not done. We hear no more of sufferings after
they became a part of Baltimore Yearly Meeting.

---

[1] *Collections of Acts,* 1814, 436.
[2] *Ibid.,* 542.
[3] *Collection of Laws,* 1808, II., 109; see also act of Jan. 21, 1807,
which confirms this, *Ibid.,* II., 143.
[4] See also *Friends' Miscellany,* VII., and same in Niles's *Register,*
VII., 90, supplement.

To the hardness of the law of distress the officers added by taking more. The following sufferings were reported:

	Demanded.	Taken.
1807	$287.03	$378.16
1810	262.50	388.97
1811	170.59¼	405.65
1813		401.85
1814	111.50	180.30
1816	1,622.02	2,444.09
1817	61.86	69.00
1818	218.73	268.35
1819	126.75	160.75
1820	94.50	145.45
1823	185.69	247.47
1824	61.34	107.42
1825	106.11	167.77
1826	42.50	47.00
1827	80.25	109.40
1829	99.75	71.75
1830	66.00	78.30
1831	43.50	65.75
1832	99.00	104.12½
1833	59.25	100.55
1840	23.00	21.56
1841	64.25	32.25
1842	7.80	
1844	8.00	2.50

CHAPTER IX.

SOUTHERN QUAKERS AND SLAVERY.

"Stitch away, thou noble Fox," wrote Thomas Carlyle, "every prick of that little instrument is pricking into the heart of slavery and world worship and the mammon god."

If it be lawful for us to speak of men of destiny; if men are born to accomplish a certain purpose; if God in His wisdom raises up nations to a certain end, then this is true of institutions as well. The mission of Quakerism has been to the slave. In this struggle Quakers appealed to the universal conscience of mankind. Here they ceased to be propagandists of faith and became propagandists of action. They announced their opposition to the system when it had no other opponents, and they steadfastly maintained their testimony until its last traces were swept from the English-speaking world.

As early as 1675 William Edmundson wrote an epistle to Friends in Virginia, Maryland and other parts of America, in which he denounced the holding of slaves.[1] In 1693 George Keith published his testimony against slavery in a pamphlet having Bradford's imprint and the title: An exhortation and caution to Friends concerning buying and keeping of negroes, given forth by M. M. of Philadelphia. In 1699 we find Thomas Story and other Friends taking an interest in the slaves. He found some of them in Friends' families, some were convinced of the Truth, and in other places he urged the necessity of freeing those who had been baptized.[2] William Penn took the same view of slavery and made attempts to improve the condition of the slaves by legal enactments. As early as 1688 German Friends in Germantown, Pa., issued a protest

---

[1] Janney. III., 178.   [2] *Ibid.*, III., 66-67.

against slavery, which was sent up to the Yearly Meeting, but " It was adjudged not to be so proper for this meeting to give a positive Judgement in the Case, It having so General a Relation to many other Parts." In 1696 the Yearly Meeting advised " that Friends be careful not to encourage the bringing in of any more negroes." In 1727 the London annual epistle censured those Friends who engaged in the importation of· slaves. With these points as a basis, the struggle was kept up in the northern colonies. It worked a little faster in New England, and slave-holding was made a disownable offense about 1770. In 1755 Philadelphia Yearly Meeting reiterated its former advice against the importation or buying of slaves, and in 1776 made slave-owning a disownable offense. Many individual Friends had been led to manumit their slaves. One of the most earnest in this anti-slavery crusade was Warner Mifflin, who was born on the Eastern Shore of Virginia about 1745, and from his fourteenth year began to consider this question. By 1775 he had advanced far enough to manumit his own slaves, induced his father to do the same, and even paid his slaves for their services.[1]

This question was a cause of trouble, more or less, to all Friends traveling in the South. We have the tocsin sounded in 1754 by Samuel Fothergill and Joshua Dixon, who landed on the shores of the Delaware in the autumn of that year and traveled south. "Maryland is poor; the gain of oppression, the price of blood is upon that province—I mean their purchasing, and keeping in slavery, negroes." Friends had here decreased in numbers, had mixed with the world and were unfaithful "to their testimony against the hireling priests." In various parts the very appearance of Truth had been almost destroyed. There was a great scarcity of ministers. "I know not more than two in the province . . . and they were neither negro-keepers nor priest- ·

---

[1] Janney, III., 178, 317, 426-428. For a summary of the early efforts of Friends and others in this matter see the early chapters of Clarkson's *History of the Abolition of the Slave Trade.*

payers. This very much describes also the state of Virginia, only I think I may add, the visitation of Divine truth seems more effectually received in various parts of this province than the former, and a spring of living ministry to edification; but here the youth are those whom the King of heaven delights to honor. North Carolina is the next. There are a great many Friends in a part of it contiguous to Virginia [Albemarle]; some truly valuable Friends, but few; yet many who offer a sacrifice which costs them nothing. The largest body of Friends here seems to me the weakest; they have been a lively people, but negro purchasing comes more and more in use among them." There were, however, "some brethren and true members ingrafted into the Vine; though worldly-mindedness and lukewarmness have seized upon many." South Carolina had only two meetings. In Charleston "there are few who bear our name and fewer who deserve it."[1]

Slavery was the central question in the life of John Woolman. He visited Virginia and Carolina for the second time in 1757. He complained bitterly of the small care shown the slaves in their social relations. The Virginia Yearly Meeting had recently considered the query of the Philadelphia Yearly Meeting: "Are there any concerned in the importation of negroes, or buying them after imported?" Their answer to this query was unsatisfactory, for they had altered it to: "Are there any concerned in the importation of negroes or buying them to trade in?" This admitted the right to buy them for their own use and was displeasing to Woolman. He spoke against the change; it was not altered, although some "manifested a concern in regard to taking more care in the education of their negroes." Their action weighed heavily on his spirits. It appeared to him "that through the prevailing of the spirit of this world, the minds of many were brought to an inward desolation; and instead of the spirit of meekness, gentleness and heavenly

---

[1] *Memoir of Fothergill*. 282-283.

wisdom, . . . a spirit of fierceness, and the love of dominion too generally prevailed." He wrote an epistle to the new settlement of Friends at New Garden and Cane Creek against slavery, and found trouble because of this subject in the meetings in eastern North Carolina.[1]

The history of slavery agitation among the Virginia Quakers divides itself into three pretty distinct periods: The first, closing in 1765, we may call the period of amelioration. It took the form of more attention to bodily comforts. It was inspired as much, doubtless, by economic as philanthropic motives. It does not seem to have looked directly to liberation. (2) The period of emancipation, closing practically with the century. (3) The second period of amelioration, when the attention of Friends was drawn to the condition of the liberated blacks, and when efforts were made to improve their economic and intellectual condition, and to encourage masters, who were not Friends, in the work of emancipation.

The first mention of slavery that I have found in the annals of the Southern Quakers occurs in 1722, when the Virginia Yearly Meeting propounded the query: "Are all Friends clear of being concerned in the importation of slaves or purchasing them for sale, do they use those well they are possessed of, and do they endeavor to restrain from Vice, and to instruct them in the principles of the christian religion?"

The next is in 1739, when the same meeting sent a note to their brethren in North Carolina, inquiring if they used their negroes well, etc. In 1740 the Yearly Meeting recommended to those who hold slaves "to use them as fellow creatures" and not to make "too rigorous an exaction of all their labour." It was also decided that Friends could not go patroling to keep blacks in subjection.

Woolman's position and presence precipitated some discussion. In 1758 there is a complaint in the Virginia meet-

---

[1] *Journal*, 73-78.

ing that some were not careful to teach Christianity to their negroes, and the Virginia discipline of that year directs "that none amongst us be Concerned in importing, buying, selling, Holding or Overseeing slaves, and that all bear a faithful testimony against these practices." In 1759 we have the first of a long series of complaints, continuing as long as the Virginia Yearly Meeting existed, that there was a general deficiency in the education of the negroes. It is noticeable that Southern Friends manifested much anxiety for the education of the negro from very early times.

In 1760 the meeting asked: "Are all Friends clear of being concerned in the importation of slaves, or purchasing them for sale, do they use those well which they are possessed of, and do they endeavor to restrain them from vice, and to enstruct them in the principles of the christian religion."

Again in 1764: "It having been weightily recommended in this meeting to Friends who are possessed of negros, impartially to consider their situation; and as the reports from the quarterly meeting state there is a general deficiency in most places in instructing them in the principles of the christian Religion, it is the weighty concern of this meeting earnestly to recommend to the quarterly and monthly meetings, to have that unhappy people more immediately under their care and notice; and that they not only advise their masters and mistresses to use some endeavors towards their education, but also make a diligent inspection into their usage clothing and feeding, earnestly desiring that their state and station may more and more become the particular care and concern of each individual."

In January, 1765, Benjamin Ferris traveled in the South with William Reckitt, who was on a second visit. It is easy to recognize the key-note. "We came to Curles, and lodged at a Friend's house, where riches, negroes and grandeur abound, which makes very poor fare for a christian mind; but he was hospitable and kind to us . . . Had a meeting at Black Creek. . . . Here I had an opportunity of very close conversation on the subject of slave keeping with a Friend who at times appeared in public by way of ministry . . . . at Somerton a small meeting, and, like most others, poor and low. Indeed how can it be otherwise, while oppression is continued, and the gain thereof coveted after! . . . I have been at times much oppressed on account of Friends in this province [North Carolina] and in Virginia, so far countenancing the slave trade, as to hold those excused who purchase them; and have endeavored . . . to impress on the minds of Friends the necessity of shutting the door against the increase of slaves among them by purchase." The state of the church in Carolina was low, " so, that the prospect at present is very discouraging and painful; and the wound seems so deep that I have been ready to conclude it is incurable in the present generation." [1]

The activity of Virginia Friends was hastened and turned more directly toward emancipation by the visit of John Griffith, another anti-slavery apostle, who was among the meetings in Virginia and Carolina in 1765. After attending most of the meetings he remarks: " Alas! great deadness, insensibility, and darkness were felt to prevail amongst them; close labor, in great plainness, was used, shewing the cause thereof; amongst other things, that which appeared none of the least was their keeping negroes in perpetual slavery. I was often concerned to use plainness in families where I went in respect to this matter, and am satisfied truth will never prosper amongst them, nor any others, who are in the practice of keeping this race of mankind in bondage. It is too manifest to be denied, that the life of religion is almost lost where slaves are very numerous; and it is impossible it should be otherwise, the practice being as contrary to the spirit of christianity as light is to darkness." [2]

From this time Virginia Friends were active. In 1766,

---

[1] *Journal,* in *Friends' Miscellany*, XII., 253-260.
[2] *Journal*, 379-380.

" it having been weightily proposed to this meeting to endeavor to put a stop to the further purchases of negroes,
after solid consideration it is concluded to recommend the
subject by an epistle to quarterly and monthly meetings for
them to consider and report their sense thereon to the
next Yearly Meeting."

Cedar Creek Monthly Meeting seems to have taken the
lead. At a meeting held in December, 1766, they appointed
a committee to investigate. It reported in May, 1767,
" agreeable to a minute of the last yearly meeting concerning the slave trade, together with the unhappy consequences, this meeting has collected the sentiments of most
of the Friends belonging to the same which is willing and
desirous that some steps be taken to relieve those people
from that perpetual slavery which they are now involved
in, and think that George Fox's advice to Friends in Barbadoes, and the advice in the printed epistle from London
of 1758, seems the most likely to take effect."

But when the matter came up for consideration in the
Yearly Meeting of 1767: " By answers from the Quarterly
Meetings to the minute and epistle from last Yearly Meeting respecting the putting a stop to the further purchase
of negros, it appears that Friends are divided in their sentiments concerning the steps to be immediately taken in that
important matter, which being solidly considered, and several
weighty remarks made thereon, it is left for further consideration at the next sitting of this meeting." Friends
were requested not to encumber themselves with further
purchases. All were encouraged to treat and clothe their
slaves well, also to allow them to hire their time and to
pay them wages as servants.

In 1768 it was reported to the Yearly Meeting that
Friends were for the most part clear " of importing or buying negros." Some Friends were also willing to release
their slaves if way could be made for it. It was agreed
that no Friends from this time should purchase a negro or
other slave without being guilty of a breach of the dis-

cipline. In 1767 the Isle of Wight Monthly Meeting passed
a minute that no Friend should purchase a slave without
leave of the monthly meeting, and in February, 1769,
Cedar Creek Monthly Meeting said: "This meeting having considered the unhappy state of negroes and it appears that Friends present are unanimously agreed that
some steps may be taken to relieve them from slavery as
the quarterly and yearly meeting may point out." In
March, 1770, James Crew was disowned for buying a slave.
In December, 1772, Shadrack Stanley was disowned for the
same offense, and twelve copies of Benezet's treatise on
slavery were ordered to be distributed to persons in authority.

In 1769 it was reported that some Friends were burthened
with the keeping of slaves; the next year the query was
adopted: "Are Friends clear of importing or buying negros,
or other slaves, and do they use those well which they are
possessed of, endeavoring to restrain them from vice, and
to instruct them in the principles of the christian religion?"
The climax was reached in 1772, when a minute was sent
down to the monthly meetings that those members were
to be disowned who purchased slaves "with no other view
but their own benefit or convenience."

In the meantime efforts had begun in 1769 toward a
change in the Virginia law against emancipation. In 1770
Friends report that some of their number had discussed
this law with members of the Assembly, who confessed it
was bad, but manifested little disposition toward altering it.

There were free negroes in Virginia as early as 1668.
The first law in regard to emancipation was passed in 1691,
and under it no negro or mulatto could be set free under a
penalty of £10, unless the person freeing him should obli-
gate to pay for his transportation out of the country within
six months.[1] The law of 1723 provided that no slave should
be set free thereafter "except for some meritorious services,
to be adjudged and allowed by the governor and council

[1] Hening. III., 87, 88.

for the time being, and a licence thereupon first had and obtained." If slaves were set free contrary to this law, it was the duty of the church-wardens to sell them and apply the money to parish uses.[1] This law was re-enacted in 1748.[2]

The Virginia Quakers did not meet with success. The law was not repealed, but their efforts had influence, for they probably encouraged the Burgesses, who about this time appealed to the British crown against slavery.[3] The same year, 1770, we find the Standing Committee of North Carolina Friends considering "the most prudent steps for Friends to take to show their approbation and good liking to the prudent steps which the Virginia Burgesses have taken in presenting a very pertinent address to the throne of Great Britain to put a stop to that most iniquitous practice of importing negroes from Africa and making them slaves in the colonies."

In North Carolina there does not seem to have been as much discussion of slavery during the early period as in Virginia. It first appears in North Carolina in 1758, and within fourteen years was the leading question of the day. There the fight was longer, was more stubbornly contested, resulted in the removal of many negroes from the State, and materially influenced the development of Quakerism itself. In 1758 the North Carolina Yearly Meeting asks: "Are all that have negroes careful to use them well and encourage them to come to meetings as much as they reasonably can?" At the same time special meetings were provided for them, and renewed annually for several years.

In 1768 North Carolina Friends interpret the section of the discipline in regard to negroes as a prohibition of buying negroes to trade upon or of those that traded in them. The meeting advises Friends not to buy or sell in any case that

---

[1] Hening. IV., 132.   [2] *Ibid.*, VI., 112.
[3] See this petition in *Collections* of Virginia Historical Society, VI., 14. In 1770 a number of Virginia gentlemen entered into an agreement to import no slaves into Virginia unless they had been twelve months on the continent.

can be reasonably ... d, as the "having of negroes is
become a burden t such as are in possession of them."
In 1769 Friends wer uneasy about their members purchasing negroes and desire an absolute prohibition of the traffic,
but in 1770 we find instead the following query: "Do Friends
bear witness against the iniquitous practice of importing
negroes; or, do they refuse to purchase of those who make
a trade or merchandise of them? Do they use those they
inherit well," etc.

In 1772 Friends were not to buy negroes except of
Friends, or to prevent the parting of husband and wife, or
parent and child, "or for other reasons" that might be
approved by the monthly meeting. They were not to sell
to slave-buyers, and address the Legislature: "Being fully
convinced in our minds and judgments beyond a doubt or
scruple, of the great evil and abomination of the importation of negroes from Africa: by which iniquitous practice
great numbers of our fellow creatures with their posterity are
doomed to perpetual and cruel bondage; without any regard
being had to their having forfeited their natural right to liberty and freedom, by any act of their own or consent thereto
otherwise than by mere force and cruelty, impresses our
minds with such abhorance and detestation against such
a practice, in a christian community; where experience fully
makes it manifest that instead of their embracing true religion, piety, and virtue, in exchange for their natural liberty, that they are become nurseries to pride, and idleness,
to our youth in such a manner that morality, and true piety,
is much wounded where slavery abounds; to the great grief
of true christian minds.

"And therefore we cannot but invite our fellow subjects;
and more especially the representatives in North Carolina
(as much lies at their doors for the good of the people and
prosperity of the province) to join heartily with their prudent brethren the burgesses of the colony of Virginia in
presenting addresses to the throne of Great Britain in order
to be as eyes to the blind, and mouths to the dumb; and

whether it succeeds or n   .e the secret satisfaction in our own minds o   ur best endeavor, to
have so great a torrent of evil,   ially stopped, at the
place where it unhappily had the permission to begin."

From this time on there were individual cases of tender
conscience among North Carolina Friends. Some masters
began to desire to free their slaves, and it was agreed that
this might be done " by applying to the monthly meeting,
and likewise advises the monthly meetings to appoint proper
persons to assist such Friends in drawing instruments of
writing for that purpose, and likewise to judge whether the
persons proposed to be set free is able to get their own live-
lihood, and the clerk is desired to send copies of this judgment to each monthly meeting."

In 1775 " Friends of the western quarter, being uneasy
under the consideration of keeping our fellow men in bondage and slavery, desire this meeting may revise the query
relating thereunto and make such alteration thereon as may
relieve some distressed minds."

The year before, 1774, Thomas Nicholson's " Liberty and
Property " had appeared, in which he urged an alteration
in the law restraining the freeing of slaves. In the Yearly
Meeting of 1776, as a result of the work of a committee,
some Friends declared their resolution to set their slaves
free. The Yearly Meeting also " earnestly and affection-
ately advised " all who held slaves " to clense their hands
of them as soon as they possibly can." No Friend was
permitted to buy or sell any slave, or hire any save from
persons in unity; and " any member of this meeting who
may hereafter buy, sell or clandestinely assign for hire any
slaves in such manner as may perpetuate or prolong their
slavery " was to be testified against. A committee was appointed to assist Friends in the case.

In 1777 the committee " appointed last yearly meeting to
assist such Friends as appear disposed to release their negroes from a state of bondage being called on to render an
account of the progress made therein, report, that they

found great willingness, even beyond their expectation, to promote the work and that a considerable number have been set free by those who had them in possession, about forty of which have since been taken up and sold in consequence of an act of assembly passed at Newbern in the third or fourth month last (which was after said negroes were manumitted) which seems to put a stop to that work at present, although they believe several friends who yet have negroes in their possession, are very uneasy in remaining in a practice they are convinced is not consistent with justice, or doing as they would be done unto."

The law of which Friends complain here was "An act to prevent domestic insurrections and for other purposes," passed in 1777.[1] It was a re-enactment of the law of 1741. The act of 1741, "Concerning servants and slaves," is the first one of the kind in North Carolina.[2] It is itself a transcript of the Virginia law of 1723, with alterations in detail only. No negro or mulatto slave could be set free on any pretence whatsoever, "except for meritorious services, to be adjudged and allowed of by the county court and licence thereupon first had and obtained." If slaves were freed otherwise than in accord with this law, the churchwardens were instructed to sell them at public vendue if found in the province at the expiration of six months. If they returned to the province after leaving it they might also be sold. The law practically amounted to a permission to emancipate, coupled with the requirement to then remove them out of the province.

The law of 1777 re-enacted in substance that of 1741. Slaves could be freed only under license from the county court for meritorious services. If freed in any other way they could be arrested by any freeholder, turned over to the sheriff, and kept in jail until the next term of court which should order them to be sold.

Acting under this law, the county courts of Perquimans

---

[1] Iredell, 288. [2] Davis's *Revisal*, 1773, pp. 75-87, 256.

and Pasquotank arrested negroes who had been liberated
before the act of 1777 and sold them again into slavery.
Friends claimed that this was an *ex-post-facto* law, and employed a lawyer, paying him £64, to fight the case, presumably in the county court. They then carried it to the
superior, which was, in reality, the supreme court, and paid
their lawyer £600. They won their case. The superior
court said the lower court had exceeded its jurisdiction
and ordered that its proceedings be quashed. But the Legislature in 1779 came to the relief of the lower court, confirmed the sales they had made, and further authorized the
county courts to proceed against all slaves who had been thus
illegally liberated before the passage of the act of 1777 " in
the same manner as if such slaves had been set free after
the passage of the same." [1]

The next year the former owners of these slaves presented
a memorial to the Legislature about this law and declared
it also *ex-post-facto*, but the matter does not seem to
have been pressed. They advanced as arguments for their
side of the case that many negroes had been manumitted
in Virginia since 1775 and had not been resold; but if this
was the case, it was a matter of pure grace on the part of
the church-wardens, for the law of 1748 was still in force.

There was a marked tendency, however, in Virginia toward emancipation. There was also continued discussion
among Friends until 1773, when the Yearly Meeting de-
clares that " it is our clear sense and judgment that we are
loudly called upon in this time of calamity and close trial
to minister justice and judgment to black and white, rich
and poor, and free our hands from any species of oppression. . . . We do therefore most earnestly recommend to
all who continue to withhold from any their just right to

---

[1] Iredell's *Revisal*, 371. The preamble of this act recites that these
negroes had been freed after the 16th April, 1775, and before the
passage of the new act in 1777, "notwithstanding the same was
expressly contrary to the laws of this state." Reference is had
here clearly to the law of 1741.

freedom, as they prize their own present peace and future happiness, to clear their hands of this iniquity, by executing manumissions for all those held by them in slavery who are arrived at full age, and also for those who may yet be in their minority,—to take place when the females attain the age of eighteen, and the males twenty-one years." [1]

In 1779 they renewed their appeal. Friends who continued to own or to hire slaves were to be "admonished and advised" to stop. The monthly meetings were again taking the lead and urging on the Yearly Meeting. At a monthly meeting held in Caroline County, Va., 8th of 5th mo., 1773: "By a report from Camp Creek preparative meeting it appears the Friends of that meeting are desirous there should be a prohibition of Friends hiring negroes; believing that practice to be attended with the same covetous disposition as the purchasing of them."

At a monthly meeting held at South River, Va., 20th day of 9th mo., 1777: "This meeting appoints William Johnson and Christopher Anthony to assist those Friends appointed to labor with such Friends as still hold their negroes in bondage, to convince them if possible of the evil of that practice and its inconsistency with our christian profession."

A committee was appointed in 1779 to take these things into consideration, and without the consent of this committee the monthly meeting was not to disown members because of the question of slavery. It was suggested also that a committee be appointed to assist such as had been manumitted, to instruct them in religion, in education, in worldly affairs, etc.

In 1780 it was ordered that those who continued "to hold their fellow creatures in bondage" were to "be particularly visited and labored with." The committee reported progress the next year and was continued; some still held them, and such were not to be employed in the services of the church.

---

[1] Janney, III., 433.

Finally, way opened to Friends in 1782, when a new law on the subject was passed. This law had been introduced in 1781, but had been defeated by a combination of its opponents. The leader of this opposition was Benjamin Harrison. Robert Pleasants remarks in his *Letter Book* that forty of Harrison's negroes had gone off with the British, and intimates that this was punishment for his opposition to emancipation.

The law of 1782 gave all slave-owners the power to emancipate by will after death or by acknowledging the will while still alive, in open court, provided they agreed to support all the aged, infirm and young persons thus set at liberty.[1]

This was the beginning of the end. The great body of Friends did not hesitate when the law allowed emancipation and protected those emancipated. The Yearly Meeting had appointed a committee of visitation in 1779 whose duty it was to visit and labor with those members who declined to emancipate. The committee reported progress from year to year; many were persuaded; some were refractory and held back for a time. In 1784 the Upper Quarterly Meeting said: "It appears to be the unanimous sense and judgment of the Yearly Meeting that the monthly meetings should extend further care to their members who hold slaves, as they may apprehend may be necessary and where such endeavours prove ineffectual they may exclude them from the right of membership. . . . It also appears by said extracts that the education of negroes is very much neglected, although it is generally believed to be an indispensable duty, wherefore this meeting recommends this weighty matter to the particular care and notice of the monthly meetings, who are requested to send up an account how far they have proceeded on this business."

In 1785 the query took the form: " Do any Friends hold slaves, and do all bear a faithful testimony against the prac-

---

[1] Hening, XI., 39, 40.

tice, endeavoring to instruct the negroes under their care in the principles of the christian religion."

In 1786 those Friends who acted as overseers of slaves on plantations were to be treated as possessing slaves and were to be disowned.

In 1788 it was inserted in the discipline "that none amongst us be concerned in importing, buying, selling, holding or overseeing slaves, and that all bear a faithful testimony against the practice." During the same year Cedar Creek Monthly Meeting disowned thirteen persons for holding slaves, and in some cases where Friends had sold slaves they were required to redeem them and restore them to liberty. The work of Friends was also strengthened in 1787 by the visit of Sarah Harrison to the southern meetings. Her principal work was done in eastern North Carolina and Virginia. She and her party visited many slaveholders. They wrote manumissions which numerous masters were induced to sign, and she gave, no doubt, a strong forward impulse to the emancipation movement.[1]

About 1790 an Abolition Society was formed in Virginia. One of its leaders and its president was Robert Pleasants, whose interesting and noteworthy *Letter Book* has been mentioned already. This society soon numbered (1791) eighty members, and these were not all Quakers. Methodists are mentioned as being particularly prominent in it, and the absence of Baptists is noted. In 1791 it sent a petition to the Virginia Assembly against slavery. It also petitioned Congress in that year, as did the Yearly Meeting. Pleasants wished to stop the trade from Virginia to Africa for slaves. He corresponded with Patrick Henry, and quotes him as saying in 1776 that some prominent men were in favor of abolishing slavery altogether; he wrote to George Washington, Thomas Jefferson, James Madison, St. George Tucker, and others, and obtained a respectful hearing from all. He also contributed to the public press

[1] *Memoir.* in *Friends' Miscellany.* XI.. 97-216.

of Virginia on slavery and the slave trade. He urged that
a law for gradual emancipation be passed, under which
the children of slaves, born after a certain date, should be
free. Pleasants lived to hear the encouraging report in 1796
that there was no complaint of Friends holding slaves when
they could be lawfully liberated.[1]

Robert Pleasants was the son of John Pleasants of Henrico County. John Pleasants was for many years clerk of
the Upper Quarterly Meeting, and by will, dated August
12, 1771, freed all of his slaves, under limitations partially
required by law but chiefly dictated by considerations for
the welfare of the negroes. He desired the emancipation
of those of his slaves who were thirty years old, of others
when they should attain that age, and of the issue of all
at that age. He made provision for the maintenance of
those above forty-five. Through existing legal restrictions
the testament was inoperative, and the slaves remained in
the possession of his heirs until 1800, when by a decree of
the High Court of Chancery of Virginia, under date of
March 19, the freedom of several hundred of the slaves originally freed, and of their issue, was confirmed.[2]

Robert Pleasants died on April 4, 1801, aged 79. He is
spoken of in the monthly meeting memorial as "an indul-
gent and prudent master." He was a philanthropist as well.
He emancipated eighty slaves. In a memorial to the Governor and Council of Virginia he says that he "did, about
the year 1777, place divers of his Negroes on lands of his
own, at a small distance from his habitation, and for their
encouragement to industry, and to remove every inducement to theft and dishonesty, supported them for the term
of one year, and allowed them the full benefit of their labor."

He also united with other Friends in soliciting the Legis-

---

[1] In 1798 two persons were reported, in answer to the Yearly
Meeting queries, as still holding slaves, "one of which appears to
be a peculiar case and the other under notice."

[2] See Brock's Prefatory Note to the fourth charter of the Royal
African Company of England, in *Collections* Va. Hist. Soc., VI., 16.

lature in behalf of the slaves, and "through his patronage
and interposition in their favor in courts of law," had the
liberty of several hundred established.[1]

He was also interested in establishing schools for the
negroes. We have already referred to the effort to establish a school in 1759 mentioned by him. He circulated,
presumably about 1782, or earlier, " Proposals for Establishing a free school for the Instruction of the Children of Blacks
and people of Color," in which it was "earnestly recommended to the humane and the benevolent of all denominations, chearfully to contribute to an Institution calculated to
promote the spiritual and temporal interest of that unfortunate part of our fellow creatures, in forming their minds in the
principles of virtue and religion, and in common or useful
literature; Writing, Cyphering and Mechanic arts, as the
most likely means to render so numerous a people fit for
freedom and to become useful citizens." He proposed to
establish the school on a tract of his own land called
" Gravely [or Gravelly] Hills," situated three miles from
Four Mile Creek, Henrico County, and containing 350
acres, the whole revenue from which was to go toward its
support; or in the event that the school was located elsewhere, to give £100 to it. Ebenezer Maule, another Friend,
subscribed £50. Mr. Brock says that he does not know
the results of this proposition,[2] but from the memorial on
the life of Pleasants we learn that he appropriated the rent
of 350 acres of land and £10 per annum to be laid out in a
free school for the negroes. We know also that a few years
after his death there was a school at Gravelly Run under
care of Friends. It is reasonable to conclude that the wishes
of Robert Pleasants met with some degree of fulfillment
within a few years after his death.

In 1801 the Yearly Meeting decided to call them "black
people" instead of negroes, and there is frequent mention
of them in the records. In 1802 Friends discussed the ques-

---

[1] M. M. *Memorial.*　　[2] *Colls.*, Va. Hist. Soc., VI., 18.

tion of a petition against the internal slave trade. Two years
later they said that from defects in the law free negroes were
carried out of the State and sold, and in 1812 they complain of a new law which restrained emancipation. In 1813
a case arose where some Indians had been made slaves;
suits were brought in their behalf by Friends and were won.
This was also done in various instances for negroes.[1]

Money was subscribed by English Friends toward the
education of negroes, and in 1832 an address to Congress
was discussed. They made some effort to create a healthy
anti-slavery sentiment. About 1827 they reprinted the chapter in Raymond's *Political Economy* on Slavery. But they
were not abolitionists. They believed an attempt by the
General Government to interfere with slavery would cause
excitement and alarm. The power over slavery, they said,
was in the States.

In 1836 the Yearly Meeting attributed excitement on the
question of slavery to abolition societies, and said that this
had raised the people of the United States almost as one
man against them and had "closed the door of usefulness"
on behalf of the negro. They bear witness that the desire
to emancipate was becoming more general in Virginia. One
of the last things done by the Virginia Yearly Meeting is to
warn Friends against the extremes of the abolitionists (1838).

Under the Virginia Half Yearly Meeting, the Meeting for
Sufferings became a sort of executive committee whose
chief duty was to look after the interest of the negroes, to
see to it that they got their freedom when they had a right
to it, to provide for removal of the freedmen to free States,
and to ameliorate their condition under the criminal laws.
Negroes must be freed by will in Virginia, and it might
happen that this was not known until the will was probated,
and then only to a few besides the parties concerned, who
sometimes agreed to ignore this part and divide the slaves

---

[1] The law requiring negroes to leave the State within a year or be
sold as slaves seems not to have been enforced until 1828

among themselves. Friends interested themselves in such cases, and as soon as it was brought before the courts the freedom of the negroes was at once ordered. This brought Friends into disrepute among their neighbors, and public opinion on this point forced the removal of some to the West.

Slavery was not a subject which attracted much attention among Virginia Quakers, comparatively speaking, after the beginning of the nineteenth century. The Society had by that time succeeded in clearing its own skirts of the institution. It never became a slaveholder as it did in North Carolina. It waged few battles with the Legislature in the shape of petitions, it did not appeal to the courts as often, nor to the Federal Government, nor did it seek to forward the colonization of blacks. It was weaker, less virile, less aggressive, and less successful in the amount and character of work accomplished.

The harsh law passed by the North Carolina Assembly in 1779 seems to have paralyzed the hands of Friends for the time. Little was done in the next few years, but the Society was organizing for better work. Its first objects were (1) to clear the Society of slavery, and (2) to secure the rights of those who had been manumitted.

In 1780 Friends agreed not to hire negroes except such as were manumitted and were yet minors or the property of orphans in unity. In 1781 some slaves were still held in bondage " and their instruction in piety much neglected." The Yearly Meeting of 1781 provided for the disownment of those who persisted in holding slaves after being labored with. This was elaborated in 1782, when the Yearly Meeting gives it as their judgment that the monthly meetings shall continue to labor with such as hold slaves, in love and tenderness, " endeavoring to convince them of the iniquity thereof, but after such care has been fully extended and to no purpose then the monthly meeting shall apply to the committee appointed out of the quarterly meeting for that purpose which shall assist them in laboring with such; but if after all their endeavors prove fruitless and they still persist on to hold them in slavery the monthly meeting may with the consent of the said committee testify their disunion with them." These instructions were renewed by the Yearly Meeting in 1783, and the sixth query was altered so as to read: "Are Friends clear of importing, purchasing, disposing of, or holding mankind as slaves, and do they use those well, who are set free and are under their care, through non-age or otherwise endeavoring to encourage them in a virtuous life?"

This recommendation had its effect. Friends visited their members to discuss the matter; a number were released, and the prospect was that others would soon be freed. The work of persuasion was to be continued. Cases also demanded the attention of Friends where negroes, after being freed, had been taken to Virginia and sold. On one occasion a committee was sent there to investigate. In 1786 the Yearly Meeting repeats the query of 1783. In 1787 committees were appointed to "labor with such Friends as remain in the practice of holding their fellow men in a state of slavery, endeavoring to convince them of the iniquity of such practice," and if they still refused they were to be disowned.

From the time of the Revolution on, the burthen of the journal of every Friend who visited the South is always the same—slavery. Some of these travelers in North Carolina made use of novel means to serve the slave. Thus Hugh Judge, who visited North Carolina in 1784, writes about central North Carolina: "After meeting we went home with a woman Friend, whose husband was not a member, but very kind to Friends. We had some friendly conversation with him concerning his holding a black man in bondage and proposed to him to set him free, his wife being very willing; but he discovered an unwillingness to let him go free, and we labored with him till late bed-time. When we parted I told him to think deeply of it till morning, when I expected he would be willing to set him free. In the morning, I desired Isaac Jacobs to write a manumission and soon after it was done, the man came in. After a pause, it was proposed that he should sign it, which he did, and had it witnessed by several Friends." [1]

In 1787 Warner Mifflin attended the committee of North Carolina Yearly Meeting in a visit to the North Carolina Assembly with a "well written petition" on the subject. They were unsuccessful, but continued their work. In 1788 that body, reciting that the act of 1777 was "found by experience not to answer the good purposes by said act intended," because the power to arrest manumitted slaves was limited to freeholders and was made optional with them, provided that any justice, on information from any freeman, should issue a search-warrant to the sheriff, whose duty it was to search for the slave, and if found he was to be cast into jail and proceeded with as before. [2]

In 1786 we find one of the North Carolina quarterly meetings sending a committee to the Assembly of Georgia with a petition "respecting some enlargements to the enslaved negroes." We do not know its fortune. It probably had no visible effect. [3] From this time on for the next few years various petitions were sent to the State Legislature, but they were without visible effect. They were induced to send another petition by reason of a new law passed in 1795, which had compelled all emancipated slaves to give bond of £200 for their good behavior while they remained in the State. This was virtual expulsion, and was, no doubt, intended as such. [4] On the subject of these laws Friends sent up a new petition to the Assembly in 1796.

---

[1] *Journal*, 32-48. [2] Iredell. 637.

[3] The Georgia law of 1801 provided that slaves should be manumitted only by application to the Legislature for that purpose. There is no indication in Cobb's *Digest* (1851) of any earlier law on the subject. The Quaker petition to the North Carolina Assembly of 1787 says manumission was allowed in all the States except North Carolina and Georgia. Stephen Grellett says that when traveling in Georgia in 1825 he was told by the Bishop of the Methodists that they were considering the advisability of making a law requiring all of their members to free their slaves.

[4] Martin's *Revisal*, 1804, II., 79.

Joshua Evans, who was then engaged on his trip to the South, was in Raleigh at the time the petition was presented and assisted them. His account of the treatment he received is of interest and value. "We attended the house of common council, and had a number of private conferences with members, who received us friendly, but seemed mostly opposed to the freedom of the black people. My great Master endued me with an innocent boldness, in which I could use much freedom of conversation with the leading men. . . . I was therefore the more free to make use of private opportunities with the members of the Legislature and others; there being now here a large number of the first rank, called gentlemen, most of them being men in some office, civil or military. These opportunities were generally to my satisfaction, and I thought the respect they showed me was marvelous. . . . At the tavern where we put up, there were about fifty boarders, all men of note; and as they had private rooms, a number of them invited me, if at any time I was weary of noise, and wished to be more retired, freely to come into their rooms and sit with them, and that they should be pleased if I would do so. All this seemed to be favorable towards furnishing me with opportunities, when my mind was so engaged, to touch on their cruel laws and the hardships to which the poor blacks were subjected in that government. . . . My hints to them on the subject, were in a way of plain dealing, and so well received, that many of them kindly invited me to come and see them, if I should come near their dwellings. It was unexpected to my companion and myself, that when he came to settle for our tavern expenses whilst here, the man would take no pay for my board, he was so well pleased with the visit." [1]

The petition itself is as follows:

" The remonstrance and petition of the people called Quakers from the Yearly Meeting held in Pasquotank County,

[1] *Journal,* in *Friends' Miscellany.* X., 144-146

" That your remonstrants feel their minds impressed with sorrow, that such injustice and cruelty should be perpetrated under sanction of law, in any christian community, as have been exercised towards numbers of the African race of people in this state, who after they were emancipated from motives purely conscientious, have been taken up, without being chargeable with the commission of any offence, and sold into abject slavery, divers being thereby far separated from their nearest connections in life. We believe such proceedings to be contrary to the laws of nature; and that it will surely incur the wrath of the Almighty, who is no respecter of persons, having ' made of one blood all nations of men,' and sent his son into the world that all might be saved; for ' He tasted death for every man,' agreeable to the holy scriptures so that all people, whatever their complexions may be, are objects of his mercy. For a legislative body of men, professing christianity, to be so partial, as thus to refuse any particular people the enjoyment of their liberty, under the laws of the government wherein they live, even when the owners of such slaves are desirous, from religious motives, that they might enjoy their personal freedom, as the natural right of all mankind, is so incompatible with the nature of a free republican government, and repugnant to the spirit of the christian religion, that the present case, perhaps, all circumstances considered, hath never been paralleled in christendom: yet we hope divine wisdom may enable this house to exercise the power vested in them, to the honor of the most High, and the welfare of the State, that piety and virtue may be promoted, and injustice with other vice and immorality suppressed. Therefore we earnestly entreat and request that you may please to give your attention to this important and interesting subject, and pass an act whereby the free citizens of this state, who are conscientiously scrupulous of holding slaves, may legally emancipate them, and the persons so liberated be under protection of law; such a reasonable request we hope will not now be rejected, as we have no mo-

tive herein but a sincere desire that mercy, justice and equity
may be put in practice, and are respectfully your friends." [1]

The petition of the Quakers was rejected and a new law
passed (November, 1796), seemingly in defiance. The Assembly, " to amend, strengthen and confirm " the acts against
emancipation, re-enacted " that no slave shall be set free in
any case, or under any pretence whatsoever, except for meritorious services, to be adjudged of and allowed by the county
court and license first had and obtained therefor." [2] Further,
the Quakers in eastern North Carolina found themselves
presented by the grand jury in Edenton " as the authors of
the common mischief in this quarter," for great peril and
danger was caused by their proceedings, the idea of emancipation was openly held out to the slaves, their minds were
corrupted and alienated from service, " runaways are protected, harboured and encouraged by them. Arsons are
committed without probability of discovery."

---

[1] The following is a copy of an emancipation paper "such as
Friends used to give their slaves when they set them free, according
to the discipline of the Society, and the dictates of the witness of
truth in their own breasts":

"I Joseph Jordan of Northampton county in North Carolina from
mature deliberate consideration and the convictions of my own
mind being fully persuaded that freedom is the natural right of all
mankind, and that no law moral nor divine has given me a just
right to or proper [ty] in the persons of any of my fellow creatures,
and being desirous to fulfill the injunction of our Lord and Saviour
Jesus Christ, by doing to others as I would be done by, do therefore declare, that having under my care a number of negroes
named and aged as followers [the names and ages are here inserted]
I do for myself my heirs Executors and administrators, hereby
release unto so many of them as are come of age, men twenty one,
and women eighteen, all my right interest and claim or pretensions
of claim whatsoever, as to their persons or any estate they may
hereafter acquire, and those now under age to partake of the same
liberty and estate as they come to the ages as above written without
any interruption from me or any person claiming for, by, from or
under me. In witness whereof I have hereunto set my hand and
seal this tenth day of the eighth month in the year of our Lord one
thousand seven hundred and eighty four.
                                    "JOSEPH JORDAN Seal."
"Sealed and delivered in the presence of
Samuel Parker & Aaron Lancaster."

[2] Martin's *Revisal*, II., 88.

It was in answer to these charges and to the enactment of 1796 that the Quakers addressed a petition to the Assembly of 1797 which towers in the plain and simple grandeur of its appeal to that body, not directly for the slave, but for the rights of freemen which had been denied to themselves: " But after some of the African race of people, were, from laudible motives liberated, they have (in consequence of several laws of this state), been since reduced to abject slavery: Now, that such laws, so opposite to the spirit of liberty, should exist, and be rigorously executed in this particular state, when no such are adopted in any of her sister states, we desire may claim your serious consideration.

"Therefore we earnestly request, that you may please to give your attention to this important subject, and grant an act whereby the free citizens of this state, who are conscientiously scrupulous of keeping mankind in slavery, may emancipate them, and the persons so liberated be under the protection of the law: it is not to enjoin a general emancipation, or to compel any to liberate their slaves, that we have solicited you, but only that liberty of conscience in that respect, may be tolerated; which we conceive to be reasonable, and are not apprehensive that such an equitable step will be injurious, or against the interests of the state."

Little seems to have been done for the next few years,[1] and the committee that waited on the Legislature in 1815 found it " in an unfavorable disposition towards our Society and pointedly opposed to any law or measure being

---

[1] It is curious to note that just at this time, when they were making such eloquent appeals for the right of liberating slaves, a colored man appealed for admission into the Society. The Yearly Meeting recommended that the quarterly meeting " attend to the discipline in that respect without distinction of color." and it seems that he got in, but after several years of waiting. Thomas Shillitoe says negroes were members of Newbegun Creek meeting in 1829. After the Civil War there were a number of applications for membership from colored men, but they seem to have been rejected because of an insufficient knowledge of Friends' principles.

taken on behalf of the black people." This was no doubt
due to the position of the Friends in the matter of bearing
arms in the war of 1812.

The laws against emancipation were as rigid as ever. In
1801 the Assembly had further required all masters liberating their slaves to enter into bond that the slaves so liberated should not become a charge to the parish.[1] The act
of 1818 changed the law so far as to invest the superior
court instead of the county court of pleas and quarter sessions with the power of emancipation.[2] It was not till 1830
that a general emancipation law was passed. Under this
law, persons desiring to free slaves were required to file a
petition in the superior court stating the name, sex and age
of each, and praying permission to emancipate the same. He
was to show that he had given public notice of his intention to
file such a petition at least six weeks before its hearing. He
was also to enter into bond of $1,000 for each slave that they
would demean themselves correctly while within the State,
and that they would leave it within ninety days. Slaves
could be freed by will, provided the executor went through
the same formula. Slaves might also be freed for meritorious
service. Such freedmen were not required to leave the
State.[3] This remained the law of emancipation until the
War.[4]

The rigidity of North Carolina law caused North Carolina
Quakerism to take a form which it assumed nowhere else.
The institution itself became a slaveholder. This movement
began in 1808. The Yearly Meeting of that year appointed
a committee of seven to have under care all suffering cases
of people of color. This committee seems to have evolved
a system under which certain parties were authorized to act
as agents and to receive assignments of slaves from mas-

[1] Martin's *Revisal*, II., 179.
   Potter and Yancey's *Revisal*, II., 1446.
[3] *Laws of North Carolina*, 1830, ch. 9, pp. 12-14.
[4] See *Revised Statutes*, 1837, I., 585-587 ; *Revised Code*, 1855, 573-
575.

ters who wished to be rid of them. This custom lasted
until the Civil War. Its object was to give virtual freedom
to the blacks when actual freedom was not recognized by
the State; to ameliorate their condition, and to transport
them to the free States. The agents or trustees thus appointed had full power over the negroes thus placed under
them, to hire them out, receive their wages, etc.; they might
"act discretionary with particular characters, and if they or
any of them will not comply with the directions of the
agents, after the necessary care has been taken, they may
give them up to a course of law," or "they may be subjected by the most moderate means that will effectually reduce the object to industry for the benefit of himself or her-
self."

This step was not taken, however, until consultation had
been had with some of the best legal talent in the State.
Under date of December 3, 1809, Judge Gaston says: "By
the act of 1796, Chapter 11,[1] it is made lawful for any religious society or congregation in the state to elect any
number of their body, as trustees which trustees and their
successors in office shall have full power to purchase and
hold in trust for their society or congregation any real estate,
and to receive any donations of whatever kind, for the use
and benefit of such society or congregation; to this power
of making purchase and receiving donations there is but
one limitation, which is, that under this act, no single congregation or society shall hold more lands than shall amount
in quantity to 2,000 acres and in value to £200 per year. It
necessarily follows that donations of personal property, such
as money, slaves &c. may be receiv'd to any amount,—
such donations cannot be set aside by any persons claiming under the donors, nor can they be impaired by any one:

---

[1] This act, entitled "An act to secure property to religious societies or congregations of every denomination," was passed because
"several donations have been given by divers persons for the use
of promoting sundry religious societies and congregations in this
state, and no person being legally authorized to receive and appro-
priate the same agreeable to the intention of the donor."

unless by the creditors of the persons who have made such
gifts fraudulently to defeat the recovery of just debts, or
by those who can show a superior and paramount title to
the property given, nor are they liable for the debts of the
individual trustees to whom the conveyance is made,—for
the act especially provides that conveyances and donations
in the manner above mentioned shall be valid in law to
convey to the society or congregation the absolute estate
of the property comprehended in the instrument of conveyance or gift. And if the absolute estate therein be vested
in the society, of course there is none in the trustees through
whose medium the transfer is effected or at most a legal and
not a beneficial interest."

The Society also took the precaution to secure from Judge
Gaston a draft of the proper form for such gifts. This was
not different from the form used in making bequests to
other religious societies. The character and extent of the
responsibility of the master for the acts of the slave was
also closely examined.

The system did not at first meet with much favor, and
the Yearly Meeting was anxious to know the general mind
on the subject. As a result we find the following action by
the Yearly Meeting of 1809: "And it is further the result
of the committee that as the agents appointed last yearly
meeting have had assignments executed to them to a considerable amount in number of people of color, they are
directed to place minors and others of them in stations suit-
ing their condition so as there may be a probability of their
being instructed in virtue morality and useful employment
in life, and if opportunity offers for their freedom that they
use exertions for their emancipation, and the authority of
agents appointed last Yearly Meeting for the different quarters shall in future cases cease till next Yearly Meeting, and
it is recommended down to the quarters to send up the
general mind how to act in future in the aforesaid cases."

Cane Creek Monthly Meeting, taking this matter into consideration, in accord with the direction of the last quarterly

meeting, recorded under date of April 7, 1810: " It is agreed that the authority of the agents appointed by the Yearly Meeting be suspended or entirely cease, and that no more people of color be received in that way by the Yearly Meeting."

But it is evident that this proposed suspension of the authority of the agents was not the general mind, or at any rate remained so only a short time. On the other hand, the Society went vigorously to work to carry out the idea; for we find in 1814 that more than three hundred and fifty negroes had already been transferred to the agents. In 1822, John Kennedy assigns thirty-six negroes to the committee; Joseph Borden assigns eighteen; and the heirs of Thomas Outlaw, fifty-nine. There were then four hundred and fifty in their hands.[1] Their gifts came from all parts of the Yearly Meeting, and persons other than Quakers began to make them assignments, for the Yearly Meeting of 1822 found it necessary to forbid the agents to receive negroes from any except members of Society.

The central aim of this movement was to send the negroes thus put into the hands of Friends to free governments. As early as 1814 forty had been sent to Pennsylvania, but it was not deemed permissible for Friends to purchase slaves with the view of sending them to free governments when it was judged their masters had received a reasonable remuneration.

In 1822 a committee was appointed to examine the laws of some of the free States " respecting the admission of

---

[1] We have one instance as early as 1799, when Thomas Wadsworth, of Charleston, S. C., liberated his slaves, gave them fifty acres of land each, and put them under the care of Bush River Meeting. By the South Carolina law of 1722 the manumitted slave had to leave the province in twelve months or lose his freedom. In 1735 the time was reduced to six months, unless the manumission was approved by the Legislature. The law of 1800 required proof of the good character of the slaves to be liberated and their ability to earn their living, and that the deed of gift be registered. In 1805 Catherine White gave her negroes to Rich Square Monthly Meeting.

people of color therein and if thought necessary to consult
the Legislature of such state, the situation of which appears
most favorable ... and that Friends endeavor to remove them
as fast as practicable." The next year the committee reported that there was nothing "in the laws of Ohio, Indiana
and Illinois to prevent the introduction the people of color
into those States." The agents were thereupon instructed
to remove them "as fast as they are willing to go," and
$200 was appropriated for the work that year.

Friends were divided as to the most desirable place for
their wards. Some favored Ohio and Indiana, some Philadelphia, and others Hayti or Liberia; but the distance of
Liberia and the scarcity and uncertainty of the news made
the negroes uneasy and many refused to go there. These
objections were also true to a less extent of Hayti.

There were five hundred negroes under care in 1824, and
seven hundred and twenty-seven had been received in all.
In 1826 some six hundred were under care; of these, three
hundred and sixteen were willing to go to Liberia; one
hundred and one to the West; fifteen to Philadelphia; ninety-
nine wished to stay at home, and seventy-eight were involved in lawsuits. A summary report in 1830 says that
six hundred and fifty-two had gone to free governments at
an expense of $12,769.51, and four hundred and two were
then under care. There were three hundred under care
in the Eastern Quarter in 1834, and in that year one hundred and thirty-three were sent to Indiana. Two years before Friends had paid a wagoner $300 to take a load of
negroes from Core Sound, N. C., to Indiana.

From about 1835 slavery becomes less important; it was
turned over to the care of the Meeting for Sufferings. The
"African fund" was $3,375.05 in 1837. It was replenished
from time to time and was used to assist negroes to free
governments. In 1856 it was but $353.12. Eighteen ne-
groes were still under care of the Society in 1856. It is
probable that North Carolina Yearly Meeting continued

to hold negroes in its corporate capacity until the Emancipation Proclamation.

Friends were also instrumental in securing the liberty of such slaves as were entitled to it by the will of their masters, and brought suit from time to time for this purpose. A suit of this kind was tried in Carteret County as late as 1854. They sometimes paid the charges against such negroes and thus set them free. They were also accustomed to purchase such slaves as their masters were willing to part with at a low price, take them to free governments and accept their notes in discharge of the obligation. They urged the free women to go West and leave their slave husbands, using, no doubt, the arguments that were used when husband and wife were separated by the slave-trader.

But Friends showed occasionally a selfish desire to be rid of slaves without any corresponding care as to what should be done with them when they were free. Thus Joseph Hoag, a Vermont Friend, who visited the South in 1812, says that many Quakers who had removed from eastern North Carolina to the West had freed their slaves and then left them unprovided for, thus making them a burden to those who remained. In 1825 the number thus left neglected was put at ninety-five. Hoag says also that when a Quaker married outside of Society and took slaves as his wife's dower he became the worst of all classes to deal with.[1]

Friends also sought to assist the negro through the American Colonization Society. During the years 1825 to 1831 North Carolina Yearly Meeting was particularly interested in the work of this Society. Although some members, like Levi Coffin,[2] looked on it as little more than an adjunct of the slave power, the Society of Friends worked in harmony with it. The exchange of letters between the two was frequent and of the most friendly character.[3]

---

[1] *Journal*, 177, 180.   [2] *Reminiscences*, 75, 76.
[3] Jeremiah Hubbard and Allen Hill were delegates from Friends in North Carolina to its annual session in Washington in 1832.

Friends acted as a sort of collecting agency for the Colonization Society and contributed more than $2,000 to its funds. This money was collected from the meetings and individuals to the northward, and a considerable part came from England. In 1826 nearly $5,000 was given to North Carolina Yearly Meeting with which to send negroes out of the State. Acting under the advice of the Colonization Society and of Benjamin Lundy, a vessel was fitted out and sailed from Beaufort, N. C., for Hayti. She carried one hundred and nineteen emigrants. John Fellsee and Phineas Nixon were appointed to go with them. They report that of the one hundred and nineteen persons, fifty-four were sent by the agents of the Yearly Meeting, fifty-five were sent by members of Society, eight were free persons intermarried with slaves, and two were the slaves of persons not in Society and were sent by them. They landed at Aux Cayes, were received with cheerfulness, and provided with four months' provisions out of the government stores. " There were a number of applications made to them and us for them to live with the different applicants, but they were generally desirous of living as near together as they conveniently could; and they mostly went on the farms of a few of the principle [*sic*] men of the place. It is customary among the landholders of the Island to have their farms cultivated by tenants, who are allowed a small provision ground, to raise fruits, vegetables, &c. for the support of their families and to have one half of the salable produce of the farm they cultivate besides; and these conditions were granted to the emigrants, altho they were unacquainted with the systems of cropping there." The bad character developed by earlier American emigrants to Hayti had compelled the Haytians to require new immigrants to establish a good character before they were allowed to hold land in fee simple. This these immigrants were disposed to undertake to do, and the committee suggested that the Yearly Meeting petition the President of Hayti in their behalf for a grant of land. Good news was received the next year.

President Boyer was so well pleased that he wanted twenty
more negroes with their families to work on his sugar plantations, and was willing to advance money for their expenses.
Another planter was ready to employ from one hundred to
six hundred on the same terms.

In 1826 a ship with some fifty emigrants from eastern
North Carolina sailed for Africa; the brig Doris sailed with
sixty-seven on board in 1827.

X There was some effort to educate the negroes who came
under Friends' care. In 1816 Friends opened a school for
two days in the week to last three months, and report two
years later "that some of them can spell and some few
read." It was agreed that their education was to be extended until the males could "read, write and cypher as
far as the rule of three, and those of the females to read
and write." Levi Coffin tells how he and his cousin Vestal
Coffin undertook in the summer of 1821 to organize a
Sunday school for the blacks at New Garden. Some masters were induced to allow their slaves to attend, and these
were learning to spell in words of two or three letters, when
other masters became alarmed, for it made their own slaves
discontented and uneasy; they threatened the terrors of the
law; the slaves were kept at home and the school was
closed.[1]

These threats were perhaps intended for effect and nothing more, for it does not seem that there were at that time
any specific laws in North Carolina forbidding education
to the slave, but later, during the period 1830-35, the Legislature and the Constitutional Convention of 1835, moving in
harmony with the strong reaction against the slave which
had already set in, the momentum of which reaction was
sharply accelerated by the horrors of the Nat Turner insurrection in August, 1831, put an end to this phase of activity
by disfranchising the free negro and forbidding him to teach
or to preach; it disarmed both slave and free negroes, and

---

[1] *Reminiscences,* 69-71.

forbade slaves to be taught, figures excepted, under a penalty varying from $100 to $200 if a white person was the
teacher, with twenty to thirty-nine lashes for a free negro,
and thirty-nine lashes for a slave teacher. Friends presented a memorial against this law, but it was without effect.[1]

North Carolina Friends petitioned Congress in behalf of
the negroes as early as 1816, but their efforts, viewed in
their larger aspect, met with small success. The reason
seems to have been first of all in the negroes themselves.
They did not appreciate these efforts. Some who had been
set free were involved in lawsuits to reduce them to slavery
again; some had intermarried with slaves not in Society;
some had married free blacks; some were unwilling to leave,
and while others would agree to remove, " little confidence
is put in what they agree to."[2] But the worst is not yet.
The States of Illinois and Indiana, alarmed at the numbers
of blacks that were threatening to pour in on them by reason of the North Carolina Quakers, hastened to pass acts,
Illinois in 1831, and Indiana a little later, forbidding masters to carry negroes there for the purpose of giving them
freedom, and also forbidding negroes already free to migrate thither.[3] We know, moreover, that Western Friends
were not free from blame in this matter. There is among
the records of Friends at New Garden a summary of a letter from Samuel Charles to Jeremiah Hubbard and Henry
Ballinger, under date of 10th of 5th month, 1826, " pur-
porting that the prejudice against a coloured population, was
as great in Indiana, as in North Carolina, and that there

---

[1] *Laws of North Carolina*, 1830-31, chapt. 6. For an account of
the struggle over the disfranchisement of the free negro by the
Constitutional Convention of 1835, see my paper in the *Political
Science Quarterly* for Dec., 1894, on *The History of Negro Suffrage
in the South.*

[2] The last statement was omitted from the *Narrative* of their
work printed in 1848, p. 35.

[3] These acts were incorporated into the Illinois Constitution of
1848 and the Indiana Constitution of 1851. The free negroes in
Indiana in 1850 were 11,262 ; in Illinois, 5,436 ; in Virginia, 54,333 ;
in North Carolina, 27,463.

was as much of it in the minds of members of our Society
there as in other people, that they say as others do that
they ought to be free, but they do not want them there, and
he says notwithstanding, that is called a free state, a free
black person is not allowed as much priveledge there by law,
as in North Carolina." When a company reached there
about 1837 they found they could not stay; they turned to
Pennsylvania, but they were not allowed to remain there
either, and it was not until they reached Africa that they
found a resting place.

In 1832 Friends report little or no opening for negroes
in the North. This feeling of hostility to the unfortunate
blacks is well illustrated by the following letter from Edward Bettle, of Philadelphia, to Nathan Mendenhall, of
North Carolina, under date of May 21, 1832: "Thy favour
of the 15th, just came to hand this morning and in the
absense of father from the city, I opened it, and am con-
municating the contents relative to the black people, to
some of the Friends who are mentioned in thy letter—they
all united in the earnest desire that no more of the blacks
may at present be sent to these parts, as the effect of such
a measure would probably be desastrous to the peace and
comfort of the whole coloured population of Pennsylvania.
A law was before our Legislature at its last session,
which the friends of the negroes had great difficulty in pos-
poning, making similar provisions to the law of Indiana,
to which thou has refered, and containing the further most
obnoxious provision that all free people of colour now resident in Pennsylvania should be obliged to carry passes in
traveling from one county of the state to another, and that
should give security against becoming chargeable to the
public, whenever they might change their residence from
one part of the state to another. This act was brought before our Legislature in consequence of the arrival at Chester
I believe of some fugitives from Southamton, Virginia after massacre there—the public mind here is more roused
even among respectable persons against these poor people,

than it has been for several years, and on the 27th, of this
month, an adjourned session of the Legislature will take
place; when the bill I have just alluded to is again to be
taken up and I have no doubt if your blacks arrive here
(as they will if now shiped) while the subject is under discussion that very circumstance will be the means of causing
the passage of a bill which will bring the utmost trouble
upon the coloured population in our state and at the same
time prevent any such persons from other states ever emi-
grating to Pennsylvania.

" This same law is also very severe in its provisions against
fugitive slaves, repealing some very good acts passed a few
years ago upon that subject, and thus leaving the kidnap-
pers, fair scope for their nefarious labours. Under all these
circumstances, we do sincerely hope you may not have
shiped the blacks when this reaches you. An expedition
is to sail to Liberia from Norfolk in a short time as I am
informed, perhaps you might get your company into that
ship.   Very respectfully thy friend

EDWARD BETTLE."

The cause of the slave also received some assistance
during a part of this period, particularly between 1816 and
1835, from a number of manumission societies in central
North Carolina. These societies were most numerous and
aggressive in Guilford County. Quakers did not claim control over these organizations, nor were they conducted as
Quaker bodies, but Quaker influence was paramount in
their development and growth, and any study of Quakerism
in North Carolina which does not deal with them in detail
would be defective.

The minutes of the central, or general, society have recently come to light. They begin with July, 1816, which
seems to have been the date of the first general meeting.
Branches were already existing, for four branches, Centre,
Caraway, Deep River, and New Garden, all in or near Guil-

ford County, were represented at this meeting. Moses Swaim, who afterwards published a remarkably strong paper on the subject of abolition, was made president. One hundred and forty-seven members were reported. Most of them have Quaker names, but the records show few traces of Quaker phrases and methods of procedure. There was a president, secretary, and treasurer, and they performed the regular duties of their respective offices. Membership was limited to " free white males." The constitution, as originally proposed, contained a provision that any member who should vote for a member of the Legislature not in favor of emancipation should be impeached, but this provision was stricken out. Committees were appointed to correspond with the Manumission Society of Tennessee. The latter had been organized about this time; was, doubtless, also largely under the influence of Friends, and two delegates from Tennessee were present at one of the meetings. The society agreed also to address the Baptists, Methodists, Presbyterians and Moravians in the section. The meetings were to be held in the meeting-houses at Centre and Deep River alternately, in April and October.

The branch meetings from which this central organization had sprung were, beyond doubt, the work of Charles Osborn (1775-1850), one of the greatest of the anti-slavery agitators. Osborn was born in North Carolina, August 21, 1775. He removed at nineteen with his parents to Tennessee. He began to preach about 1806, and visited most meetings in the South during the next few years. He was the first man in America to proclaim the doctrine of immediate and unconditional emancipation. In December, 1814, he was engaged in the organization of the Tennessee Manumission Society,[1] with which the North Carolina so-

---

[1] In 1797 a powerful appeal for the abolition of slavery was published as a communication in the *Knoxville Gazette.* It called a meeting at a town in Washington County in March, 1797. to form a Manumission Society. The communication bears evidence of having been written by a Quaker. (Humes. *Loyal Mountaineers of Tennessee*, p. 32.) On January 5, 1824, Mr. Blair, of Tennessee, pre-

Clearing.

ciety kept up a close correspondence. The years 1814 and 1815 were spent largely in this work. We learn from his journal that he organized such societies in Guilford County, N. C., in 1816 (pp. 137-147). In that year he removed to Mount Pleasant, O., and in August, 1817, published the first number of *The Philanthropist.* This was the first journal in America to advocate unconditional emancipation.[1] He abstained from the use of all slave-grown produce, and in 1842-43 joined anti-slavery Friends in Indiana. His work in North Carolina seems to have been to plant the seeds of emancipation societies among the Quakers and others, and these at once developed the greater strength that comes with union.

There was soon division, however, within the Manumission Society. One part favored the American Colonization Society and decided to open communication with it. They even went further and decided in 1817 to change the name of their society to "Manumission and Colonization Society." Levi Coffin gives an interesting account of this fight in his *Reminiscences* (pp. 75-76): "The last convention that I attended was held at General [Alexander] Gray's in Randolph County. He was a wealthy man and owned a

---

sented a memorial to the House of Representatives from the ninth convention of the Manumission Society of Tennessee, praying Congress to adopt measures for the prevention of slavery in future in any State where it was not then allowed by law and for its proscription in States yet to be formed and admitted to the Union.

[1] It was not until after the present volume was ready for the press that I had the opportunity to see George W. Julian's paper on *The rank of Charles Osborn as an anti-slavery pioneer* (Indianapolis, 1891). I am gratified to know that I have arrived by an independent examination of the records at the same conclusion as Mr. Julian. He says (p. 4): "Our accepted histories and manuals agree in according to William Lloyd Garrison the honor of first proclaiming, on this side of the Atlantic, the doctrine of 'immediate and unconditional emancipation.' They also agree in awarding to Benjamin Lundy the credit of publishing the first anti-slavery newspaper of this century, and of being the pioneer abolitionist of the United States. These statements are now received without question, and supported by Johnson's 'Life of Garrison,' Greeley's 'History of the American Conflict,' Wilson's 'Rise and Fall of the Slave Power,' Von Holst's 'Constitutional and Political History of

number of slaves, but was interested in our movement. The meeting was held in his large new barn, which was covered but not weather-boarded, and which afforded ample room for the assembly. Quite a number of slave holders were present who favored gradual manumission and colonization. They argued that if the slaves were manumitted, they must be sent to Africa; it would not do for them to remain in this country; they must return to Africa, and this must be made a condition of their liberty. A motion was made to amend our constitution, so that the name of our organization would be 'Manumission and Colonization Society.' This produced a sharp debate. Many of us were opposed to making colonization a condition of freedom, believing it to be an odious plan of expatriation concocted by slave holders, to open a drain by which they might get rid of free negroes, and thus remain in more secure possession of their slave property. They considered free negroes a dangerous element among slaves. We had no objection to free negroes going to Africa of their own will, but to compel them to go as a condition of freedom was a movement to which we were conscientiously opposed and against which we strongly contended. When the vote was taken, the

---

the United States,' and various other authorities. It is the chief purpose of this paper to controvert these alleged facts, and to show that Charles Osborn, an eminent minister in the Society of Friends, proclaimed the doctrine of immediate and unconditional emancipation when William Lloyd Garrison was only nine years old, and nearly nine years before that doctrine was announced by Elizabeth Heyrick in England ; and that Mr. Osborn also edited and published one of the first anti-slavery newspapers in the United States, and thus entitled to take rank as the real pioneer of American abolition."

He substantiates the first claim on the evidence : 1. of Rachel Swain, sister-in-law of Osborn, who was present when he organized the Tennessee Manumission Society in December, 1814, and who says that its object was immediate and unconditional emancipation : 2. by Rev. John Rankin, a native and resident of Tennessee up to 1817, who bears testimony to the same thing : 3. by the testimony in the *Reminiscences* of Levi Coffin, the president of the Underground Railroad and himself a native of Carolina ; 4. by the document published in 1843 and reviewing certain proceedings of Indiana Yearly Meeting in dealing with Mr. Osborn ; 5. by the memorial of Osborn adopted by the Society of Anti-Slavery Friends

motion was carried by a small majority. We felt that the
slave power had got the ascendancy in our Society, and
that we could no longer work in it. The convention broke
up in confusion and our New Garden branch withdrew to
itself, no longer cooperating with the others. Our little
anti-slavery band, composed mostly of Friends, continued
to meet at New Garden until the majority of the members
emigrated to the west, preferring to live in a free state."

But notwithstanding these troubles and withdrawals, the
society went on with its work; in 1818 it undertook to enforce the laws against kidnapping, and discussed sending a
delegation to the American Convention for the Abolition
of Slavery, but this was indefinitely postponed, and a motion
to petition the Legislature in behalf of the free blacks was
also lost. In April, 1819, sixty-five members were reported
from the Centre branch; Deep River had forty-eight; New
Garden, sixty; Caraway, forty-two; Reedy Fork, thirty-one;
Springfield, thirty-five; total, two hundred and eighty-one.
From 1819 to 1825 there were frequent meetings, but little
was done; the society spent much of its time in discussing
what its name and constitution should be; it dallied much
with the American Colonization Society, and once contri-

of which he was a member : 6. by his opposition to the incorpora-
tion of the colonization idea into the Tennessee Manumission Society : 7. by his opposition to colonization in general.

Osborn issued the prospectus of his *Philanthropist* from Mount
Pleasant, O., in 1816. The first number appeared August 29, 1817.
Its publication was continued until the eighth of October, 1818.
"The tone of the paper was earnestly moral and religious. He devoted its columns considerably to the interests of temperance and
peace, but the burden and travail of his heart was slavery. I speak
by authority, having the bound volumes of the paper before me.
It was just such a paper as Elijah P. Lovejoy was murdered for
publishing in Illinois twenty years later. Benjamin Lundy, then
residing at St. Clairsville, was one of its agents, as the paper shows.
The subject of slavery is discussed from eighty to ninety times,
making an average of nearly twice in each number." The paper
was sold to Elisha Bates (doubtless the same man who had been
prominent among Friends in Virginia and had recently migrated
to the West), but as Lundy did not like the anti-slavery character
which the paper now assumed, he began the publication at Mount
Pleasant, in January, 1821, of the *Genius of Universal Emancipation*.
He soon removed this paper to Tennessee, as we shall see.

buted $20 to its funds; committees were appointed to do
various things that were not done, and were continued to
do the same thing the next year. Some interest in the education of the negro was also manifested; the funds were
reported to be $47.07½, this was to be increased and the
proceeds were to be devoted to his education, but two years
later it had been increased by only $2.62.

The society received a new impulse from the anti-slavery
agitation of Benjamin Lundy, who removed from Ohio to
Tennessee in 1821 and published there for three years *The
Genius of Universal Emancipation.*[1] He delivered his first
public address against slavery at Deep Creek, North Carolina, in 1824; held some fifteen or twenty anti-slavery meetings and organized twelve or fourteen abolition societies.
He removed his paper to Baltimore, and for six months
William Swain, of North Carolina, was his assistant.[2]

In April, 1824, the president of the society reviews the
progress of the doctrine of abolition; notes the recent organization of an abolition society in Virginia; and says
there were twenty branches to the one in Tennessee with
some seven hundred members. Subscriptions to Lundy's
paper were encouraged, new branches were reported, and
good Quaker names, like Mendenhall, Coffin, Hubbard,
Gardner, Nixon, Stocker, Wilson, White, Hiatt, Stanley and

---

[1] Lundy (1789–1839) was also a Quaker and was born in New
Jersey. He removed to Wheeling, Va., at 19 years of age, and, as
we have seen, contributed on slavery to Osborn's paper. *The Philanthropist.* We have seen also how his paper, *The Genius,* grew out
of Osborn's sale of the earlier journal. The *Life* of William Lloyd
Garrison, by his children (I., p. 88), says that Elihu Embree, also a
Friend, had begun a small octavo monthly newspaper, called *The
Emancipator,* at Jonesborough, Tenn., in 1820, but Embree soon
died, and early in 1822 *The Genius* was removed, at the earnest
solicitations of Embree's friends, to Greenville, Tenn., and printed
on the press of the late *Emancipator.* Humes (p. 33) gives a version
somewhat different from the above. He says that in March, 1819,
the *Manumission Intelligencer,* weekly, was issued at Jonesboro.
Its publication gave place the next year to *The Emancipator,*
monthly, by Elijah Embree, one of two Quaker brothers from
Philadelphia, who manufactured iron near Elizabethton.

[2] *Life, Travels, and Opinions,* 22–23.

Piggott, become frequent. The term "colonization" is
dropped from the title and the society became more active.
The abolition element had again gotten control. At their
meeting in September, 1825, eighty-one delegates reported
from twenty-eight branches, as follows: New Garden, Deep
River, Centre, Caraway, Springfield, Deep Creek, Westfield,
Trotter's Creek, Cane Creek, Emanuel Branch (?), Ebenezer
Branch, Rocky River, Uhwarrie, Newberry, Maire's Creek,
Tabernacle, South Fork, Muddy Creek, New Salem, Shi-
loah, Union, Hunting Creek, Prospect, Bethel, and Dover;
while eight branches were not represented: Reedy Fork,
Brushy Creek, Hillsborough, Greensborough, Beans
Shoals (?), Rehoboth, Mount Olivet, and Mure's Chapel.
At this time we find fifteen branches reporting four hundred
and ninety-seven members. If we take this as a basis of
estimation, there were probably some 1,150 members in the
State. They sent material to Lundy for the *Genius*, and
the president's address for this year was published in the
Western Carolinian, of Salisbury. Much anti-slavery matter
was published by William Swaim, a young man of rare talent, in the Greensboro *Patriot*, a paper which he had just
founded. Levi Coffin says: "He advocated the manumission of slaves, and though he met with a storm of opposition and was assailed by other papers, he continued his
course boldly and independently. He received letters from
various parts of the State full of threats and warnings.
These he published in his paper, and replied to them in
editorials. Many public speakers and writers engaged in
discussion with him, but they could not cope with him, and
generally retired from the combat much worsted."[1]

The emancipation society said that there were then no
newspapers in the State that were earnestly engaged in defending slavery, but contemplated establishing a press of
its own.[2] A number of questions were propounded and discussed, such as the cost of suppressing the slave trade; the

<hr />

[1] *Reminiscences*, 73, 74.   [2] Moses Swaim, in annual address, 1826.

cost and extent of the internal slave trade; to what extent should emancipation to Hayti be encouraged? to Liberia? One question is of particular interest to us. In answer to the question whether the majority of the citizens of North Carolina opposed slavery, they estimate that two-sixtieths were for immediate emancipation; three-sixtieths for gradual emancipation; four-sixtieths supported schemes of emigration, etc.; thirty-six sixtieths were ready to support schemes of emancipation; three-sixtieths had neither thought on nor cared for the subject; nine-sixtieths opposed emancipation because impractical; three-sixtieths were bitterly opposed to emancipation.[1]

In 1826 twenty-three branches reported about 1,000 members. It was thought there were some 1,600 members in all. Some of them, as we have seen, were slaveholders, for many slaveholders favored gradual emancipation. We find four female branches mentioned. They had their headquarters at Jamestown, Springfield, Kennet, and Centre, all Quaker strongholds. In 1827 forty branches were reported; they sent Benjamin Swaim as a delegate to the Abolition Society and also sent a memorial to Congress. From this time on the society began to fail; members began to grow careless and the branches did not send representatives. It met for the last time at Marlborough, in Randolph County, July 25, 1834. They voted to continue their meetings, but did not. They had been drawing closer to the Free Produce Society of Pennsylvania and to similar abolition movements. The temper of the times was changing in North Carolina, and the Manumission Society drifted until it ceased to have an organization save as a part of the Underground Railroad.

Such was the contribution of North Carolina Friends toward the solution of this much-vexed problem. They failed

---

[1] Poole. *Anti-Slavery Opinion before* 1800 (p. 72). quotes Lundy in saying that in 1827 there were 130 abolition societies in the United States, of which 106 were in the slave States. There were eight in Virginia, twenty-five in Tennessee with a membership of one thousand, fifty in North Carolina with three thousand members.

to accomplish the end aimed at, but it was not for lack of
effort. They contributed of their energy and money, and
were not less lavish with the leaders whom they gave to the
anti-slavery cause. Most notable among these, perhaps,
were Charles Osborn, Vestal Coffin and Levi Coffin. The
work of Charles Osborn has been noticed already. Vestal
Coffin organized the Underground Railroad near the present Guilford College in 1819. Addison Coffin, his son, entered its service as a conductor in early youth, and still sur-
vives in hale old age, the last of the men who served it
prior to 1836. Vestal's cousin, Levi Coffin, became an anti-
slavery apostle in early youth and continued unflinching to
the end. His early years were spent in North Carolina,
whence he helped many slaves to reach the West.[1] In 1826
he followed them. Here he worked incessantly, and was
for thirty years the reputed president of the Underground
Railroad.

Thus did the South give of its own sons to the solution
of the problem. Southern men had been the ones to exclude slavery from the Northwest Territory; they had voted
to abolish the slave trade after 1808; and the next genera-

---

[1] It should be noted that such action as this on the part of individuals was disavowed by the Society as a whole. In 1843 the
North Carolina Yearly Meeting, in order " to make known our long
established practice and utter disapproval of such interference any-
way whatever," condemns those Friends who had given " shelter
improperly" to slaves. The Rich Square Monthly Meeting was still
more distinct in its position. In 1843 it says : " Whereas it is a well-
known testimony of the Society of Friends that they do not allow
their members to hold slaves or in any way interfere with the system of slavery further than by petition, reason, and remonstrance
in a peaceable manner. And it having through report come to the
knowledge of the body of Society that some one or two of the members thereof have suffered themselves to be so far overcome through
sympathy as to allow and give shelter improperly to one or more
slaves and thus occasioned several of their fellow members to be
accused of the like improper conduct we have therefore thought it
due to ourselves and to the people at large of the country in which
we live thus to make known our long established practice and utter
disapproval of such interference in any way whatever, while at the
same time we do not in the least degree relinquish our testimony to
the injustice of slavery."

tion was to furnish many of the men who were most useful in its final destruction.

It is to be noted also that during the whole of this period the anti-slavery sentiment was strong in Virginia. This sentiment is shown clearly by the great debates in the Virginia Assembly in January, 1832, on the question of gradual emancipation. This debate was precipitated by the Nat Turner insurrection in August, 1831. Emancipation was advocated by most of the leading men of the day, including Mr. Moore, of Rockbridge; Mr. Rives, of Campbell; Mr. Preston, who was afterwards in Taylor's cabinet; George W. Summers, afterwards member of Congress; Thomas J. Randolph, the grandson of Jefferson; Thomas Marshall; James McDowell, Jr., afterwards governor of Virginia and member of Congress; and Charles J. Faulkner, M. C. and minister to France. While there were members who denied the advisability of action, there were none who defended the principles of slavery. The *Whig* and the *Enquirer* were both equally vehement in their denunciations of the institution.

It would be an error, however, to assume that Friends in Virginia were responsible for any large part of this strong feeling toward emancipation. They did their duty in this respect just as they did in North Carolina, but they were too few in numbers and not widely enough distributed geographically to be of great influence; besides, the most of their members had gone to the West.

It is also worthy of note that Carolina Friends were both abolitionists and colonizationists, while Virginia Friends were neither, but emancipationists instead. The action of Virginia Friends in the matter of slavery was far more temperate. They condemned both the colonization and abolition movements; North Carolina Friends worked at first with the colonization movement, and from that drifted into the more comprehensive program of abolition.

After the beginning of the present century the appeals to the State Assembly by North Carolina Yearly Meeting become fewer. In 1816 they sent their first petition to Congress, and from 1835 slavery becomes relatively less important, while the use and abuse of whiskey, distilling, etc., become more so. This had been the case in the Virginia Yearly Meeting since about 1800.

This change seems to have been due to two causes. In the first place the people of North Carolina by reason of the invention of the cotton-gin were beginning to assume a reactionary attitude in favor of slavery. This reaction was hastened by Nat Turner's rebellion, which checked the rising tide of emancipation, caused the South to be armed, made her people more sensitive, and predisposed them against agitation of the question.

In the second place, and this is the principal reason, Friends were considerably reduced in numbers in North Carolina. Those who remained were more indifferent to the question and were less able to cope with the growing power of the institution; for its most earnest opponents were already gone. Southern society was becoming more and more divided into the slaveholding aristocracy and the proletariat. The economic competition of the two was becoming more oppressive. The non-slaveholding middle class was disappearing. They had risen to the ranks of the aristocracy or had sunk to that of the proletariat; or, which was more frequently the case, had gone to the West. This brings us to the migration.

CHAPTER X.

SOUTHERN QUAKERS AND THE SETTLEMENT OF THE MIDDLE WEST.

The greater expansion of the American Republic was made possible by the victory of George Rogers Clark in 1778-79. Organization of this Northwest Territory began as soon as the Revolution terminated. It was perfected in the Ordinance of 1787. This Ordinance provided for not less than three, nor more than five, States north of the Ohio River: Ohio, Indiana, Illinois, Wisconsin, Michigan, have been the resultant States. Thus were laid the foundations of what is to us the Middle West, perhaps better known as the Old Northwest. The feature of vital importance to the Society we are studying was that under this Ordinance neither slavery nor involuntary servitude, except for crime, was to be allowed in any of this territory, and with a legal guarantee in the organic law of the territory it became a fit home for men who found themselves driven to migration by the institution in the South.

Population began to flow into the country at once. The first permanent settlement was at Marietta, Ohio, in 1788. In 1800 the Northwest Territory, including Ohio, had 50,240 inhabitants. Ohio was erected into a separate territory in 1800, and admitted into the Union in 1803. After cutting off Ohio the remaining country was erected into Indiana Territory; Michigan was set off in 1805, and Illinois in 1809. In 1810 Indiana had 24,520 people, and Illinois 12,282, which also included Wisconsin and a part of Minnesota.

The country was rich in natural resources. There were no grave obstacles in the way of its peaceful conquest save Indians and distance. The first were overcome as their

eastern fellows had b⸱een, and the other was lessened by
providing a new and improved roadway. Before this was
done, settlers made their own roads with axes, guarding
themselves in the meanwhile from attacks by the savages.
Since the settlement of the Middle West there has been
a complete reversal of the relations between roads and migration. Railroads are now built into new sections to open
them up for occupation. They now precede settlement; then
roads followed settlement. The great road to follow the
western migration was the Cumberland or National Road.
It extended from Cumberland, Md., through Wheeling, Va.,
across the Ohio River into Ohio and Indiana. It was begun in 1806; was completed to Wheeling in 1821; reached
Columbus in 1827 and Indianapolis in 1830. With this
road completed, Friends of Virginia and the Middle States
found traveling much easier than in earlier days, but Friends
have always shown a defiant enthusiasm in overcoming difficulties.

It does not appear that this route was used much by emigrants from North Carolina. There were several routes for
parties removing from central North Carolina, and many
Friends who proposed going west from eastern North Carolina first went up into the central part of the State.

1. One route was by what was known as the Kanawha
road. This led through a rough, mountainous country for
most of the way. "Crossing Dan River, it led by Patrick
C. H., Va., to Marberry's Gap in the Blue Ridge mountains,
thence across Clinch Mountain, by way of Pack's Ferry on
New River, thence over White Oak mountain to the falls
of the Kanawha, and down that river to the Ohio, crossing
at Gallipolis."[1]

2. Another route was known as the Kentucky road. By
this road the traveler crossed the Blue Ridge at Ward's Gap,
crossed New River near Wythe C. H., Va., thence by way
of Abingdon, thence through Cumberland Gap, and through
Kentucky to Cincinnati.[1]

[1] Levi Coffin's *Reminiscences*. 34, 60.

3. A third route was by way of Poplar Camp and Flour Gap; through Brownville and Lexington, Ky., and across the Ohio at Cincinnati, Lawrenceburg or Madison. This route was very rough.

4. The fourth was known as the Magadee route and lay over the Virginia turnpike, which had been built from Richmond to the Ohio at the mouth of the Kanawha. This was a favorite route from 1810 until the age of railroads. Emigrants from the eastern part of North Carolina would sometimes go to Richmond direct, while others would strike the pike at Lynchburg or Fincastle, while still others from Carolina would turn off the pike at Lewisburg, go by another pike route to Wheeling and cross the Ohio there. It is said that as many went by this route as by all the other routes.[1]

The first emigrants to the West went on horseback with pack-horses. They followed the buffalo trails, for where a buffalo could go a horse could go. All the women and the boys above twelve carried guns, and sentries were stationed at certain points, but whether this was a custom of Quakers we are not told. When two-horse wagons and two-wheeled carts came into use a little later it was necessary to double or treble the teams in crossing the mountains; a man was put at each wheel to push; there were from two to four behind for the same purpose and two to chock.[2] These vehicles were usually covered with muslin or linen. Some had no paint, but were pitched with tar instead, while the horses were hitched to them with husk collars and rawhide traces.[3] The movers took with them cooking utensils and provisions; traveled in the day;

---

[1] Addison Coffin, in *Guilford Collegian,* Vol. IV., 1891-92. He says also that the emigrants carried most of the money in circulation out with them, and that as late as 1840 notes on the Bank of Cape Fear or on the State Bank of North Carolina were considered as good as gold even in Cincinnati. For a valuable treatment of the Kentucky route, see also Speed's *Wilderness Road* (Louisville, 1886).

[2] Coffin, as above.

[3] *Annals of the Pioneer Settlers of the White Water Valley.*

camped out at night, and went singly or in companies. The women rode in the wagons or on horseback, and these companies were frequently followed at a short distance in the rear by runaway negroes who took this opportunity to make their way to the land of freedom.[1]

When we come to study these Quaker migrations in detail there is little to differentiate those of one State from those of another. They went in substantially the same way, but owing to difference in location pursued different routes. The more southern Quakers frequently took the Kanawha or the Kentucky route. Virginia Quakers would follow the more northern routes, and in the later period the Cumberland road. There is little difference in time either; but at first North Carolina Quakers went very largely to Tennessee, while Virginia Quakers, being nearer, went directly to Ohio. In this way Virginia Quakers took possession of Ohio, while North Carolina Quakers pressed on to Indiana. The differences in destination and time give us sufficient reason to narrate the Virginia migration first.

As early as 1769 some Friends from Virginia had founded Union Town on a tributary of the Monongahela in Pennsylvania, and when Zebulon Heston and John Parish were returning from a mission to the Indians in Ohio in 1773, they had some religious service with Friends in that newly settled district. Warrington and Fairfax Quarterly Meeting, to which these Friends belonged, reported to the Yearly Meeting, in 1776, that eighteen families of Friends were then residing west of the Alleghanies about Redstone, Union Town and Brownsville. They are mentioned in the records of Western Quarterly Meeting in 1777. A committee from Hopewell Monthly Meeting visited them in 1780 and reported that there were more than 150 persons there. This committee allowed them to hold a regular meeting in the new schoolhouse on the west side of the Monongahela River. Friends who settled near Redstone in Fayette

---

[1] Levi Coffin's *Reminiscences*, 34 passim.

County left their certificates at first with Hopewell Monthly Meeting. Westland, in Washington County, established in 1782, was the second meeting. Westland Monthly Meeting was established in 1785, and Thomas Scattergood mentions four particular meetings in 1787. There was a rapid increase from this date. Martha Routh mentions eight particular meetings and two monthly meetings in 1795. Ten years later it was computed that there were not less than eight hundred families of Friends who had migrated to Ohio alone.[1]

The first of the settlers going West stopped naturally in Ohio. As there were then no Friends' meetings in that territory, they left their certificates at Westland and Redstone in western Pennsylvania. The first certificate to Westland which I have discovered is dated June 24, 1785: it comes from Fairfax Monthly Meeting, Virginia, and is for John Smith. It is to be noted also that most certificates to Westland and Redstone came from Virginia meetings. The migrations of Carolina Friends to this part of the West were few until after the establishment of the Ohio meetings. After 1785 certificates from Virginia monthly meetings to Westland and Redstone became numerous; about half of them represent families, some of them being young couples who turned to the West for their fortunes. Others had numerous children; many were young men and maidens; but no period of life seems to have been without representatives. It is literally true to say that there were emigrants from the cradle to the grave. Those Friends who took certificates to Westland and Redstone were but the advance-guard of the western migration. They continued to go to these meetings for a year or two longer; thus South River sent twelve to Westland in 1801, and the southern Goose Creek sent fifteen in 1801 and 1802, of which

---

[1] See Sutcliff's *Travels in America*, 235 ; Bowden. II., 378–79 : T. Scattergood's *Journal*, in *Friends' Library*, VIII., 14–17 : Martha Routh's *Journal. ibid.*, XII., 440, and *Records* of Hopewell Monthly Meeting.

thirteen were for families, besides a considerable number
sent before the beginning of the present century. Meetings
were soon established within the Territory, and then Westland soon disappears as a stopping-place. Thus, in 1802,
we find certificates from South River to "Concord Monthly
Meeting, Northwest Territory," but this name almost immediately gives place to "Concord Monthly Meeting, State
of Ohio," and the migrations at once become very numerous. During the first ten years of the century most of
the emigrants went from Crooked Run, Hopewell, South
River and the two Goose Creek Monthly Meetings; during
the second decade they went from Hopewell, South River
and the southern Goose Creek Monthly Meetings. The
migration from the northern Goose Creek and Hopewell
became active again about 1825, and continued so until
1836. The meetings in Virginia which belonged to Baltimore Yearly Meeting were the first to send out settlers, for
they were nearer the western country and had less to hold
them in the way of local associations. From 1812-16 there
was a considerable migration from the lower meetings of
the Virginia Yearly Meeting. Again, 1824-34, migration
from lower Virginia was sharp. From such records as I
have been able to examine I have found that between 1801-
40 there left the Virginia meetings for the West 349 families and 363 single persons. In the latter class there were
many young women, and they took care that their certificates bore witness to the fact that they were clear both
of debt and marriage entanglements. These were all Quakers, but it probably does not represent all of them. It
represents those only whose certificates of removal I have
seen, and I have not seen all the records, for some have
been lost. Of the meetings belonging to the Virginia
Yearly Meeting, South River furnished the greater number
of emigrants. I explain this as due in part to the foreign
element among the Quakers in this section. From this
meeting there went eighty-six families and forty-three single persons, their removal covering the whole forty years.

In the same way migrations from the southern Goose Creek began with the century, were to Westland first and then to Ohio. These removals sapped the life of the meeting and it was laid down in 1814. In 1811 the movement began among all the lower meetings. It is impossible for us to say how much the figures presented a little later might have been modified by others which have been lost. Emigrants from Virginia went largely to Ohio. Those who took certificates to Indiana meetings belong to the later period. There was also a tendency—we can hardly speak of it more definitely than a tendency—for Friends from the same section to settle close together in the new country. This was true both of families and neighborhoods. The greater part of these removals take place early in the century, but some lingered in their old homes until near the middle. In 1857 a number had then recently removed from Fairfax Quarter, Virginia, and settled at Prairie Grove, near Mount Pleasant, Iowa.[1]

The first migration from North Carolina to the West was not made to the region north of the Ohio, nor was its purpose to escape from slavery. The general movement from North Carolina westward began as early as 1768. These adventurers passed over the Alleghany Mountains and laid the foundations of Tennessee. Others followed closely in their wake because of the political and economic troubles that culminated in North Carolina in 1771 in the War of the Regulation. In this struggle we have seen that Hermon Husband, formerly a Friend, was a leader. We cannot tell how many Friends were in this migration. We are certain there were some.

We are certain that the expansion of Quakerism toward the South was checked by the Revolution. But the migratory spirit of the Quaker was irrepressible, and his line of movement was simply deflected from the South to the West. As early as 1784 we find indications that Friends were

---

[1] *Memoirs* of S. M. Janney, 162.

then at Nolichucky in eastern Tennessee. They left their
certificates with New Garden Monthly Meeting. In 1787
Friends located at Lost Creek, near Holston River, requested
from that monthly meeting the right to hold meetings. But
their request was refused, and complaint was lodged that
Friends had settled on lands the title to which was still
in dispute with the Indians.[1] They were therefore reported
back to the monthly meetings from which they came and
were advised to move off the Indian lands. But these settlers were something more than Friends; they were pioneers as well and had imbibed the spirit of their surroundings, for in 1791 a committee reports that these Friends had
not paid the Indians for their lands and were also holding
meetings without authority. This tendency to move was
so strong and caused Friends so much trouble that the
Western Quarterly Meeting passed the following minute
in 1792: "Taking into consideration the case of Friends
removing to the back settlements & the difficulty and danger some have been reduced to and trouble they have
brought on Friends thereby, For preventing of which this
meeting do give it as our sense & judgment that no Friend
do remove and settle out of the limits of a Monthly Meeting without first applying to and having consent of the
Monthly and Quarterly Meeting to which they belong:
which bounds the Quarterly Meeting is to be the judge of."
     But the minutes of Friends in quarterly meeting assem-
bled were powerless against the spirit of migration. In
1795 a monthly meeting was established at Nolichucky, in
Greene County, under the name of New Hope; in 1796 a
meeting-house was erected at Lost Creek, in Jefferson
County; in 1802 the two were established as New Hope
and Lost Creek Quarter and still report to North Carolina
Yearly Meeting. These emigrants were drawn mostly from
meetings in central North Carolina. Thus we find among

---

[1] For an account of some of these disputes see my paper on
General Joseph Martin and the War of the Revolution in the West.

them, 1795-1806, from Cane Creek Monthly Meeting, members of the families of Marshall, Hodgins, Maxwell, Pearce, Stanfield, Phillips; from New Garden, Thornburgh, Macy, Barnard; from Springfield, Mendenhall, Beales, Hayworth, Reece, Beard.

Peter Yarnall visited these meetings in 1796. Early the next year Joshua Evans was among them. His journal will give us an idea of the difficulties to be encountered in going West, and also of the number of Friends beyond the mountains. Evans had visited all the meetings in Georgia and South Carolina, and from the latter State " set out with a prospect of trying to get to Tennessee, beyond the Alleghany mountains, having four Friends from Bush River who had given up to go with, and assist me. With two horses to my light wagon, we travelled about fifty miles the first day, and camped in the woods, near the head of the river Seluda. Next day we crossed the Blue mountain, and camped again in the woods. The wind blew cold, but I felt inward comfort and support, which was as a staff to lean upon. Next morning we set forward, and in the evening reached a house where we were kindly entertained. This was refreshing to my body: for I had not been much used to lodge in the woods. . . . On the fourth of fourth month [1797], after going about thirty miles, we arrived at New Hope, in the Tennessee country; and the next day were at their fourth day meeting of Friends, where a marriage was accomplished. We then traveled about sixty miles, a part of the road being very bad, to Lost Creek, where a number of our Friends are settled. . . . Traveling about eighteen miles, I had a meeting with a few Friends at Grassy Valley, beyond Holstein river; and in the evening, another opportunity with Friends only, to good satisfaction. . . . I was at a meeting called Limestone, which was a comfortable season. Having been at the farthest part of my journey in Georgia and Tennessee, we came about 150 miles in four days to Little Reedy Islands; the roads in places being very difficult. In traveling along, we saw and met very many people, men, women and children, going towards new settlements. . . . My concern was increased, on beholding brethren and fellow professors too incautious in respect to such hasty removals." They then visited the settlement of Friends in Grayson County, Va., which were in part a product of the new westward impulse.

"We passed on to a place called Chestnut Creek, on the Blue Ridge, where were a few Friends, with whom we had a comfortable meeting next day. . . . We then had meetings at Big Reedy Island, and Little Reedy Island, also one near the top of the Blue Ridge at a private house not far from Ward's Gap, which was comfortable to me. Coming down this high mountain, ... we came again into North Carolina. . . . I was likewise concerned to caution Friends against a disposition that leads to unsettlement, and to ramble farther out into remote places . . . . to show the great impropriety of the professors of Truth, suffering their minds to be captivated with the love of a rambling, lazy life, or going to new settlements to seek a maintenance by hunting, &c."[1] This was for North Carolina the beginning of the westward migration. From Tennessee many drifted on, like Charles Osborn and William Williams, to the Northwest.[2]

The leader and organizer of the Carolina hegira was Thomas Beales. He was the brother-in-law of Richard Williams, the first Quaker settler at New Garden, N. C. He came from Pennsylvania or Maryland to North Carolina. His first connection with the West we find noted in the journal of one of the exiles in Virginia in 1777-78:

---

[1] Evans's *Journal*, in *Friends' Miscellany*, X., 1837, 158-162.
[2] Williams was a native of Chatham County, N. C., and had gone to Tennessee about 1800. In 1814 he removed to Indiana: "and having no company but our own family, we passed along with much quietude and satisfaction, all things doing well with us. We arrived in nineteen days on the Elkhorn fork of the White Water, in Wayne county, where we have settled ourselves down in the woods, and feel satisfied in mind. We are four miles from White Water Monthly Meeting, of which we are members and two miles from our meeting for worship."—*Journal*, 171-172.

"11th day of 11th month.—Thomas Bails and William Robinson, from New Garden, in North Carolina, visited us. They were on their way to perform a religious visit to the Indians, for which they appeared to be under proper qualifications and resignation of mind; leaving all, and at the risk of their lives engaging in this service from a sense of duty and universal love to mankind, engaged our sympathy and desire that they should be preserved in this time of difficulty and danger in the arduous undertaking. Thomas Bails expects to spend the greater part of his days among the Indians; and having visited them before, he will be useful among them."[1] They returned home the next year, and in 1779 "Thomas Beales proposes removing near the Ohio river to be near the Delaware Indians." But the committee of Western Quarterly Meeting on his case reported that the "time of his removal is not yet come." In 1780 the Quarterly Meeting agreed for him to go West to make inspection as to the advisability of removing his family. In 1782 it was reported that he had removed and with him several other families, and he then requested liberty to appoint meetings. He is said to have been the first white emigrant to settle in Ohio. He died near Chillicothe, Ohio, in 1801, and was buried in a coffin dug out of a log, for no dressed timber was available and there was not a saw-mill within hundreds of miles.[2]

The example of Beales and of those who accompanied him had its effect. As early as 1792 the tendency of Friends to travel and settle in unexplored countries was also recognized by New Garden Quarterly Meeting, and a minute was passed by this meeting, as had been done by Western Quarter, forbidding such settlements except with the consent of the monthly and quarterly meetings, which were to have power to fix the limits of settlement; and as late as 1799 the Yearly Meeting " recommends to the quarterly and

---

[1] Gilpin's *Exiles in Virginia*, 183.
[2] Levi Coffin's *Reminiscences*, 10.

monthly meetings to attend more strictly to the discipline in respect to Friends removing without the limits of any established meeting." We can easily imagine the amount of restraining influence this minute would exercise. We have seen already that there were Friends in eastern Tennessee; a number of meetings had been recently established in Grayson County, Va., and in 1798 Westfield Monthly Meeting requests advice on the removal of some of its members to the Scioto River "or thereaway." But the committee to whom the matter was referred wisely left Friends to do as they thought best in the matter.

The first considerable movement of Friends from North Carolina direct to the West, excluding the migration to Tennessee, but contemporary with it, was not from the section of country where Thomas Beales was best known and had most influence, but from the section further to the east. It came from the Contentnea Quarter. It was emphatic and sweeping in its character. It was literally a migration.

Fortunately for the historian, a letter written from Concord, Ohio, by Borden Stanton, one of the leaders of this migration, to Friends at Wrightsborough, Ga., who were also thinking of going West, and who did so at a later period, has been preserved. It reveals to us the motives, the troubles and trials of these modern pilgrims to an unknown land. It is dated 25th of 5th month, 1802: " Dear Friends,—Having understood by William Patten and William Hogan from your parts, that a number among you have had some thoughts and turnings of mind respecting a removal to this country; and . . . . as it has been the lot of a number of us to undertake the work a little before you, I thought a true statement (for your information) of some of our strugglings and reasonings concerning the propriety of our moving. . . .

" I may begin thus, and say that for several years Friends had some distant view of moving out of that oppressive part of the land, but did not know where until the year

1799; when we had an acceptable visit from some traveling Friends of the western part of Pennsylvania. They thought proper to propose to Friends for consideration, whether it would not be agreeable to best wisdom for us unitedly to remove northwest of the Ohio river,—to a place where there were no slaves held, being a free country. This proposal made a deep impression on our minds. . . .

" Nevertheless, although we had had a prospect of something of the kind, it was at first very crossing to my natural inclination; being well settled as to the outward. So I strove against the thoughts of moving for a considerable time . . . . as it seemed likely to break up our Monthly Meeting, which I had reason to believe was set up in the wisdom of Truth. Thus, I was concerned many times to weigh the matter as in the balance of the sanctuary; till, at length, I considered that there was no prospect of our number being increased by convincement, on account of the oppression that abounded in that land. . . .

" Under a view of these things, I was made sensible, beyond doubting, that it was in the ordering of wisdom for us to remove; and that the Lord was opening a way for our enlargement, if found worthy. Friends generally feeling something of the same, there were three of them who went to view the country, and one worthy public Friend. They traveled on till they came to this part of the western country, where they were stopped in their minds, believing it was the place for Friends to settle. So they returned back, and informed us of the same in a solemn meeting; in which dear Joseph Dew, the public Friend, intimated that he saw the seed of God sown in abundance, which extended far north westward. This information, in the way it was delivered to us, much tendered our spirits, and strengthened us in the belief that it was right. So we undertook the work, and found the Lord to be a present helper in every needful time, as He was sought unto; yea, to be as ' the pillar of cloud by day and the pillar of fire by night': and thus we were led safely along until we arrived here."

The story of their departure from their old homes can be given substantially in their own words: "It appears by a copy of the minutes of a monthly meeting on Trent River, in Jones County, N. C., held in the ninth and tenth months, 1799, that the weighty subject of the members thereof being about to remove unitedly to the territory northwestward of the Ohio River, was and had been before that time, deliberately under their consideration. And the same proposal was solemnly laid before their Quarterly Meeting held at Contentney on the ninth of the tenth month; which, on weighing the matter and its circumstances, concluded to leave said Friends at their liberty to proceed therein, as way might be opened for them: yet the subject was continued till their next Quarter. And they having (before the said Monthly Meeting ceased) agreed that certificates be signed therein for the members, to convey their rights respectively to the Monthly Meeting nearest to the place of their intended settlement showing them to be members whilst they resided there; such certificates for each other mutually were signed in their last monthly meeting held at Trent aforesaid, in the first month, 1800; which was then solemnly and finally adjourned or concluded; and their privilege of holding it, together with the records of it, were delivered up to their Quarterly Meeting, held the 18th of the same month, 1800."

They stopped first at the settlement of Friends on the Monongahela River, in Fayette and Washington counties, Pennsylvania, to prepare for their new settlement over the Ohio. They brought their certificates with them, laid their circumstances, with extracts from the minutes of their former monthly and quarterly meetings in Carolina, before Redstone Quarterly Meeting, and received the advice and assistance of Friends there.

"Thus they proceeded and made their settlement in the year 1800; and were remarkably favored with an opportunity to be accommodated with a quantity of valuable land, even at the place which was chosen for their settlement by the Friends who went to view the country, before the office was opened for granting lands in that territory." Borden Stanton continues: " The first of us moved west of the Ohio in the ninth month, 1800; and none of us had a house at our command to meet in to worship the Almighty Being. So we met in the woods, until houses were built, which was but a short time. In less than one year, Friends so increased that two preparative meetings were settled; and in last twelfth month, a Monthly Meeting, called Concord, also was opened, which is now large. Another preparative meeting is requested, and also another first and week day meeting. Four are already granted in the territory, and three meeting houses are built. Way appears to be opening for another Monthly Meeting; and I think, a Quarterly Meeting.

. . . . " I may say that as to the outward we have been sufficiently provided for, though in a new country. Friends are settling fast, and seem, I hope, likely to do well." [1]

This seems to have been the first considerable migration from North Carolina to the West. It seems also to have been the only case on record where a whole meeting went in a body. But it was not the only case of removal from Contentnea Quarter. Removals from this Quarter, either to the West or to the upper meetings of the same Quarter, continued until Carteret, Beaufort, Hyde, Craven and Jones counties were depopulated of Quakers and the meetings there laid down. Friends in these counties now reported to Core Sound Monthly Meeting, in Carteret County. Migration from Core Sound began in 1799, when Horton Howard, secretary of the monthly meeting, took a certificate to Westland. Josiah Bundy and Joseph Bishop also

<hr/>

[1] *Friends' Miscellany*, XII., 216-223. Stanton writes, Nov. 5, 1803, that he was then on his way to visit Southern Friends. He was doubtless instrumental in continuing the work of removal. See also *Records* of Contentnea Quarterly Meeting.

removed to Westland that year. In 1802 ten parties ask
for certificates; no destination is given, but we are justified
in assuming that it was Westland or Concord. In 1802-04
the movement was to Concord, Northwest Territory. There
was then no more migration till 1831, when it was renewed,
turning now to Wayne County, Ind. The monthly meeting
was suspended in 1841 from lack of members. Stephen
Grellet, who was among them in 1825, reports that there
were then only about twenty Friends within the limits of
the monthly meeting and that some of the meetings were
kept up by the old negroes alone. Migrations began from
Contentnea Monthly Meeting in 1800. Between 1800 and
1815 we find thirty-six certificates issued. Two were to
Redstone, one to Indiana, and all the rest to Ohio, most
of them to Concord. Between 1815 and 1838 we find seventy-four certificates, all to Indiana with two exceptions.
The movement was greatest in 1823, 1825, 1826, 1828, 1831,
1832. The largest year was 1825. At the January meeting in that year ten certificates were asked for, which represented thirty-six persons in all. Again at one meeting
in 1826 five certificates, representing twelve persons, were
asked for; in 1831 ten certificates represented twenty-seven
persons.

The foregoing covers all that we know concerning the
migration from Contentnea Quarter. When we turn to the
records of the Eastern Quarter we find the same story repeated. During the first decade of the century there was
a considerable number of removals from Sutton's Creek
Monthly Meeting, in Perquimans County, to the meetings
in central North Carolina, in Guilford and Randolph counties. As we have already seen, this was in many cases only
a preliminary chapter in the further removal to the West.
Between 1797 and 1811 there were twenty-two certificates
of this character granted, nearly all of them being to Back
Creek, in Randolph County. We find also that thirteen
were given by Symons's Creek, 1803-11, to meetings in

central North Carolina; four were given by Piney Woods, 1804-11; and six by Jack Swamp, 1800-02.

The direct migration from northeastern North Carolina to the West does not begin until 1812. In 1811 Zachariah Nixon visited Ohio and Indiana. The effects of this trip are immediately visible. In July, 1812, he applies for certificates for himself and four sons to White Water, Ind. Five other certificates were also asked for. In August there were eight others ready to go. In 1816 applications were made for sixteen certificates; in 1816 it was six; in 1818, six. These people went mostly to White Water, Lick Creek, and Blue River, and to a certain extent the emigrants of any one year settled within the verge of the same meeting. In 1812 it was White Water; in 1814 it was Lick Creek; in 1816-18 it was Blue River; in 1831-35 it was Milford. The effect of these migrations was soon painfully manifest. In 1835 Sutton's Creek Monthly Meeting was laid down and the meeting itself was attached to Symons's Creek Monthly Meeting.

This meeting comes next, and its history has been already prefigured in the one just given. A considerable number had removed to central North Carolina before 1810, and in 1811 the definite migration to the West began. The result was as usual, the particular meeting at the Narrows was laid down in 1839, the one at Newbegun in 1845; in 1846 but fifty-five members were reported at Symons's Creek; in 1854 Little River preparative meeting was laid down, and in the same year, while the preparative meeting and the meeting for worship at Symons's Creek were kept up a little longer, the monthly meeting was laid down and the faithful remnant was joined to Piney Woods.

The same story is largely true of Piney Woods Monthly Meeting. Between 1806 and 1830 we find twenty-nine certificates of removals to the West. We know that the migration was kept up beyond that date, and this alone of all the monthly meetings in northeastern North Carolina has been able to stand the constant drain on its members—this constant recruiting for the West. It became the heir of all the meetings that were suspended in Perquimans and Pasquotank counties, and in 1890 had a membership of three hundred and thirty-eight. Within the last generation a new meeting has been established at Up River, in Perquimans County. This meeting, with Piney Woods, now represents all that is left of Friends in what were the first Quaker counties of the State. In 1800 there were three strong meetings in Pasquotank, with one monthly meeting; in Perquimans County there have been eight particular meetings. These are now reduced to two particular meetings, which are included in one monthly meeting.

Rich Square and Jack Swamp monthly meetings belong to the Eastern Quarter. Westward migration begins from Rich Square in 1802, but the movement never took full possession of this meeting as it did of others. They seem to have been better situated and better satisfied with their surroundings than other Friends, and hence there were few who tried their fortunes in the West. Not so with Jack Swamp meeting, however. The movement began in 1800 to central North Carolina; in 1805 it turned to the West. The monthly meeting was laid down in 1812.

Fortunately for this work, the records of one monthly meeting have been preserved entire, and thus enable us to tell accurately what the migration from that particular locality was. These are the records of New Garden Monthly Meeting. We shall take the period 1801-66, two generations, covering the period of the struggle against slavery and the removals affected by it. It was here also that Thomas Beales had preached his crusade against slavery and had proclaimed the West as a promised land. As we have already seen, a number of persons had gone West before the opening of the nineteenth century. But it was still undertaken with fear and trembling. In 1802 William Hunt asks advice about going West. The meeting leaves him at his liberty. During the first of these years there were a few certificates to Westland. Up to 1815 nearly all go to Ohio, but after 1815 most go to Indiana. After a careful examination it appears that two hundred and forty-five certificates were granted by New Garden Monthly Meeting to meetings in Ohio and Indiana between 1801 and 1866. The following schedule representing single persons and families will illustrate the migration to the two States:

	OHIO.		INDIANA.	
	Families.	Single Persons.	Families.	Single Persons.
1801-11	37	22	4	I
1812-19	15	5	21	4
1820-26		I	36	16
1827-46			29	19
1847-66			20	15
1801-66	52	28	110	55

After studying these figures we must be astonished at the remarkable vitality which has been shown by this meeting in withstanding this constant strain on its members.

New Garden Monthly Meeting was not alone among the meetings of central North Carolina in contributing to the population of the West. In 1824 a monthly meeting was established at Hopewell, about six miles from New Garden, by New Garden Quarter. It was laid down in 1848. During its life of twenty-four years thirty-seven certificates, representing twenty-three families, had been asked for. All of them went to Indiana without exception. The meeting disappeared as rapidly as it rose.

Other offshoots of New Garden were the monthly meetings of Westfield (settled 1787) and Mount Pleasant (settled 1801). The latter was composed of meetings that lay principally in Grayson County, Va. It seems to have been itself one of the preliminary steps in this system of State-building and lasted but a single generation. In 1813 it was visited by William Williams: "Attended New Hope [Tenn.] Monthly Meeting; and on first day had a large meeting at the same place, wherein I had service to good satisfaction; and on second day, had a meeting at Limestone [Tenn.]—nearly silent. Then, the four following days, we rode to the settlement of Friends in Grayson county, Virginia; and stopped at the house of our kind Friend, Samuel Chew; he and most of his family being gone to meeting, we were kindly received by his daughter Alice. On seventh day we attended 'Mount Pleasant Monthly Meeting, which was a favored one; as was also the meeting on first day, at the same place; so that we were made to rejoice in the Lord, and joy in God the giver of all good.

"Second day, the first of the third month. We had a highly favored meeting near where Friends formerly held Maple Spring meeting. This last mentioned meeting had been laid down, by reason of so many Friends moving over the Ohio. On third day we had a meeting at Friends' meeting house, called Fruit Hill."[1]

We have the records of the Mount Pleasant Woman's Monthly Meeting, 1802-25; most of these emigrants went to Ohio. This large proportion may be due to their association with the members of Virginia Yearly Meeting in Campbell and Bedford counties. Mount Pleasant Monthly Meeting was laid down in 1830, but it was not the only one to decay. Westfield Monthly Meeting, its nearest neighbor on the south, lost between 1801-22 fifty-nine members, including thirty-six families. They went West and the monthly meeting was laid down in 1832. This left but one remaining monthly meeting in Westfield Quarter, and the quarter disappears the same year.

Deep River is, and has been, one of the strongest monthly meetings. Its record of migration begins with 1811 and extends to 1860. As usual, they are all to Indiana except ten, which are divided between Tennessee, Ohio and Illinois. Between 1811 and 1845 the movement was quite uniform. The favorite objective point was the White Water meeting, Ind. Deep River, like New Garden, has had sufficient vitality to withstand this constant drain on its strength.

---

[1] *Journal*, 129-131.

Between 1816 and 1860 seventy-one certificates were granted by Dover Monthly Meeting; nearly all went to Indiana; a few stopped in Ohio; a few others went on to Illinois.

The same story is true of the monthly meeting of Cane Creek. This is the oldest monthly meeting in central North Carolina. It dates from 1751. Before and during the Revolution it contributed largely to the meetings in South Carolina and Georgia. After the return of peace the emigration continued, but was deflected to the West. Quakers went from Cane Creek to Tennessee perhaps as early as 1784. In the nine years between 1795, the date of the settling of the first monthly meeting, and 1804, we find twelve certificates to New Hope and Lost Creek monthly meetings. In 1804 the first parties went to Ohio. Five certificates were granted that year to Miami; seven were granted in 1806; sixteen in 1807. The first one to Indiana was granted in 1811. White Water was the first favorite; then comes Lick Creek; the migration was diminished, but not ended in 1836, the time limit of the records to which I have had access.

The last monthly meeting in central North Carolina whose full records I have seen is that of Springfield. Its history is like that of the others. It was settled in 1791. Migration began to Tennessee in 1795. In 1798 Westland became an objective point; Concord, O., is first mentioned in 1803; the favorite stopping-place was Miami, in Warren County. In 1811 they turned to White Water, Ind., and from this time nearly the whole stream of migration poured into that State. The records of Spring Monthly Meeting I have seen only for the period 1831-39, but this was enough, the story is the same.

This completes the survey of the meetings in North Carolina. When we turn to the meetings in South Carolina the result is the same. We shall find that they were not less aggressive and not slower than their brethren in North Carolina. We have already quoted the letter sent by Bor-

den Stanton in 1802 from Ohio to Wrightsborough, Ga.
A similar influence was brought to bear on South Carolina
Friends. The leader in this crusade was Zachariah Dicks.
He is in many respects a typical incarnation of the history
of Southern Quakerism. Born in Pennsylvania, he came
to North Carolina about 1754 and settled in the Cane Creek
section when it was still small. Here the greater part of
his life was spent. He visited the meetings, preached among
them and was a leader in the Society. He visited Europe
between 1784 and 1787. He visited South Carolina between 1800 and 1804; finally removed to Indiana and died
there. His visit to the South Carolina meetings was full
of moment to them. "He was thought to have also the
gift of prophecy. The massacres of San Domingo were
then fresh. He warned Friends to come out from slavery.
He told them if they did not their fate would be that of
the slaughtered islanders. This produced a sort of panic
and removals to Ohio commenced."[1] South Carolina was
also visited in 1800 by Joseph Cloud, another prominent
minister of North Carolina Yearly Meeting. He had traveled in Europe, but particular stress is laid on the fact that
he had been to visit meetings on "the western waters."
The records of the Society tell us the object and result of
his trip to South Carolina.

In 1802 New Garden Quarterly Meeting had established
a monthly meeting at Piney Grove, in Marlborough County,
S. C., on the borders of North Carolina. These Friends
began migrating in 1805, when one family went to Ohio;
another followed in 1809; in 1812 thirteen certificates were
granted, all to Ohio. In 1815 the migrations broke up the
monthly meeting.

The fortunes of Bush River Monthly Meeting, the most
distinctive and strongest of the South Carolina meetings,
are more pathetic still. Ramsay[2] says their removal was

---

[1] O'Neall, *Annals of Newberry,* 40.
[2] *History of South Carolina,* ed. 1859, II., 39.

due largely to the heavy importation of slaves before the
limiting date of 1808. They sold their lands, worth from
ten to twenty dollars per acre, for from three to six dollars,
and departed, never to return.[1] Their own records can
best tell the mournful tale. These records are very imperfect.
They have felt the tooth of time and the hand of fire. They
end practically with 1806, but they tell us enough. The
migration began in 1802 and the first emigrants took certificates to Westland. In 1803 certificates to Miami, Ohio,
are found, and with five exceptions all the certificates granted
1803-06 are to Miami or Little Miami. There were thirty-
nine certificates to Miami in 1805; there were forty-two to
Miami and Little Miami in 1806. Between 1803 and 1806,
with a half-dozen in 1807, there were one hundred granted
by Bush River Meeting to meetings in Ohio, and nine had
been granted to Westland prior to 1803. Of these certificates eighty-six stood for families. Fire—that enemy of
history—got in its work on the records from 1807, and
we must turn to the records of New Garden Quarter for
the end. Bush River Quarter had already disappeared.
In 1808 the committee of New Garden Quarterly Meeting
report that Bush River Monthly Meeting " appears to be
in a low declining state." It seems to have been abandoned about 1808, but not formally laid down until 1822;
they still had the privilege of holding a meeting for worship
as late as 1837. Friends at Cane Creek, S. C., declined to
undertake to hold a meeting after 1809, and others had
been laid down before this time. The committee reported
in that year that there were some five families (including
persons without family), representing eighteen persons, at
Cane Creek, in Union District, and thirty-two families, representing one hundred and thirteen persons, at Bush River.
They were joined to New Garden Monthly Meeting.
Wrightsborough Monthly Meeting had already been suspended, and nineteen certificates were granted by New Gar-

---

[1] O'Neall, 40.

den in 1809 to some of its remaining members to go to the West.

Thus ends the career of Friends in South Carolina and Georgia. They had been there for two generations, and never, perhaps, has a religious faith disappeared so quickly from such a large expanse of territory as did the Quakers from these two States. In 1799 they were quite strong, especially in South Carolina. Between 1797 and 1799 Abijah O'Neall and Samuel Kelly, Jr., bought the military land of Jacob Roberts Brown, which lay mostly in Warren County, Ohio, near Waynesville. O'Neall visited and located the land, and in 1799 "commenced his toilsome removal to his western home. When about starting he applied to Friends for his regular certificate of membership, &c. This they refused him, on the ground that his removal was itself such a thing as did not meet their approbation."[1] Ten years later they had practically disappeared from both South Carolina and Georgia. The cause was the same— slavery.

To illustrate this emigration more graphically the following tables have been prepared, which will serve as a summary for the last few pages. The first table shows the number of removals during each decade between 1800 and 1860 and indicates the States to which the emigrants went. This table covers all the Quaker records that have been accessible to the writer. The second table gives a list of the principal western meetings to which these certificates were directed. It shows that the influence of Virginia Friends was pre-eminent in Ohio, while the same was true of North Carolinians in Indiana. Following these tables is a list of the principal Quaker families that went to the West, with the meetings to which their certificates were directed.

---

[1] O'Neall, 39.

MONTHLY MEETINGS.	Before 1801.	1801 to 1810.		1811 to 1820.		1821 to 1830.		1831 to 1840.		1841 to 1851.		1851 to 1860.		REMARKS.
	TO PA.	O.	L.	O.	L.	O.	L.	O.	L.	O.	L.	O.	L.	
Alexandria (1815–51)				4		2		8		14	1	4	1	24; since laid down.
Cedar Creek (1811–42)				9		5		2						16; since laid down.
Crooked Run (1787–1807)	18	53												87; end of M. M.; 16 to Pa. 1801–10.
Fairfax (1785–1814)	0	22		2	2 to Pa.	4		1		1		1		44.
Goose Creek, North (1801–40)	20	31		16	1	12	9	38	2 to Pa.	3	3			141; 3 to Pa., 1811–30; since laid down.
Goose Creek, South (1801–14)		14		17										46; end of M. M.; removals to Pa. before 1800, and 15, 1801–10.
Gravelly Run (1801–40)			13 to Pa.	36	1	30	2	10	5					46; since laid down.
Hopewell (1785–1850)	62	20				14	3		2	3	3	1		167; 2 to Pa., 1811–20.
South River (1801–40)		44	15 to Pa.	42	2	10	3	4	12					129; removals to Pa. also before 1800; since laid down.
Western Branch (1806–33)		8		13	2	7	3	8	1					53; since laid down.
White Oak Swamp (1811–36)				11		15		11						38; since laid down.
NORTH CAROLINA Y. M.		111												111; end of M. M. practically.
Bush River, S. C. (1801–07)														156; 12 to Tenn. before 1800.
Cane Creek, N. C. (1796–1837)		43		5	31	1	47	1	23					111.
Contentnea (1800–43)	2	31				1	43		20					46; end of M. M.
Core Sound (1799–1840)	13	12		3	8	1	20	2	21	2	30			89.
Deep River (1808–60)					27	1	6	10	21		13	9	3	71.
Dover (1802–60)		17		9			6		24					37; end of M. M.
Hopewell (1824–48)							12		18					26; end of M. M.
Jack Swamp (1805–12)		43		51	1		2							99; end of M. M.; Women Friends.
Mt. Pleasant, Va. (1802–25)						2	61		19				25	195.
New Garden (1801–60)		12	1	31	10	1	8	1	4		1			38; end of M. M.
Piney Grove, N. C. (1805–15)		2	1	15	36		7		22					29.
Piney Woods (1802–30)		6		4	16	1	39		26	1	1		2	31; 1 to Iowa, 1851–60.
Rich Square (1802–60)	1	11		2	6		5	1	11		3	1	1	22; no other period seen.
Spring (1831–39)									7	7				150; 6 to Tenn. before 1800.
Springfield (1785–1850)		24		1	44									51; end of M. M.
Sutton's Creek (1812–35)		3		1	38	1								49; end of M. M.
Symons's Creek (1803–54)		37		10	22	1								54; end of M. M.
Westfield (1801–22)		19			7						1			19; end of M. M.
Wrightsborough, Ga.														2178 certificates, of which perhaps 1400 represent families.

Monthly Meeting.	Before 1801. VA.	Before 1801. N.C.	1801 to 1810. VA.	1801 to 1810. N.C.	1811 to 1820. VA.	1811 to 1820. N.C.	1821 to 1830. VA.	1821 to 1830. N.C.	1831 to 1840. VA.	1831 to 1840. N.C.	1841 to 1850. VA.	1841 to 1850. N.C.	1851 to 1860. VA.	1851 to 1860. N.C.	Remarks.
Westland, Pa	91	….	45	3 & N.C. 9	7	….	1	….	….	….	….	….	….	….	148
Redstone, Pa	33	….	19	….	30	29	7	….	2	….	….	….	….	1	62
Ohio	….	….	7	26	2	….	1	2	20	1	….	1	….	….	142 } M. M's. not specified or miscellaneous.
Concord, O	….	….	65	41 & N.C. 1	31	….	3	1	1	1	….	….	1	….	111
Miami, O	….	….	35 & Ga. 7	86 & N.C.	19	8	6	….	….	….	….	….	….	….	258
Fairfield, O	….	….	6	42	8	32	1	42	….	34	1	1	….	1	106
Middleton, O	….	….	28	N.C. 2	17	10	13	54	3	15	2	….	….	2	50
Short Creek, O	….	….	13	13	1	10	7	18	3	6	1	….	….	….	70
Stillwater, O	….	….	4	2	….	….	13	21	22	53	….	3	….	2	29
Springborough, O	….	….	….	….	….	….	7	25	19	4	….	….	….	….	46
Plainfield, O	….	….	3	4	20	14	26	25	2	26	….	7	….	….	35
Center, O	….	….	1	20	9	….	6	32	….	1	1	2	….	….	40
Salem, O	….	….	18	….	2	….	5	4	….	36	….	3	….	8	28
Indiana	….	….	….	….	….	10	3	….	13	13	….	….	….	….	106 } M. M's. not specified or miscellaneous.
White Water, Ind	….	….	….	….	….	117	2	6	2	6	2	….	1	2	198
Lick Creek, Ind	….	….	2	….	….	56	2	….	….	8	….	….	….	….	91
New Garden, Ind	….	….	….	….	….	13	1	….	7	2	….	3	….	….	79
Blue River, Ind	….	….	….	….	….	39	….	….	3	….	….	….	1	….	68
Milford, Ind	….	….	….	….	….	4	3	….	3	26	….	7	….	….	68 (now Dublin.)
Honey Creek, Ind	….	….	….	….	….	8	4	….	4	1	1	….	….	….	40
White Lick, Ind	….	….	….	….	….	….	….	….	….	36	….	2	….	….	72
Duck Creek, Ind	….	….	….	….	….	….	1	6	….	13	….	3	….	….	24
Spiceland, Ind	….	….	….	….	….	….	2	4	….	6	….	5	….	8	19
Springfield, Ind	….	….	….	….	….	….	….	….	….	8	….	….	….	….	14
Silver Creek, Ind	….	….	….	….	3	7	2	4	….	2	….	….	….	….	18
															1912 certificates, proportion of families the same.*

* The difference between the number of the certificates in this table and in the previous one is due to the fact that when only a few certificates were given to a particular monthly meeting it was, in many instances, ignored entirely and not placed under the general headings, "Ohio" and "Indiana."

This covers the records of the meetings that have been accessible to me. It does not include the list of removals from the monthly meetings of New Hope and Lost Creek in Tennessee; nor of Centre, Back Creek, or Deep Creek, in North Carolina, and of Spring only in part. The reader must be cautioned further that these figures do not include women and children; they stand for heads of families or single persons. Further, some Friends went West without taking certificates, and others settled where there were no meetings, and so neglected taking them for this reason. The records used were incomplete in many places; some were inaccessible to the writer, and many have been destroyed. Fortunately for the student there is still another opportunity to show that these are figures below the true numbers. The Quakers, in the careful way that characterizes all their dealings with their own history, have registered these certificates at both ends of the line. The records of White Water Monthly Meeting, Ind., will illustrate the extent of this movement. Timothy Nicholson, of Richmond, Indiana, who left North Carolina in 1855, writes me that between 1809, the time that White Water Monthly Meeting was established at Richmond, and 1819, the records of the Friends show one hundred and twenty certificates for Friends from Cane Creek and Piney Grove Meetings, S. C., certificates for a thousand Friends (presumably including the women and children) from North Carolina, mostly from Guilford County, and eighty-five from eastern North Carolina, chiefly from Pasquotank and Perquimans counties. Miami and West Branch Meetings in western Ohio were established several years before the White Water Meeting, and many Friends from Virginia and the Carolinas settled there. Further, hundreds of Friends removed from the east to the central part of North Carolina between 1800 and 1830, and from here went on to the West; between 1815 and 1860 hundreds of others went direct from eastern North Carolina to Ohio, Indiana and Illinois. Mr. Nicholson thinks it safe to say that if twelve hundred went to Richmond, Ind.,

direct between 1809 and 1819, not less than six thousand
went from these four Southern States between 1800 and
1860, of whom at least three-fourths went from North Carolina. In the same way Eli Jay writes me that the records
of Miami Monthly Meeting show that about twelve hundred
members were received by certificate in 1804, 1805 and 1806.
They nearly all came from Virginia, North and South Carolina, Georgia and Tennessee. South Carolina contributed
the greatest number, as we have seen.

In the following lists the attempt has been made to give
the names of those families which were the leaders in the
westward migration, or which furnished the most recruits
to it, from the various monthly meetings in the East. The
names of the meetings to which the particular families went
have also been given, in most cases, with an approximation
of the date. Thus HOPEWELL MONTHLY MEETING, Va.,
sent to *Westland* in Washington and *Redstone* in Fayette
County, Pa., between 1786 and 1803, members of the family
of Faulkner, Perviance, Townsend, Sidwell, Berry, Mills,
Blackburn, Branson, Hodge, Lewis, Brock, White, Bailey,
Smith, Roberts, Wells, Morris, Finch, Antrim; *to Concord*,
O., it sent (1803-05): Lupton, Piggot, Jenkins, Pickering,
Miller, Ellis, Steer, Bevin; *to various other monthly meet-
ings in Ohio* (1804-   ): McPherson, George, Walter, Wick-
ersham, White, Walton, Wilson, Allen, Adams, Branson,
Cope, Crampton, Faucett, Hackney, Janney, Lloyd, Little,
Lupton, Pickering, Steer, Smith, Swayne, Townsend, Taylor.

FAIRFAX MONTHLY MEETING.—*To Redstone and West
land* (1785-1833): Smith, Stokes, Wharton, Davis, Hough,
Ward, Mitchner, Plumber, Shine; *to Middleton* (1803-19):
Smith, Sidwell, Beal, Beeson, Nutt, Payson, Whitaker,
Bunting; *to Short Creek*, Harrison County, O. (1803-22):
Lacy, Ball, Hague, Rattekir, Wood, Schuley; *to other Ohio
meetings* (1807-44): Wright, Richardson, Connard, Wilkin-
son, Wood, Swayne, Janney, John, Myers, Wilson.

GOOSE CREEK MONTHLY MEETING (northern).—*To Concord* (1805-08): Evans, Pancoast, Sinclair, Spencer, Gregg,

White, Whiteacre, Canby, Dillon, Smith; *to Salem*, in Columbiana County, O. (1806-07): Craig, Smith, Canby, Janney, Gilbert; *to Plainfield*, O. (1810-19); Hough, Smith, Schirley, Musgrave, Dillon, Hatcher; *to other meetings*, nearly all in Ohio (1820-54): Talbott, Buchanan, Rose, Hampton, Hughes, Nichols, Bradfield, Trehern, Mead, Wilson, Birdsall, Brown, Shoemaker, Taylor.

CROOKED RUN MONTHLY MEETING.—*To Westland and Redstone* (1787-1803); Cadwalader, Reyley, Hank, Russel, Berry, Wright, Hunt, Richards, Mullen, Updegraff, Lupton, Wood, Evans, Cleaver, Yarnell, Painter, Dillhorn, Taylor, Holloway, Penrose, Miller; *to Concord* (1803-06): Faucett, Pickering, Wright, Lupton, Piggott, Holloway, Branson, Como, Smith, Wright, Sharp; *to Miami*, Warren County, O., but in Indiana Yearly Meeting (1805-07): Whitacar, McKay, Taylor, Smith, Cleaver, Garwood, Pusey, Harris, Rhea.

ALEXANDRIA MONTHLY MEETING.—*To Plainfield* (1815-24): Homer, Far, Faulkner; *to Allum Creek*, Morrow County, Ohio (1833-34): Elliott; *to New Garden*, Wayne County, Ind. (1833-39): Myers, Janney, Davis; *to Honey Creek*, Vigo County, Ind. (1840): Russell;[1] *to others* (1815-51): Grubb, Neale, Patterson, Schofield, Ellen, Cemby, Sands, Little, Miller, Ross.

GOOSE CREEK MONTHLY MEETING (southern).—*To Westland* (1801-03): Oliphant, Erwin, Lewis, Morlan, Richards, Whitaker, Pidgeon, Schooley, Wright, Parsons, Sinclair; *to Concord* (1802-06): McPherson, Bond, Coffee, Broomhall, Pidgeon; *to Miami* (1812-14): Johnston, Johnson, Anthony, Lewis, Cadwallader, Harris; *to other Ohio meetings:* Embree, Rhodes, Morlan, Cole, Pennock, Curl, Perdue.

SOUTH RIVER MONTHLY MEETING.—*To Westland* (1801-02): James, Hanna, Baugham, Harris, Holloway, Terrell, Stratton, Ferrall, Carle, Via, Tellus; *to Concord* (1802-05):

---

[1] Honey Creek Monthly Meeting has either been laid down or its name has been changed.

Pidgeon, Gregg, Bloxom, Wildman; *to Salem* (1805-07): Stanton, Carle, Macy, Gurrell, Fisher; *to Miami* (1806-19): Johnson, Bloxom, Terrell, Morman, Butterworth, Fisher, Dicks, Lodge, Butler, Davis, Welch, Bailey, Lewis; *to Fairfield*, Highland Co., O. (1809-21): Barum, Timberlake, Burgess, Johnson, Stanton, Anderson, Coffey, Bloxom, Holloway, Plumer, Sparkman, Fox, Perdue; *to other meetings, mostly in Ohio:* Redder, Miliner, Holloway, Fisher, Ferrall, Early, Moorman, Stratton, Johnson, Preston, Burgess, Ballard, Terrell, Lea, Cox, Cadwalader, Butler, Morgan, Bailey, Lynch.

CEDAR CREEK MONTHLY MEETING.—*To Salem* (1812-23): Stanley, Blackburn; *to Short Creek* (1813-41): Moorman, Terrell, Maddox, Hargrave, Creek; *to others* (1812-   ): Anthony, Johnson, Wilkins, Blackburn, Bates, Jordan, Leadbetter.

GRAVELLY RUN MONTHLY MEETING.— *To Springboro* (1826-29): Peebles, Hunnicutt, Bailey, Binford, Lewis, Stanton, Walthal; *to others* (1822-30): Butler, Thomas, Peebles, Binford, Wrenn, Johnson, Hunnicutt, Sems, Watkins; nearly all to Ohio.

WHITE OAK SWAMP MONTHLY MEETING.—*To Ohio*, meetings not specified (1811-36): Ratcliff, Crew, Ladd, Harrison, Bates, Hockaday, Hargrave, Terrill, Andrews, Binford, Johnson, Ricks; most of these went to Short Creek.

WESTERN BRANCH MONTHLY MEETING.—*To Concord* (1805-33): Bond, Morlan, Curl, Johnson, Anthony, Lewis, Larow, Moorland, Perdue, Howell, Powell, Butler, Stanton, James, Draper, Ricks, Chapel, Hunnicutt, Trotter, Ricks, Lawrence; *to Indiana* (1829-33): Hare, Draper, Johnson, White, Hunnicutt, Andrews, Butler.

SYMONS'S CREEK MONTHLY MEETING.— *To White Water*, Wayne Co., Ind. (1811-24): Morris, Symons, Trueblood, Tatlock, Bundy, Henby; *to Lick Creek*, in Orange County, Ind. (1815): Trueblood, Morris; *to Blue River*, in Washington County, Ind. (1816-32): Trueblood, Symons, Jordan, Morris, Cosand, Pritchard, White, Delon; *to Milford* (now

Dublin), Wayne Co. (1829-44): White, Perisho, Bundy, Pike, Lamb, Albertson, Trueblood, Parker; *to other meetings* (1811-54): Bogue, Sanders, Bundy, White, Trueblood, Elliott.

SUTTON'S CREEK MONTHLY MEETING.—*To White Water*, (1812-31): Nixon, Newby, Cox, Henby, Draper, Bogue, Guier, Haskett, Chappel; *to Lick Creek* (1814): Newby, Evans, Draper, Bogue, Willard, White, Lacy, Haskett, Chawner; *to Blue River* (1815-31): Newby, Cox, Hollowell, Albertson, White, Moore, Charles, Hollowell, Cosand; *to others* (1820): Charles, Fletcher, Draper, Chappel, Nicholson, Albertson, Haskett, Wilson, Nixon, Henby.

PINEY WOODS MONTHLY MEETING.—*To Ohio* (1806-28): Goodwin, Smith, Harrel, Lamb, Elliott, Thornton, Bogue, Moore, Newby; *to White Water* (1816-30): Saint, Lamb, Wilson, Moore, Bundy; *to other Indiana meetings*(1816-): Elliott, Lamb, White, Newby.

RICH SQUARE MONTHLY MEETING.—*To Short Creek* (1805-41): Parker, Judkins, Peele; *to other Ohio meetings* (1802-25): Brown, Outland, Wilson, Patterson; *to White Water* (1819-26): Parker, Hall, Binford; *to other Indiana meetings* : Baker, Parker, Peele, Beamon, Outland.

JACK SWAMP MONTHLY MEETING.—*To Short Creek* (1805-11): Patterson, Maremoon (or Moreman), Taylor; *to other Ohio meetings* (1805-12): Patterson, Maremoon, Hicks, Crew, Reams.

CORE SOUND MONTHLY MEETING.—*To Westland* (1799-1802): Howard, Bundy, Bishop, Dew, Ward, Mace, Stanton, Williams; *to Concord* (1802-04): Harris, Thomas, Scott, Williams, Mace; *to New Garden* (1832): Davis, Harris, Hubbard, Perisho, Wilson, Mace, Fodra.

CONTENTNEA MONTHLY MEETING.—*To Redstone* (1800): Thomas, Arnold; *to Concord* (1802-05): Hall, Edgerton, Outland, Doudna, Albertson, Dodd, Bailey, Morris; *to other meetings in Ohio* (1805-34): Copeland, Bundy, Collier, Cox, Price, Hollowell, Hobson, Spivy, Thomas, Peele, Hall, Jinnett; *to New Garden* (1822-32): Arnold, Fulghum,

Horn, Woodward, Barker, Bogue, Hall, Harris; *to Honey Creek* (1822-31): Cox, Arnold, Musgrave, Lancaster, Pike; *to Bloomfield* (1832-38): Morris, Outland, Overman, Horn, Hollowell, Colyer, Davis; *to other meetings in Indiana* (1820-36): Cook, Newson, Parker, Davis, Arnold, Morris, Cox, Bishop, Coleman, Jinnett, Harris, Fellow, Hall, Barker, Arnold, Woodward, Overman, Kean, Boswell, Peele, Pike, Bundy.

CANE CREEK MONTHLY MEETING.—*To Miami* (1804-07): Edwards, Hobson, Stout, Doan, Cox, Kenworthy, Jones, Cloud, Carter, Morrisson, Grave, Harvey, Newlin, Ratcliff, Pettott, Morrow, Rineand, Johnson, Hadly; *to other meetings in Ohio* (1805-09): Stanton, Haydock, Cox, Hadly, Baker, Clark, Hussey, Hasket, Moffit, Hale, Ratcliff: *to White Water* (1811-24): Farlow, Moffit, Doan, Gifford, Cox, Corner (or Comer?), Ratcliff, Hadley, Allen, Carter, Williams, Ward; *to Lick Creek* (1814-34): Doan, Freeman, Dixon, Stout, Hadly, Rubottom, Wells, Gifford, Atkinson, Siler, Farmer, Moon, Marshall, Moore, Carter, Cox, Moffitt, Stuart; *to White Lick*, in Morgan County, Ind. (1824-37): Hadly, Marshall, Allen, Johnson, Cashet, Pickett, Hinshaw, Hobson, Vestal, Anderson, Lindley, Hockett, Dixon, Hill, Carter; *to other meetings in Indiana* (1822-37): Hobson, Pickett, Newlin, Wheeler, Hinshaw, Wells, Hadly, Pike, Faust, Dixon, Hill, Stout, Hills, Puckett, Branson.

NEW GARDEN MONTHLY MEETING.—*To Miami* (1804-09): Dillon, Leonard, Ozburn, Moore, Baldwin, Hoggatt, Hester, Hodgson, John, Witty, Stanley, Hunt, Simmons, Knight, Thornburgh, Stephens: *to Center*, O. (1807-11): Hodgson, Starbuck, Cox, Thornburgh, Dillon, Moore, Hiatt, Coffin, Haskins; *to Fairfield*, Highland Co., O. (1808-11): Hoggatt, Baldwin, Starbuck, Hoskins, Thornburgh, Hiatt; *to other meetings in Ohio* (1803-31): Hines, Hodgson, Perkins, Starbuck, Williams, Thornburgh, Flanner, Macy, Bunker, Low, Brown, McMuir, James, Jenkins, Russell, Knight, Swain, Blizzard, Jessop, Coffin, Hunt; *to White Water* (1810-37): Benbow, Baldwin, Clark, Jessop,

Hunt, Macy, Puckett, Cook, Hiatt, Williams, Johnson, Un-
thank, Davis, Hubbard, Swain, John, Coffin, Moore; *to
Blue River* (1816-24): Wilson, Hague, Macy; *to Silver Creek,*
now *Salem,* in Union County, Ind. (1817-30): Gardner,
Jessop, Macy, Bernard; *to New Garden* (1820-55): Jessop,
Baldwin, Evans, White, Coffin, Unthank, Claton, Wilson;
to Honey Creek (1820-24): Dicks, Hunt, Cox; *to West
Grove,* Wayne Co., Ind. (1821-28): Coffin, Hunt, Jessop,
Gordon, Baldwin; *to Silver Creek* (1822-33): Macy; *to Mil-
ford* (1824-44): Hiatt, Coffin, Hubbard, Unthank, White,
Clayton, Moore, Jessop, Stanley, Hunt; *to other meetings
in Indiana* (1821-60): Farmer, Jessop, Stephens, Osborn,
Hunt, Johnson, Benbow, Claton, Knight, Russell, Dennis,
Moore, Canon, Hollingsworth, Coffin, Stanley, Swain, Has-
kins, Edwards, Foster, Hellam, Mendenhall, Woody, Clark,
Davis, Macy, Grey, Wilson, Rayl, White.

SPRINGFIELD MONTHLY MEETING.—*To Miami* (1804-10):
Mendenhall, Smith, Millikan, Wright, Kersey, Tomlinson,
Bundy, Hoggatt, Arnold, Harlan; *to other meetings in Ohio*
(1803-32): Pidgeon, Reece, Newby, Kersey, Bundy, Tomlin-
son, Mendenhall, Wright, Kellum, Beard, Harlan, Millikan,
Spears, Spencer, Hoggatt; *to White Water* (1811-31): Nixon,
Mendenhall, Munden, Hoggatt, Symons, Hitchcock, Kersey,
Millikin, Gilbert, Cook, Morris, Bell, Kendall, Moore, Pear-
son, Bundy, Springs, Newby, Bond, Frazier, Garrett;
to Lick Creek (1813-21): Weeks, Coffin, Cook, White,
Kersey, Tomlinson, Blair; *to Blue River* (1816-30): Blair,
Coffin, Morris, Hoggatt, Cox, Overman, Beals, Bundy,
Haworth, Albertson; *to Milford* (1824-31): Boon, Kersey,
Kendal, Hodson, Mendenhall; *to White Lick,* Hendricks
and Morgan counties, Ind. (1825-50): Hodson, Beeson,
Hoggatt, Kendal, Carter, Beals, Mendenhall, Albertson,
Turner, Hunt, Harlan, Stalker; *to other meetings in Indiana :*
Gilbert, Hodson, Barnet, Wickersham, Haworth, Boon,
Bond, Kersey, Frazier, Gordon, Harlan, Mendenhall, Ken-
dall, Hockett.

DOVER MONTHLY MEETING.—*To Ohio meetings* (1825-

49): Hunt, McPherson, Ballard, Horney; *to Blue River* (1816-36): Meredith, McPherson; *to White Water* (1827-34): Brown, Stanley, Norton, Meredith, Jessop; *to Duck Creek,* Henry Co., Ind. (1829-37): Henley, Stanley, Bownan, Coffin, Dean; *to New Garden* (1831-38): Meredith, Eaves, Gurley, Horney; *to other Indiana meetings* (1830-59); Bowren, Camness, Pidgeon, Rich, Stanley, Harrold, Perkins, Starbuck; *to Vermillion,* Vermillion Co., Ill. (1831-33): Meredith, Stanley, Gardner.

WESTFIELD MONTHLY MEETING.—*To Miami* (1804-14): Carr, Worley, Burris, Sumner, Beeson, Bond, Harrold, Williams; *to Fairfield,* Highland Co., O. (1807-10): Burris, Grigg, Sumner, Horton, Puckett, McKinney, Beeson, Harrold, Hoggatt, Carson, Bond, Small; *to Fall Creek,* Highland Co., O. (1812-17): Ballard, Hiatt, Bond, Carson, Jessop; *to White Water* (1817-22): Denny, Puckett, Jessop, Chandler; *to New Garden* (1819-20): Puckett, Jackson; *to Springfield* (1822): Beales, Cook.

HOPEWELL MONTHLY MEETING.—*To White Water* (1824-38): Hiatt, Coffin, Stanley, Middleton, Edwards, Rayl; *to White Lick* (1825-33): Hale, Edwards, Perkins; *to Milford* (1826-45): Macy, White, Edwards, Hunt; *to Walnut Ridge,* Rush Co., Ind. (1844-45): White, Ray, Cannaday; *to other meetings in Indiana :* Baldwin, Meredith, Perkins, Clark, Rayl, Macy, Hodgins.

DEEP RIVER MONTHLY MEETING. — *To Ohio meetings* (1811-37): Pike, Pegg, Cook, Jones, Stafford, Hubbard; *to White Water* (1811-59): Morris, Johnson, Gardner, Harris, Jessop, Horney, Pegg, Cook, Mills, Stewart, Clark, Pearce, Springer, Brown, Saunders, Ham, Mendenhall, Hiatt, Brooks, Baldwin, Elliott, Johnson, Beard; *to Lick Creek* (1814-21): Stanley, Henley, Howell; *to Blue River* (1815-26): Coffin, Bundy, Stalther, Jessop, Starbuck, Pittman, Wilson; *to White Lick* (1826-44): Coffin, Jessop, Vestal, Thomas, Hubbard; *to Milford* (1829-57): Brown, Nixon, Coffin, Hubbard, Pitman, Brothers; *to Springfield* (1830-40): Beeson, Baldwin, Coffin; *to Duck Creek* (1833-42):

Beeson, Thomas, Robertson, Coffin; *to Walnut Ridge*
(1837-60): Coffin, Clark, Pitts, Moore; *to other Indiana
meetings* (1822-): Coffin, Stafford, Johnson, Thomas,
Pugh, Mendenhall, Hiatt, Cosand, Moore, Bundy, Fisher.

MOUNT PLEASANT MONTHLY MEETING. — *To Westland*
(1802): Bradford; *to Miami* (1803-09): Hiatt, Pope, Pick-
rell, Hosier, Suffring, Bailey, Williams, Jessop, Hill, Overman, Small, Paxson, Bond, Ballard; *to Concord* (1805):
Vinon, Davis, Bundy, Woods; *to Fairfield* (1807-19):
Hiatt, Chalfant, Reece, Betts, Hunt, Green, Pearson,
Newby, Stanley, Ballard, Jessop, Robinson, Bond, Pig-
gott, Perisho, McPherson, Hockett, Green, Bryant, Bently;
to other Ohio meetings (1804-24): Thomas, Lundy, Bond,
Ballard, Sumner, Beek, Pierce, Stalker, Scooly, Green,
Gray, Williams, Robinson, Pierson, Wildman, Ward, John-
son, Pike, Lewis, Cary, Hunt, Anthony, Hiatt, Betts,
Bundy, Jones, Chew, Davis; *to White Water* (1810-12):
Lundy, Thornbrough, Coffin, Bond, McLean, Potter, Davis,
Farmer, Commons, Hoggatt; *to Lick Creek* (1814-21):
Carter, Williams, Davis.

SPRING MONTHLY MEETING.—*To Bloomfield*, Park Co.,
Ind. (1831-39): Newlin, Lindley, Morison, Harvey, Sergent,
Carl, Woody, Andrew, Hadley; *to White Lick* (1831-37):
Lindley, Turner, Hadley, Thompson; *to other Indiana
meetings* (1831-38): Piggott, Hadley (these records were
seen for 1831-39 only).

PINEY GROVE MONTHLY MEETING. — *To Ohio meetings*
(1805-12): Stafford, Mendenhall, Beauchamp, Thomas,
Marine, Moorman, Harris, Morris, Lingagar, Almond; *to
White Water* (1812-15): Beauchamp, Thomas, Baldwin,
Parker, Wilents, Knight, Moorman; *to Lick Creek* (1815):
Morris, Dauson, Thomas, Mendenhall.

BUSH RIVER MONTHLY MEETING.—*To Westland* (1802-
03): Pugh, Jay, Kelly, O'Neal, Mills, Peaty, Horner,
Wright; *to Miami* (1803-07):[1] Evans, Cate, Compton,

[1] Some of these certificates are addressed to Little Miami Monthly
Meeting, but they were all evidently intended for Miami Monthly

Bridgers, Brooks, Jenkins, Davis, Coppock, Pearson, Gaunt, Nichols, Furnas, Ellyman, Coats, Teague, Kelly, Hollingsworth, Henderson, Cook, Jay, Comner, Jones, Mote, Wright, Thomas, Cox, Insco, Farmer, Miles, McCool, Peaty, Vernon, Compton, Weisner, Mills, Stedom, Cammack, Cave, Benbow, Hasket, Thompson, McClure, Lewis, Brown, Bartin; *to other Ohio meetings* (1805-   ): Galbreath, Marmaduke, Mendenhall.

WRIGHTSBOROUGH MONTHLY MEETING (including some emigrants from Bush River and Cane Creek, S. C.).— *To Miami* (1802-1810): Farmer, Maddox, Thomson, Hart, Mendenhall, Stubbs, Green; *to other Ohio meetings*: Butler, Hollingsworth, Moore, Jay, Pearson, Killey, Henderson, Williams, Brooks.[1]

No section in the West represents, perhaps, more distinctly the effects of this Southern migration than does Wayne County, Indiana, and White Water Monthly Meeting, which is within its limits. This county is on the eastern border of the State and has Richmond for its county-seat. One of its Carolina pioneers was David Hoover, of Randolph County, N. C. The personal history of this man and of his family is typical of the hundred-year history of the Society of Friends which I here seek to present. " I was born," he says in his autobiography, " on a small watercourse, called Huwarrie, a branch of the Yadkin River, in Randolph County, North Carolina, on the 14th day of April, 1781." His opportunities for education were very

---

Meeting, which is near the Little Miami River, Warren County, O. It was the first monthly meeting set up in Western Ohio, and was established by Redstone Quarterly Meeting in October, 1803.

[1] Were the means at hand it would be an exceedingly interesting study to find out how many descendants of these Quakers who left the South because of slavery became prominent in service of the Union during the Civil War. Lucy Norman, the mother of Edwin M. Stanton, removed from Stevensburg, Culpeper County, Va., to Ohio, with a Quaker family named Starr. The family of Senator George E. Pugh, of Ohio, went from South Carolina. Gen. Solomon Meredith was a Guilford County (N. C.) Quaker, and the father of George W. Julian, the Free-Soil candidate for Vice-president in 1852, migrated from Randolph County, N. C.

limited; he had no chance to read a newspaper, and he never
saw a bank-note until a man. " If my information is correct,
my grandfather, Andrew Hoover, left Germany when a boy,
married Margaret Fouts, in Pennsylvania, and settled on
Pipe Creek, in Maryland. There my father was born, and
from thence, now about one hundred years ago [*c.* 1754], he
removed to North Carolina, then a new country. He left
eight sons and five daughters, all of whom had large families.
Their descendants are mostly scattered through what we call
the Western country. . . . My father had a family of ten
children, four sons and six daughters. In order to better
our circumstances he came to the conclusion of moving to
a new country, and sold his possessions accordingly. He
was then worth rising of two thousand dollars, which at
that time, and in that country, was considered very considerably over an average in point of wealth. On the 19th of
September, 1802, we loaded our wagon and wended our way
toward that portion of what was then called the Northwest-
ern Territory which constitutes the present State of Ohio. . .
After about five weeks' journeying, we crossed the Ohio
river at Cincinnati. . . . We pushed on to Stillwater, about
twelve miles north of Dayton, in what is now the county of
Montgomery. A number of our acquaintances had located
themselves there the previous spring. There we encamped
in the woods the first winter. . . . Our object was to find a
suitable place for making a settlement and where but few or
no entries had been made. But a small portion of the land
lying west of the Great Miami, or east of the Little Miami,
was settled at that time. We were hard to please. We
Carolinians' would scarcely look at the best land, where
spring-water was lacking. . . . Thus time passed on until
the spring of 1806, when myself and four others, rather

<hr/>

¹It is worthy of note that Friends are almost the only citizens of
North Carolina who recognize that they have the right to this form
of the name instead of those across the line. It is the rarest thing
for Quakers to speak of themselves as "North Carolinians." They
are nearly always simply "Carolinians," and in Quaker parlance
"Carolina" still means the Old North State.

accidentally, took a section line some eight or ten miles
north of Dayton, and traced it a distance of more than
thirty miles, through an unbroken forest, to where I am now
writing. It was the last of February, or first of March, when
I first saw White Water. On my return to my father's I
informed him that I thought I had found the country we
had been in search of. Spring-water, timber and building
rock appeared to be abundant,[1] and the face of the country
looked delightful. In about three weeks after this, my
father, with several others, accompanied me to this 'land of
promise.' As a military man would say, we made a recon-
noissance. . . . It was not until the last of May or the first
of June that the first entries were made. John Smith [from
Perquimans County, N. C.] then entered south of Main
Street, where Richmond now stands, and several other tracts.
My father entered the land upon which I now live, I having
selected it on my first trip, and several other quarter-sections.
About harvest of this same year, Jeremiah Cox reached here
from good old North Carolina [Randolph County] and purchased where the north part of Richmond now stands. If I
mistake not, it had been previously entered by John Meek,
the father of Jesse Meek, and had been transferred to Joseph
Woodkirk, of whom J. Cox made the purchase. Said Cox
also entered several other tracts. Jeremiah Cox, John
Smith, and my father were then looked upon as rather
leaders in the Society of Friends. Their location here had
a tendency of drawing others, and soon caused a great rush
to White Water, and land that I thought would hardly ever
be settled was rapidly taken up and improved. Had I a
little more vanity I might almost claim the credit . . . of
having been the pioneer of the great body of Friends now to
be found in this region, as I think it very doubtful whether
three Yearly Meetings would convene in this county, had
I not traced the line before-mentioned."[2]

---

[1] These are the chief characteristics of his old home section in
North Carolina.
[2] *Memoir* of David Hoover, written by himself and edited by Isaac
H. Julian.

Hoover had been preceded in 1805 by John Endsley, who came from South Carolina. He traveled between South Carolina and Wayne County, Ind., seven times, five of the trips being made on horseback. Other North Carolina Friends soon followed Hoover. Elijah Wright, Benjamin Hill, Robert Hill and David Railsback came in 1806 or 1807; Ralph Wright, Charles Hunt, Isaac Beeson, Benjamin Maudlin, in 1807; Jesse Bond settled in 1808 on a farm where Earlham College now is; John Burgess and Isaac Julian (father of George W. Julian) came in 1808, the latter from Randolph County. There were also a few emigrants into the section from South Carolina and Virginia. Many North Carolina Quaker names became common in the county, such as Anderson, Bunker, Beeson, Beard, Bogue, Clark, Elliott, Fouts, Hubbard, Hiatt, Harris, Hough, Henly, Jessop, Johnson, Jordan, Morris, Mendenhall, Newby, Nicholson, Nixon, Overman, Peele, Pike, Starbuck, Swain, Symons, Vestal, White, Wilson, Williams.

Many of these came from Guilford and Randolph counties. Center and New Garden townships were laid out in the new county, and the names of the North Carolina localities from which the immigrants came were soon stereotyped, such as "Guilford County, near Clemmons's store," or "Beard's hat shop," or "Deep River settlement of Friends," or "Dobson's cross roads."[1]

In the same way the first settlers of Henry County, Indiana, another Quaker stronghold, came from Maryland, Virginia, North Carolina, Pennsylvania, Ohio and Kentucky, beginning about 1819. The biographical history of the pioneers of Henry County indicates that a majority were born in Virginia and North Carolina.[2]

These records illustrate the character and extent of the migrations from North Carolina. In point of territory, the western Yearly Meetings, beginning with Ohio, were set

---

[1] *History of Wayne County, Indiana.* 1884 : Andrew W. Young's *History of Wayne County, Indiana.* 1872.
[2] *History of Henry County, Indiana.* 1884.

off from Baltimore Yearly Meeting, but the parent meeting, in reality, is North Carolina Yearly Meeting, as Stanley Pumphrey recognizes in his journal. He says: " I believe that fully half the Friends in the West are of Carolina descent, and many of the most prominent men, like Charles F. Coffin, Dr. Dougan Clark and Dr. William Nicholson, are natives of Carolina."

This view of the case agrees literally with what was written me recently by Addison Coffin, a man of close observation and inquiring mind, an actor in the migration, and one who has investigated the subject for himself. He writes under date of January 16, 1894: " Two or three years ago the Historical Society of Wayne and Henry County, Indiana, asked me to assist them in getting a list of family names known to have emigrated from North Carolina to Indiana in the first half of this century. I succeeded in furnishing over three hundred; in many instances twenty or more families of one name migrated; my list began moving in 1806, when there was quite a large number left the State; again, from 1818 to 1819. After the agitation and settling of the Missouri Compromise, thousands left the State, a very large per cent being Quakers; again, as a result of the South Carolina nullification frolic other thousands left; then when the legislature disfranchised the free colored men,[1] and forbade masters from educating their slaves,[2] the tide of emigration increased and flowed without ceasing till the rebellion." Mr. Coffin estimates that in 1850 one-third of the population of the State of Indiana was composed of native Carolinians and their children in the first generation.

These emigrants were not all Friends, for there were many other enemies of slavery in the South. There were among them many of the middle class of the white population who did not own slaves, who could not come into economic competition with slave labor, who realized that their own labor was degraded by the presence of slaves, and who

[1] By the revision of the State Constitution in 1835.
[2] Law of 1830-31.

sought to escape its influence by removal. These are they who were called by negro slaves in the South and by some historians "poor white trash"; by the negroes from contempt because they owned few or no slaves; by the historians from ignorance, and the latter have also represented that they were not lovers of liberty. Whatever the origin of the word, there is the clearest evidence that it was used before the war by the slaves alone. It perhaps started with house servants in the more aristocratic families, for these servants were the greatest aristocrats in all the South. So far as my observation goes, and that of my correspondents in various parts of the country, the term originated with and was used almost exclusively by the negroes.

There certainly would have been the greatest inconsistency in the use of the term by well-to-do slaveholders, for many of them had risen by their own energy and pluck from the ranks of this same class to independence and affluence. Nothing can be more unjust than to speak of "poor whites" as a class without energy, character or ambition. Such is not the case. They are men who have always had a fierce, even an unreasoning, love of liberty. They are the representatives of the men who stood behind the English barons at Runnymede; they plucked victory from the French at Crecy, Poictiers and Agincourt. They are the men who braved the heat of the day in the Revolution. They furnished the bone and sinew of both armies in the American conflict. Their typical representatives are Jackson, Johnson and Lincoln. These were the men who left Virginia, the Carolinas and Georgia by thousands, because there was no liberty with slavery. These are the men—many Quakers, many not—who contributed with their brain and their brawn to the making of the central West.

CHAPTER XI.

We have now come to the turn in the tide for Southern Quakerism. From the beginning of the nineteenth century the decline of the Society is visible. It has disappeared entirely from South Carolina and Georgia. It has become very weak in Virginia. It has disappeared also from certain parts of North Carolina. There are now no Quakers in Pasquotank County, where there were three meetings in 1800 and one meeting in 1850. Craven, Carteret and Jones counties reported four meetings in 1800 and one in 1850. There are none to-day. It has disappeared from the Cape Fear section. Its members have become fewer in number in Perquimans and Northampton. We can also trace a movement westward even within the limits of the State. There has been an effort to get away from the sea-coast, probably for the same reason as the westward migration, for the slaves were more numerous in the eastern counties. It has grown in Johnston, Wayne, Guilford and Randolph counties, the last two being now the banner Quaker counties of the State. Guilford now contains twenty per cent and Randolph twenty-two per cent of their total population in the State.

In Virginia, Quakerism is strongest in the counties of Frederick, Loudoun and Fairfax, where a majority have accepted the Hicksite view. It has disappeared from Surry, Prince George, Charles City, Hanover, Louisa, Bedford and Campbell. There are three meetings in Southampton, one in Nansemond and one in Henrico. With the beginning of the present century there is a visible change in the tone of the Virginia minutes. The invariable answer to the second of the annual questions is, " no new meeting-houses

built or meetings settled." Then it becomes necessary for
Friends to appoint committees to look into the condition of
certain meetings. In 1807 the meeting at Black Creek
in New Kent County was suspended, and Friends were
appointed to sell the meeting-house and the lot on which it
was located. In 1809 I find that " the committee continued
to sell Black Creek meeting-house reported that no person
had yet offered to purchase it—the committee is discontinued and the house given to Friends in that neighborhood
to pull down or otherwise apply to their private benefit." [1]
Black Water Monthly Meeting was laid down in 1806; Bennett's Creek meeting was laid down in 1821. A new meeting was established in Prince George County in that year
by the name of Binford, but this turn was only temporary
and it was laid down in 1826. Seacock meeting was laid
down in 1821; Stanton's in 1829, when there were only two
families there, and Burleigh in 1832. These four composed
a part of Gravelly Run Monthly Meeting, told on its organization and it too was laid down in 1832. These were not
isolated cases of decay. Fothergill tells us that Friends
had almost disappeared from the Eastern Shore of Virginia
as early as 1736. About 1750 the Chuckatuck meeting was
reduced to a faithful few. But their time was not yet. In
1814 the Goose Creek Monthly Meeting, which dates from
1794 in the prosperous years of the Society, was laid down
and its few remaining members turned over to South River
Monthly Meeting. In 1817 the Western Quarterly Meeting,
whose organization in 1797 indicated the direction in which
Quaker migration was going, was also laid down, for the
wave had passed its limits, surmounted the Alleghanies, subdued the wilderness, and spread itself into the valley of the
Mississippi.

The Hicksite Separation.

In the meantime the Hicksite controversy had culminated
in 1828. It is not within the province of this paper to enter

---

[1] A meeting of the same name still exists in Southampton County.

into a detail of events leading up to this movement which had a very unfortunate influence on the Society. It arose from a difference in theological beliefs, and each party claimed to represent the original views of Fox and his followers. The separation began in Philadelphia Yearly Meeting, and extended to those of New York, Ohio, Indiana and Baltimore. It did not extend to the Virginia or North Carolina Yearly Meetings. It is only with the separation in Baltimore Yearly Meeting that we are concerned. The orthodox party lost all of their meetings within the bounds of this Yearly Meeting that were located in Virginia, except a part of the meeting at Hopewell, and the meeting-house at this place has been used jointly by the two branches up to the present time. In 1832 an almanac of the Hicksite[1] Friends reported ten meeting-houses as then in use by themselves in Northern Virginia. In Hopewell Monthly Meeting were Hopewell, Centre, Berkeley, Middle Creek, The Ridge, and Dillon's Run; Fairfax made a monthly meeting by itself; Goose Creek Monthly Meeting had Goose Creek and South Fork; Alexandria Monthly Meeting had Alexandria meeting, with Washington on the other side of the river. In recent years there has been a greater relative growth of the orthodox branch in this section. The census of 1890 put the number of orthodox Friends at ninety-six and the number of Hicksite Friends at five hundred and six.

One of the best known members of the latter party was Edward Stabler, who was one of the most prominent of Virginia Friends. His father removed from York, England, to Pennsylvania, then settled in Petersburg, Va., and there the son was born on September 18, 1769. The son learned the business of tanning, but went into the drug business, first in Leesburg, Va., and in 1791 in Alexandria, Va. He

---

[1] As all persons acquainted with the history of Friends are aware, this name is not recognized by this branch of the Society. The terms Hicksite and orthodox are used here as in popular parlance, to distinguish the two. It is not the province of this paper to discuss the question as to which branch is nearer the teachings of Fox.

became a prominent leader in the Society. He visited the more southern meetings in 1804, and in 1806 began to preach. From this time on he was largely engaged in the work of the ministry, particularly in the Northern, Eastern and Middle States, and was very useful in helping to suppress the improper use of spirituous liquors among Friends. He died in Alexandria, January 18, 1831. His life has been published by his son.

Besides Samuel M. Janney, of whom a sketch has been given in another connection, this branch of the Society had another prominent representative in this section in Benjamin Hollowell. He was not a native, but spent much time in Alexandria and in Washington City, where he was well and favorably known from his connection with educational work and for his scientific publications. Between 1824 and 1858 he conducted the Alexandria (Va.) Boarding School, and numbered among his pupils many sons of slaveholders, including Gen. Robert E. Lee and Gen. Edmund Kirby-Smith. His autobiography has been published.[1]

The Laying Down of Virginia Yearly Meeting.

Although, as has been said already, the separation did not extend to the Virginia or to the North Carolina Yearly Meetings, it is safe to say that its influence on those meetings was bad. In the meantime the Virginia Yearly Meeting was growing weaker year by year. In 1829 they write their North Carolina brethren that their meeting is small and continues to annually decrease on account of the migration of Friends to other States, where slavery does not exist, and "from the departure of many of our youth from the Testimonies and simplicity of our ancestors," and Thomas Shillitoe says there were only two acknowledged ministers within the Yearly Meeting at that time. In 1830 they invite Baltimore and North Carolina Yearly Meetings to send

---

[1] See the valuable paper on "Education in the Religious Society of Friends," by Edward H. Magill, LL. D., in *Proceedings* of the Religious Congress for Friends [Chicago, 1893]. 8°.

delegates to sit with them and confer with their committee on the advisability of laying down the Yearly Meeting, a step which, they say, had hitherto never been known. The committee reported that time for dissolution had not yet come, but in consideration of their weak state Baltimore and North Carolina were invited " to extend their christian regard toward this meeting." The committees were again present in 1832 and made the same report, also in 1833, but the time was not yet. In 1834 the Yearly Meeting was transferred from Gravelly Run, where it had been held for many years alternately with Cedar Creek, to Somerton in Nansemond County. There was a poetic fitness in this change; it was as if the old man, weary of the troubles and trials of life, had come home to die, for Nansemond had been the scene of their early trials and triumphs. Here Fox and Edmundson had labored and here some of their earliest meetings were held. The Yearly Meeting dragged on for a few years longer. In 1843 committees from the Yearly Meetings of Philadelphia, Baltimore, and North Carolina met Virginia Friends to advise on the situation. The last Yearly Meeting was convened at Somerton in the 5th month, 1844. The Virginia Yearly and Quarterly Meetings were then suspended and Friends were constituted a Half Yearly Meeting with the powers of a quarterly meeting, which now meets alternately at Black Creek, Southampton County, and in Richmond. It reports to Baltimore Yearly Meeting.

Thus, after an independent organization of nearly a hundred and fifty years, the Virginia Yearly Meeting ceased to exist as a separate body. It had seen the colony of Virginia grow from a feeble folk, oppressed with political bondage and religious bigotry, into a great and flourishing commonwealth cherishing civil and religious liberty as the cornerstones of its system. But they saw one cancerous spot in its social system; they had rid themselves and had sought to rid the State of this incubus; they had failed; slavery proved too powerful for Friends; they left the mother-State to her fate.

Causes of the Decline of Southern Quakerism.

This brings us directly to enumerate and discuss very briefly the causes which have led to the decline of Southern Quakerism.

I. The removal of Friends to the West. This removal was itself the result of at least three causes. The Quakers were Teutons. The old love of adventure was strong in their breasts as it was in the breasts of those who did not accept their religious views. The influence of this spirit in extending the area of their settlements is acknowledged by John Churchman, John Griffith and other traveling ministers. It was the same spirit that had led to the discovery and settlement of America. It was an historic force. These Quakers, all unconsciously, were carrying out the spirit of their race. It was the same as the spirit which took the Angles and Saxons to Britain; which drove the Franks and later the Normans into Gaul; led the Ostrogoths into Italy, the Visigoths into Spain, and the Vandals to Africa. This was the first heart-beat, as von Ranke calls it. The second heart-beat leads the descendants of these same Teutons to the Holy Land on the Crusades; when their day was over the struggle was kept up in Spain against the Moors; and the discovery of America was one of the results of the fall of Grenada. (2) Along with this historic spirit went the economic spirit —a search for more land and better land than was then available in the older States, for the best lands had been exhausted by continuous crops, and fertilizers were not extensively used. To show that these two reasons would have led many to emigrate it is only necessary for us to study the development of Old England, or New England, or the Middle Colonies, or the Germany of to-day. (3) It may be an open question as to how many of these particular emigrants would have gone West had there been no slavery in the South. But that slavery did have an overwhelming influence in the case under discussion no one can deny.

II. Dissensions within the Society. As we have seen, the

Hicksite schism divided and therefore weakened the Society in Northern Virginia.

III. Disownments for slight offenses, like marrying out of Society, and persistent efforts to force all men into the same narrow mould, which is so visible in the earlier records of the Society, have both cost it dear.

IV. Two elements have prevented the growth of the Society. On the one hand, its extreme spirituality has been a load on the Society. No body of Christians has come so near fulfilling, perhaps, the injunction to worship in spirit and in truth as have Friends. This deep spirituality is too high for most men. Their deficiencies must be supplied by forms and ceremonies. On the other hand, Quakers were the radicals of the Reformation. They abominated above all things the forms, ceremonies and rituals of the Roman Church; they were equally as uncompromising with those of the English Church. But in their very effort to escape from the Scylla of ritualism they fell into the Charybdis of stiffness and inflexibility. They developed forms and ceremonies of their own which were no less ritualistic than those of the Roman Church, and which were adhered to with such tenacity that the expression "rigid as a Quaker" became a by-word in the English-speaking world. To have no forms, no rites, no symbols, no liturgies is the root of Quaker forms. Their entire history is full of the adoption of external signs as the witness of the ministry of the spirit. Wearing sackcloth on the body and ashes on the head, as was sometimes done in early times, and a difference in dress, tell the very same story as the alb and cassock of the priest The use of the thee and thou, the broad-brim hat, the curved coat, the sing-song tone of address, the wearing of hats in court, disownment of those who marry outside of Society, all point to the same effort to indicate a coming out from the world.' These things,

---

' It is but just for us to say, in answer to a part of these criticisms, that more things were worn for mere fashion in the seventeenth century than now. It was against these excesses that the Quaker

so utterly insignificant by the side of the deep spirituality for which the Society has always stood, have been abandoned to a large extent. Quakers are not now generally known by their speech or their dress; but this was not the case until recent years, and the outsider, when first coming in contact with them, experienced, in many cases, a vague feeling of dread, and this feeling has repelled many who might have been attracted by their spirituality and by their strong insistence on moral character.

V. Aggressiveness of other denominations. The most careless perusal of the journals of the traveling Friends from the time of the Revolution will convince the reader that Friends were being absorbed, as it were, slowly and imperceptibly, into the greater body of their more aggressive and vigorous rivals, the Methodists and Baptists. The journalists note frequently that their congregations are made up principally of outsiders; when denominations are given they are almost always Methodists and Baptists. These attended their meetings, entertained their preachers and absorbed their members. The completeness of this can be seen clearly in the journal of Samuel M. Janney, who notes the fact that there had been Friends in Culpeper, Orange and Albemarle counties, Virginia, in the closing years of the eighteenth century; but in 1841-42 they had disappeared. The Methodists had taken their place.

It is true to say that Quakerism was absorbed in Virginia and North Carolina to a great extent by the Methodists. But it would be far from the truth to think that Quakerism thus disappeared leaving no trace behind. The influence which it has exerted on Southern Methodism has been very profound. It is probably accurate to call the Methodist Church the heir of the Quakers. Indeed it is entirely within the bounds of historical accuracy to say that the

---

protested ; that his garb has become peculiar, in part, because he has not chosen to change with the seasons ; that his style is tending to become the fashion again. The student will recall what a near approach was made to the coat of the Quaker in the coats that were the fashion in the spring of 1894.

foundations of Methodism in Virginia and North Carolina
were laid by Edmundson and Fox rather than by Whitefield
and Robert Williams. The beginnings of Methodism are
much nearer 1672 than 1772. Methodism was a return
toward the forms of primitive Quakerism. With them, as
with the Methodists a century later, religion took the form
of excessive emotion. The convicted sinner shook from
head to foot: there were many groans and sighs and tears;
then a sudden change, with a " sweet sound of thanksgiving
and praise." [1] In other words, the Quakerism of the Revolutionary period was beginning to lose that aggressive and
exuberant vitality that characterized it at the time of the
death of Fox. It was sinking into that quietism which had
characterized English Friends since the beginning of the
eighteenth century. The continued enthusiasm of American
Friends explains why the system retained its aggressive
vitality and grew in. numbers for almost a century after
English Quakers had reached their maximum in numbers.
When this spirit disappeared American Quakerism began
to lose numbers relatively. The early Methodists were simply leading their Quaker hearers back to the good old days
of the past.

The relations between Southern Quakers and Southern
Methodists have usually been very cordial.[2] Quakers
seldom abandon outright the scenes of former habitations.
They have returned to them in after years, have found few
of their own members still alive, but have received a warm
welcome at the hands of Methodists and others. Thus,
although their last meeting in Pasquotank County, N. C.,
was laid down in 1854, they continued to visit and to
preach among the Methodists there for nearly a generation.[3]

---

[1] Samuel Fothergill, *Essay on the Society of Friends.*
[2] Thus the Quakers of Carver's Creek Monthly Meeting gave their
meeting-house to the Methodists who were then coming into that
section of North Carolina. The latter now have a church on the
site of the Quaker meeting-house, and this is one of the strongest congregations in the county.—Private information from C. M. McLean,
Esq., Elizabethtown, N. C.   [3] Personal recollections.

In the same way Friends left Carteret County, N. C., for the West, 1830-40, and regular services were suspended then, but Friends visited the section until their own meeting-house had perished from decay. They then held meetings in private houses or in the Methodist church, which was always open to them. A touching story is told of the three or four Quaker families who still lived in the section. One took up his residence in the meeting-house until he could erect a dwelling, and as long as the meeting-house stood this man and the two or three other families met regularly on Wednesdays and Sundays for silent worship.

The North Carolina Yearly Meeting since 1844.

It follows then that from the time of the laying down of the Virginia Yearly Meeting in 1844 until the present there has been but one Yearly Meeting within the bounds treated in this volume. This is the North Carolina Yearly Meeting, covering North Carolina and Tennessee, for as early as 1826 all reference to South Carolina and Georgia as comprising a part of the Yearly Meeting had been dropped. The history of Southern Quakerism since 1844 is little more than the history of the Society in those two States.

This Yearly Meeting has been particularly free from internal dissensions; neither the early controversy with John Perrot nor the later schisms of the New Lights or Ranters; nor Hicks; nor such a division on the question of slavery as occurred in Indiana in 1843, has ever occurred within it. It has perhaps had less internal disorder than any other Yearly Meeting in America. While others were torn and weakened by internal strife, this went on in its work quietly and undisturbed. This immunity from divisions has helped it to show that wonderful vitality on which I have already remarked, and to maintain its absolute if not relative strength.

The majority of Friends both in Virginia and North Carolina accepted the views advanced by Joseph John

Gurney during his visit to America, 1837-40. He was in
North Carolina and Virginia in 1837 and in Georgia and
South Carolina in 1840. The "Beacon" controversy in
England was an outgrowth of Gurney's views. He advocated the Bible as "the only divinely appointed means and
rule of salvation." His opponents claimed that he not only
tended toward the Episcopacy, but some even said he was
an Episcopalian.[1] In England the "Beacon" controversy
gave rise to what were known as "Evangelical Friends."
In America the split began in New England and extended
to other meetings. The Society was divided in New England into a larger body who followed Gurney, and a
smaller body. Indiana and North Carolina Yearly Meetings
were great admirers of Gurney; and his character, as seen
from his memoirs, seems to have been thoroughly lovable.
In 1849, Baltimore, North Carolina and Indiana Yearly
Meetings recognized the larger or Gurneyite body in New
England, and these, with New York Yearly Meeting, caused
a joint conference to assemble in Baltimore, whose object
was to secure recognition of the "Larger Body" of New
England Friends by Philadelphia and Ohio Yearly Meetings and thus restore harmony and unity. There was
another meeting in 1851, which issued an address, and one
in 1853; in 1852 deputations from Baltimore and North
Carolina attended Philadelphia and Ohio Yearly Meetings.
But all these efforts failed. The trouble culminated in a
separation in Ohio in 1854, in which the larger body, as in
New England, accepted the views of Gurney, while the
smaller body rejected these views.[2] The latter, from the

[1] Philadelphia Yearly Meeting disclaimed officially the views of
J. J. Gurney, and adopted in April, 1847, *An Appeal for the
Ancient Doctrines* (Phila., 1883, 8°). This appeal was also adopted
by Ohio Yearly Meeting.
[2] See Hodgson's *The Society of Friends in the Nineteenth Century.*
This book is written from the extreme conservative standpoint.
For Gurney's views see the Declaration of Faith attached to his
Memoirs, II., also II., 109-115, 219-221. For the action of Baltimore
and North Carolina Yearly Meetings see Baltimore *Minutes,* 1845-55,
N. C. Y. M. *Minutes,* 1849-53, and the *Document* giving the address

name of their leader in New England, have since been distinguished from the other party by the title of Wilburites.

This trouble will also help to explain a tendency which is now visible among some members of the meetings in eastern North Carolina, particularly among those of Rich Square. Gurney did not stay among these meetings long, and his influence seems to have been small. They have had but little infusion of new blood, and are, therefore, more conservative than the western meetings. They resist the attempt to introduce modern methods, and there is a desire apparent to separate these meetings from the North Carolina Yearly Meeting and to join them to Philadelphia Yearly Meeting.

With the exception of these troubles, the Society in North Carolina has little history to record up to the Civil War. Those men were then coming on the scene in whose hands the Society has been until the present. The organization moved on quietly, and there is little in its records out of the ordinary. The main questions discussed were schools and the use of spirituous liquors. Now and then the question of slavery comes up, but seldom; they did not see their way in 1846 to make an order against voting for slaveholders, nor was it thought expedient in 1852 to take action on the question whether Friends should use slave products or not; one Friend is reported as holding slaves and others hired slaves; but the days of the slavery agitation were over. There was found to be but one effective protest against the system—migration.

---

of the committee in 1849. (New York. 1850.) See also *Some Account of the Late Separation in Ohio Yearly Meeting,* which favors the Gurney party (Wheeling, 1855), and the *Narrative* of the secession in New England "Larger Body," or Gurney party (Providence, 1845). An examination of the causes of the separation in New England was made by the meeting for sufferings of Philadelphia Yearly Meeting, followed by an expostulation to both bodies to review and retrace their steps, at the same time allowing the rights of membership, so far as Philadelphia Yearly Meeting was concerned, to both bodies. A copy of this examination was sent in MS. to each body. The Smaller Body published it.

A newer question and one which is still vital to the Society, was the use of intoxicating liquors. Each year the number of all members was reported and their position on this subject was given. These reports enable us to give the numbers of the Society who were over eighteen years of age. In 1847, one thousand six hundred and thirty-six members are reported and two hundred and forty-five used intoxicants; in 1848, two thousand and twenty-four are reported; in 1849, two thousand and fifty-six. In 1850 there were one thousand nine hundred and forty-six members divided among the quarters as follows: Eastern, two hundred and eighty-eight; Western, three hundred and forty; New Garden, one hundred and ninety-three; Contentnea, fifty-four; Lost Creek, two hundred and thirty-six; Deep River, four hundred and fourteen; Southern, four hundred and twenty-one. In 1851 there were two thousand and six members; in 1852, one thousand seven hundred and twenty-five and over; 1853, one thousand seven hundred and seventy-four; 1854, one thousand seven hundred and fifty; 1855, one thousand seven hundred and eighty-one; 1856, one thousand six hundred and seventy-nine; 1857, one thousand five hundred and seventy-eight; 1858, one thousand seven hundred and eight; 1859, one thousand six hundred and two; 1860, one thousand five hundred and thirteen. From this time the number falls off rapidly, perhaps in part from emigration caused by the war and in part by the lack of more perfect statistics. In 1861 there were one thousand four hundred and sixty-one; 1862, one thousand and seventy-two; in 1863 the number reached its lowest point, one thousand and thirty; in 1864 it had gone up to one thousand six hundred and seventy-four, representing seven hundred and eighty-seven families and parts of families; in 1865 it was one thousand seven hundred and ninety-six.

But the matters of most interest to us are those dealing with the intellectual life. The first and least successful of these was an effort in both Virginia and North Carolina toward the establishment of monthly meeting libraries. The weakness of the Virginia meetings probably prevented

any important action on the subject, but in 1838 the Yearly
Meeting provided that the interest on the fund which had
been given to the Society by Ann Scott, after paying the
expenses of the sessions of the Yearly Meeting, should be
devoted to the purchase of books. Within the North Carolina Yearly Meeting the question was first agitated in 1829,
and we find that " the Meeting for Sufferings being brought
under exercise on account of the great want there is within
the limits of this Yearly Meeting of books of information
on the principles and doctrines of the Society of Friends,
propose a plan by which each of the monthly meetings,
within our borders, may be supplied with a suitable library
of books." As a result of this conference a committee was
appointed to correspond with the meeting for sufferings in
regard to the character of books and terms; such as had
suitable books were requested to donate them to the libraries, and those who had no books to give were requested to
subscribe liberally to the book fund; each monthly meeting
was to send to the meeting for sufferings a list of the books
it had, a list of those it wanted, and to make an annual
report to the same; the meeting for sufferings was to super-
vise the purchase and to send to the monthly meetings lists
of suitable books.

There was another general effort for libraries in 1836;
in that year £60 was received from England for books; but
these efforts, worthy as they were, seem to have met with
little encouragement. There was, however, at least one
exception to this fortune. Levi Coffin [1] tells us of his efforts
in this direction in connection with a school he taught at
Deep River: "In the early part of 1826 we organized a
library association at my school-house, calling it the Naze-
reth Library Association. We got several of the prominent
men of the neighborhood interested in this work, and succeeded in getting a small, yet good collection of books
with which to start our library. We then made up a considerable sum of money, and having, by the aid of Jeremiah

---

[1] *Reminiscences*, 105.

Hubbard and others, made out a list of valuable books, we sent by Abel Coffin, who was going to Philadelphia, and purchased others. This was the beginning of what grew in time to be a large and interesting library. When my school closed, I made a donation of my stock and interest in the library to the association."

Closely associated with the movement for libraries comes a similar movement looking to better educational facilities. Up to this time there were no higher institutions of learning in the State that were in any sense distinctively Quaker. Secondary institutions were also wanting among them, and their primary schools were generally poor.

During the previous generation, Friends in North Carolina, engaged as they had been in their long-drawn and stubbornly contested fight against slavery, had had little time to think of their own more immediate needs. But with the beginning of the fourth decade of the century the tide turned more sternly against the negro, and Friends then became more self-conscious. They seem to have been thoroughly aroused to their situation by a report to the Yearly Meeting in 1831: "There is not a school in the limits of the Yearly Meeting that is under the care of a committee of either monthly or preparative meeting. The teachers of Friends' children are mostly not members of our Society and all the schools are in a mixed state." A committee was appointed to prepare an address on the subject of education to subordinate meetings. Jeremiah Hubbard, who already had a school at New Garden, was one of the prime movers in the question. Funds were collected from this country and England and a school was located at New Garden in Guilford County. It was chartered in 1833 and was called New Garden Boarding School. It was to be governed by a body of trustees chosen from each quarter; was co-educational; took only boarders, and only the children of Friends.[1] But the last clauses were soon repealed. The number of

---

[1] Nereus Mendenhall says Governor Morehead was reported to have founded the celebrated Edgeworth Seminary in Greensboro because his children were not received at the Boarding School.

students who were not Friends is very noticeable; it continued large during the war, and in 1865 reached 70 per cent, for many men were glad to send their younger sons here to save them from conscription in the Southern armies. The first superintendents were Dougan and Asenath Clark.[1] It was opened August 1, 1837, with 25 boys and 25 girls, and had been preceded in 1835 by Belvidere Academy in Perquimans County, which was under the care of the Eastern Quarter and is still in successful operation as an institution for secondary instruction.

Reports were made annually to the Yearly Meeting from New Garden Boarding School. In 1845 the average number of pupils for the year was thirty-four and one-half. In 1850 there had been ninety-four pupils in the school during the past year, of whom forty were not members of Society. There were one hundred the next year; one hundred and twenty-eight in 1853; one hundred and forty-three in 1854; one hundred and seventy-nine in 1855; one hundred and sixty-three in 1856, of whom eighty-two were not Quakers; one hundred and fifty-nine in 1857; one hundred and thirty-nine in 1858, of whom only sixty were Quakers. As the war period drew on, from sickness, the panic of 1857, and other causes, numbers declined. The institution had never paid expenses and there was a chronic complaint of lack of funds. Its accounts were carelessly kept, were unreliable, and the matter became so serious that it was necessary to appoint an agent to look into its affairs. In 1860 a committee from Baltimore and Indiana Yearly Meetings was sent down to confer over the matter. The debt, which was placed at $27.245.52 in 1861, was all assumed by the Yearly Meeting, and this body set heroically to work to pay the whole. Some $15,000 was received from

---

[1] Dougan Clark was born in Randolph County, N. C., October 3, 1783. He was a Methodist preacher for three years, but became a minister of Friends in 1817. He visited Ohio and Indiana in 1822 and Ohio again in 1828. In 1834 he visited Philadelphia. New England and Canada Yearly Meetings, and Great Britain and Ireland in 1844. He was superintendent of New Garden Boarding School for six years and died August 23, 1855. His wife was a daughter of Nathan Hunt (*q. v.*).

other Yearly Meetings for this purpose, and in 1865 the debt
was reported as finally settled. The school had been turned
over in 1861 to Jonathan E. Cox to be conducted as a private enterprise; this was successfully accomplished and on
a gold basis. With the return of peace Friends were ready
to assume its management again with a clean balance-sheet
and with the promise of a still greater degree of usefulness
than it had had in the past.

This institution is the head of Quaker education in the
South, but this is not all. It has had its legitimate influence
on the grades below. In 1851 it is reported that there
were then eight hundred and four Quaker children in North
Carolina Yearly Meeting between five and sixteen, and three
hundred and thirty-six between sixteen and twenty-one. Of
this number one thousand one hundred and four were
receiving some education, and one thousand and thirty-eight
had received some education the year before. These children had been taught in one hundred and thirty schools.
All of these were co-educational; sixteen were taught by
female members of Society and twenty-eight by male members, while eighty-six had been taught by outsiders. In
1853 there were but eight children over five who were not
receiving an education. In 1855 there were one thousand
and sixty children between five and twenty-one, and we have
the pleasing information that "there are none over five
years of age but who are in the way of receiving some education." Sunday schools were also inaugurated during this
period. No other religious denomination in these States
can probably show an educational record covering as thoroughly the whole body of its communicants as Friends.
The good work of primary and secondary education went
on till the dark days of the Civil War, often under the most
trying circumstances, for William Evans tells us that he saw
a log school-house in Lost Creek Quarter, Tennessee, about
1840, that had no windows and no fireplace; the fire was
built in the middle of the room and the smoke got out as
it could.[1]

---

[1] *Journal*, 405-415.

Friends in the Civil War.

During the Civil War Friends suffered no little. This was natural. They were within the limits of the Confederacy; they refused to fight; they were known to have circulated abolition literature, and some of them had been punished for the same; and while they steadily refused to join the Federal forces, their well-known views on the question of slavery made them, of necessity, unfriendly to the South, and the Society served as a refuge, to a limited extent, for men who wished to escape conscription. But North Carolina Friends did not refuse to pay the taxes levied by the State, " believing that upon the government rests the responsibility of how they expend this tribute or custom." Nor did they refuse to contribute to the needs of the sick and suffering soldiers.

Friends within the compass of Hopewell Quarter in Northern Virginia were the greatest sufferers. They were within the territory contended for by both armies. Their meeting-houses were occupied by Federal and Confederate troops by turns; some were used as hospitals during the greater part of the war. They suffered also from requisitions. Sheridan's raid into the Valley of Virginia cost Friends of Goose Creek Monthly Meeting about $80,000 and Fairfax Monthly Meeting about $23,000 in property burned and live stock driven off; but the value of the latter was at a later period refunded by the Federal Government.[1]

Some of the young Friends in the North joined the Federal armies. "In the South," to quote Stanley Pumphrey, " there were not the same motives for laying aside peace principles as prevailed in the North. The Friends were loyal to the Union, and with their pronounced anti-slavery views could look with no sympathy upon the founding of a new polity, of which the leaders avowed that slavery should be the corner-stone. Accordingly I did not hear of more than one member who was ever known to take active part

---

[1] Janney's *Memoirs*, 188-235.

in the Southern army." Janney says that a few families in
Hopewell Quarter "allowed their sympathies with the
Southern people to lead them astray."[1] Quakers within
the verge of the old Virginia Yearly Meeting seem to have
sympathized with the South more than those of any other
section. This was natural, as they, because of their fewness
in numbers, were more controlled by circumstances. But
they maintained a position of absolute neutrality. After
reading carefully the minutes of the Richmond meeting
through the whole of the war period, I found nothing to
indicate that they were so much as aware that a war was
going on until November, 1864, when it is reported that by
reason of the excitement caused by the attack of the Federal
Army on Richmond some of their members had been unable
to attend meetings.

Stanley Pumphrey continues in his journal: "Considering
how obnoxious their principles must have been to the Confederate government, it is to their credit that they often
showed so much disposition to be lenient towards Friends.
In twelfth month, 1861, a few months after the outbreak
of hostilities, an attempt was indeed made in the Carolina
Legislature to pass an act by which every free male person
above sixteen years of age, would have been required, under
penalty of banishment within a month, publicly to renounce
allegiance to the United States, and also to promise to support, maintain and defend the Independent Government of
the Confederates."[2] But the enactment of the proposed
test oath was successfully opposed. In the course of his
speech against the test Gov. Graham said: "This ordinance
wholly disregards their [the Quakers'] peculiar belief, and
converts every man of them into a warrior or an exile.
True, they are allowed to affirm, but the affirmation is
equivalent to the oath of the feudal vassal to his lord, to
'defend him with life and limb and terrene honor.' . . . This
ordinance, therefore, is nothing less than a decree of banish-

[1] *Memoirs.* 189.   [2] *Memories of Stanley Pumphrey.* 137–162.

ment to them. . . . Upon the expulsion from among us of such a people, the civilized world would cry, shame!"[1]

In July, 1862, a conscription act passed the Confederate Congress which ordered every man between eighteen and thirty-five into the army. The North Carolina Meeting for sufferings had a called session and drew up memorials to the State Convention and to the Confederate Congress. The latter was presented by John Carter and Nereus Mendenhall. It was laid before the Senate by Hon. William T. Dortch and before the House by Hon. J. R. McLean. The committee continue: "We were treated with respect by every one with whom we conversed on the subject, and by some, with tenderness of feeling. We may particularly mention William B. Preston, of Virginia, chairman of the committee on military affairs for the Senate, and William Porcher Miles, chairman of a similar committee for the House. On an interview with the former, he told us to make ourselves entirely easy on the subject; that the Senate committee, in acting upon it, were unanimously in favor of recommending an entire exemption. He said that some were for requiring us to furnish substitutes, but that he was well aware that we could not conscientiously do that, and that nothing but a clear and full exemption would meet our scruples. Miles, chairman of House committee, invited us to a hearing, in their room, before the committee at large, and took pains to arrange the sittings as much as possible to suit our convenience. We here had the very acceptable company and assistance of John B. Crenshaw, who labored faithfully in word and doctrine."

They did not secure what they desired, however. Friends were exempted from military service by Congress only on the payment of $500 each into the public treasury. Strictly, to the Quakers this was no favor at all, for they were no more willing to pay the fine than to go into the army itself. In taking action on this proposed exemption the committee

---

[1] See *Speech* of Governor Graham, delivered December 7, 1861, pp. 10, 11. Raleigh, 1862.

report: " While, in accordance with the advice issued by
our last Yearly Meeting, ' we do pay all taxes imposed on
us as citizens and property holders, in common with other
citizens, remembering the injunction, tribute to whom
tribute is due, custom to whom custom'; yet, we cannot
conscientiously pay this specific tax, it being imposed upon
us on account of our principles, being the price exacted of
us for religious liberty." To this statement of principle
they add: " Yet do we appreciate the good intentions of
those members of Congress who had it in their hearts to
do something for our relief; and we recommend that where
parents, moved by sympathy, or young men themselves
dreading the evils of a military camp, have availed themselves of this law, that they be treated in a tender manner."[1]

It is reasonable to conclude from the tone of this report
that those Friends who preferred to clear themselves by
paying the requisite sum were not held to a strict account
by the Society. But there were cases where Friends declined to pay the ransom, and to escape conscription were
compelled to hide in the woods in caves, or " dug-outs,"
and were subject to no little hardship. There were also
cases where Friends were drafted into the army and on their
refusal to perform military duty were treated harshly, even
cruelly, but it is probable that such instances were few in
number.

The class to suffer most were those who were convinced
of Friends' principles after the beginning of the war. The
Society was thus liable to become a refuge for men who
were for any reason unwilling to fight, and the term " war

---

[1] Some North Carolina Quakers who went to Indiana to escape
being conscripted into the Confederate Army found themselves
drafted into the Federal Army, and had to pay an exemption fine
to keep out of service. One of these was Albert W. Brown, of
Northampton County.

Hon. George W. Julian writes me, under date of September 18,
1895, concerning the Indiana Quakers : " The large body of Quakers
whose Yearly Meetings are held in Richmond not only have a good
anti-slavery record, but a record for patriotism. I think it is con-
ceded that in proportion to their number they had more soldiers in
the war for the Union than any other religious denomination."

Quaker" became a term of reproach. No provision had been made for them under the Confederate exemption act, and we have record of several cases of much suffering. It is but just to say, however, that the Society did not allow itself to become a refuge for men whom it thought to be insincere, and that many of these newly-convinced Friends remained faithful to the cause which they had espoused.[1]

---

[1] See Pumphrey as above; *Sufferings of Friends*, 1868, and an interesting article on *The Cave Dwellers of the Confederacy* (*Atlantic Monthly*, October, 1891), by David Dodge (O. W. Blacknall). The fortune of Southern Quakers has been treated exhaustively by Fernando G. Cartland in his *Southern Heroes or the Friends in War Time* (Cambridge, 1895), 8°, pp. 480, with portraits; and in novel form by Lydia C. Wood in *The Haydock's Testimony* (Philadelphia, 1890).

ADDITIONAL NOTE ON EMIGRATION FROM SOUTH CAROLINA AND GEORGIA.

Since Chapter X. was put into type I have seen a copy of the second edition of O'Neall's *Annals of Newberry* (Newberry, S. C., 1892). The original work of Judge O'Neall is reprinted in full (8°, pp. 326), and to this a second part is added by John A. Chapman, A. M. (pp. 327-816, + vii). Among other material of much value the new part contains a supplementary paper by David Jones, of Ohio, on "The Friends and their Migration to Ohio" (pp. 329-358). From this paper a few additional facts are gathered (see the present volume, pp. 266-268). Z. Dicks visited Wrightsborough and Bush River in 1803. From the former he advised removal and predicted an internecine war within the lives of children then living. At Bush River he began his warning in a well built meeting house, erected only five years before with full expectation of long continued occupancy, and where Judge O'Neall says he often saw 500 Friends assembled, with the ominous words: " Oh, Bush River! Bush River! how hath thy beauty faded away and gloomy darkness eclipsed thy day!" These Friends and those from Georgia removed mostly to Miami, Warren and Clinton counties, O., and from there have spread over the West. Mr. Jones then gives a number of sketches of the leaders in the emigration, including members of the families given on pp. 279-280. The Bush River property still belongs to the Society, and an effort has been recently made to revive the Society and rebuild the meeting-house. White Lick meeting-house was on the public road leading from Newberry C. H. to Long's Bridge on Little River, between Deadfall and the bridge, and within 200 yards of the residence of Mr. G. Henry Werts. The house was built of large hewn logs, and was also known as Coate's Meeting House.

CHAPTER XII.

THE RENAISSANCE OF NORTH CAROLINA YEARLY MEETING.

A list of the active meetings within the limits of the Yearly Meeting in 1869 has been preserved. This list may be taken as substantially representing the condition of Quakerism at the close of the war. It may also be taken as a measure of the weakness of the Society superinduced by slavery. This list should be compared with the other list given in the appendix where present conditions are indicated.

This list is reproduced from the "Book of Meetings" for 1869:

EASTERN QUARTER: *Monthly Meetings:* (1) Rich Square, (2) Piney Woods; Meetings for worship: (1) Rich Square, (2) Piney Woods, (2) Up River.

WESTERN QUARTER: *Monthly Meetings:* (1) Cane Creek, (2) Centre, (3) Spring; Meetings for worship: (1) Cane Creek, (1) Rocky River, (2) Providence, (2) Centre, (3) Spring, (3) Chatham, (3) South Fork.

DEEP RIVER QUARTER: *Monthly Meetings:* (1) Deep River, (2) Springfield, (3) Deep Creek; Meetings for worship: (1) Deep River, (2) Springfield, (2) Pine Woods, (3) Deep Creek, (3) Hunting Creek, (3) Forbush Creek.

SOUTHERN QUARTER: *Monthly Meetings:* (1) Back Creek, (2) Marlborough, (3) Holly Spring; Meetings for worship: (1) Back Creek, (2) Little River (now Hopewell, near by), (2) Marlborough, (2) Salem, (3) Holly Spring, (3) Pine Ridge, (3) Bethel.

NEW GARDEN QUARTER: *Monthly Meetings:* (1) New Garden, (2) Dover; Meetings for worship: (1) New Garden, (2) Dover.

CONTENTNEA QUARTER: *Monthly Meetings:* (1) Neuse, (2) Nahunta; Meetings for worship: (1) Neuse, (2) Nahunta, (2) Falling Creek.

LOST CREEK QUARTER: *Monthly Meetings:* (1) New Hope, (2) Lost Creek, (3) Newberry; Meetings for worship: (1) New Hope, (2) Lost Creek, (3) Newberry.[1]

The Work of Baltimore Association.

The State of North Carolina had the good fortune to be comparatively free from the horrors of war until toward the close of 1864. As the terrible realities of war began to draw nearer to the Quakers in that year, many of them began to seek homes, friends and relatives in the West. Before the war closed these emigrants usually went West by way of Baltimore. They frequently arrived there in a destitute condition and were forwarded to the West by Baltimore Friends.

After the war closed and the usual routes of travel were open, the emigration began again with renewed strength. The man most prominent in this new migration was Addison Coffin, a native of Guilford County, and born of Quaker parents in 1822. He became connected with the Underground Railroad as early as 1835, and the experience acquired in those days stood him in good stead in later years. On the third of May, 1843, he set out from North Carolina for Indiana on foot. He reached Richmond, Indiana, in twenty-one days. This was the first of three trips from North Carolina to Indiana on foot, and each was made over a different route. His travels have extended into many parts of the West—to the Pacific, to Yucatan and Central America, to Europe and the Holy Land, and are not yet finished. After the war was over he chartered trains and organized a new migration. This migration, unlike those

---

[1] Within the limits of the old Virginia Yearly Meeting there was the Virginia Half-Yearly Meeting with two monthly meetings: (1) Cedar Creek and (2) Lower, with four meetings for worship: (1) Richmond, (1) Cedar Creek, (2) Black Creek, (2) Somerton. At Hopewell there was also a monthly meeting (orthodox) consisting of the meeting for worship of the same name, and several meetings of Hicksite Friends.

at the beginning of the century, was consciously organized
and made use of modern methods. Mr. Coffin says that
between 1866 and 1872 he carried ten trains of emigrants
each year from North Carolina to Indiana. They numbered
more than fourteen thousand in all; nearly one-half were
under ten years of age. Three out of five of his emigrants
have made a success, while the other two were no worse off.
But their children, having the advantage of schools, have
done well. He has seen four of his barefoot Carolina boys
become members of the Indiana Legislature. Others have
met with success, particularly in Iowa and Kansas.

All of these emigrants were by no means Quakers; there
were some five hundred among the emigrants carried West
by Mr. Coffin; but a general western exodus of Friends
was threatened, and its consequences, had the movement
not been checked, would have been very harmful to central
North Carolina in removing a valuable class of its citizens.

The man who, of all others, realized the importance of this
movement, and who saw more clearly than others the necessity of keeping these Friends in their old homes, was Francis
T. King of Baltimore. It was he who conceived the plan
afterwards put into execution. His own liberal contributions and the contributions of Friends throughout the world,
many of whose yearly meetings he visited in the interests
of this cause, and his constant personal service, made possible its realization. Francis Thompson King was born in
Baltimore in 1819, and was a member of Baltimore Yearly
Meeting. He spent a number of years in business, then
retired from active life and devoted himself to the public
service of his native city in the broadest and best sense of
this term. He accepted positions of trust in connection
with the public works and charitable institutions of the city,
and performed similar duties outside the State. During the
winter of 1863, although a strong Union man, he was
intrusted by Southern sympathizers in Baltimore with
$20,000 for the relief of Confederate prisoners confined in
Fort Delaware, and although accountable to no one for the

money, faithfully performed the trust. When this new
migration of Friends to the West began, Mr. King realized
that if the Southern States were to recuperate their forces
they must do it by developing their own energies and
resources, and began to use his influence to induce Friends,
who chiefly represented the numerous class of small farmers,
to retain their old homesteads and build up the waste places
instead of carrying their industry and money out of the
State. He felt that the Society of Friends, with their anti-
war principles, could help both parties without suspicion,
as their message was one of peace and reconciliation to all.
To check this new migration, therefore, " The Baltimore
Association of Friends to advise and assist Friends in the
Southern States" was organized in the spring of 1865.
Francis T. King was made president; Isaac Brooks, secretary; Jesse Tyson, treasurer; with an executive committee
composed of Francis T. King, John C. Thomas, Dr. James
Carey Thomas, Jesse Tyson, Francis White and Dr. Caleb
Winslow, of whom the last two were natives of North Carolina. Their work of relief began in Contentnea Quarter,
which had just been devastated by Sherman's army. The
Association shipped them carloads of provisions and boxes
of goods of all descriptions, including agricultural tools and
household utensils of all sorts. But this assistance was not
of the sort that pauperizes, for the object of the Association
was to put their aid into such forms as would elevate Friends
and make them self-sustaining. Its object was to help them
first to educate their children and then to improve their lands.
Many of those who had already gone to the West were
induced to return and further migration was discouraged.
This great work was only made possible through the personal devotion which Mr. King gave to it. He made about
thirty-five journeys to North Carolina at a time when travel
was very difficult, and the success of the reorganization of
this large and comparatively isolated region depended greatly
on the personal inspiration of the open-air meetings which
he held in villages, arousing the discouraged inhabitants to
improve their exhausted farms and educate their children.

The Boarding School was reorganized; money was appropriated for repairs and for paying the expenses of the children of Friends who had suffered most by the war. In 1866 the school was clear of debt and reported one hundred and twenty-six students. But it did not prosper greatly, and the number of students fell off largely during the next few years. A normal school for the training of teachers was opened this year. They secured capable instructors from the North; the tuition was free; teachers of all denominations and from various sections attended. Their work had marked influence, for some of their teachers were employed to give instruction in the State normals and were sought for by other institutions.

The first annual report made to Baltimore Yearly Meeting in October, 1866, showed that $22,554.31 had been expended as follows: Repairs of New Garden School, furniture and tuition of thirty-six pupils, $4,817.50; for thirty primary and one normal school and aid to new school-houses, $4,710.36; relief to families and individuals, $12,936.40; office expenses, $90.05. During the second year nearly $19,000 was expended.

The greatest efforts of Baltimore Friends were put on the development of primary schools. In 1865 Friends in North Carolina had no schools, no good school-houses and no books. Mr. King attended the Yearly Meeting in 1865 and told Friends to start such schools as they could with the materials at hand, and that a superintendent would be sent them as soon as the proper man could be found. In a few weeks Prof. Joseph Moore, of Earlham College, Ind., was chosen and arrived on the scene of his labors in December, 1865. He labored in this field for three years and was then succeeded by Allen Jay, also of Indiana, who took up the work of Professor Moore and conducted it successfully for eight years. In 1866 there were over thirty schools that received aid or entire support from the Baltimore Association. In 1868 they reported forty schools with 2,588 pupils; of these 1,430 were the children of Friends, and the average duration of the school year was six months and a half. In 1870 there were forty-one schools with 2,774 children, 1,233 being Friends, and the average length of the school term was five months. Fifty-four teachers were employed, and most of the schools were reported as self-sustaining. In 1871 there were forty schools, 2,415 pupils and sixty-two teachers, fifty-six of the latter being natives. This work lay principally in the Quaker localities of central North Carolina and received the hearty commendation of all regardless of party. Governor Worth, a representative of Nantucket stock, but not a Quaker, said that this movement was the most important phase of reconstruction that had come to his knowledge.

Friends also emphasized and developed religious and educational work in the Sunday-school. These were then given an impetus forward which they have not since lost. In 1867 a normal school for the especial training of Sunday-school teachers was organized, and the experiment was repeated with success the next year.

In the same way much attention was given to the schools for the freedmen. A committee had been appointed at an early date to take charge of this affair, and in 1867 reported six day and twenty-two Sunday-schools for them, with an estimated attendance from 1,600 to 2,000. In 1869 twenty-four day-schools and thirty-five Sunday-schools are reported with 1,707 pupils. Dr. J. M. Tomlinson was appointed superintendent in 1869. In 1870 he reported fourteen schools with five hundred and sixty pupils, and these were administered at an outlay of $1,161.74. The next year the pupils had increased to eight hundred and eight, the schools to sixteen, with an average length of four and a half months, and the expenses to $1,308.61. Both fell off in 1872, and from that time reports from these schools are uncertain.

Baltimore Friends also put some $6,000 into an orphan house for colored orphans in Richmond and then transferred its management to the colored pastors of the city.

But school education was not the only form of the helpful

activity of the Baltimore Association. They probably did
as much for agriculture as they had done for the schools.
In 1867 they purchased the farm of Nathan Hunt, near High
Point and in Guilford County, N. C., named it " Swarthmore
farm," and put it under the care of William A. Sampson, a
practical farmer. This model farm, with improved implements, artificial manures, grasses, selected seeds and selected
stock, became a practical school of agriculture, and demon-
strated to Friends the great but neglected wealth of the
soil; a widespread interest in agriculture was awakened;
farmers' clubs were organized; the superintendent gave occasional lectures before them on agricultural topics, and the
farm was visited by farmers from all parts of the State. In his
fifth report in 1872, Superintendent Sampson estimates that
the influence of this farm was felt for fifty miles around. He
considered the main features of this influence as coming
from the more extended use of clover, for it was estimated
that 15,000 acres of land had been put in because of the successful example set at Swarthmore farm; the next advantage
was in the use of better implements and in better drainage.
It was in connection with this work that a bone-mill, probably the first in the South, was erected. This farm was
also of service in stopping the westward migration.

In 1872 Baltimore Association closed most of its work.
The crisis had then passed. Friends and others were recov-
ering from the effects of the war. The schools were mostly
self-supporting, and as soon as this point was reached there
was no need of further aid. The schools were then placed
under the care of an executive committee of the Yearly
Meeting. They numbered thirty-eight, with sixty-two
teachers and 2,358 pupils, and it was said that probably
not one Friend's child in North Carolina or Tennessee had
been overlooked. The work was continued by North Carolina Friends, and in 1880 their superintendent could say with
pride that there was probably no Quaker child between
seven and twenty-one who could not read and write. The
work was also carried on satisfactorily among the meetings
in Tennessee.

During the last few years of its existence the work of the Association was devoted mainly to the improvement of the New Garden Boarding School. The buildings were remodeled and improved; new apparatus was provided; an endowment was started, and the end of the work was the rechartering of the institution as Guilford College.

The total expenditures of the Baltimore Association up to 1887, when it dissolved, may be divided as follows: For physical relief, including net cost of model farm, $36,000; for schools (1865-1876), $60,000; for schools (1877-1883), $12,000; for Guilford College (1883), $15,000; for Guilford College on endowment fund (1883), $8,000; for aid in repairing or building meeting-houses, $7,300; total, $138,300.

Francis T. King was appointed to visit every Yearly Meeting in America to collect these funds, and the funds administered by Baltimore Association were the contributions of the Quaker world, as will be seen from the report of receipts at the end of the second year in October, 1867:

From London Yearly Meeting	$22,494
From Dublin " "	10,761
From New York " "	4,899
From New England Yearly Meeting	3,606
From Philadelphia " "	1,515
From Baltimore " "	1,034
From Indiana " "	1,213
From Ohio " "	452
From Iowa " "	318
From Western " "	200
From interest on deposits	2,294

Total contributions for the first two years, $48,786.52

Baltimore Association acted as a sort of trustee in the collection and administration of this great charity. The activity and influence of Francis T. King have been promptly and properly acknowledged, for a large and commodious building has been dedicated to his memory at Guilford College within the last few years.[1]

In the same way and during the same period, Philadelphia Friends were engaged in supporting schools in North Carolina for the freedmen. In 1869 they report twenty-nine schools with some forty teachers. It is estimated that they reached an enrollment of 2,000 for a number of years, and that $6,000 was spent in this work. The Philadelphia Association of Women Friends also did educational work in Tennessee. Since 1874 New York Friends have spent some $18,000 on schools for whites as well as colored children.[2] They have also established a high grade school for colored pupils in High Point, N. C. New England Yearly Meeting has a college for colored people at Maryville, Tenn., and Indiana Yearly Meeting has one at Helena, Ark.

North Carolina Friends in 1875.

The following account of Carolina Friends was written in 1875 by Stanley Pumphrey, but the description is too gloomy to be taken for the Yearly Meeting as a whole. " The most enterprising left a worn-out soil not naturally fertile, and went West, leaving the less energetic on the old patrimonial homes. Their houses are often built of logs, and an upper story is the exception. The whole domestic arrangements are on a scale of startling simplicity. The produce raised on the farm supplies the table, bread made of Indian corn meal, and pork, being the staple food, and the garments are often home-spun. Allen Jay assured me that many of the Friends did not handle fifty dollars in the year. The entire absence of windows from the dwellings is by no means an unusual experience.[3] . . . As for the

---

[1] Partly from materials kindly furnished me by Miss E. T. King, of Baltimore. See also Cartland's *Southern Heroes*, Chapter 24.

[2] See the extensive discussion of this phase of educational work in Dr. Charles Lee Smith's *History of Education in North Carolina.*

[3] There was a section in the counties of Yadkin, Iredell and Surry where the great lack of windows was about as stated above, and perhaps in one small section in Randolph County ; elsewhere the

meeting houses, the better class are like barns, others are like poor sheds. They are often built of logs, roughly mortised together, and the spaces filled with mud. The lowest log is placed on piles of stones, and in one case the pigs had worked their way between these piles of stones and rendered the meeting house utterly untenantable."[1]

The result of this visit was an appeal to Friends in England for help toward building better meeting-houses. Pumphrey says that the North Carolina Yearly Meeting had then built sixteen new meeting-houses since the war, that twelve more were needed, and four had been left unfinished for lack of funds. In the Southern Quarter, which is entirely within the limits of Randolph County, he reports that out of the ten meetings there were but two creditable houses. To this appeal for aid Friends of England and Ireland responded liberally and more than £1,000 was contributed. This fund was also administered through the Baltimore Association, and up to 1885 had been of service in Canada and in eight States, including North Carolina, Virginia, Tennessee, Florida, Arkansas and Texas.

Conclusion.

The history of Carolina Friends during the last twenty years has been one of quiet and steady growth. There are few events that rise above the level of the whole. The most important of these, perhaps, was the rechartering of New Garden Boarding School, January 25, 1889, and its

---

"entire absence of windows" was the rare exception. But the statements of Pumphrey are not surprising, for he was shown the worst parts of the Yearly Meeting, the object being to enlist the sympathies of English Friends.

[1] *Memories* of Stanley Pumphrey, pp. 128, 131, 168-170. Oh that the early Quakers had written journals like this one! See also *Minutes* of Baltimore Yearly Meeting, 1884, 1895. Thomas Shillitoe said in 1828 that the Quarterly Meeting at Westfield was held in a log house in November and that they sat with both doors open for light; there was no convenience for making a fire, and they "found it to be a great exercise of patience to endure the cold." It was the same way at Sutton's Creek meeting-house, and at Wells daylight came through in twenty places.—*Friends' Library.* III.

reorganization as Guilford College. It had graduated its
first class as Friends' School in 1886. Its first class as a
college was graduated in 1889. It is now well attended, well
manned, in some lines is probably as well equipped for
advanced work as any institution in the State, and under the
presidency of L. L. Hobbs has won recognition as one of
the best and most progressive institutions in North Carolina.'

Friends have increased very largely in numbers since the
war. In 1866, one thousand seven hundred and eighty-five
members above eighteen years of age were reported, and
a general migration to the West was threatened; in 1869 it
was two thousand and one: in 1870 it was two thousand
and sixty-eight; in 1876, owing probably to defects in the
earlier reports, the number had jumped to four thousand
two hundred and seventy-five, of whom one hundred and
seventy-three were received by request. During the ten
years 1876-1886 inclusive, the only years for which the
proper statistics are to be had, it is found that almost the
whole of the net gain in membership to the Society came
from those who were received by request, the births and
certificates received about equaling those lost by death,
disownment, certificate and resignation.

The following tables will show the state of the meetings
as reported by the Quarters to the Yearly Meeting.

<hr/>

'Statistics of secondary education as reported to North Carolina
Yearly Meeting in August, 1895: Academies under care of Friends,
six: average time taught, eight months; value of property, $9,000;
no endowments; value of apparatus, $60; total enrollment, five
hundred and twenty; financial aid received, about $800; Friends
enrolled, about one hundred and fifty; tuition received, $1,776.25;
school buildings, seven; acres of land in school premises, forty;
teachers, fourteen; advanced pupils, sixty-one: pupils preparing for
college, five. These academies have been graded so as to fit pupils
for Guilford College.

1883. QUARTERS.	Number of Meetings.	Number of Members.	Received by Request.	Received by Certificate.	Received by Birth.	Total.	Lost by Disownment.	Lost by Certificate.	Lost by Resignation.	Lost by Death.	Total.	Gain.	Loss.
Eastern · · ·	5	696	1	1	18	20	..	2	3	10	15	5	
Western · ·	8	818	15	8	22	45	3	1	2	11	17	28	
New Garden.	3	260	9	3	4	16	..	6	.	4	10	6	
Deep River ·	11	897	66	6	12	84	4	6	3	6	19	65	
Contentnea ·	7	593	61	..	10	71	4		10	10	24	47	
Southern · ·	9	675	..	5	9	14	..	10	1	3	14	..	
Lost Creek ·	8	941	24	16	11	51	1	5	7	10	23	28	
Friendsville.	2	505	..	..	9	9	1	15	1	5	22	..	13
Totals · ·	53	5385	176	39	95	310	13	45	27	59	144	166	13

QUARTERS. 1894.	Number of Meetings.	Male Members.	Female Members.	Additions.	Subtractions.
Eastern · · · · · · · · · · · ·	4	274	262	9	12
Western · · · · · · · · · · ·	11	409	431	35	15
Southern · · · · · · · · · · ·	10	478	498	55	88
Deep River · · · · · · · · ·	7	361	414	32	71
New Garden · · · · · · · · ·	5	225	252	64	19
Contentnea · · · · · · · · ·	8	277	285	18	10
Friendsville · · · · · · · · ·	2¹	198	204	61	58
Yadkin Valley · · · · · · · ·	8	489	409	261	26
Totals · · · · · · · · · · ·	55	2711	2755	535	299
1895.					
Eastern · · · · · · · · · · · ·	4	310	314	11	19
Western · · · · · · · · · · ·	10	387	401	26	12
Southern ² · · · · · · · · · ·	10	478	498	55	88
Deep River · · · · · · · · ·	6	300	346	26	30
New Garden · · · · · · · · ·	4	216	225	16	51
Contentnea · · · · · · · · ·	8	285	305	14	11
Friendsville · · · · · · · · ·	2¹	383	390	48	33
Yadkin Valley · · · · · · · ·	10	531	645	123	27
Totals · · · · · · · · ·	54	2890	3084	319	271

Final total of members for 1892 · · · · · · · · · · ·5301
Final total of members for 1894³ · · · · · · · · ·5702
Final total of members for 1895 · · · · · · · · · ·6022

¹ Report of 1892, but evidently too small a number.
² Report of 1894; none made in 1895.
³ No statistics in 1893.

The growth of Southern Friends since the war has been, so far as can be seen, a healthful growth. This applies to Tennessee as well as to North Carolina, for in the former State Friends have more than doubled since 1860, and they have now secured a footing in Florida, Arkansas, Louisiana and Texas. This increase in numbers is due largely to the fact that modern methods are beginning to be employed. Much attention is given to evangelistic and mission work, and this accounts for large accessions in various quarters. In addition to this, Sunday-schools, temperance, peace, Indians, orphans, education, and similar matters are now taking the place of that one absorbing question with which this paper has been principally concerned, and which more than anything else drove Friends to plant the banner of civilization in the Valley of the Mississippi, now their stronghold. With this question settled, with increasing numbers and increasing wealth, with better methods and the same unconquerable enthusiasm, there is reason to hope for a future brighter than the past.

The North Carolina Yearly Meeting now includes the meetings in that State and Friendsville Quarter, in Tennessee. It is still one of the largest meetings in the United States, being sixth in numbers. Its daughter, Indiana Yearly Meeting, stands first.[1] North Carolina Yearly Meeting has suffered most of all, perhaps, from emigration. It can look on all the Yearly Meetings in the West and say

---

[1] The statistics of Quakers in the United States, according to the census of 1890, is as follows, by States: Orthodox:—Ark., 338; Cal., 1,009; Col., 38; Del., 122; D. C., 19; Fla., 70; Ill., 2,015; Ind., 25,915; Ind. Ter., 468; Iowa, 8,146; Kans., 7,762; La., 66; Me., 1,430; Md., 525; Mass., 1,560; Mich., 1,433; Minn., 305; Mo., 615; Neb., 782; N. H., 413; N. J., 982; N. Y., 3,644; N. C., 4,904; O., 10,884; Okl., 108; Or., 766; Penn., 3,490; R. I., 617; S. D., 266; Tenn., 1,001; Tex., 120; Vt., 251; Va., 387; W. Va., 50; Wis., 154; total, 80,655. Hicksite:—Del., 622; D. C., 40; Ill., 440; Ind., 1,376; Io., 440; Md., 1,547; Mich., 25; Neb., 198; N. J., 2,279; N. Y., 3,331; O., 1,187; Penn., 10,001; Va., 506; total, 21,992. Wilburites:—Ind., 489; Io., 1,539; Kan., 495; Mass., 28; O., 1,676; Penn., 30; R. I., 72; total, 4,329. Primitive:—Mass., 14; N. Y., 103; Penn., 106; R. I., 9; total, 232.

By Yearly Meetings: Orthodox:—Baltimore, 1,012; Ind., 22,105; Iowa, 11,391; Kans., 9,347; New England, 4,020; N. Y., 3,895; N. C.,

with truth, " these are my children." It has seen its members
go forth and become leaders in the Middle West. It has
given to Western Friends such leaders as Thomas Beales,
said to have been the first white emigrant to settle in Ohio;
William Williams, Dougan Clark, Elijah Coffin, Charles F.
Coffin, Charles Osborn, who first advocated unconditional
emancipation in his paper, *The Philanthropist,* the first
abolition journal in America, when William Lloyd Garrison
had just entered his teens. And it gave them Vestal Coffin,
the founder, and Levi Coffin, for thirty years the president,
of the Underground Railroad. This is a part of North Carolina's contribution to the settlement of the West and to the
abolition of slavery. Her influence has extended to the
Pacific, where California Yearly Meeting has been organized
within a year. And these young children still turn to the
mother meeting for guidance; for the first president of Whittier College, the new Quaker institution on the Pacific, was
John W. Woody, who went from the same meeting from
which so many men great in the annals of Quakerism have
gone,—from New Garden Monthly Meeting, Guilford
County, North Carolina.

5,905; O., 4,733; Philadelphia. 4,513; Western, 13.734; (Cal. and
Wilmington Yearly Meetings—the latter composed of meetings in
west and southwest Ohio—were organized since the census was
taken); total, 80,655. Hicksite :—Baltimore, 2.797; Genesee, 751;
Ill., 1,301; Ind., 1,743; N. Y., 2,803; O., 568; Philadelphia, 12,209;
total, 21.992. Wilburites :—Iowa. 714; Kans., 495; New England,
100; O., 2.451; Western. 569; total, 4,329. Total Quakers in United
States, 107,208. For detailed statistics of Southern Quakers see
Appendix I.

APPENDIX I.

Detailed Statistics of Southern Quakers according to Census of 1890.

	Organizations.	Church edifices.	Approx. seating capacity.	Halls, etc.	Seating capacity	Value of church property.	Communicants.
North Carolina.							
Alamance	2	3	1,400	. .	. .	$2,500	263
Chatham	5	2	850	sh. 2 ph. 1 } 3	150	1,100	278
Davidson	1	1	300	. .	. .	500	50
Guilford	6	6	2,900	. .	. .	13,600	987
Iredell	1	1	200	. .	. .	300	65
Moore	1	1	200	. .	. .	200	45
Northampton . . .	2	2	1,000	. .	. .	1,100	292
Perquimans	2	2	1,200	. .	. .	2,000	338
Randolph	10	8	4,000	h. 1	300	5,000	1,077
Robeson	1	1	75	. .	. .	200	10
Sampson	1	1	250	. .	. .	600	78
Surry	2	2	750	. .	. .	1,900	255
Wayne	7	7	2,400	. .	. .	4,850	758
Yadkin	6	6	1,950	. .	. .	3,000	408
	47	43	17,475	4	450	36,850	4,904
Tennessee.							
Blount	5	5	1,525	. .	. .	6,100	528
Greene	1	. .	. .	h. 1	100	. .	79
Jefferson	6	1	600	sh. 5	375	2,500	275
Knox	1	1	350	. .	. .	400	25
Loudon	1	1	500	. .	. .	400	76
Monroe	1	. .	. .	sh. 1	75	. .	18
	15	8	2,975	7	550	9,400	1,001
Totals for North Carolina Y. M.	62	51	20,450	11	1,000	$46,250	5.90

	Organizations.	Church edifices.	Approx. seating capacity.	Halls, etc.	Seating capacity	Value of church property.	Communicants.
VIRGINIA (to Balto. Y. M.)							
Frederick Co. . . .	1	1	350	. .	. .	$600	34
Henrico	1	1	400	. .	. .	8.000	58
Loudoun.	1	1	400	. .	. .	3,500	62
Nansemond	1	1	300	. .	. .	1,200	27
Southampton . . .	3	3	850	. .	. .	1.600	206
	7	7	2,300	. .	. .	$14.900	387
ARKANSAS.							
Benton (to Kan. Y.M.)	2	1	100	h. 1	100	$150	106
Phillips (to Ind.Y.M.)	2	2	400	. .	. .	1,800	205
Washington (to Kan. Y. M.)	1	. .	. .	ph. 1	. .	. .	27
	5	3	500	2	100	$1,950	338
FLORIDA (to Ind. Y. M.)							
Alachua · · · . . .	1	1	300	. .	. .	$1,000	45
Marion	1	1	75	. .	. .	200	25
	2	2	375	. .	. .	$1,200	70
LOUISIANA (to Iowa Y. M.)							
Acadia · · · · · ·	1	. .	. .	sh. 1	75		66
TEXAS (to Iowa Y. M.)							
Crosby · · · · · ·	1	. .	. .	sh. 1	150		120
HICKSITES (to Balto. Y.M.) **VIRGINIA.**							
Fairfax · · · · · ·	1	1	200	. .	. .	$600	53
Frederick · · · · ·	4	4	1,700	. .	. .	4.700	123
Loudoun · · · · ·	2	2	1,300	.	.	8,000	330
	7	7	3,200			$13.300	506

APPENDIX II.

Time and Place of holding Yearly Meetings in Virginia and North Carolina, 1702–1895.

Year.	Virginia Yearly Meeting.	Month.	North Carolina Yearly Meeting.	Month.
1702	Pagan Creek(LevyNeck) [Isle of Wight Co.]	7		
1703	Levy Neck (same as P. C.)			
1704	Levy Neck, at "Public M. H."		Mentioned by Y. M. records of 1755	
1705	Levy Neck			
1706	Levy Neck	7		
1707	Levy Neck	7		
1708	Levy Neck	7	"In North Carolina" .	
1709	Levy Neck	7	"In North Carolina" . .	8
1710	Levy Neck	7	"In North Carolina" . .	8
1711	Chuckatuck (Nansemond Co.)	7	"In North Carolina" . .	8
			"In North Carolina" . .	8
1712	Levy Neck	7	"At Perquimmans". . .	6
1713	Chuckatuck	7	"At Perquimmans". . .	8
1714	Levy Neck	7	"At Perquimmans". . .	8
1715	Chuckatuck	7	"At Perquimmans". . .	8
1716	Levy Neck	7	"At Perquimmans". . .	8
1717	Chuckatuck	7	"At Perquimmans". . .	8
1718	Levy Neck	7	"In North Carolina" . .	8
1719	Chuckatuck	7	"At Paquamons"	8
1720	Levy Neck	7	"In North Carolina" . .	8
1721	Chuckatuck	7	"In North Carolina" . .	8
1722	Levy Neck	7	"At paquamons"	8
1723	Chuckatuck	7	Not given.	8
1724	Levy Neck	7	Perquimans	8
1725			Perquimans	8
1726			Perquimans	8
1727			Perquimans	8
1728			Perquimans	8
1729			Perquimans	8
1730			Perquimans . . .	8
1731			In North Carolina . . .	8
1732			In North Carolina . . .	8
1733			In North Carolina . . .	8

Year.	VIRGINIA YEARLY MEETING.	Month.	NORTH CAROLINA YEARLY MEETING.	Month.
1734			Perquimans	7
1735			Perquimans	8
1736			North Carolina	8
1737	Chuckatuck	7	Perquimans	8
1738	Western Branch M. H. .	7	Perquimans	8
1739	{ M. H. near John Murdaugh's	7	Not given	8
1740	Chuckatuck	7		
1741	Western Branch	7	Perquimans	8
1742	{ Nansemond (= Chuckatuck ?)	7	Not given	8
1743	Nansemond	7	Not given	8
1744	Nansemond	7	Not given	8
1745	Nansemond	7	Perquimans	8
1746	Waynoak, Charles City co.	7	Perquimans	8
1747	Nansemond	7	Perquimans	8
1748	Henrico Co. (Curles ?) .	7	Perquimans	8
1749	Nansemond	7	Perquimans	8
1750	Curles	7	Perquimans	8
1751	Nansemond.	3	Perquimans	8
1752	Curles	5	Perquimans	10
1753	Isle of Wight	6	Old Neck	10
1754	Curles	6	Old Neck	10
1755	Western Branch	5	Old Neck	10
1756	Curles	6	Old Neck	10
1757	W. Br. (Isle of Wight Co.)	5	Old Neck	10
1758	Curles	5	Old Neck	10
1759	{ W. Br. (of Nansemond river, but in Isle of Wight Co.)	6	Old Neck	10
1760	Curles	5	Old Neck	10
1761	Black Water in Surry Co.	5	Old Neck	10
1762	Curles	5	Old Neck	10
1763	Black Water	5	Old Neck, Perquimans co.	10
1764	Curles	6	Old Neck, Perquimans co.	10
1765	Black Water	5	Old Neck, Perquimans co.	10
1766	Curles	6	Old Neck, Perquimans co.	10
1767	Black Water	6	Old Neck, Perquimans co.	10
1768	Curles	5	Old Neck, Perquimans co.	10
1769			Old Neck, Perquimans co.	10
1770			Old Neck, Perquimans co.	10
1771			Old Neck, Perquimans co.	10
1772			Old Neck, Perquimans co.	10
1773			Old Neck, Perquimans co.	10
1774			Old Neck, Perquimans co.	10
1775			Old Neck, Perquimans co.	10
1776			Old Neck, Perquimans co.	10
1777			Old Neck, Perquimans co.	10

Year.	VIRGINIA YEARLY MEETING.	Month.	NORTH CAROLINA YEARLY MEETING.	Month.
1778			Old Neck, Perquimans co.	10
1779			Old Neck, Perquimans co.	10
1780			Old Neck, Perquimans co.	10
1781	Curles and Waynoak		Old Neck, Perquimans co.	10
1782			Old Neck, Perquimans co.	10
1783	Curles and Waynoak		Old Neck. Perquimans co.	10
1784	{ Black Creek, Southampton Co.		Old Neck, Perquimans co.	10
1785			Old Neck. Perquimans co.	10
1786			Little River, Perq. Co.	10
1787			Centre, Guilford Co.	10
1788			Wells. Perquimans Co.	10
1789			Centre	10
1790			Symons's Creek	10
1791			New Garden	10
1792			Symons's Creek	10
1793	Waynoak	5	New Garden	10
1794	Black Creek	5	Symons's Creek	10
1795	Waynoak	5	New Garden	10
1796	Black Water	5	Symons's Creek	10
1797	Waynoak	5	New Garden	10
1798	Black Water	5	Little River	10
1799	Waynoak	5	New Garden	10
1800	Black Water	5	Little River	10
1801	Waynoak	5	New Garden	10
1802	Black Water?	5	Little River	10
1803	Waynoak	5	New Garden	10
1804	Black Water	5	Little River	10
1805	Waynoak	5	New Garden	10
1806	Black Water	5	Little River	10
1807	Waynoak	5	New Garden	10
1808	{ Gravelly Run, Dinwiddie Co.	5	Little River	10
1809	Waynoak	5	New Garden	10
1810	Gravelly Run	5	Little River	10
1811	Waynoak	5	New Garden	10
1812	Gravelly Run	5	Little River	10
1813	Waynoak	5	New Garden	10
1814	Gravelly Run	5	New Garden	10
1815	Waynoak	5	New Garden	10
1816	Gravelly Run	5	New Garden	10
1817	Waynoak	5	New Garden	10
1818	Gravelly Run	5	New Garden	11
1819	Waynoak	5	New Garden	11
1820	Gravelly Run	5	New Garden	11
1821	Waynoak	5	New Garden	11
1822	Gravelly Run	5	New Garden	11
1823	Waynoak	5	New Garden	11

Year.	VIRGINIA YEARLY MEETING.	Month.	NORTH CAROLINA YEARLY MEETING.	Month.
1824	Gravelly Run	5	New Garden	11
1825	Waynoak	5	New Garden	11
1826	Gravelly Run	5	New Garden	11
1827	Waynoak	5	Guilford County	11
1828	Gravelly Run	5	New Garden	11
1829	Waynoak	5	New Garden	11
1830	Gravelly Run	5	New Garden	11
1831	Waynoak	5	New Garden	11
1832	Gravelly Run	5	New Garden	11
1833	Cedar Creek	5	New Garden	11
1834	{ Somerton, Nansemond Co.	5	New Garden	11
1835	Cedar Creek	5	New Garden	11
1836	Somerton	5	New Garden	11
1837	Cedar Creek	5	New Garden	11
1838	Somerton	5	New Garden	11
1839	Cedar Creek	5	New Garden	11
1840	Somerton	5	New Garden	11
1841	Cedar Creek	5	New Garden	11
1842	Somerton	5	New Garden	11
1843	Cedar Creek	5	New Garden	11
1844	Somerton	5	New Garden	11

From 1845 to 1879 inclusive, North Carolina Yearly Meeting was held regularly at New Garden; in 1880 at Friendsville, Tenn.; 1881-83 at New Garden; since 1883 it has been held regularly at High Point, N. C., in August.

APPENDIX III.

LIST OF FRIENDS' MEETINGS IN THE SOUTHERN STATES.

In the following list is given the name of every meeting
of which the author has been able to find mention during the
progress of his work. Such facts as may help to fix the
limits of the period each was in existence, its location,
the superior meetings to which each belonged, etc., are
added. The list here given should be compared with the map.
Most of the principal meetings will be found on the map, but
all mentioned in the following list will not be found located
there, for the reason that it has been found impossible to get
sufficiently accurate data in many cases. In all such cases
the location has been indicated as nearly as possible. Some
of the data given is only approximate and there are doubtless some errors and omissions in the list. The author will
be thankful for any corrections or additions. The names
printed in *italics* are of meetings no longer in existence.

Yearly Meetings:
  Baltimore (Orthodox); from 1789 to date.
  Baltimore (Hicksite); from 1828 to date.
  North Carolina; settled 1698, to date.
  Philadelphia; from 1732 to 1789, when its territory
    was transferred to Baltimore.
  Virginia; settled about 1698, laid down 1844.

Quarterly Meetings:
  Bush River; N. C. Y. M.; settled 1791, laid down
    about 1808; included all meetings in South Caro-
    lina and Georgia; had Bush River, Cane Creek
    and Wrightsborough M. M.'s.
  Chester; Phila. Y. M.; Hopewell and Fairfax M. M.'s
    in northern Virginia, were joined to this Q. when
    first organized; superseded by Western Q.

Chuckatuck; Va. Y. M.; was cut out of the Lower
Quarter in 1706 for Surry, Levy Neck and Chuckatuck and was to serve as a sort of middle ground
between the Upper and Lower Quarters; this meeting gives place to the Lower Quarter again.

Contentnea; N. C. Y. M.; settled 1788 and opened
1789; had in 1793 Contentnea, Core Sound and
Trent M. M.'s and included all Friends in Carteret,
Hyde, Craven, Jones, Beaufort and Edgecombe
counties; now includes those in Johnston, Sampson, Greene and Wayne counties, N. C., and has
Woodland, Nahunta and Neuse M. M.'s

Deep River; N. C. Y. M.; settled 1818; then composed of Deep River and Springfield M. M.'s; now
has Springfield, High Point and Deep River
M. M.'s.

Eastern; N. C. Y. M.; settled about 1681; for
meetings in Pasquotank, Perquimans and Northampton counties; has always included all the M.
M.'s in northeastern N. C.; and has Piney Woods
and Rich Square M. M.'s.

Fairfax; Baltimore Y. M.; settled 1769; superseded
Western; for meetings in Frederick, Fairfax and
Loudoun counties, Va.; now made up of Alexandria, Fairfax, Goose Creek and Hopewell M. M.'s
(all H.).

Friendsville; N. C. Y. M.; settled 1871; includes all
meetings in Eastern Tennessee.

Lost Creek; N. C. Y. M.; settled 1802; laid down
1888; meetings transferred later to Friendsville Q.

Lower; Va. Y. M.; settled as early as 1696; laid down
1844; also called Black Water and by the names
of the various meeting-houses at which it was held
from time to time; for meetings in lower Virginia.

New Garden; N. C. Y. M.; settled 1787, opened 1788;
then composed of New Garden, Deep River, Bush
River, Wrightsborough and Westfield M. M.'s;

now has New Garden, Greensboro and Dover
M. M.'s.

Southern; N. C. Y. M.; settled 1819; then composed
of Back Creek, Holly Springs and Marlborough
M. M.'s; now of Back Creek, Marlboro, Science
Hill and Holly Springs M. M.'s.

Upper ; Va. Y. M.; settled about 1700, laid down
1844; also called Cedar Creek; for Upper Virginia
meetings.

Western ; Va. Y. M.; settled 1797, laid down 1817;
for Goose Creek and South River M. M.'s.

Western; Phila. Y. M.; settled 1758; included meetings in northern Virginia.

Western; N. C. Y. M.; settled 1759; first had Cane
Creek and New Garden M. M.'s; Dunn's Creek
M. M. was added in 1760; after 1788 had only
Cane Creek and Centre; now has Spring, Cane
Creek and Centre; for Alamance, Chatham and
parts of Randolph counties, N. C.

Westfield; N. C. Y. M.; settled 1803, laid down 1832;
had Westfield, Mt. Pleasant and Deep Creek
M. M.'s; for Surry and Stokes, N. C., Grayson and
Carroll counties, Va.

Yadkin Valley; N. C. Y. M.; settled 1887; has Deep
Creek, East Bend, Hunting Creek, Harmony
Grove, in Yadkin County, and Westfield and
White Plains M. M.'s, in Surry County, N. C.

[Note: a = ante; c = circa; p = post.]

Monthly Meetings.	State.	Yearly Meeting.	Present or last Quarterly Meeting.	Settled (established).	Laid down (suspended/ended).	Remarks.
Alexandria (H)	Va.	Bal.	Fairfax	c. 1805	....	Has particular meetings of Woodlawn and Washington (D.C.)
Back Creek	N. C.	N.C.	Southern	1793	....	In Randolph Co.; has B. C. and Hopewell.
Black Water	Va.	Va.	Lower	1757	1807	Surry Co.; had B. W. and Stanton meetings.
Bush River	S. C.	N.C.	Bush River	1770	c. 1822	Newberry Co.; practically abandoned c. 1808.
Camp Creek	Va.	Va.	Upper	....	l. d.	Louisa Co.; have records 1739-1773.
Cane Creek	N. C.	N.C.	Western	1751	....	Alamance and Chatham Cos.; has C. C., Rocky River, Edward's Hill, Burlington.
Cane Creek	S. C.	N. C.	Bush River	c. 1773	c. 1808	Newberry (?) and Union Cos.
Caroline	Va.	Va.	Upper	1739	1853(?)	Same as Cedar Creek.
Carver's Creek	N. C.	N.C.	Eastern	c. 1746	c. 1797	Bladen Co.; Friends request M. M. 1743.
Cedar Creek	Va.	Va.	Upper	1739	1853(?)	Hanover, Louisa and Caroline Cos.
Centre	N. C.	N. C.	Western	1772	....	Guilford and Randolph Cos.; has C. and Providence.
Chuckatuck	Va.	Va.	Chuckatuck	....	l. d.	Mentioned 1683.
Contentnea	N. C.	N. C.	Contentnea	c. 1748	c. 1856	Wayne Co.; superseded by Nahunta.
Core Sound	N. C.	N.C.	Contentnea	1733	1841	Carteret and Hyde Cos.
Crooked Run	Va.	Bal.	Fairfax	a. 1783	1807	Warren Co.
Curles	Va.	Va.	Upper	c. 1698	l. d.	First name for Henrico M. M.
Deep Creek	N. C.	N.C.	Yadkin Valley	1793	....	Yadkin Co.; has D. C.
Deep River	N. C.	N.C.	Deep River	1778	....	Guilford Co.; has D. R.
Denby	Va.	Va.	Lower	c. 1716	l. d.	New in 1716; probably a variant name only.
Dover	N. C.	N.C.	New Garden	1815	....	Guilford Co.; has D.
Dunn's Creek	N. C.	N.C.	Western	c. 1746	1772	"On Cape Fear," probably in Cumberland Co.
East Bend	N. C.	N.C.	Yadkin Valley	c. 1832	....	Yadkin Co.; has E. B. and Forbush Creek.
Fairfax (H)	Va.	Bal.	Fairfax	1744	....	Fairfax Co., settled by Chester Q., Phila. Y. M.; has F.
Falling Creek	N. C.	N.C.	Contentnea	c. 1748	....	Changed to Contentnea, 1772; near Kinston.
Fredericksburg	S. C.	N.C.	Western	c. 1750	1782	At Camden, on Wateree; see Wateree.
Friendsville	Tenn.	N. C.	Friendsville	a. 1876	....	Blount Co., 11 mi. w. Maryville; has F.

Monthly Meetings.	State.	Yearly Meeting.	Present or last Quarterly Meeting.	Settled (established).	Laid down (suspended).	Remarks.
Goose Creek (H)	Va.	Bal.	Fairfax	a.1786		Fairfax and Loudoun Cos.; held at Lincoln; orthodox branch l. d. c. 1861.
Goose Creek	Va.	Va.	Western	1794		Bedford Co.; set off from South River.
Gravelly Run	Va.	Va.	Lower	1819		An earlier m. m. transferred to this place.
Greensboro	N.C.	N.C.	New Garden	1891		Has meeting in Greensboro.
Harmony Grove	N.C.	N.C.	Yadkin Valley	1894		Yadkin Co.; has H. G.
Henrico	Va.	Va.	Upper	c.1698		Henrico Co.; formerly called Curles, &c.
Hickory Creek	Tenn.	N.C.	Friendsville		c.1880	Knox Co., Tenn., about 20 mi. w. Knoxville.
Hickory Valley	Tenn.	N.C.	Friendsville		1893	Loudon Co., Tenn., 10 mi. e. Loudon.
High Point	N.C.	N.C.	Deep River	1892		Guilford Co.; has H. P.
Holly Springs	N.C.	N.C.	Western	1790		Randolph Co.; has H. S., Pine Ridge, Bethel, Prosperity.
Hopewell (H)	Va.	Bal.	Fairfax	1735		By Chester Q. M., Phila. Y. M.; now has H., Center, Ridge, Back Creek.
Hopewell	N.C.	N.C.	New Garden	1824		Guilford Co.
Hunting Creek	N.C.	N.C.	Yadkin Valley	1891		Yadkin and Iredell Cos.; has H. C. and Winthrop.
Isle of Wight	Va.	Va.	Lower		l. d.	Have records 1767-71; probably a variant name.
Jack Swamp	N.C.	N.C.	Eastern	1794		Northampton Co.
Lincoln (O)	Va.	Bal.	Baltimore	1887		For Loudoun Co.; the small m. m. here before the war was known as Goose Creek (O); has L. and Silcott's Springs.
Lost Creek	Tenn.	N.C.	Lost Creek	1797		Jefferson Co.
Long Creek	Tenn.	N.C.	Friendsville	1894		Jefferson Co., first settled 1890; has L. C.
Maple Grove	N.C.	N.C.	Friendsville	1894		Washington Co., 4 mi. w. Jonesboro; has M. G.
Marlboro	N.C.	N.C.	Southern	1816		Randolph Co.; has M., Cedar Square, Poplar Ridge, Plainfield.
Maryville	Tenn.	N.C.	Friendsville	1801		Blount Co.; has M.
Mount Pleasant	Va.	N.C.	New Garden	c.1826		Grayson Co., Va., and parts of Surry (?) Co., N. C.; changed to Chestnut Creek, 1818.
Nahunta	N.C.	N.C.	Contentnea	c.1856		Wayne Co.; took place of Contentnea.
Nansemond	Va.	Va.	Lower	a.1702	l. d.	Nansemond Co.

Name						Notes
Neuse	N.C.	N.C.	Contentnea	1841	. .	Sampson and Wayne Cos.; has N., Bethany, Bethesda and Oakland.
Newberry	Tenn.	N.C.	Lost Creek	a.1809	l. d.	Blount Co., Tenn.
New Garden	N.C.	N.C.	New Garden	1754	. .	Guilford Co.; has N. G.
New Hope	Tenn.	N.C.	Friendsville	1794	l. d.	Greene Co.; has N. H. Meeting.
Pagan Creek	Va.	Va.	Lower	a.1702	l. d.	Probably a variant name.
Piney Grove	S. C.	N.C.	New Garden	1802	1815	Marlborough Co., S. C., Anson and Richmond Cos., N. C.
Piney Woods	N.C.	N.C.	Eastern	1791	. .	Perquimans Co.; has P. W. and Up River.
Rich Square	N.C.	N.C.	Eastern	1760	. .	Northampton and Hertford Cos.; has R. S. and Cedar Grove.
Science Hill	N.C.	N.C.	Southern	1894	. .	Set off from Back Creek; has S. H.
Short Creek	Tenn.	N.C.	Lost Creek	. .	l. d.	Mentioned 1822; Jefferson Co.
Southland	Va.	Bal.	Fairfax	c.1789	l. d.	Culpeper Co.
South River	Va.	Va.	Upper	1757	1858	Campbell Co. and Bedford (?) Co.
Spring	N.C.	N.C.	Western	1793		Alamance and Chatham Cos.; has S., Chatham, South Fork, Plainfield.
Springfield	N.C.	N.C.	Deep River	1791	. .	Randolph and Davidson Cos.; has S., Pine Woods, Archdale, Oak Forest.
Surry	Va.	Va.	Lower	a.1702	l. d.	Probably a variant name.
Sutton's Creek	N.C.	N.C.	Eastern	1794	1835	Perquimans Co.; grew out of Wells.
Symons's Creek	N.C.	N.C.	Eastern	c.1803	1854	Pasquotank Co.
Trent	N.C.	N.C.	Contentnea	1792	1800	Jones and Craven Cos.
Union	N.C.	N.C.	Westfield	. .	l. d.	Ment'd 1818; Stokes Co.
Wainoak	Va.	Va.	Upper	a.1702	l. d.	Ment'd 1813–1835; probably same as Henrico.
Warwick	Va.	Va.	Lower	c.1750	c.1782	Ment'd 1703; same as York?
Wateree	S. C.	N.C.	Bush River	c.1764	. .	At Camden, Fredericksburg township, Kershaw Co.
Wells's	N.C.	N.C.	Eastern	c.1794	. .	Perquimans Co., superseded by Piney Woods.
Western Branch	Va.	Va.	Lower	c.1806	1833	Isle of Wight Co.
Westfield	N.C.	N.C.	Westfield	1787	1832	Re-established; Surry Co.; has W. and Charity Mission.
White Oak Swamp	Va.	Va.	Upper	c.1780	c.1839	
White Plains	N.C.	N.C.	Yadkin Valley	c.1886		Surry Co., N. C., and Patrick Co., Va.; has W. P. and Blue Ridge Mission.
Woodland	N.C.	N.C.	Contentnea	new		Wayne Co.; has W. and New Hope.
Wrightsborough	Ga.	Ga.	Bush River	1773	c.1803	McDuffie and Warren Cos., Ga.
York	Va.	Va.	Lower	a.1702	l. d.	Discontinued soon after; same as Wainoak? As York?

Particular meeting, meeting for worship or congregation.	State.	Yearly Meeting.	Present or last Quarter.	Present or last Monthly Meeting.	Settled (established).	Laid down (suspended).	Remarks on Location, etc.
Alexandria (II)	Va.	Bal.	Fairfax	Alexandria	a.1825	c.1856	In Alexandria, Va.
Amelia	Va.	Va.	Upper	Cedar Creek	a.1779	l. d.	A few Friends there, 1787; same as Genito?
Appomattox	Va.	Va.	Upper	Curles (?)	1718	l. d.	Ment'd 1718; probably near Burleigh.
Archdale	N.C.	N.C.	Deep River	Springfield	new	. . . .	Randolph Co.; 19 mi. n. w. Asheboro.
Back Creek (H)	Va.	Bal.	Fairfax	Hopewell	1759	. . . .	Frederick Co.; 9 mi. n. w. by w. Winchester.
Back Creek	N.C.	N.C.	Southern	Back Creek	1785	. . . .	Randolph Co.; 5 mi. w. Asheboro.
Banister	Va.	Va.	Western	Goose Creek (?)	c.1798	l. d.	In Pittsylvania or Halifax Co.; ind'l'g. m. 1798; new M. H. in place of old 1799.
Barker's	N.C.	N.C.	Deep River	Deep River	. . . .	l. d.	Ment'd about 1800 and in 1884.
Bath	N.C.	N.C.	Eastern	Core Sound (?)	. . . .	l. d.	Ment'd 1746; indications that it was then a M. M.
Bear Creek	N.C.	N.C.	Contentnea	Contentnea	c.1788	l. d.	Wayne Co.; new M. H. 1793; 10 mi. n. e. Goldsboro; close to Hood's Swamp?
Bear Garden	W.Va.	Bal.	Fairfax	Hopewell	1766	l. d.	Hampshire Co.; c.19 mi. n.w. Winchester, Va.
Beaver Dam	Va.	Va.	Upper		a.1780	l. d.	Close to Swamp m., probably in lower Henrico Co.
Beaver Dam	S. C.	N.C.	Bush River	Bush River	. . . .	l. d.	Existence doubtful; B. D. Creek is in Newberry Co.
Beech Spring	N.C.	N.C.	Eastern	Piney Woods	. . . .	p.1845	Perquimans Co.; M. H. to be sold 1850.
Bennett's Creek	Va.	Va.	Lower	West'n Branch	. . . .	1821	Nansemond Co.; about 10 mi. nearly n e. Suffolk.
Berk's Fork	N.C.	N.C.	. . . .	Springfield	a.1798	l. d.	Randolph Co.; n. w. corner? Same as Kennet?
Berkeley (II)	W.Va.	Bal.	Fairfax	Hopewell	. . . .	l. d.	Jefferson Co.; 18 mi. n. e. Winchester; same as Bullskin?
Bethany	N.C.	N.C.	Contentnea	Neuse	c.1868	. . . .	Wayne Co.; 15 mi. w. Goldsboro.
Bethel	Va.	Bal.	Va. Half	Yearly M.	. . . .	. . . .	Southampton Co.; about 8 mi. s. e. Jerusalem.
Bethel	N.C.	N.C.	Southern	Holly Springs	. . . .	. . . .	Randolph Co.; 6 mi. s. e. Asheboro; deed to M. H. 1821.

Bethel	Tenn.	N. C.	Deep River	Maryville		c. 1887	Blount Co.; 9 mi. s. Maryville.
Bethesda	N. C.	N. C.	Contentnea	Neuse			Sampson Co.; n. w. part, near Dunn.
Binford	Va.	Va.	Lower	Gravelly Run	1821	c. 1826	Prince George Co.
Black Creek	Va.	Va.	Upper	Henrico	c. 1699	1807	New Kent Co.
Black Creek	Va.	Va.	Lower	West'n Branch	1807		Ment'd 1766; Southampton Co.
Black Water	Va.	Va.	Lower	Black Water		1807	Surry Co.
Blue Ridge	Va.	N. C.	Yadkin Valley	White Plains	c. 1886		Patrick Co.
Blue's Creek	N. C.	N. C.	New Garden	Deep River		l. d.	Ment'd 1792; Yadkin Co.
Boice's	N. C.	N. C.	Eastern	Piney Woods		1825	Perquimans Co.
Brooklyn	Tenn	Tenn	Friendsville	Friendsville		l. d.	Blount Co.; 7 mi. n. w. Maryville, laid down "several years since."
Brush Creek	N. C.	N. C.	Western	Cane Creek		l. d.	M. for w. 1796; same as Ridge; and near Rocky River m.
Buffkin's	Va.	Va.	Lower		a. 1701	l. d.	Nansemond Co.; On So. Branch N. River.
Bull Run	N. C.	N. C.	New Garden	New Garden	a. 1793	l. d.	Called also Sherborn; Guilford Co.; 6¼ mi. s. New Garden.
Bullskin	W.Va.	Bal.	Fairfax	Hopewell	1785	l. d.	Jefferson Co.; 5 mi. s. e. Charlestown.
Burk's Fork	Va.	N. C.	Westfield	Westfield		l. d.	Ment'd 1812; Grayson Co.
Burleigh	Va.	Va.	Lower	Black Water	1722	1832	Prince George Co.; first to Curles M. M.
Burlington	N. C.	N. C.	Western	Cane Creek	1893	l. d.	Alamance Co.; 2 mi. w. Graham.
Bush Creek	Va.	Bal.	Fairfax	Fairfax	1755	l. d.	
Bush River	S. C.	N. C.	Bush River	Bush River	c. 1767	c. 1808	Privilege of holding m. not withdrawn in 1837; Newberry Co.; 8 mi. n. w. Newberry.
Camp Creek	Va.	Va.	Upper	Camp Creek	a. 1739	c. 1800	Louisa Co.; about 11 nearly s. w. Louisa C. H.
Canada Creek	Tenn.	N. C.	Lost Creek			l. d.	Ment'd in 1812 by Joseph Hoag.
Cane Creek	N. C.	N. C.	Western	Cane Creek	1751		Alamance Co.; 14 mi. s. Graham.
Cane Creek	S. C.	S. C.	Bush River	Cane Creek	1774	1808	"On waters of Tiger River," Union Co.
Caroline	Va.	Va.	Upper	Cedar Creek	a. 1739	p. 1833	In Caroline Co.
Carver's Creek	N. C.	N. C.	Eastern	Carver's Creek	c. 1740	c. 1797	or earlier; Bladen Co.; 18 mi. below Elizabethtown; on Cape Fear R.
Cedar Creek	Va.	Va.	Upper	Cedar Creek	c. 1722	p. 1833	Hanover Co.; new M. H. 1797.
Cedar Grove	N. C.	N. C.	Deep River	Deep Creek	1775		
Cedar Grove	N. C.	N. C.	Eastern	Rich Square	1873		Northampton Co.

Particular meeting, meeting for worship or congregation.	State.	Yearly Meeting.	Present or last Quarter.	Present or last Monthly Meeting.	Settled (established).	Laid down (suspended).	Remarks on Location, etc.
Cedar Square	N. C.	N. C.	Southern	Marlboro	. . . . .	l. d.	Randolph Co.; 14 mi. n. w. Asheboro.
Center (II)	Va.	Bal.	Fairfax	Hopewell	a.1779	l. d.	Now held in Winchester.
Centre	N. C.	N. C.	Western	Centre	1757	. . . .	Guilford Co.; 11 mi. nearly s. Greensboro.
Charity Mission	N. C.	N. C.	Yadkin Valley	Westfield	new	. . . .	Surry Co.; 2¾ mi. n. w. Westfield m.
Charleston	S. C.	. . .	. . . . .	. . . . .	c.1680	c.1837	See text for full account.
Chatham	N. C.	N. C.	Western	Spring	. . .	. . . .	Deed for M. H. 1824; Chatham Co.; 15 mi. nearly n. Pittsboro.
Chestnut Creek	Va.	N. C.	Westfield	Mt. Pleasant	179?	l. d.	Friends there in 1781; in Grayson Co.
Chuckatuck	Va.	Va.	Lower	Chuckatuck	. . .	l. d.	"General M. H. at C." 1674; very weak 1761; Nansemond Co.
Olub Foot Creek	N. C.	N. C.	Contentnea	Core Sound	. . .	l. d.	Ment'd 1797; in Carteret Co.?
Concord	N. C.	N. C.	Western	Centre	c.1800	1853	Prep. 1806; new M. H. recently built; Guilford Co., 8 mi. s. Greensboro.
Contentnea	N. C.	N. C.	Contentnea	Contentnea	c.1772	p.1856	Wayne Co.; 15 mi. n. Goldsboro; 9 mi. n. e. Nahunta.
Core Sound	N. C.	N. C.	Contentnea	Core Sound	a.1733	l. d.	Deed to M. H. 1737; Carteret Co.; 6 mi. n. Beaufort.
Corinth	Va.	Bal.	Va. Half	Yearly M.	. . .	l. d.	Southampton Co.
Crooked Run	Va.	Bal.	Fairfax	Crooked Run	c.1760	c.1807	Warren Co., 9 mi. s. Winchester.
Culpeper	Va.	Bal.	Fairfax	Crooked Run	1778	l. d.	Culpeper Co.; first to Hopewell M. M.
Curles	Va.	Va.	Upper	Henrico	1700	l. d.	Lower Henrico Co.
Deep Creek	N. C.	N. C.	Yadkin Valley	Deep Creek	a.1793	. . . .	Yadkin Co.; 4 mi. n. Yadkinville.
Deep River	N. C.	N. C.	Deep River	Deep River	1760	. . . .	Guilford Co.; 12 mi. s. w. Greensboro; mid-week m. 1753.
Dillon's Run (II)	W. Va.	Bal.	Fairfax	. . . .	a.1820	l. d.	Hampshire Co.; 6 mi. w. Capon Bridge.
Disco	Tenn.	N. C.	Friendsville	Friendsville	. . .	recent	Blount Co.; 14 mi. w. Maryville.
Dixon's	N. C.	N. C.	Western	Spring	a.1805	l. d.	Ment'd 1805; probably settled c. 1800.

	N. C.				1793	. . .	
Dover	N. C.		New Garden	Dover	1793	. . .	Guilford Co.; 16 mi. w. Greensboro; formerly called Upper Reedy Fork.
Douglass's . .	Va.		Upper	Cedar Creek (?)	c. 1750	c. 1800	Orange Co.; same as Orange?
Dunn's Creek .	N. C.		Western	Cane Creek	a.1746	1781	Supposed to have been near Fayetteville.
East Bend . .	N. C.		Yadkin Valley	East Bend	a.1882		Yadkin Co.; 15 mi. n. e. Yadkinville.
Edisto . . .	S. C.		Bush River	Bush River	c. 1754	c. 1806	See text for full account.
Edward's Hill .	N. C.		Western	Cane Creek			Chatham Co.; about 15 mi. w. Pittsboro.
Eno	N. C.		Western	Spring	1754	1847	Orange Co.; 1 mi. n. Hillsboro; prep. m. 1761.
Fairfax (H) . .	Va.	Bal.	Fairfax	Fairfax	1733		M. H. built 1741; new M. H. 1763; Loudoun Co., 7 mi. w. of n. Leesburg.
Falling Creek .	N. C.		Eastern	Falling Creek	a. 1748	1772	Removed to Contentnea, 1772; near Kinston, Lenoir Co.
Fuositt's . .	Va.	Bal.	Fairfax	Hopewell		l. d.	Ment'd 1777; same as Mt. Pleasant? A reg. m.?
Flat Creek . .	Tenn.		Lost Creek	. . . . . .		l. d.	Granger Co.; ment'd 1809; seems to have been a regular m.
Forbush Creek .	N. C.		Yadkin Valley	East Bend	a.1845		Yadkin Co.; 9 mi. n. e. Yadkinville.
Fork Creek . .	Va.		Upper	Cedar Creek (?)		l. d.	Louisa Co.; about 16 mi. east of CampCreek m.
Fountain Spring .	Tenn.					l. d.	Regular m.?
Fredericksburg .	S. C.		Western	Fredericksburg	c. 1750	1784	Camden, Kershaw Co.; same as Wateree?
Friends' Mission	Va.		Yadkin Valley	White Plains	1886		Patrick Co.; 10 mi. n. Mt. Airy, N. C.; prep. m. 1894.
Friendsville . .	Tenn.		Friendsville	Friendsville	1797		Blount Co.; 11 mi. w. Maryville.
Fruit Hill . .	Va.		Westfield	Mt. Pleasant		l. d.	Prep. m. c. 1800; Grayson Co.; near Burk's Fork.
Gap	Bal.		Fairfax	Fairfax	1755	l. d.	Hillsborough, Loudoun Co.
Genito	Va.		Upper	Cedar Creek	a.1804	p.1833	Fluvanna Co., n. w. corner; same as Amelia?
Goose Creek (II)	Bal.		Fairfax	Goose Creek	1756	l. d.	Lincoln, Loudoun Co.
Goose Creek . .	Va.		Western	Goose Creek		l. d.	Bedford Co.; 10 mi. s. e. Bedford City; new M. H. 1792.
Grassy Valley .	Tenn.		Lost Creek	Lost Creek	1800	l. d.	Blount Co.
Gravelly Run .	Va.		Lower	Black Water	early	l. d.	Dinwiddie Co.; about 4 mi. e. Dinwiddie.
Greensboro . .	N. C.		New Garden	Greensboro	new	. . .	Guilford County.

Particular meeting, meeting for worship or congregation.	State.	Yearly Meeting.	Present or last Quarter.	Present or last Montly Meeting.	Settl-(est. ablished).	Laid down (suspended).	Remarks on Location, etc.
Gum Swamp . . .	S. C.	N. C.	New Garden	Piney Grove	. .	1829	Deed dated 1743; Marlborough Co.; 12 mi. n. e. Bennettsville; not a reg. m. 1798.
Halifax	Va.	Va.	Upper	South River (?)	1759	l. d.	Halifax Co.; true name unknown; same as Banister, or Kirby's?
Harmony Grove .	N. C.	N. C.	Yadkin Valley	Harmony G've	new	l. d.	Yadkin Co.; 1½ mi. n. w. Yadkinville.
Hedgecock's Creek	N. C.	N. C.	Western	Cane Creek (?)	. .	l. d.	Chatham Co.; title to this M. H. to be looked up 1829.
Henderson's . . .	S. C.	N. C.	Bush River	Bush River	a.1798	1805	Probably in n. e. part Newberry Co.; also called Allwood's.
Hering Creek . .	Va.	Va.	Upper	Curles	. .	l. d.	Ment'd 1708; probably a variant name.
Hickory Creek . .	Tenn.	N. C.	Friendsville	Friendsville	. .	c. 1880	Knox Co.; about 20 mi. w. Knoxville.
Hickory Valley . .	Tenn.	N. C.	Friendsville	Friendsville	. .	1893	Loudon Co.; 10 mi. e. London.
High Point . . .	N. C.	N. C.	Deep River	High Point	1787	. .	Guilford Co.; 16 mi. s. w. Greensboro.
Hill's Creek . .	Va.	Va.	Western	South River	. .	l. d.	In Campbell Co.
Hinshaw's . . .	N. C.	N. C.	. . . . .	. . . .	. .	. .	Ment'd by C. Osborn, 1824; in Randolph or Guilford.
Holly Springs . .	N. C.	N. C.	Western	Holly Springs	a.1769	c. 1821	Reestab. after 1845; Randolph Co.; 11 mi. s. e. Asheboro.
Holly Springs .	N. C.	N. C.	Contentnea	Contentnea	. . .	l. d.	Deed 1813; ment'd 1821 as weak.
Hood Swamp . .	N. C.	N. C.	Contentnea	Nahunta	new	. .	Wayne Co.; about 10 mi. n. e. Goldsboro.
Hopewell (II) . .	Va.	Bal.	Fairfax	Hopewell	1732	. .	Frederick Co.; 6 mi. n. Winchester; same house occupied by both branches.
Hopewell . . .	N. C.	N. C.	New Garden	New Garden	1793	l. d.	Guilford Co.; 6 mi. n. w. New Garden; also called Lower Reedy Fork.
Hopewell . . .	N. C.	N. C.	Southern	Back Creek	1885	. .	Randolph Co.; 6 mi. s. w. Asheboro.
Howard's . . .	Va.	Va.	Upper	Curles	c. 1702	early	Probably a regular meeting; also called Old Man's Neck.

	N. C.	Va.	Yadkin Valley	Hunting Creek	1801	1828		Remarks
Hunting Creek	N. C.		Western			1828		Re-established 1843; Yadkin Co.; 10 mi. s. w. Yadkinville.
Ivy Creek		Va.		Goose Creek?		c. 1799	l. d.	New M. H. in place of old, and indulged m. 1799; in Campbell Co.?
Jack Swamp	N. C.		Eastern	Rich Square		c. 1771	l. d.	Northampton Co.; M. H. built 1775, sold 1844.
Johnson's		Va.	Lower	West'n Branch			l. d.	Isle of Wight Co.; 12 mi. s. w. I. of W. C. H.
Kennet	N. C.		Deep River	Springfield		c. 1800	1867	Guilford Co.; 14 mi. w. of s. Greensboro; same as Berk's Fork?
Kirby's		Va.	Western	South River?	1759			"On Dan River", in Halifax Co.?
Langley's		Va.	Upper	Cedar Creek				Regular meeting?
Leesburg		Bal.	Fairfax			c. 1807		At Leesburg in Loudoun Co.
Levy Neck		Va.	Lower			a. 1700	l. d.	Public M. H. there 1704; also called Pagan Creek; Isle of Wight Co.
Liberty	N. C.		Deep River	Deep River				Possibly same as Cedar Grove, in —— Co.
Lick Creek	Tenn.		Lost Creek	New Hope		c. 1850		Greene Co.; 6 mi. n. Greenville.
Limestone	Tenn.		Lost Creek	New Hope		a. 1798	l. d.	Washington Co.; 5 mi. s. w. Jonesboro; M. H. repaired 1850.
Lincoln (O)	Bal.		Baltimore	Lincoln		c. 1884		Loudoun Co.; 8 mi. w. Leesburg; known before war as Goose Creek (O) m.
Little River	N. C.		Eastern	Symons's Cr'k	c. 1700			Perquimans Co.
Little River	N. C.		Southern	Back Creek		1854		Randolph Co.; 7 mi. s. w. Asheboro.
Little River	S. C.		Bush River	Bush River		c. 1875		M. asked for 1774; Newberry Co.; 10 mi. w. Newberry.
Little's Creek	N. C.		New Garden	Piney Grove	new			Ind'g'd m. 1802; probably in Anson Co.
Long Creek	Tenn.		Friendsville	Long Creek				Jefferson Co.; 7 m. n. Dandridge.
Long Hill	N. C.		Deep River	Deep Creek	1815			In —— Co.
Long's	N. C.		Western	Cane Creek	l.			M. for w., near John Long's in Cane Creek prep. m.
Lost Creek	Tenn.		Lost Creek	Lost Creek	a. 1798			Jefferson Co.; M. H. built 1796.
Lower Reedy Fork	N. C.		New Garden	New Garden	1795		l. d.	Guilford Co.; see Hopewell.
Lower Ridge (II)		Va.	Fairfax	Hopewell	175		l. d.	Frederick Co.; 9 mi. n. w. Winchester.
Lower Trent	N. C.		Con:entnea	Core Sound?	c. 175		l. d.	M. H. built 1791; near mouth of Buck Horn Branch, in Jones Co.; usually called Trent.

Particular meeting, meeting for worship or congregation.	State.	Yearly Meeting.	Present or last Quarter.	Present or last Monthly Meeting.	Settled (establ'd).	Laid down (suspended).	Remarks on Location, etc.
Lynchburg . . .	Va.	Va.	Western	South River?	c.1810	l. d.	Mt. H. built c. 1810.
Maple Grove . .	Tenn.	N. C.	Friendsville	Maple Grove	1807	a.1813	Washington Co.; 5 mi. w. Jonesborough.
Maple Spring . .	Va.	N. C.	Westfield	Mt. Pleasant	1796	. .	Grayson Co.
Marlboro . . .	N. C.	N. C.	Southern	Marlboro	. .	. .	Randolph Co.; 11 mi. n. w. Asheboro.
Maryville . . .	Tenn.	N. C.	Friendsville	Maryville	. .	. .	Blount Co.
Mattamuskeet .	N. C.	N. C.	Contentnea	Core Sound	c.1793	p.1810	Mt. H. to be built 1793; ment'd 1810; Hyde Co.
Mendinhall's . .	Ga.	N. C.	Bush River	Wrightsbor'gh	c.1773	c.1808	Variant name of Williams's Creek?
Merchant's Hope	Va.	Va.	Upper	Curles	a.1700	early	Prince George Co.
Middle Creek (H) .	W.Va.	Bal.	Fairfax	Hopewell	a.1771	l. d.	Berkeley Co.; 18 mi. n. Winchester.
Mill Creek . . .	Va.	Phila.	Western	Hopewell	1759	1762	Another meeting settled 1766.
Mill Creek . . .	Va.	N. C.	Western	Cane Creek	. .	l. d.	Randolph Co.
Mt. Pleasant . .	Va.	Bal.	Fairfax	Crooked Run	a.1778	l. d.	Frederick Co.; 9 mi. s. w. Winchester; same as Fawsitt's?
Mt. Pleasant . .	Va.	N. C.	Westfield	Mt. Pleasant	1797	1817	Grayson Co.
Mt. Pony . . .	Va.	Bal.	Fairfax	Southland	a.1779	l. d.	Culpeper Co.; called later Southland.
Muddy Creek . .	Va.	Va.	Lower		c.1680	a.1736	Northampton Co.; Eastern Shore.
Muddy Creek . .	N. C.	N. C.	New Garden	Deep River	c.1771	l. d.	Prep. m. 1785; 2 mi. s. Kernersville, Forsythe Co.
Mud Lick . . .	S. C.	N. C.	Bush River	Bush River	a.1798	1806	Newberry Co.; on Mud Lick Creek?
Nahunta . . .	N. C.	N. C.	Contentnea	Nahunta	1797	. .	Wayne Co.; 12 mi. n. w. Goldsboro.
Nansemond . .	Va.	Va.	Lower		c.1672	l. d.	Nansemond Co.
Narrows . . .	Va.	Va.	Eastern	Symons's Cr'k	c.1680	a.1839	Pasquotank Co.; Eastern Shore.
Nassataolox . .	N. C.	N. C.	Contentnea	Neuse	c.1789	1736	Northampton Co.; Eastern Shore.
Neuse	N. C.	N. C.	Eastern	Symons's Cr'k	early	. .	Wayne Co.; 6 mi. w. Goldsboro.
Newbegun Creek .	N. C.	N. C.	New Garden	New Garden	early	1845	Pasquotank Co.; M. H. sold 1850.
Newberry . . .	N. C.	N. C.			1811	p.1837	Guilford Co.; "On head of Deep River"; 4 mi. w. New Garden.
Newberry . . .	Tenn.	N. C.	Lost Creek		. .	p.1841	Blount Co.

Meeting	State	Y. M.	Quarterly Meeting	Monthly Meeting	Set up	Laid down	Remarks
New Garden	N. C.	N. C.	New Garden	New Garden	1751		Guilford Co.
New Hope	N. C.	N. C.	Contentnea	Woodland	c. 1878		Wayne Co.; 7 mi. s. e. Goldsboro.
New Hope	Tenn.	N. C.	Friendsville	New Hope	c. 1792		Greene Co.; 10 mi. e. Greenville; first called Nolichucky.
New Salem	N. C.	N. C.	Westfield	Westfield		l. d.	Deed 1815; Randolph.Co.
North Providence	?	N. C.			1801	1809	"On big Creek of Dan"; Va. or N. C.?
North River	W. Va.	Bal.	Fairfax			l. d.	Hardy Co.; 50 mi. w. Winchester.
Oak Forest	N. C.	N. C.	Deep River	Springfield		recent	Randolph Co.; 16 mi. n. w. Asheboro.
Oak Grove	Tenn.	N. C.	Friendsville	Friendsville	c. 1880		Blount Co.; 9 mi. w. Maryville.
Oakland	N. C.	N. C.	Contentnea	Neuse		l. d.	Wayne Co.; 10 mi. w. Goldsboro.
Old Neck	N. C.	N. C.	Eastern	Sutton's Creek	1735		Perquimans Co.
Opeckon	Va.	Phila.	Chester	Nottingham	a. 1780	l. d.	Frederick Co.; same as Hopewell.
Orange	Va.	Va.	Upper	Cedar Creek?	1774	l. d.	Orange Co.; 8 mi. n. w. Gordonsville; same as Douglass's?
Padgett's Creek	S. C.	N. C.	Bush River	Cane Creek	c. 1700	l. d.	Union Co.; perhaps near Tiger River.
Pagan Creek	Va.	Va.	Lower		1755	c. 1799	Isle of Wight Co.; also called Levy Neck.
Pee Dee	S. C.	S. C.	New Garden	Piney Grove			Marlborough Co.; same as Gum Swamp?
Pine Ridge	N. C.	N. C.	Southern	Holly Springs	1791		Randolph Co.; 13 mi. s. e. Asheboro; deed for M. H. 1826.
Pine Woods	N. C.	N. C.	Deep River	Springfield	c. 1797	1815	Davidson Co.; 12 mi. n. of e. Lexington.
Piney Grove	S. C.	S. C.	Western	Piney Grove	a. 1794		Marlborough Co.; 9 mi. n. Bennettsville.
Piney Woods	N. C.	N. C.	Eastern	Piney Woods			Perquimans Co.; 9 mi. n. Hertford.
Plainfield	N. C.	N. C.	Western	Spring	1894		Chatham Co.; 14 mi. n. w. Pittsboro; 3 mi. s. w. South Fork m.
Plainfield	N. C.	N. C.	Southern	Marlboro			Randolph Co.; 9 mi. n. w. Asheboro.
Poplar Ridge	N. C.	N. C.	Southern	Marlboro			Randolph Co.; 16 mi. n. w. Asheboro.
Prosperity	N. C.	N. C.	Western	Holly Spring			Moore Co.; n. w. part; n. side Deep River.
Providence	W. Va.	Bal.	Western	Hopewell	1733		Berkeley Co.; called also Tuscarora, and later Mill Creek.
Providence	N. C.	N. C.	Western	Centre	c. 1792		Randolph Co.; 14 mi. e. of n. Asheboro.
Rayburn's Creek	S. C.	S. C.	Bush River	Bush River	a. 1798	c. 1805	Laurens Co.; about 8 mi. s. Laurens C. H.
Reedy Island	N. C.?	N. C.	New Garden	Westfield	a. 1798	l. d.	Surry Co., N. C.? Same as Mt. Pleasant?

Particular meeting, meeting for worship, or congregation.	State.	Yearly Meeting.	Present or last Quarter.	Present or last Monthly Meeting.	Settled (estab-lished).	Laid down (susp-ended).	Remarks on Location, etc.
Richmond	Va.	Bal.	Va. Half	Yearly M.	1795	. . .	M. H. built 1797; indulg. m. 1795; reg. m. set. 1801.
Richmond Co.	N. C.	N. C.	Western	Piney Grove	. . .	l. d.	M. H. land ment'd 1844 and 1846. Possibly Piney Grove, just across S. C. line, is meant; see Rocky Fork.
Rich Square	N. C.	N. C.	Eastern	Rich Square	1753	. . .	Northampton Co.
Ridge (H)	Va.	Bal.	Fairfax	Hopewell	a.1805	. . .	Frederick Co.; 4 mi. n. w. Winchester; formerly called Upper Ridge to distinguish it from Lower Ridge (q. v.).
Ridge	N. C.	N. C.	Western	Cane Creek	c.1796	1830	Chatham Co.; also known as Brush Creek.
Round Creek	Va.	N. C.	Westfield	Mt. Pleasant	1832	l. d.	In Grayson or Carroll Co., Va.
Rocky Fork	N. C.	N. C.	New Garden	Piney Grove	1804	l. d.	Is this the Richmond Co. meeting?
Rocky River	N. C.	N. C.	Western	Cane Creek	1754	. . .	Chatham Co.; 21 mi. n. w. Pittsboro; prep. m. 1796.
Rocky River	S. C.	N. C.	Bush River	Bush River	. . .	l. d.	Prep. m. 1797; to Cane Creek M. M.?
Rocky Spring	S. C.	N. C.	Bush River	Bush River	a.1793	1805	Newberry Co.; now a Baptist M. H.
Salem	S. C.	N. C.	Southern	Marlboro	a.1813	1885	Randolph Co.; 10 mi. n. Asheboro.
Sandy Branch	N. C.	N. C.	New Garden	Piney Grove	a.1837	l. d.	Anson Co.; deed for M. H. land 1775.
Sandy Creek	N. C.	N. C.	Western	Cane Creek	1780	1795	Randolph Co.
Sandy Springs	N. C.	N. C.	New Garden	New Garden	1801	1822	Guilford Co.; near New Garden.
Science Hill	N. C.	N. C.	Southern	Science Hill	. . .	. . .	Randolph Co.; 9 mi. s. w. Asheboro.
Seimino	Va.	Va.	Lower	Black Water	c.1690	p.1805	York Co.; near York River? Now M. H. 1799.
Seacock	Va.	Va.	Lower	South River	a.1801	1821	Sussex Co.
Seneca	Va.	Va.	Western	New Garden	a.1795	l. d.	Campbell Co.; new M. H. and prep. m. 1795.
Sherborn	N. C.	N. C.	New Garden	New Garden	a.1793	1829	Called also Bull Run; Guilford Co.
Silcott's Springs(O)	Va.	Bal.	Baltimore	Lincoln	a.1894	. . .	Louloun Co.; 11 mi. s. of w. Leesburg.
Smith's Creek	Va.	Phila.	Fairfax	Crooked Run	a.1770	l. d.	
Somerton	Va.	Va.	Va. Half	Yearly M.	c.1672	. . .	Nansemond Co.

Name	State	Y. M.	Quarterly Meeting	Monthly Meeting	Estab.	Disc.	Remarks
South Pork (II)	Va.	Bal.	Fairfax	Goose Creek	1769	c.1810	Loudoun Co.; 16 or 18 mi. s. w. Leesburg.
South Fork	N. C.	N. C.	Western	Spring	1818	....	Chatham Co.; 12 mi. n. w. Pittsboro; prep. m. 1835.
Southland	Va.	Bal.	Fairfax	Southland	a.1789	l. d.	Stevensburg, Culpeper Co.; called first Mt. Poney.
South River	Va.	Va.	Upper	South River	a.1757	p.1858	Campbell Co.; new M. H. 1795; near Lynchburg?
Spring	N. C.	N. C.	Western	Spring	1773	. . .	Alamance Co.; 14 mi. s. Graham.
Springfield	N. C.	N. C.	Deep River	Springfield	1773	. . .	Guilford Co.; near High Point.
Stafford	Va.	Va.	Fairfax	Crooked Run	a.1779	l. d.	Stafford Co.; perhaps near Stafford P. O.
Stanton's	Va.	Va.	Lower	Black Water	a.1804	1829	Sussex Co.; 8 mi. nearly e. Sussex C. H.
Summerfield	N. C.	N. C.	New Garden	New Garden	c.1873	l. d.	Guilford Co.; l. d. in a few years.
Surry	Va.	Va.	Lower			l. d.	Surry Co.; a variant name?
Sutton's Creek	N. C.	N. C.	Eastern	Sutton's Creek	a.1794	1835	Perquimans Co.
Swamp	Va.	Va.	Upper	Henrico	c.1700	l. d.	Henrico or Charles City Co. ? Same as White Oak Swamp?
Swan Creek	N. C.	N. C.	Westfield	Deep Creek	1809	. . .	Yadkin Co.; western part.
Symons's Creek	N. C.	N. C.	Eastern	Symons's Cr'k	c.1700	1854	Pasquotank Co.
Tallassee	Tenn.	N. C.	Deep River	Maryville	. .	c.1888	Monroe Co.; 28 mi. s. Maryville.
Tar River	N. C.	N. C.	Contentnea	Contentnea	1758	1794	Edgecombe Co.; perhaps near Tarboro; to Rich Square M. M. till 1782.
Taylor's Creek	Va.	Va.	Western	South River ?	1802	l. d.	New M. H. 1802; in Mecklenburg Co., n. e. Boylton.
Trotter's Creek	N. C.	N. C.	Western	Cane Creek	. .	1837	S. e. corner Guilford Co.; ment'd 1825.
Turner's Creek	S. C.	N. C.	Bush River	Bush River	. .	l. d.	Newberry Co.; 6¼ mi. s. w. Newberry; *possibly* a m. was located here.
Turner's Swamp	N. C.	N. C.	Contentnea		c.1789	c.1829	New M. H. 1793; probably on lower edge Wayne Co.
Tuscarora	W. Va.	Bal.	Western	Hopewell	1733	1758	Berkeley Co., see Providence. Said by Kercheval to have been the place where the gospel was first preached w. of Blue Ridge Mts.
Tyson's	N. C.	N. C.	Western	Cane Creek	a.1763	l. d.	On Deep River, Chatham Co.
Uwharrie	N. C.	N. C.	Southern	Back Creek	1793	c.1870	Randolph Co.; 14 mi. s. w. Asheboro.

Particular meeting, meeting for worship, or congregation.	State.	Yearly Meeting.	Present or last Quarter.	Present or last Monthly Meeting.	Settled (estab- lished).	Laid down (susp- ended).	Remarks on Location, etc.
Union	N. C.	N. C.	Westfield ?	. . . . .	a.1818	l. d.	M. H. sold 1841; Stokes Co.
Up River . . .	N. C.	N. C.	Eastern	Piney Woods	c.1867	. . .	Perquimans Co.; 14 mi. n. e. Hertford.
Upper Goose Creek	Va.	Va.	Western	Goose Creek	1792	1813	Bedford Co.; 15 mi. n. w. Bedford City; M. H. 1792.
Upper Ridge (H) .	Va.	Bal.	Fairfax	Hopewell	a.1805	. . .	Same as Ridge, q. v.
Upper Trent . .	N. C.	N. C.	Contentnea	Trent	c.1791	c.1800	Jones Co.; 20 mi. from Lower Trent.
Upper Reedy Fork	N. C.	N. C.	New Garden	New Garden	1793	. . .	Guilford Co.; now known as Dover.
Vick's	Va.	Va.	Lower	West'n Branch	a.1796	l. d.	Southampton Co.; 10 mi. s. w. Jerusalem ; new M. H. 1796.
Wainoak . . .	Va.	Va.	Upper	Henrico	a.1718	l. d.	Henrico Co.
Ward's Gap . .	Va.	N. C.	Westfield	Mt. Pleasant	a.1802	l. d.	Carroll Co.
Warwick . . .	Va.	Va.	Lower	. . . . .	a.1703	l. d.	Warwick Co.
Watere . . .	S. C.	N. C.	Western	Fredericksburg	c.1750	c.1790	Same as Fredericksburg; see text.
Wells's . . .	N. C.	N. C.	Eastern	Piney Woods	a.1764	p.1845	M. H. sold 1850; Perquimans Co.
Western Branch .	Va.	Va.	Lower	West'n Branch	c.1702	l. d.	Set. 1702 or earlier; Isle of Wight Co.; 7 mi. nearly s. c. I. of W. C. H.; new M. H. 1797.
Westfield . . .	N. C.	N. C.	Yadkin Valley	Westfield	c.1771	. . .	Surry Co.; 22 mi. n. e. Dobson.
Westland . . .	Tenn.	N. C.	Lost Creek	. . . . .	a.183?	c.1850	M. H. sold 1850; Greene Co.
White Lick . .	S. C.	S. C.	Bush River	Bush River	. . . .	1805	Probably in Newberry Co.
White Oak Swamp	Va.	Va.	Upper	Henrico	c.1710	a.1798	New M. H. 1723; Henrico Co.; same as Swamp.
White Plains . .	N. C.	Va.	Yadkin Valley	White Plains	new	. . .	Surry Co.; 8 mi. n. c. Dobson.
William Farmer's .	Ga.	N. C.	Bush River	Wrightsbor'gh	c.1773	c.1808	McDuffie Co.?
Williams's Creek .	Ga.	N. C.	Bush River	Wrightsbor'gh	c.1773	c.1808	Warren Co.; 8 mi. w. Wrightsborough. Seems to have been called Mendenhall's, also.
Winthrop . . .	N. C.	N. C.	Yadkin Valley	Hunting Creek	new	. . .	Iredell Co.; 18 mi. n. Statesville.
Woodland . .	N. C.	N. C.	Contentnea	Woodland	c.1870	. .	Wayne Co.; 5 mi. s. w. Goldsboro.
Woodlawn (H) .	Va.	Bal.	Fairfax	Alexandria	. . .	. .	Fairfax Co.; 3 mi. w. Mt. Vernon.
Wrightsborough .	Ga.	N. C.	Bush River	Wrightsbor'gh	1773	c.1808	McDuffie Co.; 36 mi. n. w. Augusta.

BIBLIOGRAPHY.

The sources for the history of Southern Quakerism are abundant and of the most trustworthy kind. This study has been based almost exclusively on original sources; where no authorities for statements are given, it will be understood that they are based on the manuscripts; these authorities have been quoted literally as far as possible. Secondary authorities have been used for the purpose of explanation and illustration. These sources can be divided into three classes, and while perhaps the followi. ʔ list is not exhaustive, it represents the printed material tʜat has been of actual service in the preparation of the present monograph, and presents a practically complete list of the manuscript records of the Society in these States so far as I have been able to discover them.

I.—ORIGINAL MANUSCRIPT SOURCES.

1. *Philadelphia Yearly Meeting :*
   Yearly Meeting Minutes, about 1683-1710.
   Charleston Monthly Meeting Minutes, 1718-86.
   There is a break in the Charleston records, 1737–53, with several other lesser ones.

2. *Baltimore Yearly Meeting :*
   Yearly Meeting Minutes, 1866-85 (printed).
   Alexandria Monthly Meeting Register, 1805-51.
   Crooked Run Monthly Meeting Register, 1784-1807.
   Fairfax Monthly Meeting Minutes, 1749-1844.
   Goose Creek (northern) Monthly Meeting Register, 1786-1868.

Hopewell Monthly Meeting Minutes, 1759-1845; extracts, 1748.

Nottingham Monthly Meeting Minutes, 1764-97.

These monthly meetings, with the exception of the last named, lay in Virginia and were transferred by Philadelphia to Baltimore Yearly Meeting in 1789. In the division in 1828 these records fell to the Hicksite Friends, and are kept in their fireproof vault in Park Avenue Meeting House, Baltimore. Through the loving zeal of Kirk Brown, such volumes as required it were rebound, properly labeled and shelved, and a catalogue gives the location of all the records in the vault. An exhaustive index to the contents of all the volumes in the vault is now in preparation by Mr. Brown. As far as the preservation and care of these volumes go nothing more is to be desired.

3. *Virginia Yearly Meeting:*

Book of Records of the Lower Virginia Meetings, 1673-1709.

This contains the earliest records, of any and all kinds, of Virginia Friends. It deals principally with marriages, births and deaths, and was begun by motion of George Fox.

Yearly Meeting Minutes, 1702-1836, 1838-43; Women, 1763-1825.

These volumes are imperfect. There is no trace of the records for 1724-37; those from 1737-68 are pretty generally preserved; those from 1768-91 are made up of material sent in the form of extracts from the Yearly to the quarterly and monthly meetings. Some of these parts were made up after 1800, the spelling was frequently modernized and other similar changes made. After 1791 the records have been preserved.

Yearly Meeting Correspondence, 1796-1828, 1829-40; Records of Ministers and Elders, 1758-74, 1824-53; Records of Meeting for Sufferings (Wainoak), 1811-25, (Gravelly Run) 1822-35.

Half Yearly Meeting Minutes of Ministers and Elders, 1854-60.

Quarterly Meeting Minutes:

Upper, 1783-1818, 1839-43; Women, 1786-1817, 1837-43; Western, 1797-1817.

Monthly Meeting Minutes:

Blackwater, 1796-1807.

Camp Creek Register, 1739-73.

Cedar Creek, 1739-73, 1789-91, 1791-92, 1797-98, 1811-33, 1834-68.

Cedar Creek and Caroline County, 1775-89; same as Cedar Creek.

Goose Creek (southern), 1794-1814; Women, 1794-1814; Register, 1795-1814.

Gravelly Run, 1819-32; Register, 1760-1810.

Isle of Wight, 1767-71.

Pagan Creek, 1738-74.

South River, 1757-97, 1797-1823, 1820-25, 1832-37, 1836-39; Women, 1763-1805, 1805-20; Register, 1757-1858.

Upper (Gravelly Run and Burleigh), 1800-32.

Wainoak, 1807-26, 1828-30, 1830-33, 1833-35; Women, 1830-34.

Western Branch (Isle of Wight), 1806-33.

White Oak Swamp, including Register, 1780-81; Minutes, 1781-1805, 1805-24; Women, 1762-1807; Register, 1792-1837.

To this list we must add various miscellaneous volumes that have been of service:

Records of Cedar Creek School Company, 1791-99.

Memoir and Manuscript Writings of Barnaby Nixon (1752-1807).

Manuscript Writings of Hardy Crew.

Letter Book of Robert Pleasants (d. 1802), covering the period 1754-97.

Virginia Discipline, 1758.

Minutes of Committee to Defend Freedom of People of Color, 1846-53.

All of the above volumes, together with a few others that are of little importance, are in the care of Baltimore Yearly Meeting of (Orthodox) Friends. They have a Records Committee of which John C. Thomas is chairman. The records are deposited in the vaults of the Mercantile Safe Deposit and Trust Company of Baltimore. Many of the records of Virginia Yearly Meeting have been destroyed by fire or lost through neglect. Many of the volumes that survive need rebinding; some should be copied, and the whole should be so arranged and indexed that use of them may be easier and their preservation better assured.

Besides the above records in possession of Baltimore Friends, other Virginia manuscripts have been of service as follows:

Henrico Monthly Meeting Minutes, 1692-1746.

This volume is owned by Robert A. Brock, Esq., of Richmond, Va., and was kindly placed by him at the disposal of the author.

Records of the General Court, Orders, etc., of Virginia, 1657-78 (or later).

These records are preserved only in the extracts and notes made from the originals, now destroyed by fire, by the late Conway Robinson, and are now among his MSS. which are in possession of the Virginia Historical Society. They were made available for this work through the courtesy of Philip A. Bruce, Esq., the accomplished Secretary of the Society.

Records of the General Court, Orders, etc.

Covers the period immediately succeeding the Conway MSS.; also in Virginia Historical Society Library.

Court Records of Norfolk and Princess Ann Counties in the Seventeenth Century.

Extracts kindly made for me by John W. H. Porter, Esq., and Edward W. James, Esq.

4. *North Carolina Yearly Meeting:*

Yearly Meeting Minutes, 1708-93, 1794-1837, 1835-46, 1846 to date.

The Minutes for 1805-12, inclusive, have been lost. Since 1845 these Minutes have been printed annually.

Minutes of the Meeting for Sufferings, 1757-1803, 1820-25, 1824-56.

Minutes of Standing Committee, 1757-1814, 1817-23.

Record of the Epistles, Letters, and Other Documents Directed and Belonging to the Meeting for Sufferings of North Carolina Yearly Meeting, 1826-36.

Quarterly Meeting Minutes:

Contentnea, 1793-1823, 1823-30, 1838-40; Women, 1851-75.

Deep River, 1819-70; Women, 1819-89.

New Garden, 1788-1830, 1830-88.

Perquimans, 1708-92 (same as Eastern).

Western, 1759-1866.

Westfield, 1803-32; Women, 1804-32.

Monthly Meeting Minutes:

Bush River (S. C.), 1772-83, 1783-91, 1792-1808, 1790-95; Register, 1797-1807 (3 vols.).

Cane Creek, 1751-97, 1797-1837.

Contentnea (Falling Creek, 1772), 1774-1817, 1790-95, 1814-43; Women, 1817-33.

Core Sound, 1733-91, 1791-1840; Women, 1774-1810, 1784-1804.

Deep River, 1778-1808, 1808-37, 1837-71; Women, 1778-1843, 1843-92; Register, 1779.

Dover, Women, 1815-77.

Hopewell, 1824-49; Women, 1824-48; Register, 1824.

• Jack Swamp, 1794-1812.

Mount Pleasant, Women, 1802-25.

New Garden, 1754-75, 1775-82, 1783-1800, 1801-20, 1820-31, 1831-46, 1847-70; Women, 1754-1823, 1823-67; Register, 1754-1821, 1821-48.

Pasquotank, Women, 1715-68, 1768-1841; Register, 1809-50 (continued under Symons's Creek).

Perquimans, 1681-1764 (notices some events that occurred in 1680 and has a Register of marriages and births); Register, *c.* 1677-1707; (continued under Wells's).

Piney Grove, S. C., 1802-15; Register.
Piney Woods, 1794-1802, 1802-30; Women, 1794-1836.
Rich Square, 1760-99, 1799-1830, 1831-73.
Spring, 1831-39 (all that I have seen).
These records begin as early as 1793 at least.

Springfield, 1791-1820, 1820-59, 1860-85; Women, 1790-1850, 1850-86; Register.
Sutton's Creek, 1794-1807, 1807-35; Women, 1794-1835 (continued under Piney Woods).
Symons's Creek, 1803-37, 1837-54; Women, 1768-1841, 1841-53 (continued under Piney Woods).
Wells's, 1764-94. (Grew out of the old Perquimans Monthly Meeting; was divided in 1794, a new one being established at Sutton's Creek and the old one continued at Piney Woods.)
Westfield, 1787-1823.
Wrightsborough, Ga., 1773-93; Register.

The fortunes of the records of this Yearly Meeting parallel those of Virginia. Many have perished through fire, neglect and decay, and this was made more possible by the large expanse of territory covered. These misfortunes awakened Friends to a partial realization of their value. They began the work of collecting, and the books gathered were stored in King Hall at Guilford College. This Hall was destroyed by fire, August 31, 1885. The records, some deeds and other papers were in the safe. The parchments were roasted beyond repair. The leather backs were baked and peeled from the records, and the edges of some were so charred that they crumbled at the slightest handling. This experience taught Friends a hard lesson. They have since erected a fire-proof vault on the campus of Guilford College, and have invited the lesser meetings to deposit their records there. Friends in North Carolina have not been careful enough of their history. They do not appreciate fully the great mass of invaluable material that there is in their records. They should insist that all unused record books be placed in the vault at Guilford College, and they should use all possible means to secure this end. Many of the volumes already there are very much in need of rebinding. Some must be copied soon or the action of fire and the decay of time will render them entirely illegible. Copying has been begun with the South Carolina records, but they are being modernized in spelling, etc., to suit the taste of the copyist, which should not be allowed. The whole should also be catalogued and systematically arranged on the shelves. The work of collecting these records was inaugurated by Allen Jay, of Indiana.

5. *Other Manuscript Sources:*

Minutes of North Carolina Manumission Society, 1815-35.

This volume is now the property of the North Carolina Yearly Meeting. It was discovered a few years ago, after it had been forgotten for half a century, and was deposited by Addison Coffin.

Journal of Isaac Hammer (1769-1835).

This MS. is owned by North Carolina Yearly Meeting.

Minutes of Monthly Meeting of Friends in Pasquotank, 1701-*c.* 60.

This volume got into the hands of the late Governor Swain. It then passed into the office of the Secretary of State of North Carolina, and extracts were published from it by Col. Saunders in the *Colonial Records of North Carolina*, Vols. I. and II. It was in his office as late as 1890, when it was examined by the writer. Since the death of Col. Saunders it has disappeared.

Archdale Papers. Papers relating to ye Province of Carolina:/ principally whilst John Archdale Esq: was/ Governour & Comander in chief of ye Province./ and 1694, 1695, &c. with a Draught of y^e/ Town, Mapps of ye Forts, Rivers, Coasts, &c.

This folio volume is composed of contemporary documents, many of them in the handwriting of Archdale, and deals principally with his administration in South Carolina. Its general character is like that of his *Description of Carolina*, but is more definite than that wandering performance. The volume was sold at Mr. Granger's auction, Jan. 25, 1732(33). It was once the property of the Chevalier D'Eon, and has recently come into the possession of Charles Roberts, Esq., of Philadelphia, who very kindly placed it at the disposal of the author.

Account of the State of Friends in Virginia in 1727, by Robert Jordan.

This account is mentioned and quoted by Robert Pleasants in his *Letter Book*. The original itself has disappeared.

A Journal of part of the Life, travails and labours of
that faithful Servant, And Minister of the Gospel,
Thomas Nicholson (*c.* 1715-1780).

This MS. is owned by Philadelphia Yearly Meeting, and was
placed at the service of the author by Mr. George J. Scattergood. Nicholson was a prominent Carolina Quaker, see *ante*,
pp. 141, 142.

Some Account of the Family of the Kirks, by Rachel
Price (*née* Kirk) (1763-1841).

This MS. was kindly furnished me by Mr. Gilbert Cope, of
West Chester, Pa. It deals with the settlement in Georgia.

Historical Sketch of the origin, investment and con-
tinuance of the Trust of the Estate of Friends in
Charleston, S. C., with sundry facts and circumstances relating thereto down to 1826 [continued
to 1883] by a Committee of the Meeting for Sufferings.

This MS. is owned by Philadelphia Yearly Meeting.

II.—ORIGINAL PRINTED SOURCES.

The second class of materials consists of printed matter.
This includes: (1) The journals, memoirs and other accounts
of Quaker missionaries who visited these States; (2) Laws
of the several States.

1. *Journals, Memoirs, &c.*:

The largest collection of Quaker literature in a public library
with which the writer is acquainted is that of The Friends' Historical Library of Swarthmore College, Pa. A catalogue of
this collection was printed in 1893. Many Quaker books of
value are to be found in the Pennsylvania Historical Society
Library. The libraries of both Orthodox and Hicksite Friends
of Philadelphia, the library in the Eutaw Street Meeting House,
and that in the Park Avenue Meeting House, Baltimore, and
that of Guilford College, N. C., have all been of service.
Of private libraries, it is probable that no finer collection of
Quaker books exists than that of Charles Roberts, Esq., of
Philadelphia.

Archdale, John. Description of Carolina. London, 1707.
Reprinted in Carroll's *Historical Collections* of South Carolina. New York, 1836.

Backhouse, Hannah Chapman (1787-1850). Extracts from her Journal and Letters. [London], 1858.
Visited the South in 1834.

Boweter John (*c.* 1629-1704). Journal. London, 1705.
Contains a list of American places visited.

Bownas, Samuel (1676-1753). Life. London, 1846. 16°.

Brayton, Patience (1733-1794). Life. New York, 1801. 12°.
Visited the South 1771-72.

Brookes, Edward (1758-1827). Life and Journal, in *Friends' Miscellany*, XII., 1839. 12°.
Visited North Carolina 1813.

Burnyeat, John (1631-1690). The Truth Exalted in the Writings of. London, 1691. 8°.
Cadwallader, Priscilla (1786-1859). Memoirs. Philadelphia, 1864. 16°.
Born in North Carolina; visited Virginia 1823 and 1850.

Chalkley, Thomas (1675-1741). Works. Philadelphia, 1790. 8°.
Churchman, John (1705-1777). Account of. London, 1780. 8°.
Coffin, Elijah (1798-1862). Life, with a Reminiscence by his son, Charles F. Coffin. N. p. [Cincinnati?], 1863. 8°.
Born in North Carolina; migrated to the West.

Coffin, Levi (1798-1877). Reminiscences. Cincinnati, 1876. Second edition, 1880.
Born in North Carolina; migrated to the West.

Collins, Elizabeth (1755-1831). Memoirs. Philadelphia, 1859. 16°.
Visited Virginia in 1799.

Comly, John (1773-1850). Journal. Philadelphia, 1853. 8°.
Visited the South in 1829.

Dickinson, James (1659-1741). Life, in *Friends' Library*, Vol. XII. Philadelphia, 1848. 8°.

Edmundson, William (1627-1712). Journal. London, 1774. 8°.

Ellis, William (1658-1709) and Alice. Life and Correspondence, edited by James Backhouse. Philadelphia, 1850. 12°.

Evans, Joshua (1731-1798). Journal, in *Friends' Miscellany*, Vol. X. 1837. 12°.

Evans, William (1787-1867). Journal. Philadelphia, 1870. 8°.
Visited the South 1830 and 1841.

Ferris, Benjamin (1740-1771). Journal, in *Friends' Miscellany*, Vol. XII. 1839. 12°.

Ferris, David (1707-1798). Memoirs. Philadelphia, 1825. 12°.
Visited the South in 1772.

Forster, William (1784-1854). Memoirs. London, 1865. 8°. 2 vols.
Visited the South 1820 and 1824.

Fothergill, John (1676-1744). Account of, in *Friends' Library*, Vol. XIII. Philadelphia, 1849. 8°.

Fothergill, Samuel (1715-1772), M. D. Memoirs and Letters. New York, 1844. 8°.

Fox, George (1624-1691). Epistles. Philadelphia, 1858. 16°.

— — Journal. New York, 1800. 8°. 2 vols.

Friends' Library. Philadelphia, 1837-1850. 8°. 14 vols.
A reprint of many of the old journals and of very great value.

Friends' Miscellany. Philadelphia. 12°. *c.* 1830-
c. 1840. 12 vols.

A serial publication which contains a number of the shorter
papers dealing with the history of Southern Friends and with
visits of traveling Friends among them.

Gough, James (1712-1780). Memoirs. Philadelphia, 1783. 12°.

Grellet, Stephen (1773-1855). Memoirs. Philadelphia, 1860. 8°. 2 vols.

Visited the South 1800, 1809, 1824.

Griffith, John (1713-1776). Journal. Philadelphia,
1780. 8°.

Gurney, Joseph John (1788-1847). Memoirs. Philadelphia [*c.* 1854]. 8°. 2 vols. in one.

Harrison, Sarah (1748-1812). Memoirs, in *Friends'
Miscellany*, Vol. XI., 1838. 12°.

Healey, Christopher (1773-1851). Memoir. Philadelphia, 1886. 16°

Visited the South 1818.

Hicks, Elias (1748-1830). Journal. New York,
1832. 8°.

Visited the South 1797 and 1813.

Hoag, Joseph (b. 1762). Journal. London, 1862.
12°.

Visited the South 1812, 1816 and 1823.

Holme, Benjamin (1682-1749). Epistles and Works.
London, 1753. 12°.

Visited the South in 1717.

Hoover, David. Memoir, edited by Isaac H. Julian.
Richmond, Ind., 1857. 8°.

Born in North Carolina ; migrated to the West.

Hoskins, Jane (b. 1694). Life, in *Friends' Library*,
Vol. I. Philadelphia, 1837. 8°.

Hull, Henry (1765-1834). Memoir. Philadelphia,
1864. 12°.

Visited the South in 1799.

Hunt, Nathan (1758-1853). Brief Memoir, from his Journals and Letters. Philadelphia, 1858. 12°.
Born and lived in North Carolina.

Hunt, William (1733-1772). Memoirs, chiefly from his Journals and Letters. Philadelphia, 1858. 12°.
Born in Pennsylvania or Maryland ; lived in North Carolina ; died in England. This volume is bound with the one devoted to Nathan Hunt, his son.

Janney, Samuel McPherson (1801-1880). Memoirs. Philadelphia, 1881.

Jordan, Richard (1756-1826). Journal, in *Friends' Library*, Vol. XIII. Philadelphia, 1849. 8°.

Judge, Hugh (*c.* 1750-1834). Memoirs and Journal. Byberry, 1841. 12°.

Kersey, Jesse (1768-1845). Narrative of. Philadelphia, 1852. 12°.
Visited the South 1795.

Kirk, Elisha (1757-1789). Memoirs, in *Friends' Miscellany*, Vol. VI., 1834. 12°.

Lewis, Enoch (b. 1776). Memoir, by Joseph J. Lewis. West Chester, Pa., 1882. 8°.
Visited the South 1814 and 1849.

Lundy, Benjamin (1789-1839). Life, Travels and Opinions. Philadelphia, 1847. 12°.
Compiled by Thomas Earle.

Memorials of deceased Friends. Philadelphia, 1787. 8°.

Morris, Susannah (1682-1755). Journal, in *Friends' Miscellany*, Vol. VI. Philadelphia, 1834. 12°.

Neale, Samuel (1729-1792) and Mary Neale (1717-1757), formerly Mary Peisley. Lives. Philadelphia, 1860. 12°.
Samuel visited the South 1770-71 ; Mary 1753.

Nixon, Barnaby (1752-1807). Memoirs, in *Friends' Miscellany*, Vol. XII. Philadelphia, 1839. 12°.

Osborn, Charles (1775-1850). Journal. Cincinnati, 1854. 8°.

Born in North Carolina ; removed to the West.

Phillips, Catherine (1727-1794), formerly Peyton. Memoirs. London, 1797. 12°.

Piety Promoted. Kendall's edition.

Pumphrey, Stanley (1837-1881). Memories. London [*c.* 1882]. 16°.

Reckitt, William (1706-1769). Account of. Philadelphia, 1783. 12°.

Richardson, John (*c.* 1666-1753). Account of. Philadelphia, 1783. 12°.

Routh, Martha (1743-1817). Memoir, in *Friends' Library*, Vol. XII. Philadelphia, 1848. 8°.

Savery, William (1750-1804). Journal, in *Friends' Library*, Vol. I. Philadelphia, 1837. 8°.

Scattergood, Thomas (1748-1814). Memoirs, in *Friends' Library*, Vol. VIII. Philadelphia, 1844. 8°.

Scott, Job (1751-1793). Journal. Mount Pleasant, Ohio, 1820. 12°.

Sewel, William. History of the rise, increase and progress of the Christian people called Quakers. London, 1795 and 1835. 8°. 2 vols.

This book was published early in the eighteenth century, and is practically an original authority for the period covered.

Shillitoe, Thomas (1754-1836). Life, in *Friends' Library*, Vol. III. Philadelphia, 1839. 8°.

Stabler, Edward (1769-1831). Memoir. Philadelphia, 1846. 16°.

Stanton, Daniel (1708-1768). Journal, in *Friends' Library*, Vol. XII. Philadelphia, 1848. 8°.

Story, Thomas (*c.* 1662-1742). Journal. Newcastle-upon-Tyne, 1747. 4°.

See also Life of Story by John Kendall, condensed from his Journal, London, 1786, 8°.

Sutcliff, Robert. Travels in some parts of North
America, 1804, 1805, 1806. Philadelphia, 1812.
16°.
Visited the South 1804 and 1805.

Thomas, Abel (*c.* 1737-1816). Memoir, in *Friends'
Library*, Vol. XIII. Philadelphia, 1849. 8°.

Wheeler, Daniel (1771-1840). Memoir. Philadelphia [*c.* 1845].
Visited Virginia in 1839.

Wigham, John (1749-1839). Memoirs. London,
1842. 16°.
Visited the South 1795-1797.

Williams, William (1763-1824). Journal. Cincin-
nati, 1828. 12°.
Published also in Belfast, 1839, 12°. Williams was born in
North Carolina and went to the West.

Wilson, Thomas (d. 1725). Journal. London, 1784.
16°.

Woolman, John (1720-1772). Journal. London,
1824. 8°.

Yarnall, Peter (*c.* 1755-1798). Memoir, in *Friends'
Miscellany*, Vol. II., 1832. 12°.

2. *Laws of the States :*

Hening's Statutes at Large of Virginia. Richmond,
Philadelphia and New York, 1819-1823. 8°. 13
vols.
Collection of Laws of Virginia, 1808.
Collection of Acts of Virginia, 1814.
Code of Virginia. Richmond, 1849. 8°.
Swann's Revisal of the Laws of North Carolina.
Newbern, 1752. 4°.
Davis's Revisal of the Laws of North Carolina.
Newbern, 1765. Sm. 4°.
Davis's Revisal of the Laws of North Carolina.
Newbern, 1773. 4°.

Iredell's Revisal of the Laws of North Carolina. Edenton, 1791. 4°.

Martin's Revisal of the Laws of North Carolina. Newbern, 1804. Sm. 4°.

Potter and Yancey's Revisal of the Laws of North Carolina. Raleigh, 1821. 8°. 2 vols.

Session Laws, 1785, 1803, 1830, 1832.

Revised Statutes of North Carolina. Raleigh, 1837. 8°. 2 vols.

Revised by Frederick Nash, James Iredell and William H. Battle.

Revised Code of North Carolina. Boston, 1855. 8°.

Revised by B. F. Moore and Asa Biggs.

Statutes at Large of South Carolina. Columbia, 1836-1841. 8°. 10 vols.

Revision begun by Thomas Cooper; continued by D. J. McCord.

Digest of the Laws of the State of Georgia. Savannah, 1802. Sm. 4°.

By William H. Crawford.

A Digest of the Laws of the State of Georgia, from its establishment as a British Province down to the year 1798 inclusive. Philadelphia, 1808. Sm. 4°.

By Robert and George Watkins.

Digest of Statute Laws of Georgia. Athens, 1851. 8°. 2 vols.

By Thomas R. R. Cobb.

Acts/ passed by the/ General Assembly/ of the/ Colony of Georgia,/ 1755 to 1774./ Now first printed./ Wormsloe./ MDCCCLXXXI.

III.—Secondary Authorities.

Under this head are classed a number of papers that have been of service in illustrating and expanding original authorities and in suggesting new lines of thought.

Applegarth, Albert Clayton. Quakers in Pennsylvania. Johns Hopkins University *Studies in History and Political Science*, Vol. X. Baltimore, 1892. 8°.

Book of Meetings of the Society of Friends in America. Columbus, O., 1884. 16°.

Gives a list of the various meetings throughout America, together with the times they are held, but little trouble has been taken to fix the geographical location of these meetings.

Bowden, James (d. 1887 *act.* 75). History of the Society of Friends in America. London, 1850-1854. 8°. 2 vols.

This work is of much merit and is the most extensive separate study of American Quakerism.

Bradley, Thomas (?). History of Quakers. London, 1799. 12°. 2 vols.

Published anonymously.

Brock, Robert Alonzo. Prefatory note to the fourth charter of the Royal African Company. *Collections of Virginia Historical Society*, Vol. VI. Richmond, 1887. 8°.

—— The Colonial Virginian. Reprinted from Vol. XIX. of *Southern Historical Society Papers*.

Brown, Levi K. Account of the meetings of the Society of Friends within the limits of Baltimore Yearly Meeting (Hicksite). Philadelphia, 1875. 16°.

Cabell, Mrs. Julia Mayo. Sketches and Recollections of Lynchburg. Richmond, 1858. 12°.

Published anonymously.

Cartland, Fernando G. Southern Heroes or the Friends in War Times. Cambridge, 1895. 8°.

Coffin, Addison (1822—). Emigration from North Carolina. *Guilford Collegian*, Vol. IV., 1891-92.

—— Pioneer Days in Guilford County. *Ibid.*, Vol. III., 1890-91.

Mr. Coffin has a volume in preparation on his Life and Travels.

Coffin, Charles F. Early Settlement of Friends in Indiana, *Friends' Review*, Vol. IX., 1855-56, pp. 506-508, 539-541, 553-554, 581-582, 619-620.

—— Some facts relating to the early settlement of Friends in North Carolina, the emancipation of their slaves, &c. *Ibid.*, Vol. XII., 1858-59, 532-534, 548-550.

Coffin, Elijah. Friends in North Carolina. *Friends' Review*, Vol. XIV., 1860-61, 420-421, 453-454, 470-472, 484-485, 500-501, 517-519, 531-533, 554-555, 565-567, 580-581, 613-615.

Evans, Charles, M. D. Friends in the Seventeenth Century. Philadelphia, 1875. 8°.

Chapters 10 and 22 deal with the beginnings of Quakerism in the South.

Fothergill, Samuel. Essay on the Society of Friends.

Gilpin, Thomas. Exiles in Virginia: with observations on the conduct of the Society of Friends during the Revolutionary War. Philadelphia, 1848. 8°.

Gough, John. History of the People called Quakers from their first rise to the present time. Dublin, 1789-90. 8°. 4 vols.

Volume 3, chapters 21 and 26 have some notices of the work of Edmundson. Robert Pleasants prepared an account of Virginia Friends and sent it to James Pemberton for these volumes.

Hancock, Thomas. The Peculium; An endeavor to throw light on some of the causes of the decline of the Society of Friends. London, 1859. 16°.

Harrison, Samuel A., M. D. Wenlock Christison and the early Friends in Talbot County, Md. Baltimore, 1878. 8°.

Hodgson, William. The Society of Friends in the Nineteenth Century: A historical view of the successive convulsions and schisms therein during that period. Philadelphia, 1876. 8°. 2 vols.

Janney, Samuel McPherson. History of the Religious Society of Friends. Philadelphia, 1861-68. 12 . 4 vols.

Julian, George W. The rank of Charles Osborn as an anti-slavery pioneer. Indianapolis, 1891. 8°.

McIlwaine, Henry Reid, Ph. D. The struggle of Protestant Dissenters for religious toleration in Virginia. J. H. U. *Studies in Historical and Political Science.* Baltimore, 1894. 8°.

Macy, Obed. History of Nantucket. Boston, 1835.

Mendenhall, Nereus (1819-1893). History of New Garden Boarding School, in *Guilford Collegian,* Vol. II., 1889-90.

Michner, Ezra. Retrospect of early Quakerism. Philadelphia, 1860. 8°.

O'Neall, John Belton. Annals of Newberry, S. C. Charleston, 1859. 12°.

Slavery and the Slave trade. Brief statement of the rise and progress of the testimony of the Religious Society of Friends against slavery and the slave trade. Philadelphia, 1843. 12°.
This contains some account of the proceedings within the limits of Virginia Yearly Meeting.

Smith, Charles Lee. History of Education in North Carolina. Washington, 1888. 8°.

Wasson, M. Annals of Pioneer Settlers on the White Water and its Tributaries. Richmond, Ind., 1875. 8°.
Published anonymously.

Weeks, Stephen B. The religious development in the province of North Carolina. J. H. U. *Studies in Historical and Political Science,* Vol. X. Baltimore, 1892. 8°.

—— Church and State in North Carolina. *Ibid.* Vol. XI. Baltimore, 1893. 8°.

Young, Andrew W. History of Wayne County, Indiana. Cincinnati, 1872. 8°.

INDEX.

Lankford family of Va., 77.
Larow fam. goes West, 274.
Lawrance, Richard, ment'd, 129.
Lawrence, Robert, ment'd, 26.
Lawrence fam. goes West, 274;
of N. C., 80.
Lawson, John, on causes of set-
tlement in N. C., 35.
Lea fam. goes West, 274.
Lead, Lad. *See* Ladd.
Leadbetter fam. goes West, 274.
Lee, Gen. Robert E., ment'd, 289.
Lenoir Co., N. C., Q. in, 87.
Leonard fam. goes West, 276.
Lewis, Enoch, ment'd, 137n.
Lewis, T., ment'd, 94.
Lewis fam. goes West, 272-274,
279, 280.
Liberia as place of migration,
228.
Libraries, efforts for in Va. and
N. C., 298-300; of Q. books, 352;
in wills, 129-130.
Lick Creek M. M., emigrants to,
261, 265, 274, 275, 276, 277, 278,
279.
Liddal, John, visits Va., 21.
Lillington, Alexander, ment'd,
58n.
Lillington, John, ment'd, 27n.
Lillington, Sarah, ment'd, 27n..
Limestone, Tenn., Q. at, 253,
263.
Lincoln, Abraham, a type, 285.
Lindley, Thomas, goes to N. C.,
103.
Lindley fam. goes West, 276,
279.
Lingager fam. goes West, 279.
Liquors, discussed in N. C. Y.
M., 297, 298; use of, 126-129.
Literary work of Q., 139-143.
Little fam. goes West, 272, 273.
Little Reedy Island, Q. at, 253,
254.
Lloyd fam. goes West, 272.
Locke, John, on religion in Fund.
Const. of Car., 10-12.
Lodge fam. goes West, 274.
London Yearly Epistle on S., 199.
Lords, House of, action on S. C.
laws, 160; effect of declaration
on N. C., 161.
Lost Creek M. M., Tenn., emi-
gration to, 265; Q. at, 252, 253.

Lotteries, Q. engage in, 128.
Loudoun Co., Va., Q. in, 83, 98-
100, 286.
Louisa Co., Va., Q. leave, 286;
Q. in, 320; statistics, 323.
Lovejoy, Elijah P., ment'd, 238n.
Low fam. goes West, 276.
Lowe, Emmanuel, boat restored
to, 166n.; in "Cary Rebellion,"
166; marries dau. of Archdale,
60; tried by Q., 166; ment'd,
74, 129.
Ludwell, Philip, gov. gen. of
Car., 57, 58n.
Lumbroso, Jacob, pushed by Q.,
14n.
Lundy, Benj., advises sending
negroes to Hayti, 230; agent
for *The Philanthropist*, 238n.;
influence on Manu. Soc., 239;
on no. of Abolition Societies,
241n.; preceded by Charles Os-
born, 236n.; publishes *The Gen-
ius*, 238n.; sketch, 239n.
Lundy fam. goes West, 279.
Lupton fam. goes West, 272, 273.
Lynch, Charles, sketch, 101.
Lynch, Charles, Jr., founds
Lynchburg, 101n.
Lynch, John, founds Lynchburg,
101n.
Lynchburg, founders of, 101n.
Lynch fam. goes West, 274; of
Va., 101.
Lynch law, origin of term, 101.

M

McClure fam. goes West, 280.
McCool fam. goes West, 280;
goes to S. C., 117.
McDowell, James, Jr., urges
emancipation, 243.
McDuffie Co., Ga., Q. in, 118.
Mace fam. goes West, 275.
Mace family of N. C., 87.
McKay fam. goes West, 273.
Mackie, Josias, licensed, 147.
McKinney fam. goes West, 278.
McLean, C. M., quoted, 294.
McLean, J. R., aids Q., 305.
McLean fam. goes West, 279.
Macocomocock River, ment'd,
38, 39n.
Macon, Fort, Q. help to build,
195n.

www.ingramcontent.com/pod-product-compliance
Lightning Source LLC
Chambersburg PA
CBHW030858270326
41929CB00008B/479